NEW YORK CITY
Van Cortlandt Park
THE BRONX
NY Botanical Garden
The Cloisters
Bronx Zoo
Yankee Stadium
Long Island Sound
Teterboro Airport
Hudson River
Harlem
MANHATTAN
Bronx-Whitestone Bridge
Throgs Neck Bridge
East River
Rikers Island
Central Park
Metropolitan Museum of Art
La Guardia Airport
Flushing
Rockefeller Center
Grand Central Station
Long Island City
Louis Armstrong House
Citi Field
Flushing Meadow
New York Hall of Science
Amphitheater
Corona Park
NEWARK
JERSEY CITY
East River
Forest Hills Tennis Stadium
Jamaica
One World Trade Center
Williamsburg
Newark Airport
Ellis Island
Brooklyn Bridge
Forest Park
Golf Course
QUEENS
Statue of Liberty
Governor's Island
Flatbush
East New York
Newark Bay
Brooklyn Museum
Prospect Park
Upper Bay
Spring Creek Park
Postcards 9/11 Memorial
Children's Museum
BROOKLYN
John F. Kennedy International Airport
The Narrows
Clove Lakes Park
Dyker Beach Park
Jamaica Bay
Richmond
Verrazano-Narrows Bridge
Lower Bay
Brooklyn Marine Park
US Naval Air Station
Long Beach
STATEN ISLAND
Coney Island
Rockaway Inlet
Richmondtown
Rockaway Point
Great Kills Park
Crooke's Point
Conference House
Atlantic Ocean
Raritan Bay
NORTH
WEST
EAST
SOUTH
0 1 2 3 4 5 km
0 1 2 3 miles

Orange Line 4 Grundkurs

für Klasse 8

Das Lehrbuch versteht sich als Gesamtangebot. Welche Texte und Aufgaben verpflichtend sind, wird durch die schulinternen Curricula festgelegt.

Zusatzmaterial für Schülerinnen und Schüler:
Orange Line 4 Grundkurs Workbook mit Audio-CD und Übungssoftware (ISBN 978-3-12-548184-8)
Orange Line 4 Grundkurs Workbook mit Audio-CD (ISBN 978-3-12-548384-2)
Orange Line 4 Grundkurs Vokabellernheft (ISBN 978-3-12-548194-7)
Orange Line 4 Grundkurs Vokabeltraining aktiv (ISBN 978-3-12-548314-9)
Orange Line 4 Grammatiktraining aktiv (ISBN 978-3-12-548304-1)
Orange Line 4 Klassenarbeitstraining aktiv (978-3-12-548104-6)

1. Auflage 1 5 4 3 2 1 | 21 20 19 18 17

Alle Drucke dieser Auflage sind unverändert und können im Unterricht nebeneinander verwendet werden.
Die letzte Zahl bezeichnet das Jahr des Druckes.

Herausgeber: Dr. Frank Haß, Kirchberg
Autorinnen und Autoren: Chris Caridia, London sowie
Jo Cummins, London; Wolfgang Hamm, Marktredwitz; Dr. Andrea Jessen, Tamm; Leonie Pohl, Gütersloh; Nadine Uesbeck, Dortmund; Anna Zagermann, Hattingen; Konstanze Zander, Großenehrich
Beratung: Brunhilde Biek, Leonberg; Karin Braun, Dortmund; Wilma Brings, Bedburg; Amanda Chisnell, Lollar; Sara Conway, Stuttgart; Ulf Degen, Braunschweig; Tanja Frank, Ulm; Sandra Haberland, Recklinghausen; Wolfgang Hamm, Marktredwitz; Ulrike Heringhaus, Altheim; Michael Herrmann, Ludwigsfelde; Christa Kathmann-Fuhrmann, Bonn; Dr. Margitta Kuty, Greifswald-Eldna; Grit Machut, Berlin; Michael Meisenzahl, Karlstadt; Beatrix Pierce, Eppingen; Annegret Preker-Franke, Bielefeld; Dr. Hubert Schwandt, Parchen; Christian Straukamp, Nordhorn; Ines van Hove, Oldenburg; Dieter Vilimek, Helmstadt-Bargen

Redaktion: Beate Jäger; Dr. Susanne Dyka, Nürnberg; Birgit Piefke-Wagner, Korntal-Münchingen
Herstellung: Ulrike Wursthorn

Umschlaggestaltung und Gestaltungskonzept: know idea, Freiburg; Koma Amok, Stuttgart
Umschlagfoto: Getty Images (The Image Bank), München; Getty Images (Photographer's Choice), München
Illustrationen: Marek Blaha, Offenbach; Kirill Chudinskiy, Köln sowie
Friederike Ablang, Berlin; Iris Blanck, Hamburg; Martina Burghardt-Vollhardt, Kamenz; Udo Clormann, Wiesbaden; Thorsten Droessler, Leipzig; Andreas Florian, Lübeck; Anke Fröhlich, Leipzig; Carolin Görtler, Immenstadt im Allgäu; Josef Hammen, Trierweiler; Christian Hansen, Berlin; Rob Harvey, Cirencester, GB; Carmen Hochmann, Bielefeld; Martin Hoffmann, Stuttgart; Yvonne Hoppe-Engbring, Steinfurt; Steffen Jähde, Sundhagen; Klett Archiv, Stuttgart; Hendrik Kranenberg, Drolshagen; Jeongsook Lee, Köln; Katja Leuschner, Halle; Helga Merkle, Albershausen; Lutz-Erich Müller, Leipzig; Axel Nicolai, Brauweiler; David Norman, Meerbusch; Liliane Oser, Hamburg; Sven Palmowski, Barcelona, Spain; Katja Rau, Fellbach; Anja Rieger, Berlin; Annika Sauerborn, Mainz; Sandra Schmidt, Berlin; Carolin Ina Schröter, Berlin; Friederike Schumann, Berlin; Birgit Tanck, Hamburg; Inge Voets, Berlin; Sylvia Wolf, Wiesbaden; Katrin Wolff, Wiesbaden; Steffen Wolff, Brohl-Lützing; Dorothee Wolters, Köln

Satz: Satzkiste GmbH, Stuttgart
Reproduktion: Schwabenrepro GmbH, Stuttgart
Druck: Mohn Media Mohndruck GmbH, Gütersloh

Printed in Germany
ISBN 978-3-12-548174-9 (fester Einband)
ISBN 978-3-12-548374-3 (flexibler Einband)

9 783125 481749

9 783125 483743

Orange Line 4

Grundkurs

Herausgeber: Dr. Frank Haß

Ernst Klett Verlag
Stuttgart • Leipzig

Inhalt

L = Listening S = Speaking R = Reading W = Writing V = Viewing I = Intercultural

L = Listening S = Speaking R = Reading W = Writing V = Viewing I = Intercultural

Inhalt

L = Listening S = Speaking R = Reading W = Writing V = Viewing I = Intercultural

So lernst du mit Orange Line

Hier zeige ich dir, wie du dich in deinem Buch gut zurechtfindest. Das Buch hat fünf Units (Kapitel). Jede Unit ist gleich aufgebaut.

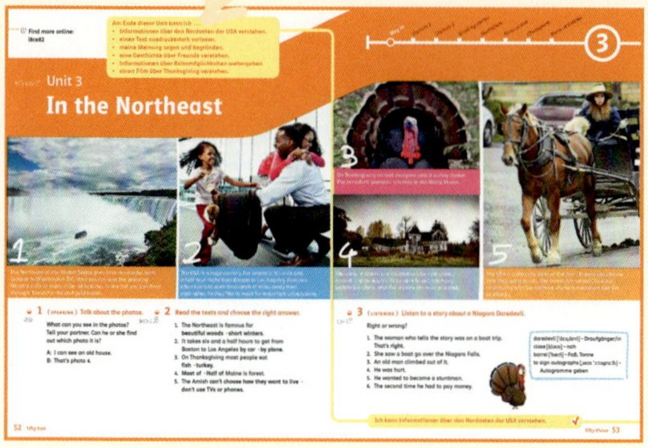

Way in

Hier steigst du in das neue Thema ein. Dazu gibt es auch einen kurzen Film.

Im gelben Kasten siehst du, was du in der *Unit* lernst.

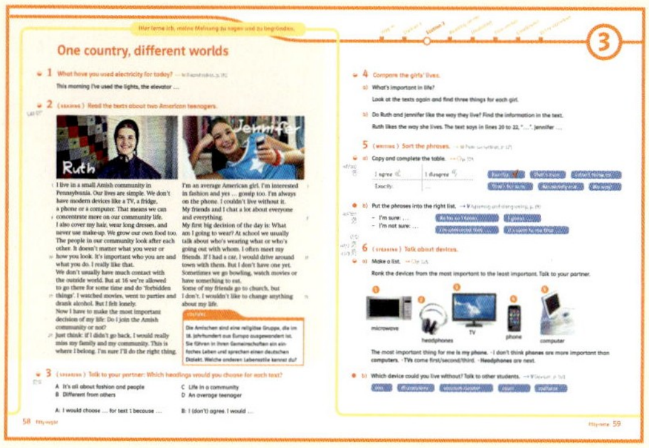

Stations

In jeder *Unit* gibt es zwei *Stations*, in denen du viele neue Dinge lernst. Diese Symbole zeigen dir, wie schwer die Übung ist und ob es im Anhang eine leichtere Variante gibt:

◒ → ○ p. 137, ●

In der *Your turn*-Aufgabe kannst du zeigen, dass du alles verstanden hast, und deine eigenen Ideen einbringen.

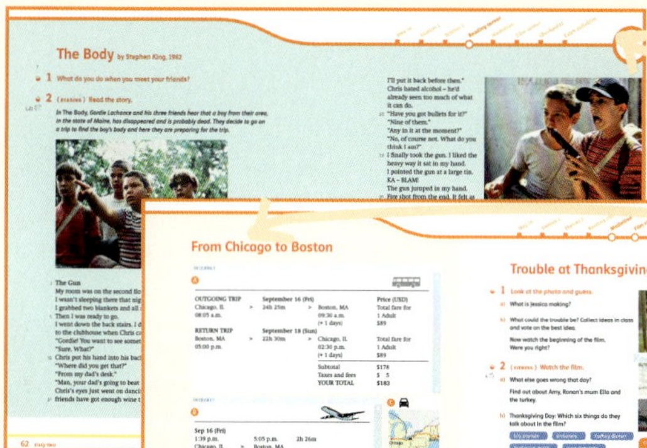

Reading corner

In der *Reading corner* gibt es verschiedene Geschichten und Sachtexte.

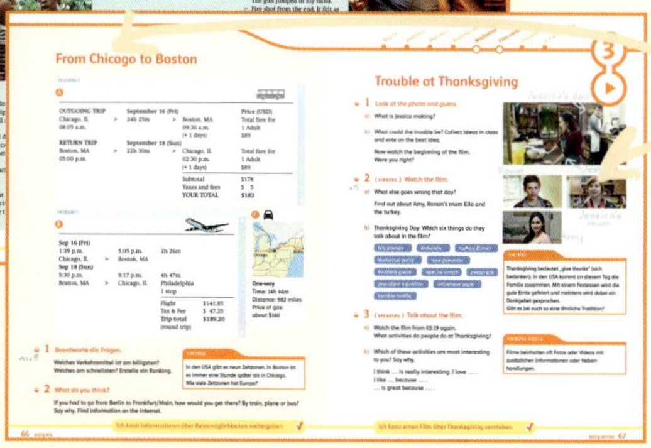

Mediation/Film corner

Auf der linken Seite geht es darum, englische Informationen auf Deutsch weiterzugeben oder umgekehrt.

In der *Film corner* geht es um einen englischen Film.

Checkpoint

Auf dieser Seite kannst du überprüfen, ob du in der *Unit* alles verstanden hast. In der *Checklist* sind alle Lernziele noch einmal aufgelistet.

Die Abschluss-Aufgabe (*task*) sollt ihr zu zweit oder in der Gruppe lösen.

Extra activities

Hier findest du zwei Seiten mit besonderen Aktivitäten, z. B. einem Spiel.

Skills

Auf einige *Units* folgt eine Doppelseite, auf der du eine bestimmte Fertigkeit (*skill*) besonders trainieren kannst, also z. B. das Lesen, Schreiben, Sprechen oder Wörterbucharbeit.

More about

Hier findest du interessante weiterführende Informationen zur Region der Unit.

Im Anschluss an die fünf *Units* gibt es noch weitere nützliche Seiten:

Extra: Hier erwarten dich weitere Lesetexte und vieles mehr.

Grammar: Hier findest du alle Regeln und Erklärungen zur Grammatik sowie weitere Übungen.

Methods: Manche Übungen könnt ihr auf eine bestimmte Art und Weise bearbeiten. Das erkennt ihr an diesem Symbol: → M
Wie es genau funktioniert, kannst du hier nachlesen.

Vocabulary: Im *Vocabulary* findest du alle neuen Wörter in der Reihenfolge, in der sie in der *Unit* auftauchen, und die wichtigsten Arbeitsanweisungen.
Im *Dictionary* sind die Wörter noch einmal alphabetisch aufgelistet: zuerst Englisch-Deutsch und dann Deutsch-Englisch.

Am Schluss des Buches findest du noch
- Sätze, die du im Unterricht sagen kannst, z. B. bei der Gruppenarbeit
- eine Liste mit den unregelmäßigen Verben.

Symbol	Erklärung
○ ◒ ●	leicht/mittel/schwer (Niveaudifferenzierung)
	individualisierende Aufgabe (natürliche Differenzierung)
→ ○ p. 131	Verweis auf leichtere Parallelübung auf der *Diff corner*-Seite
OR	Aufgabe zur Auswahl (Wahldifferenzierung)
	Entwicklung von Schlüsselkompetenzen
P	Hier entsteht ein Produkt für das Portfolio.
4/1	Verweis auf eine Übung im *Workbook*
→ G6, p. 163	Verweis auf den Grammatikanhang (*Grammar*)
→ M	Verweis auf die Methodenseite (*Methods*)
→ V	Verweis zum Wortfeld im Vokabular (*Vocabulary*)
	Partnerarbeit
	Gruppenarbeit
	Verweis auf die Lehrer-CD (Audio)
	Verweis auf die Lehrer-DVD (Film)
Find more online:	Code auf www.klett.de eingeben und Zusatzinformationen erhalten

Zoom in – The USA

Every year in fall the New England states shine in bright colors.

1

Denali (Mt. McKinley) is the highest mountain in Alaska and North America (6,190 m).

4

flag

rose

bald eagle

Name:	United States of America	**Capital:**	Washington D.C.
Population:	≈ 321,400,000 (July 2015)	**States:**	50
Area (total):	≈ 9,800,000 km² (≈ 3,600,000 sq.mi.) (3rd largest country in the world)	**Time zones:**	9
		Major rivers:	Mississippi, Missouri, Colorado
		Mountains:	Rocky Mountains, Appalachian Mountains
Currency:	US dollar		

The Midwest is a huge open area with lots of corn and soybean fields.

2

Hawaii is a surfer's paradise with perfect waves and white and black beaches.

3

Most parts of the Rocky Mountains are protected. Lots of tourists enjoy the beautiful landscape.

5

In some parts of the American South there are swamps where alligators live.

6

1 Look at the photos and read the texts.

What parts of the USA would you like to visit? Say why.

2 Look at the map at the back of the book. Find the answers.

1. Name the countries that are north and south of the USA.
2. Name the oceans that are east and west of the USA.
3. Name the sea that's south of the states of Louisiana, Mississippi and Alabama.
4. Name the state that's in the Pacific Ocean, southwest of California.
5. Name the state that's to the northwest of Canada.
6. Find out the distances from north to south and east to west.

3 Look at the photos and choose one of the places.

Find out more about it on the internet. Present some interesting facts to the class.

1. Indiana: Indy 500
2. Kentucky: Fort Knox
3. Pennsylvania: Declaration of Independence
4. Washington: Space Needle, Seattle

3

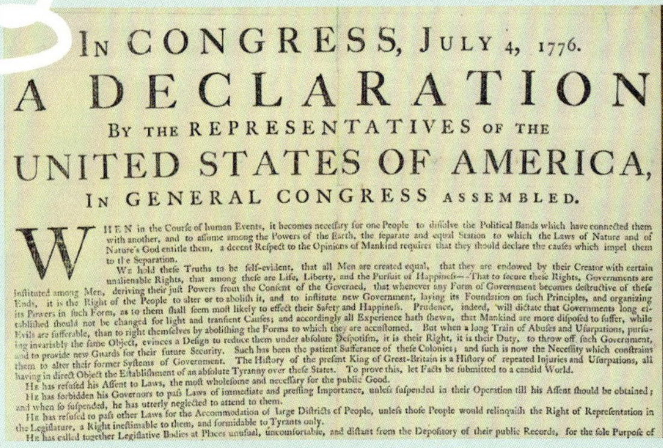

6

9

5. North Dakota: Sitting Bull
6. Alabama: US Space & Rocket Center, Huntsville
7. Colorado: Mesa Verde
8. Nevada: Las Vegas
9. New Mexico: Very Large Array

Find more online: i8ce82

Am Ende dieser Unit kann ich …
- Informationen über New York verstehen.
- interessante Orte einer Stadt präsentieren.
- einen Artikel über eine Person schreiben.
- einen Text über die Geschichte der Einwanderung verstehen.
- Informationen über Einbürgerung weitergeben.
- einen Film über Sehenswürdigkeiten in New York verstehen.

1 1,1

Unit 1

Gateway NYC

New York City (NYC) is the biggest city in the United States. Over eight and a half million people live in its five boroughs: The Bronx, Brooklyn, Queens, Manhattan and Staten Island.

One World Trade Center is the tallest building on the New York City skyline and in the USA. It replaced the old World Trade Center after the attacks on September 11, 2001.

1 Look at the photos.

a) What do you know about New York City? The photos can help you.

b) Read the texts. Then match them with these phrases.

- sports in the USA
- a special tall building
- American culture
- the biggest city in the USA
- a symbol of hope

2/1–2

2 Check the sentences.

a) Right or wrong?

1. There are eight boroughs in New York City.
2. One World Trade Center is the tallest building in the USA.
3. People in New York don't like baseball very much.
4. Hip hop and street art started in New York.
5. The Statue of Liberty was made in the USA.

b) Correct the wrong sentences.

Baseball is one of the most popular sports in the USA, and New Yorkers love it.

New York is an important center for American culture. Music, theater, dance and art are all popular. Hip hop and street art started in New York.

The Statue of Liberty was a present from France to celebrate 100 years of American independence. For immigrants it became a symbol of hope.

3 (LISTENING) Listen to a guided tour of One World Trade Center.

1,2

Choose the right answer.

1. How many people died on September 11, 2001?
   almost 3,000 • almost 1,000
2. How many people saw the events on TV?
   over two million • over two billion
3. How long does it take to travel to the top?
   six minutes • 60 seconds
4. What do visitors watch in the elevators?
   a movie about the past of NYC • a movie about the past of the USA
5. Where does the electricity for the lights in the tower come from?
   the elevators • the wind

billion ['bɪliən] – Milliarde
event [ɪ'vent] – Ereignis
elevator ['elɪveɪtə] – Aufzug; Lift
top [tɒp] – Spitze
light [laɪt] – Licht

Ich kann Informationen über New York verstehen. ✓

Hier lerne ich, interessante Orte einer Stadt zu präsentieren.

A taxi ride in NYC

1 (READING) Read the text.

1,3 3/1

David Singh: A traffic jam! It's always bad on the Brooklyn Bridge during rush hour. And last Monday they started roadwork here too. Did you know that it gets very cold here in the winters? Two years ago we had so much snow. I didn't get into the city some days. I live in Queens, but I work in downtown Manhattan.
You can get a very good look at the New York skyline from here. I never get tired of it – let me tell you about the sights.
That's One World Trade Center. Those skyscrapers over there are on Wall Street, the financial center of the world. Can you see the Empire State Building? In the 1930s it was the tallest building in the world. The view of Manhattan from the top is really fantastic.
How long are you here for anyway? If you only have one day in NYC, I say: buy a sandwich and a coffee and go for a walk in Central Park. There are lakes, playgrounds, a zoo and lots more.

Then take the subway at 86th Street and Lexington Avenue to Grand Central Station. Around the corner you can get the best hot dogs in New York. In the afternoon you should go shopping and finish the day with a Broadway show.
The lights are green at last. Let's go.

2 Collect the information.

→ M Think-pair-share, p. 173

1. What's David's job?
2. Make a list of the places and buildings from the text.
3. Find the places or buildings on the map at the front of your book.

CULTURE

Man kann sich in Manhattan nicht verlaufen, wenn man auf die Straßennamen achtet. Avenues verlaufen von Nord nach Süd; Streets von Ost nach West.
Woher haben Straßen bei euch ihre Namen?

David Singh

3 Right or wrong? Find it in the text. → M Peer correction, p. 171

1. The traffic is bad during rush hour.
   That's **right.** *(lines 1–2) "It's always bad on the Brooklyn Bridge during rush hour."*
2. David lives in downtown Manhattan.
3. In the 1920s the Empire State Building was the tallest building in the world.
4. There's a zoo in Central Park.
5. You can get the best hot dogs around the corner of Grand Central Station.

4 Find the words.

a) Choose the right word. → ○ p. 114

subway | avenue | skyline | playground | rush hour

1. street • road • ___
2. taxi • bus • ___
3. park • lake • ___
4. traffic jam • roadwork • ___
5. skyscraper • tower • ___

b) Match the words with the definitions. → V City words, p. 179

sidewalk | suburbs | construction site | parking lot

1. you can leave your car there
2. where people can walk safely
3. a place where they are building something
4. people live here, away from the city center

5 (SPEAKING) Act as a guide.

a) Present what is on the map. → ○ p. 114

3/2-3a)

Over there you can see ...
Don't miss ...
You must visit ...
Around the corner you can see ...
Look, there's ...

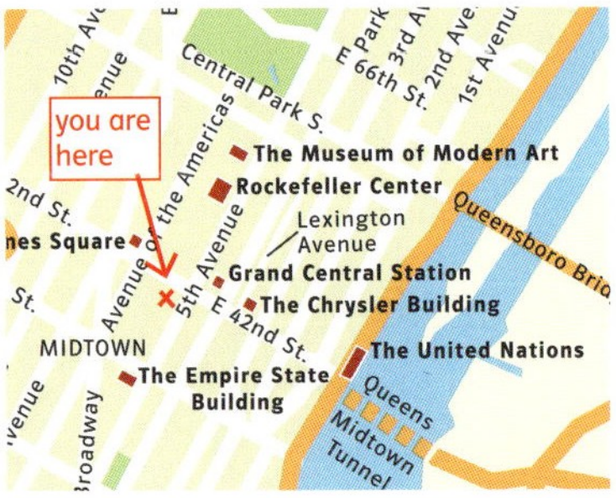

b) Show a visitor three places in your town. Bring a map or photos. → V City guide, p. 183

3/3b)

In the distance you can see ...
Have a good look at ...
Right ahead are ...

CULTURE

Ein paar Wörter unterscheiden sich im britischen und amerikanischen Englisch. Schreibweise und Aussprache sind manchmal auch anders. Viele Sprecher mischen britisches und amerikanisches Englisch.

British	American
town centre	downtown
lift	elevator
holidays	vacation

Language → G1, p. 158

Last Monday they started roadwork here.
Two years ago we had so much snow.
Did you know that?
I didn't get into the city.

Welche Zeitform ist das? Wie bildest du sie? Welche Signalwörter kennst du für diese Zeitform?

6 Complete the sentences. → M Bus stop, p. 168

4/4

1. The Statue of Liberty was a present from France in the 19th century. (be)
2. The Brooklyn Bridge —— on May 24, 1883. (open)
3. Grand Central Station —— its new name 'Grand Central Terminal' in 1913. (get)
4. In the 1980s Central Park —— a very safe place. (not be)
5. It —— eight years to build One World Trade Center, from 2004 to 2012. (take)
6. Two years ago schools in New York City —— because of heavy snow. (not open)

I was in NYC.
I wasn't in LA.
Were you there?

7 (WRITING) Tell the taxi driver's story.

a) Make sentences. Use the simple past. → ○ p. 114

4/5a)

1. be at the airport • get in

2. be cold • heavy snow

3. be in a traffic jam • talk to

4. arrive at the hotel • forget her saxophone

5. run to the hotel • look for her

6. give the saxophone back • be happy

1. Last winter I was at the airport. A woman …

b) Write an ending for the story. Here's one idea:

4/5b)

invite • concert • brilliant • great evening

8 (SPEAKING) What did they do at One World Trade Center yesterday?

a) Ask and answer questions about the people in the picture. → ○ p. 115

4/6
5/7

have a drink | eat | look at | sit | phone | take a photo

A: What did Henry eat? – B: He ate a sandwich.
B: Did Susan take a photo? – A: No, she ...

Who ate my sandwich?

b) Now Partner B closes his or her book. Partner A asks questions. Then take turns.

5/8

A: Did Lisa eat a sandwich? – B: No, she didn't. Henry did.
A: Where did Linda sit? – B: Linda ...

9 (YOUR TURN) New York City sights → V City guide, p. 183

a) Get into groups of five. Each student chooses a different borough of New York.

b) Find out information about one sight in your borough in the library or on the internet:
- What is special about it?
- When was it built? / When did it open?

c) Imagine you are a New York taxi driver and the others are tourists: Present your sight to your group. → M Tip top, p. 173

You can start like this:
We are now in ... .
Over there you can see ... .
It's ... . There is/are ... .
It was built in ... ./It opened in ... .

STUDY SKILLS

Wenn du im Internet nach Informationen suchst, gib gezielt mehrere Suchbegriffe ein, um das Ergebnis einzugrenzen, z. B. die Sehenswürdigkeit, den Stadtbezirk und „facts for kids". Kinderseiten sind übersichtlicher und sprachlich einfacher.

Ich kann interessante Orte einer Stadt präsentieren. ✓

Hier lerne ich, einen Artikel über eine Person zu schreiben.

Living the dream?

1 (READING) Read the interview with José Blanco.

1,4
6/1

Interviewer: Hello José. Can I ask you a few questions for our magazine, please?

José: Hi. Sure.

Interviewer: You're new on the baseball team. Are you happy?

José: We won the first three matches, so I can't complain.

Interviewer: There are lots of players from Latin America here. When did you immigrate to the United States?

José: That was twelve years ago. I was ten.

Interviewer: That was a big decision for your parents. They left their home and moved to a foreign place.

José: Yes, but they were very poor in Cuba. My father had been unemployed for a long time. My parents wanted to give me and my sisters the best chances.

Interviewer: What were the first years like?

José: My parents had problems because they hadn't learned English in school. But there's a strong community of Cubans here in New York. So my parents opened a small shop for other immigrants.

Interviewer: And how did you feel?

José: At the beginning I was homesick. I missed my friends. But my parents had given up a lot for me and I slowly got used to my new life.

Interviewer: When did you begin your baseball career?

José: Before I was 15, I hadn't taken any sports seriously. Then I joined the baseball team in high school and we were very successful. After I had become the star of my team, my baseball career started. I've been very lucky. I can live my dream. For most people it's much harder.

Interviewer: What about your plans for the future?

José: I'm a US citizen now and my home is here. But I plan to help people in Cuba.

Interviewer: Thank you for your time.

CULTURE

Der amerikanische Traum besagt, dass jeder Mensch durch harte Arbeit ein erfolgreiches Leben führen kann.
Ist es bei euch möglich, sich vom Tellerwäscher zum Millionär hochzuarbeiten?

2 (WRITING) Collect facts about José and his family. → M Think-pair-share, p. 173

a) Complete the fact card. Take notes. → ○ p. 115

Name: … From: … Plans: …
Job: … Lives in: …
Age: … Why they left their country: …

b) Find more facts.

Problems at the beginning: ? Why he is happy now: ?

STUDY SKILLS

Halte deine Notizen so kurz wie möglich. Schreibe nur Schlüsselwörter auf, keine ganzen Sätze.

3 (LISTENING) Listen to the interview with Angela.

1,5

Complete the sentences.

1. Angela was —— when she left the Philippines.
2. She lives with her —— in Brooklyn.
3. She had —— with the language, the culture and her papers.
4. She goes to college now and she has also got a —— .
5. Her —— had an accident, so she helps him now.

4 Imagine you want to leave your country.

6/4

a) Complete the sentences with these phrases. → ○ p. 116

6/2

chances | get used to | feel foreign | immigrate to ✓ | give up

1. Where could I go? I could immigrate to the USA.

2. It will be hard to —— my old life.

3. I hope I will have many —— in the USA.

4. I hope I won't —— and lonely.

5. I hope I can —— my new life soon.

b) Match the sentences with the same meaning. → V Going to a new country, p. 180

6/3

1. I want to emigrate from my home country.
2. I can get support from my family.
3. I hope I won't fail.

A I hope I will be successful.
B I want to leave my home country and live in another country.
C My family will help me.

5 (SONG) Empire State of Mind (Part II) Broken Down

1,6

Listen to the song. What can you find out about New York?

Ooooh, New York!
Ooooh, New York!

Grew up in a town that is famous as a place of movie scenes.
Noise is always loud, there are sirens all around and the streets are mean.
If I can make it here, I can make it anywhere, that's what they say.
Seeing my face in lights or my name in marquees found down on Broadway.
Even if it ain't all it seems, I got a pocketful of dreams.

Language detectives → G2, p. 159

Before I was 15, I hadn't taken any sports seriously.
After I had become the star of my team, my baseball career started.

Das simple past und past perfect beschreiben Ereignisse in der Vergangenheit. Das past perfect wird für das Ereignis verwendet, das weiter zurückliegt. Wie bildest du die neue Zeitform?

6 Look at the sentences and say what happened first.

7/5

1. After José's dad had lived in New York for two years, his family joined him.
2. Before José left for the USA, his grandma had died.
3. Before José moved to New York, he hadn't spoken English very often.
4. After José had been in school for a year, he joined the baseball team.
5. After José's dad had opened his own shop, lots of other Cubans came to buy things.

7 Find out about one of Angela's days.

7/6

a) Match the sentence parts. The pictures can help you. → ○ p. 116

A After Pablo had invited Angela to his party, … ✓
B Before Angela ate her pizza, …
C After Angela and Pablo had walked through the park, …
D Before Angela and Pablo went to the stadium, …
E After they had bought tickets, …

… she bought a present.

… they took the subway.

… they visited Ellis Island.

… she had ordered a milkshake.

… they had put on their fan shirts.

8/7

b) Complete the sentences about Angela. Use the past perfect.

Before Angela went to bed, she —— (call) Pablo, she —— (watch) a TV show and she —— (close) the windows.

8/8 52/1

8 (WRITING) Write sentences. Use the past perfect.

a) What had José done before his first important baseball game last summer? What hadn't he done? → ○ p. 117

1. played every day ✓
2. bought new sports shoes ✗
3. ordered tickets for my friends ✓
4. watched the other team ✓
5. phoned my dad ✓
6. eaten a big meal ✗

José:
1. Before my first big game I had played every day.
2. I hadn't bought …

b) What had Angela done before she left the Philippines? What hadn't she done?

Before Angela left the Philippines, …

ask her friends for advice | not organize a party | talk to her uncle on the phone

9 (YOUR TURN) A magazine article

→ V Presenting personal information, p. 184
→ M Writers' conference, p. 173

8/9 9/1

Collect all the information about José that you can find on page 18. Use it to write an article about José.

A Cuban-American star

José Blanco is a baseball player with a big future – that's what people tell us.

Einleitung: das Wichtigste über die Person, Interesse beim Leser wecken

José is from … . He immigrated to … when … . His parents had been … in their home country and José's dad … . José lives in … now. He is good at … . He started to take baseball seriously when … . After he had become … . Now he … . He wants to … .

Hauptteil: Details zur Person

Would you like to meet José? Write to us and win a ticket for his next baseball match.

interessanter Schluss: z. B. Frage oder Aufforderung an Leser/Leserin

Ich kann einen Artikel über eine Person schreiben. ✓

Ellis Island – a symbol of immigration

1 Why do people leave their home? → M Think-pair-share, p. 173

2 (READING) Read the text.

1,7

The United States is a country of immigrants. Between 1892 and 1954 Ellis Island was the most important gateway for twelve million immigrants. In the museum on Ellis Island visitors can look at millions of passenger lists and find out more about their personal family story.

Families often saved money for the father or the oldest son to make the journey alone. They sent for the rest of family when they had a home and a job.

The journey by ship took seven to 21 days. But conditions were very hard on board. Immigrants were poor, so they traveled third class. It was very crowded and dirty at the bottom of the ship. There was bad food and very little fresh air. Many passengers were sick.

At the end of the long trip, doctors came on board to check the passengers. Then the ship moved slowly into the harbor. The people saw the Statue of Liberty first. "No one spoke a word," said one immigrant. "It was the symbol of the big, powerful country which was our new home."

After the ship had arrived in Manhattan, they went to Ellis Island on a small boat. Here they had more checks and personal interviews. About two percent had to go back home because they had diseases or they were too weak to work.

A minority of about 20 percent stayed on the island for days or sometimes weeks for more checks, but the rest could leave after a few hours.

The immigrants' journey to the USA was now over. But they still had a long way to go.

3 Answer the questions about Ellis Island.

1. How many immigrants arrived from 1892 to 1954?
2. How long was the journey?
3. What were the conditions on the ships like? Name three examples.
4. Why did the passengers have to go to Ellis Island? Name two reasons.
5. How many immigrants could not stay in the USA?

CULTURE

Jeder, der in den USA geboren wird, hat automatisch die amerikanische Staatsbürgerschaft und einen amerikanischen Pass.
Wie ist das in deinem Land?

Immigration to the USA

From the 1840s to the 1890s most immigrants to the USA came from Britain, Ireland, Scandinavia and Germany.
Between the 1890s and the 1920s the majority of immigrants came from Italy, Greece, Eastern Europe, Russia and Turkey. Many of them came because they were poor or because there were fights in their home countries. Others came to find work or freedom.

Immigration to the USA today: 2013

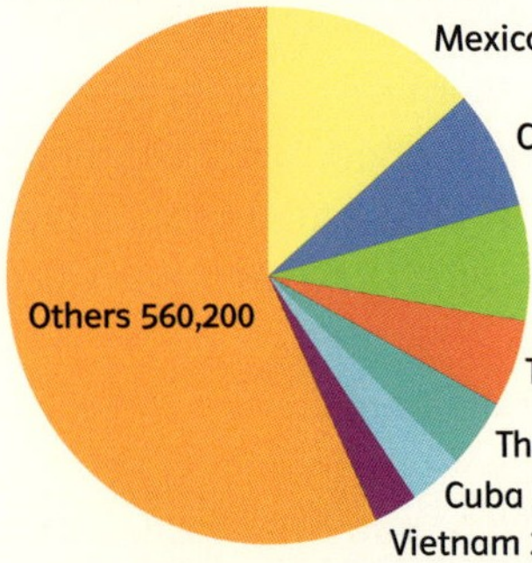

Source: Department of Homeland Security

READING SKILLS

Wenn du ein Kreisdiagramm liest, sieh dir die Beschriftungen genau an.
Achte auf die unterschiedlichen Größen der einzelnen Abschnitte innerhalb des Diagramms.

4 Look at the box and find out: Why did people immigrate to the USA?

5 (SPEAKING) Look at the chart and complete the sentences.

This chart shows the countries where the immigrants to the USA came from in … . Most immigrants came from … . The next group came from … . The third group … and … . There were also lots of immigrants from … and lots of other countries.

6 Choose one of these tasks.

a) Work with a partner. Prepare an interview with an immigrant who has just arrived. Here are some questions:

10/1-3

- Where are you from?
- Why did you choose this country?
- What was the journey like?
- What are your plans for the future?

Present your interview to the class.
→ M Dramatic reading, p. 169

OR

b) What is the country of your dreams? What do you like about the country? What don't you like? Give a short presentation to the class.
→ M 1-minute-presentation, p. 168

SPEAKING SKILLS

Interviews und Präsentationen beginnen immer mit einer Begrüßung und enden mit einem Dankeschön.

Ich kann einen Text über die Geschichte der Einwanderung verstehen.

How to become a US citizen

How do I apply for US citizenship?

- be age 18 or older
- be a permanent resident for a certain amount of time (usually 5 years or 3 years)
- be a person of good moral character
- have a basic knowledge of US government
- be able to read, write and speak basic English

Sample test questions:

1. What did the Declaration of Independence do?
2. What is the name of the President of the United States now?
3. In what month do we vote for President?
4. What is one reason colonists came to America?
5. What group of people was taken to America and sold as slaves?
6. There were 13 original states. Name three.
7. Name one Native American tribe in the United States.
8. What ocean is on the West Coast of the United States?
9. Why does the flag have 50 stars?
10. Name two national US holidays.

CULTURE

Um amerikanischer Staatsbürger zu werden, muss man einen Einbürgerungstest machen. Das ist ein mündlicher Test, in dem einem 10 von 100 möglichen Fragen gestellt werden. Von diesen zehn Fragen muss man sechs richtig beantworten. Es gibt auch einen Englischtest. Gibt es so einen Test auch in deinem Land?

Du findest die Lösungen auf S. 282.

1 Fasse die wichtigsten Punkte zusammen.

11/1-2

Was sind die Voraussetzungen, um die amerikanische Staatsbürgerschaft anzunehmen?

- Wie alt muss man sein?
- Was muss man können und wissen? Gib Beispiele.

2 What do you think?

Why do people immigrate to Germany? Give reasons.

Ich kann Informationen über Einbürgerung weitergeben. ✔

New York City, here we come!

1 Talk about New York City.

What do you already know about New York City? Make a mind map of buildings and places.

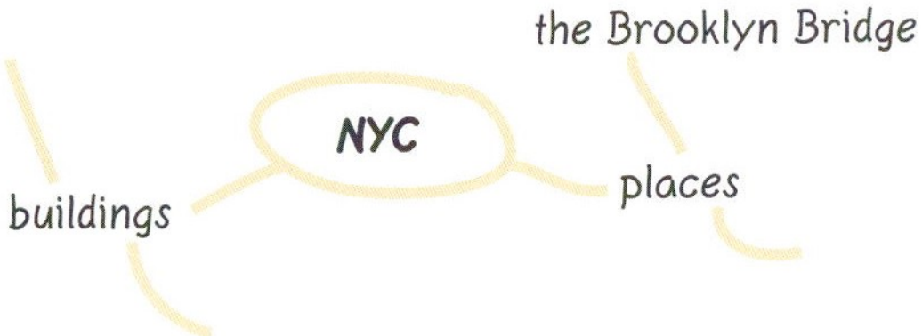

> **CULTURE**
>
> Central Park liegt im Herzen Manhattans. Es gibt dort einen Zoo, sieben Seen, eine Eisbahn, Baseballfelder und vieles mehr. Wusstest du, dass der New York Marathon im Central Park endet?
> Wo ist der nächste Park bei dir? Was kannst du dort machen?

2 (VIEWING) Watch the film.

2

a) Name the sights that Wesley and Jessica show to Ronan. Put them in the right order.

A

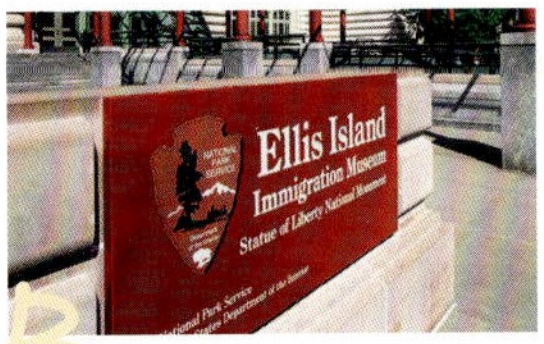

B

C

D

b) Match the facts with the pictures.

1. It's between Manhattan and Brooklyn. There were once elephants here.
2. It's not far from Little Italy and there isn't only one of these in NYC.
3. It has names on a 'Wall of Honor'. Maybe Ronan's great-grandparents were here.
4. There are no elevators here. In summer it can get very hot inside.

3 (SPEAKING) Talk about the film.

Where would you like to go in New York City? Why? Tell your partner.

I would like to go to/see/visit …
because … .
I think … is interesting. I like … .

> **VIEWING SKILLS**
>
> In einem Film sind nicht nur die Personen und die Geschichte wichtig, sondern auch die Orte und das, was man im Hintergrund sehen kann. Suche dir eine Filmsequenz aus und stelle den Ton ab. Was passiert im Hintergrund?

Ich kann einen Film über Sehenswürdigkeiten in New York verstehen. 

Checklist

Ich kann Informationen über New York verstehen. ✓

12

Ich kann interessante Orte einer Stadt präsentieren. ✓

Over there you can see .... • Look at .... • You must visit .... • Around this corner we'll come to .... • Don't miss ....

12

Ich kann einen Artikel über eine Person schreiben. ✓

immigrated to • felt foreign • was homesick • missed • had given up a lot • had many chances • got used to

13

Ich kann einen Text über die Geschichte der Einwanderung verstehen. ✓

13

Ich kann Informationen über Einbürgerung weitergeben. ✓

13

Ich kann einen Film über Sehenswürdigkeiten in New York verstehen. ✓

(TASK) A city profile

Work in groups of three students. Each group chooses an American city and finds out some basic facts about it and its population. Each group makes a poster.

Step 1

Get into groups. Choose an American city.

Choose one of America's big cities like Los Angeles. Look at the map at the back of the book to find an interesting place.

Step 2

Find the basic facts and some photos.

City: Los Angeles
State: California
Sights: Hollywood sign, Venice Beach
One interesting fact about the past: had a very long Spanish name in 1871 (El Pueblo de la Reina de Los Ángeles)

Step 3

Find the numbers.

Answer these questions with the help of the internet:

1. What's the population of the city?
2. Which ethnic groups are part of the city's population? Name the biggest ones.

STUDY SKILLS

Suche offizielle Webseiten der Regierung, um die korrekten Zahlen herauszufinden. Daten zu Städten in den USA findest du auf der Webseite des US Census Bureau. Du kannst die Angaben dort runden. Finde die größten Volksgruppen heraus und fasse die übrigen Gruppen unter „others" zusammen.

Step 4

Make a chart.

Make a chart. You can make a pie chart (A) or a bar chart (B). Remember that your chart must have a title, labels and a key. Your chart should take up about 30 percent of your poster.

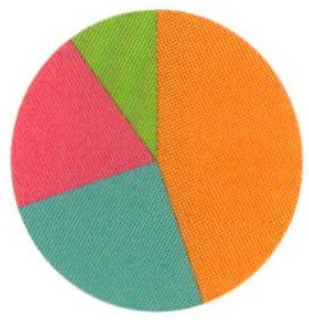

A

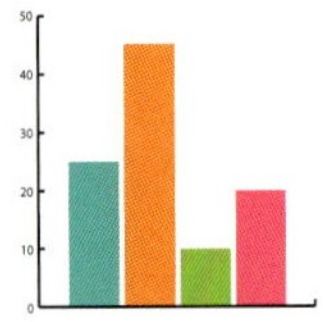

B

> **STUDY SKILLS**
>
> Du kannst Säulen- oder Kreisdiagramme auch mit einem Computerprogramm erstellen. Das ist recht einfach und sieht sauber und ordentlich aus.

Step 5

Write a short text for your chart.

This text should explain the most important information.

most | the next group | the third group | ...

Step 6

Finish your poster.

Arrange your photos, chart and texts.
Can you read everything from two metres away?
Don't forget to say where you got your information from.

> **STUDY SKILLS**
>
> Überprüfe, ob dein Poster Aufmerksamkeit auf sich zieht. Ist es gut strukturiert und sieht es gut aus?

Step 7

Put up your poster. → M Tip top, p. 173

0.7 = zero point seven

Make your own street art

Five steps to turn your schoolyard into an American Dream art gallery

You need:

a piece of paper

pens

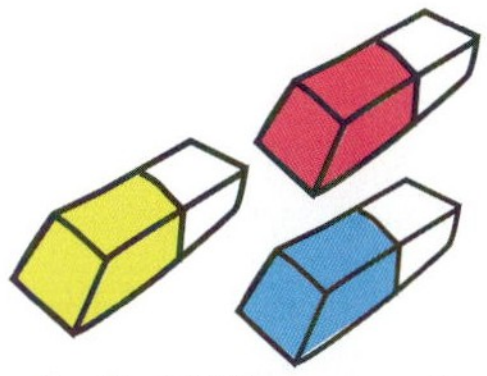
chalk (different colours)

1 Find out about the American Dream.

The American Dream

The basic idea of the American Dream is that you can be anything you want – you only have to work hard enough. Typical dreams are, for example, the dream of being happy, rich or famous. Other people dream of a house for their family or want to have a life which is better than their parents' life. Millions of immigrants have come to the United States searching for a country where their dreams can come true. Critics say that the American Dream does not exist in reality because it isn't for everyone.

2 What do you (not) like about the American Dream?

Vom Tellerwäscher zum Millionär.

3 Turn your idea into a piece of street art.

Choose one aspect of the American Dream.

You can write words or sentences and/or draw pictures. Decide the style of your piece of street art.

Here are some ideas:

1

2

3

4

4 Make a draft for your street art on a piece of paper.

5 Draw your street art in the schoolyard with chalk.

Macht Fotos, bevor der Regen eure Kunstwerke wegwischt.

Hier kannst du lernen, wie du das Internet effektiv nutzt.

INTERNET

Alaska: Denali National Park
wild and wonderful

SEARCH | MENU

Wild and wonderful Alaska is a state full of extremes – freezing winters and warm summers. You can have fantastic adventures and enjoy the amazing wildlife in the USA's most northern state. The park is also the home of Denali, the highest mountain in the United States.

▶ Park history

A The life of a Denali husky

The Denali National Park is home to a group of Alaskan huskies. They make travel and transport easier in the park. They travel on paths with the sled where cars and trucks cannot go because of the snow.

▶ Visiting the dogs

B Bears in Alaska

One reason tourists come to Alaska is to see the grizzly bears. If you are lucky enough to see them, you will never forget these large, beautiful animals.

▶ What bears eat in the wild

▶ Safety

▶ Bus tours ▶ Park alerts ▶ Contact us ▶ FAQ

Last updated: 02/20/2016
(security information)

1 Find out information.

First look at the website on the left. What could the keywords be to find a website like this? Make a list. Compare it with a partner.

Je genauer du deine Schlüsselwörter eingibst, desto eindeutiger werden deine Suchergebnisse.
Wenn du nach Tieren im Denali Nationalpark suchst, beginne mit „animals“ und „Denali National Park“.
Benötigst du spezielle Informationen, kannst du in deiner Suchmaschine auch Folgendes eingeben:
Animal Denali National Park
Large animals Denali National Park
What animals are in Denali National Park?

2 Check the information.

Look at the website on the left again. Do you think it is an official website, an ad or a blog? Give reasons.

Es ist wichtig zu wissen, woher die Informationen kommen, die du gefunden hast. Offizielle Webseiten sind verlässlicher als Werbeseiten oder Seiten von Einzelpersonen. Sieh dir immer mehrere Webseiten an.

offizielle Webseite	Werbung	Blog
- Datum, Update - Geschäfts-/Sicherheits-informationen …	- Slogan - kurz, einfach - große Fotos …	- eigene Meinung - wie ein Journal oder Tagebuch …

3 Collect information.

Read text A or B on the left. Write down the most important keywords.

17/1-3

4 Do a search.

Search for more facts about your topic. Present two interesting things.

1. List keywords.
2. Search the internet.
3. List two to three different websites.
4. Prepare a short presentation.

Here are some ideas:
- Huskies: Training? Typical day? Summer dog sledding?
- Bears: Food? Food cache? Bear spray?

Benutze deine eigenen Worte, wenn du die Informationen der Webseiten weitergibst. Kopiere nicht einfach den Text. Aber ändere keine Fakten.

Find more online:
i8ce82

Am Ende dieser Unit kann ich ...
- Informationen über den Mittleren Westen verstehen.
- das Schulleben in den USA und in Deutschland vergleichen.
- über Schülerjobs sprechen.
- einen Comic über das Highschool-Leben verstehen.
- Informationen über den Führerschein weitergeben.
- einen Film über den ersten Tag an einer neuen Schule verstehen.

3 1,8

Unit 2

Teens in the Midwest

1

The American Midwest is famous for its huge areas of farmland and small towns. The summers are very hot and the winters are very cold. In some areas there are terrible storms.

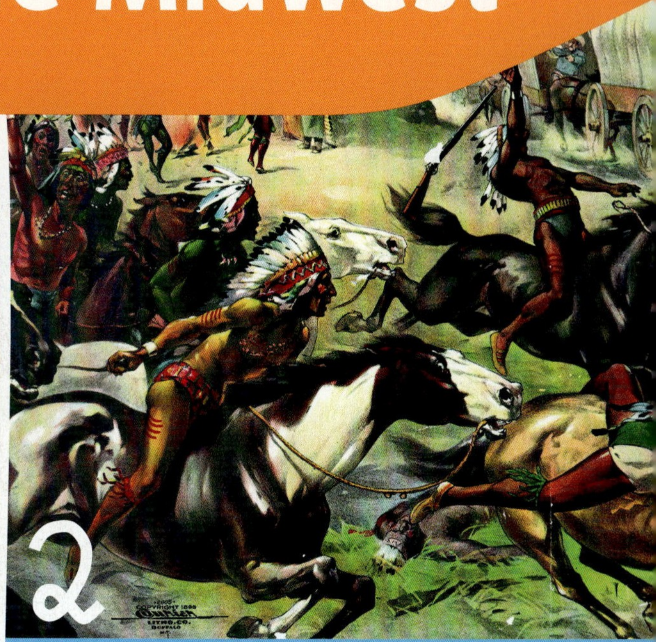

2

In the 1840s a lot of European settlers moved west. They wanted to find land and gold. The Native Americans had to sell their land and move to reservations.

1 (SPEAKING) Talk about the photos.

a) Match the photos with the headings. 18/1-2
Which two photos have the same heading?

Student jobs | The past | Country life | School life

b) Which photo do you like most?
→ M Round robin, p. 172

Photo x looks great. • I like photo x most.
I'm interested in .... • I really like ....

2 Read the texts and answer the questions.

1. What is the Midwest famous for?
   The Midwest is famous for its farmland and small towns.
2. Why did European settlers move west?
3. Where can high school students get a job?
4. What's special about the grades at American high schools?
5. When is Homecoming?

High school students over 14 often have jobs. They can work in stores, clear the tables or serve in restaurants or cafés.

American high schools are usually big. There can be over 2,000 students. They are 15 to 18 years old. They can get grades from A (very good) to F. The schedule is almost the same every day.

At the start of the new school year students celebrate Homecoming. There's a football game and a dance. Students vote for a Homecoming King and Queen.

3 (LISTENING) Listen to a radio report about a tornado.

1,9

Complete the sentences. Use five of these words:

dangerous · clouds · help · strong · cars · storm · interview

tornado [tɔːˈneɪdəʊ] – Tornado, Wirbelsturm
warning [ˈwɔːnɪŋ] – Warnung
storm chaser [ˈstɔːm ˌtʃeɪsə] – Sturmjäger/in
cloud [klaʊd] – Wolke

1. Warren is a —— chaser.
2. The wind is really —— .
3. The —— are moving very fast.
4. The situation is —— .
5. Warren wants to —— some people.

Ich kann Informationen über den Mittleren Westen verstehen. ✓

Hier lerne ich, das Schulleben in den USA und in Deutschland zu vergleichen.

A student exchange

1 What can you see in the photo?

2 (READING) Read Luise's report.

1,10

"No! An exchange year in South Dakota? That's in the middle of nowhere," I thought. But after my year there I can say that it was the best time ever.

In the beginning it was like in a movie. I had seen it all on TV. My American school was huge. Teachers usually stay in their classrooms, and students go to them for each class. So we had to put our things into our lockers. After two weeks I got used to it, and I could find the way to the classrooms by myself.

Every day school started at 8:00 with a morning message from the principal. The first class started at 8:30. I had to take Math, English, Science and History. But I could choose subjects like Astronomy and Journalism, for example. We also had six classes a week in the study hall. There we could do our homework or study. You weren't allowed to talk there. School rules were strict. Much stricter than at home. Another rule was: You weren't allowed to wear short skirts.

Classes finished at 3:30. After that there were many extracurricular activities. I wanted to join the cheerleaders. There was a lot of competition for places. Exchange students were allowed to try too, so I did. And I got a place! Awesome!

My host family was great too. They even took me on a trip to the east coast. My exchange year was fantastic, even in the middle of nowhere.

3 (WRITING) Find out about Luise's exchange year.

a) Make a mind map. → ○ p. 118

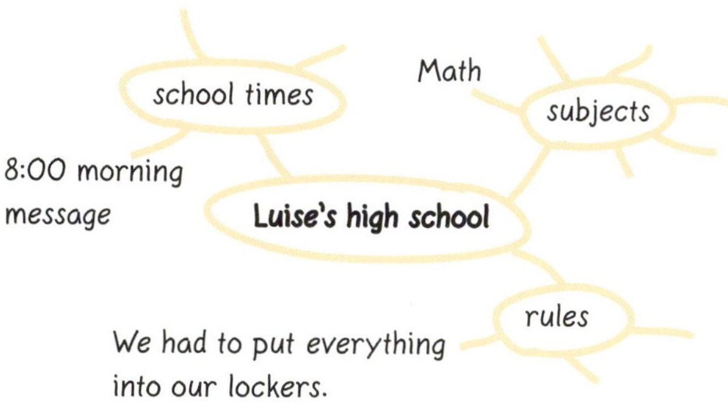

b) What did Luise like? What didn't she like? Make a list.

CULTURE

Eltern müssen ihre Kinder nicht in die Schule schicken. Sie dürfen sie auch zu Hause unterrichten. Das tun aber nur sehr wenige (ca. 3%). Gibt es Homeschooling auch in Deutschland?

19/1-2a)
4 What do these words mean?

a) Match the words with the definitions. → ○ p. 119

grade | principal | study hall | locker | exchange year

1. where students keep their things
2. the leader of a school
3. where you can do your homework or study
4. a number or letter that tells you how well you did in a test
5. a year with a host family in another country

19/2b)
b) Choose the right word. → V At American schools, p. 186

electives | detention | core subjects

1. Math and English are —— .
2. Astronomy and Journalism are —— .
3. When you have to stay at school after classes you have —— .

19/3
20/4
5 (SPEAKING) Describe a school day.

a) Describe a day at an American high school. Use the photos for help.

1

2

3

4

	Monday	Tuesday	Wednesday	Thursday	Friday
	English	English	English	English	English
2	Math	Math	Math	Math	Math
3	Science	Science	Science	Science	Science
4	History	History	History	History	History
5	Journalism	Journalism	Journalism	Journalism	Journalism
6	Astronomy	Astronomy	Astronomy	Astronomy	Astronomy

5

6

(1) In the morning most students go to school by bus. (2) Then students .... (3) At 8:00 there's .... (4) After that they .... (5) At 1:00 there's .... (6) After school ....

b) Describe a typical day at your school. Use the sentences from a) for help.

1,11
6 (SONG) Cool kids

Listen to the song. How does the singer describe the 'cool kids'?

She sees them walking in a straight line,
that's not really her style.
And they all got the same heartbeat,
but hers is falling behind.
Nothing in this world could
ever bring them down.
Yeah, they're invincible, and she's just in the background.
And she says,

I wish that I could be like the cool kids,
'cause all the cool kids, they seem to fit in.
I wish that I could be like the cool kids,
like the cool kids.

Language detectives → G3, p. 160

I had to take Math, English, Science and History.
I could choose subjects like Astronomy and Journalism.
Exchange students were allowed to try too.

Wie sagt man im simple past, dass man etwas tun
- konnte?
- durfte?
- musste?

7 (SPEAKING) Talk about school rules.

52/2 20/5-6 a) What was Luise allowed to wear at high school? What was she not allowed to wear?

INTERNET

High School Dress Code

Dos

jeans

simple T-shirts

jewellery

Don'ts

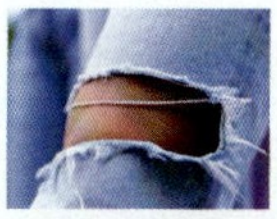

jeans with holes

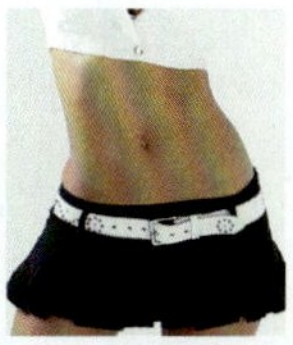

short tops

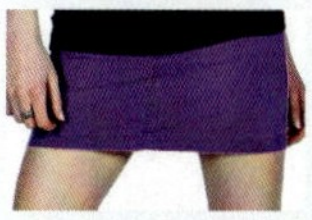

very short skirts

Luise was allowed to wear jeans. She wasn't allowed to …

21/7 b) What are you allowed to do at school? What aren't you allowed to do?
Use different verbs.

leave | stay | wear ✓ | use | …

We are allowed to wear … . We aren't allowed to wear …

8 Complete the sentences.

52/3

21/8a) a) Write the sentences about Luise and the cheerleaders. → ○ p. 120

had to | didn't have to

1. Before Luise joined the cheerleaders she had to get the right clothes.
2. She was fit, so she — worry.
3. For the first practice she — be there 15 minutes early.
4. During her first practice the cheerleaders — shout really loudly.
5. Luise learned very quickly, so she — do extra practice.

21/8b) b) What did or didn't you have to do on your first day at school after the summer holiday?

buy exercise books | do homework | get my books | get up early | …

On my first day at school after the summer holiday I had to … but I didn't have to … .

21/9 ## 9 Make sentences about Luise's life after her exchange year in the USA.

a) Say what Luise could (+) or couldn't (–) do after her exchange. → ○ p. 120

Luise
1. – get used to her old life easily
2. + understand English a lot better
3. + speak English a lot better
4. – keep in touch with all her American friends
5. + help other students with English

1. **Luise** couldn't get used to her old life easily.

b) Interview Luise about the things she could or couldn't do after her exchange. Use the phrases from part a) and make questions.

1. Interviewer: Could you get used to your old life easily?
Luise: No, I couldn't. (I missed my host family and my American friends.)

10 (YOUR TURN) A comparison → V Comparing schools, p. 190 → M Writers' conference, p. 173

a) Use your notes about American schools from page 34, exercise 3. Make a table:

	American high schools	German schools
school times	8:00 to 3:30	…
…	…	…

b) Compare American and German schools.
Give your opinion: Would you like to go to an American school? Say why (not).

1. You can start like this:
There are many students like Luise who go to an American high school for one year. What is different from schools in Germany?

2. You can go on like this:
In the USA school starts at … and finishes at … . Our school in Germany also starts at …, but we finish at … .

In American high schools students … . For German schools this is the same/different. We … .

3. You can end like this:
I would (not) like to go to an American school because … .

WRITING SKILLS

So schreibst du einen Vergleich:
1. Stelle dein Thema vor.
2. Nenne im Hauptteil drei Fakten für beide Seiten.
3. Am Ende schreibst du deine eigene Meinung.

Ich kann das Schulleben in den USA und in Deutschland vergleichen. ✓

A lesson outside school

1 Have you ever tried to earn some extra money? What did you do?
→ M Think-pair-share, p. 173

2 (READING) Read the story.

1,12 22/1

Like a lot of American teenagers Michael Adams (16) needed to earn some money. He wanted to get his driver's license soon, he needed new clothes, and he had a new girlfriend. When he read the advert for a student job in a sports store, he thought, "That's the perfect job for me. With all the customers it'll never be boring." He applied for the job.

INTERNET

Student Jobs

JIMMY'S SPORTING GOODS Lincoln, NE

Job title: Sales associate

Job type: Weekends

Education: High school

Bring your love of sports to Jimmy's.

The job interview was tough. The manager asked lots of difficult questions. "What will you do if somebody steals something?" or "What will you do if a customer complains?" Michael answered all the questions and they offered him the job. Ten hours a week and the minimum wage was OK for him.

His co-workers were very helpful. At the beginning everything was new and exciting. After two weeks, however, Michael learned that jobs have their good and bad sides. Some days were really boring. He didn't have much to do. On other days he was busy, so he didn't know what to do first.

One Saturday two students from his school came into the store. They started teasing him. "You'll miss all the fun if you work here every weekend. Just look at you. If you wear a uniform like that, you won't be one of the cool kids, ever."

Michael got angry. He got into a big argument with them and in the end he threw them out of the store.

Later that day his manager called him into his office. "I can understand you," he said. "But what will our customers think? Be more responsible. If this happens again, you'll lose your job."

3 Find the right order.

A He throws them out of the store.
B Two students start teasing Michael.
C He gets the job.
D Michael needs money.
E There's a job interview.
F He applies for a job.
G Michael's job has good and bad sides.
H The manager talks to Michael in his office.

CULTURE

Viele Amerikaner benutzen Kreditkarten, kein Bargeld. Man kann sogar einen einzigen Bagel mit der Kreditkarte bezahlen.

4 (SPEAKING) What do you think?

a) What should or shouldn't Michael say to the manager? → ○ p. 120

1. "I'm sorry."
2. "It won't happen again."
3. "But they started it."
4. "It wasn't me."
5. "I don't think you're right."
6. "Next time I'll try to be cooler."

b) Imagine you apply for the job in the sports store. Answer the manager's questions.

1. What will you do if somebody steals something? – I think I'll … .
2. What will you do if a customer complains? – I think I'll … .

call … · talk to … · say, "…"

5 (LISTENING) Listen to Marie on her first day at work at Fruit4U.

1,13
52/4

Choose the right answer.

1. Who is Stacey?
   the manager • a co-worker
2. What is Fruit4U famous for?
   the best location and the most friendly waiters • the freshest fruit and the lowest prices
3. What are Marie's working hours?
   9:30 a.m. to 3 p.m. • 9 a.m. to 2 p.m.
4. How long is Marie's break?
   30 minutes • 40 minutes
5. How can she get extra money?
   extra hours • good feedback

6 (WRITING) Practise words to describe people at work. → M Peer correction, p. 171

22/2 a) Copy and complete the table. → ○ p. 121

lazy ✓ · hard-working · helpful · responsible · unmotivated · unfriendly

+	–
…	lazy …

Welche bekannten Wörter stecken in den neuen Wörtern drin?

22/3 b) Find the opposites. → V Describing people, p. 187

confident · generous · polite · rude · selfish · shy

7 (SPEAKING) Describe the most … job.

22/4

Think of ten jobs in English. Make a list in two minutes. Then say which job is the …

most dangerous · most exciting · most boring · best-paying

A: I think a football player has got the most exciting job because **he has got a lot of fans.**
B: I don't think so. I think an actor has got the most exciting job because … .

Language → G4, p. 161

If this happens again, you'll lose your job.
If you wear a uniform like that, you won't be one of the cool kids.

Diese Sätze bestehen aus zwei Teilen, dem If-Satz und dem Hauptsatz. In welchem Teil verwendest du das simple present, in welchem Teil das will-future?

8 What does Marie think after her first day at work? Use the will-future. → M Bus stop, p. 168

23/5

1. If I watch everything that Linda does, I'll learn quickly. (learn)
2. If the customer feedback is good, I — extra money. (get)
3. If I have to cut fruit all day, I — . (not complain)
4. If a customer is unfriendly, I — polite. (stay)
5. If my friends work every weekend too, we — time for parties any more. (not have)
6. If I get sick, I — the manager. (call)

23/6

9 Complete the sentences.

a) Use the simple present. → ○ p. 121

find a job ✓ | buy two | complain | be late | steal something | need help

1. If Michael finds a job, he'll earn money.

2. If he — , he'll ask his co-workers.

3. If he — , he'll lose his job.

4. If the girl — , Michael will catch her.

5. If the man — , he'll get a new sweatshirt.

6. If the woman — , she'll get one free.

b) What will happen if Michael gets sick? Make a chain of sentences.

If Michael gets sick, he'll stay at home. If he stays at home, he … . If …

53/5 ## 10 (SPEAKING) What will you do if …?

a) Talk about next weekend. → p. 121

23/7a)

1. If I get up late,
2. If the weather is fine,
3. If it rains,
4. If I don't have any homework,
5. If my parents are away on Saturday evening,
6. If I'm too busy,

\+ I'll / I won't +

watch TV.
have a party.
go cycling.
go to the cinema.
go shopping.
have breakfast.
look for a student job.
…

b) Find a partner. Ask him or her about next weekend.

23/7b)

A: What will you do if you get up late?
B: I'll/I won't …

11 (YOUR TURN) A job for me → V Jobs, p. 191

26/1-2

Which student job would you like to do? Choose one and talk about it.

JOBS FOR TEENS

Dog walker
- work near your home
- be outside (also when the weather is bad)
- earn $10 per hour

Babysitter
- look after kids in their homes
- work very often in the evenings
- earn $12 per hour

Paperboy/girl
- work early in the morning
- every day (even on Sundays)
- earn $40 per week

I would like to work as a papergirl because
I like to get up early.
I'm a responsible person,
so this is the perfect job for me.
If I get the job, I'll buy clothes.

dog walker | babysitter | paperboy
I like … | it's the best paying job | …
helpful | hard-working | …
get tickets for … | …

Ich kann über Schülerjobs sprechen.

A first date

1 Which stereotypes of American high school characters do you know from movies and TV shows? → M Placemat, p. 171

2 (READING) Read the comic strip.

1,14

1. Dylan often thought about Abby. He really liked her. But he was too shy to ask her out on a date.

2. One day his books fell out of his locker right when Abby showed up. Scott was with her, of course. How embarrassing.

3. A few days later they had lunch together. Dylan helped Abby with her Science project. They didn't see Scott and his football friends.

4. When Dylan went to the gym, the boys attacked him. Scott pushed him really hard and Dylan couldn't do anything about it.

3 (SPEAKING) Talk about the story.

a) Do you like the story? Why (not)?

I (don't) like the story because … .

funny | boring | (not) real life | romance | stereotypes | …

b) Who is … ?

A shy
Dylan is shy. That's picture 1.
B proud
C nervous
D unfriendly
E worried
F furious
G brave
H helpful

5. A few days later Dylan asked Abby, "Are you coming to the dance with me?" And she said yes. He was very nervous when he picked her up.

6. The party was great. Everybody enjoyed the music and dancing. There was a big surprise that evening. Dylan and Abby were so proud.

7. At the end of the evening Dylan took Abby home. There it was, the perfect moment. But …

4 Retell the story.

1. Work in groups of three. Each student chooses two pictures.
2. Take notes for your pictures.
3. Tell your part of the story.

STUDY SKILLS

Wenn du einen Comic nacherzählst, benutze auch die Informationen aus den Bildern.

Photo 1
football match – Dylan – his friends – talk about Abby – shy – boyfriend – football player

Dylan and his friends talked about Abby at the football match. Dylan liked Abby but he was too shy to ask her out on a date and she had a boyfriend anyway. He was a very good football player.

5 Choose one of these tasks. → M Tip top, p. 173

a) Do Dylan and Abby stay together? What happens next? Write the last paragraph.

24/1
25/2-3

OR

b) Choose one scene. Make a freeze frame. Let other groups guess.

The next day … | Then … | After that … | In the end …

Ich kann einen Comic über das Highschool-Leben verstehen.

How to get your driver's license

Classroom Driver Ed

Length: 9 weeks

Classroom driver education is a course for all students who will be 15 years old before the last day of instruction and who have successfully completed eight out of ten courses in 8th grade. The course introduces students to basic skills of driving.
To take the written and practical driving test, please contact your local driving school.

DRIVER EDUCATION APPROVAL FORM

Name and Address of Driver Training School:

Sally's Driving School Inc., 524 Bird Highway, Park Ridge 60068 IL

Student's Full Name: (last) Jenkins (first) Caitlin (middle) Amy

Street Address: 1815, Baxendale Road

City or Town: Chicago ZIP Code: 60004 IL

Caitlin A. Jenkins 12/16/2016
Signature of Student Date

Steve M. Jenkins
Signature of Parent

CULTURE

Amerikaner haben keinen Personalausweis. Sie benutzen stattdessen ihren Führerschein. Nach fünf Jahren muss man einen neuen beantragen (aber man muss die Prüfung nicht wiederholen).

1 Berichte darüber, wie man in den USA den Führerschein macht.

27/1

2 Pass on the information in a conversation about how to get a driver's license.

27/2

A *(from Germany)*: In welchem Alter kann man bei euch in Illinois den Führerschein machen?
You: At what age … ?
B *(from Illinois)*: At the age of 15. And in Germany?
You: …
A: Mit 18. Aber man kann ihn auch schon mit 17 machen, wenn eine weitere Person mit Führerschein im Auto dabei ist.
You: …
B: So, do you need a parent's signature for that too?
You: …
A: Ja, das stimmt. Muss man in den USA auch eine theoretische und eine praktische Prüfung ablegen?
You: …
B: …

Wenn du ein bestimmtes Wort auf Englisch nicht weißt, sage es mit anderen Worten.

Ich kann Informationen über den Führerschein weitergeben.

The new kid at school

1 Talk about a new school.

a) What would you show a new kid at your school?

I would show him/her the cafeteria, … .

b) How would you feel if you were the 'new kid' at school?

I would be … .

nervous | excited | shy | …

2 (VIEWING) Watch the film.

4

a) Watch the film until 02:48. Right or wrong? Correct the wrong sentences.

1. A buddy is a teacher's favourite student.
2. CJ and Ronan are in the same homeroom.
3. Ruby has had seven detentions this year.
4. They have Math first period.
5. All students say the Pledge of Allegiance.

b) Watch the film from 02:48 to the end. Name the places that Ronan and CJ go to. Say one sentence about what they do there.

CULTURE

In den USA beginnen viele Schulen jeden Tag mit dem Treueschwur. Die Schüler stehen auf, legen ihre rechte Hand aufs Herz, sehen zur amerikanischen Flagge und geloben der Nation und Gott ihre Treue.
Hältst du einen Treueschwur für eine gute Idee? Warum? Warum nicht?

3 (WRITING) Write about the film.

Write Ronan's e-mail to Roy, his best friend at his old school, to tell him about his first day at the new school.

E-MAIL

Hi Roy,
I must tell you about my first day at school. I met CJ. He's my buddy. He's really … . We went … . Then I met … . Can you believe that …?
Bye,
Ronan

VIEWING SKILLS

Die meisten Filme beginnen mit einer Eröffnungsszene. Sie zeigt die Tageszeit, den Ort des Geschehens und die beteiligten Personen etc. an.
Sieh dir die Eröffnungsszene im Film an. Was erfährst du dort?

Ich kann einen Film über den ersten Tag an einer neuen Schule verstehen.

Checklist

Ich kann Informationen über den Mittleren Westen verstehen. ✓

28

Ich kann das Schulleben in den USA und Deutschland vergleichen. ✓

In American high schools …. • In German schools …. • In the USA most students go to school by …. • School rules … stricter. • … is the same. • But … is different.

28

Ich kann über Schülerjobs sprechen. ✓

I would like to work as a …. • I'm very/not so good at …. • If I earn money, I'll buy …. • If I work in my free time, I won't have much time for ….

29

Ich kann einen Comic über das Highschool-Leben verstehen. ✓

29

Ich kann Informationen über den Führerschein weitergeben. ✓

29

Ich kann einen Film über den ersten Tag an einer neuen Schule verstehen. ✓

❀ (TASK) A speech

Every year your class elects a class president. You would like to be the next one. Give a 1-minute speech. Then answer your classmates' questions.

Step 1

Collect ideas.

What's important for you and your class?
(good team, nice teachers, fun …)

What topics interest you?
(school trips, projects, …)

What are you good at?
(listening to …, talking to …, …)

What will you do if your class elects you?
(try to paint the classroom a new colour, have a party every month, …)

Step 2

Structure and write your speech.

→ M 1-minute-presentation, p. 168

1. How can you start your speech?
2. Why would you like to be the next class president? Use one paragraph for each topic.
3. How can you finish your speech?

WRITING SKILLS

Eine Rede hat ähnliche Merkmale wie die meisten geschriebenen Texte: Einleitung, Hauptteil, Schluss.

Auf der nächsten Seite findest du eine Vorlage für eine fertige Rede.

Step 3

Practise your speech. → M Read and look up, p. 172

Find different partners.
Practise your speech in front of them.
Read your speech a couple of times.
Then make notes and repeat your speech again and again.

SPEAKING SKILLS

Um gewählt zu werden, musst du deine Klasse überzeugen. Es ist wichtig, dass sie dir zuhört. Du kannst z. B. Dinge wiederholen, die dir wichtig sind. Sprich nicht zu schnell oder zu langsam.

Step 4

Give your speech.

- Stand straight and try to relax.
- Look at your listeners from time to time. Eye contact is important.
- Speak loudly and clearly.

Dear class,
Next Friday will be a big day for all of us. We're going to elect our class president.
I think our class is already a really good team. If you elect me, I'll .... I'll listen and .... If you have any problems, I'm sure ....
I promise ... because I'm hard-working and motivated.
You think classes could be more fun? You think we should have ...?
Come and talk to me. I'll try to talk to the teachers and the principal.
Thanks for listening. I'll be happy to answer your questions now.

Step 5

Answer your listeners' questions.

Answer the questions politely.
If you didn't understand the question, ask the person to repeat it.

High school electives

In American high schools you can choose from a number of electives, depending on your interests. They also look great on your CV. Some courses offer extra credits for your graduation.

INTERNET

< 1 > Home   < 2 > About   < 3 > News   <4 > Courses

COURSE #	DESCRIPTION	CORE SUBJECT OR ELECTIVE	OTHER INFORMATION
A022	**Astronomy**	**Elective**	

Length: 2 semesters
Credits: 2
Open to Grades: 10–12
Prerequisite: Algebra, Science

This course introduces students to our solar system, planets and galaxies. Topics include the history of astronomy, its impact on society, and the methods and tools that scientists use to locate objects in the night sky. Students are required to attend some observations in the early morning or in the evening.

COURSE #	DESCRIPTION	CORE SUBJECT OR ELECTIVE	OTHER INFORMATION
B005	**Introduction to Welding Technology**	**Elective**	**$20 Lab Fee**

Length: 2 semesters
Credits: 2
Open to Grades: 9–12
Prerequisite: –

This course introduces students to the process of making things out of metal. Students learn about different forms of metal and also how to cut and join metals. This course also makes students familiar with required safety measures. Students create individual projects as well as complete projects for school.

C011	Journalism	Elective

Length: 1 semester
Credits: 1
Open to Grades: 9–12
Prerequisite: –

This course introduces students to the fundamentals of journalism. Topics include writing, editing, layout and graphic design. Students learn different styles of journalistic writing such as news, interviews, features, sports, book and movie reviews, and blogs. They contribute articles to the school's yearbook and online newspaper. Students are required to work in teams, be ready to write articles in their free time and have to meet deadlines.

1 Which elective would you choose? Say why.

2 Think of electives for your school and write a course description.

Ihr könnt euren Gedanken freien Lauf lassen!

- Collect ideas in groups.
- Write a course description.
  Say what the course is about, what students can learn there and what they have to do.
  Write about 50 words.
- Present your course descriptions in class.
- Vote in class to find the most popular elective.

STUDY SKILLS

Verwende ein Computerprogramm zur Textverarbeitung.
Hier findest du ein paar Anregungen:
- Wähle eine Schriftart und eine Schriftgröße zwischen 10 und 14 aus.
- Hebe die Überschrift fett oder mit Farbe hervor.
- Verwende den Wortzähler und die Rechtschreibprüfung.
- Du kannst Textfelder einfügen, um deine Seite zu strukturieren.
- Du kannst ein Foto im Internet suchen und herunterladen, um deinen Text interessanter zu machen.
- Du kannst eine Seitenfarbe für den Hintergrund auswählen.

Hier kannst du lernen, wie du eine Präsentation vorbereitest und hältst.

American football

A

- Super Bowl: most famous sporting event
- first Sunday in February
- famous sporting event on TV
- like a national holiday
- final match of the season
- game first played in USA in 1869

B

C

- team of supporters
- motivate players and fans
- today: 95% girls
- dance, jump, shout loudly, do stunts
- 1–3 minutes per performance

D

- pass the ball by throwing and kicking
- allowed: running with the ball, hands
- take the ball as far as possible into the other team's half
- score: touchdown, field goal

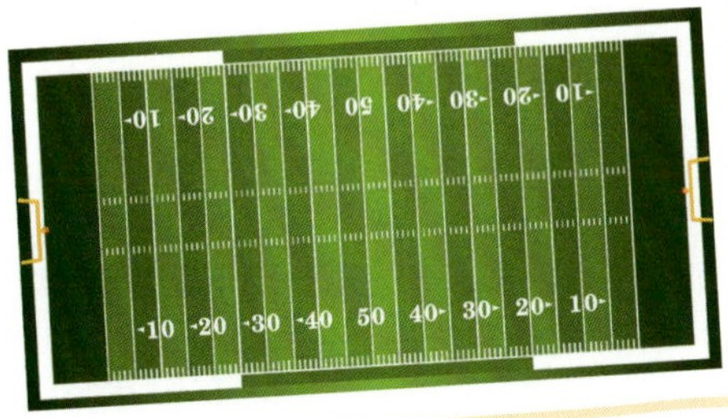

E

F

- team sport
- each team: 11 players on the field
- one game: 60 minutes (plus pauses)
- 4 quarters (one quarter = 15 minutes)

1 Organize the cards on the left.

a) Choose a heading for each card and each photo.

Equipment | General facts | Basic rules | Cheerleaders | Move and score | Performance

b) Put the information cards and the photos in a suitable order.

2 Prepare your presentation about American football.

a) Prepare your poster, transparency or computer presentation.

b) Use the prompt cards from page 50 or prepare your own prompt cards.

3 Practise your presentation.

You can practise your presentation in front of the mirror or with family and friends.

1. Give an introduction.
2. Present the different aspects of your information.
3. End your presentation. Emphasise the most important facts and come to a conclusion.

33/1-3 ## 4 Give your presentation.

Schlage neue Wörter nach. Achte darauf, dass du die richtige Bedeutung auswählst und die Wörter richtig aussprechen kannst. Überlege dir, wie du deiner Klasse unbekannte Wörter erklären kannst. Nutze dazu Fotos oder Skizzen. Du kannst manche Wörter auch umschreiben oder vormachen.

Prüfe, ob deine Präsentation gut ist:
- große Überschrift
- keine Rechtschreibfehler
- Fotos

Das sollte auf deinen Karteikarten stehen:
- nur Stichwörter (keine ganzen Sätze)
- die Erklärung neuer Wörter

Hier sind hilfreiche Redewendungen für den Einstieg:
My presentation is about … .
First, I'd like to talk about … .

So kannst du zum nächsten Punkt deiner Präsentation überleiten:
Now I'm going to talk about … .
My next topic is … .
Finally, I'm going to talk about … .

Bedanke dich bei deinen Zuhörern für ihre Aufmerksamkeit und biete an, Fragen zu beantworten:
That's the end of my presentation.
Thank you for listening. Do you have any questions?

Sieh dein Publikum an, während du sprichst. Sprich langsam, klar und deutlich. Beziehe dein Poster oder deine Folie in deine Präsentation mit ein. Achte auf die Zeit.

Find more online:
i8ce82

Am Ende dieser Unit kann ich ...

- Informationen über den Nordosten der USA verstehen.
- einen Text ausdrucksstark vorlesen.
- meine Meinung sagen und begründen.
- eine Geschichte über Freunde verstehen.
- Informationen über Reisemöglichkeiten weitergeben.
- einen Film über Thanksgiving verstehen.

5 1,15

Unit 3

In the Northeast

The Northeast of the United States goes from the border with Canada to Washington D.C. Here you can visit the amazing Niagara Falls or enjoy miles of beaches. In the fall you can drive through beautiful red and gold woods.

The USA is a huge country. For example, it's a six and a half hour flight from Boston to Los Angeles. Families often live and work thousands of miles away from each other. So they like to meet for important celebratio

1 (SPEAKING) Talk about the photos.

What can you see in the photos? Tell your partner. Can he or she find out which photo it is?

A: I can see an old house.
B: That's photo 4.

2 Read the texts and choose the right answer.

36/1-2

1. The Northeast is famous for **beautiful woods** • **short winters.**
2. It takes six and a half hours to get from Boston to Los Angeles **by car** • **by plane.**
3. On Thanksgiving most people eat **fish** • **turkey.**
4. **Most of** • **Half of** Maine is forest.
5. The Amish **can't choose how they want to live** • **don't use TVs or phones.**

On Thanksgiving almost everyone eats a turkey dinner. The president 'pardons' a turkey in the White House.

The state of Maine is a favorite location for creepy movies and books. It's 90 percent forest, not many people live there, and the winters are long and dark.

The USA is called the 'land of the free'. People can choose how they want to live. The Amish are an old Christian community who live without modern inventions like TVs or phones.

3 (LISTENING) Listen to a story about a Niagara Daredevil.

1,16

Right or wrong?

1. The woman who tells the story was on a boat trip. That's **right.**
2. She saw a boat go over the Niagara Falls.
3. An old man climbed out of it.
4. He was hurt.
5. He wanted to become a stuntman.
6. The second time he had to pay money.

daredevil ['deəˌdevl] – Draufgänger/in
close [kləʊs] – nah
barrel ['bærl] – Faß; Tonne
to sign autographs [ˌsaɪn 'ɔːtəɡrɑːfs] – Autogramme geben

Ich kann Informationen über den Nordosten der USA verstehen. ✓

Hier lerne ich, einen Text ausdrucksstark vorzulesen.

A family Thanksgiving

1 What is the biggest celebration that your family has?

2 (READING) Read the dialogue.

1,17

The Millers from Boston are getting ready for Thanksgiving dinner. Julia is in the kitchen. Her husband Mark, their son Jacob and Grandma Brenda are in the living room. Her daughter Lily lives with her boyfriend Evan in Washington D.C. They are not there yet.

Grandma: Last year we had a terrible storm. I got stuck in my car for over two hours. Do you remember?

Mark: Yes, that's right. Did you have a hard time again yesterday?

(The doorbell rings. Mark opens the door. It's their neighbor.)

Robert: Happy Thanksgiving, Mark!

Mark: You too, Robert. How are you doing?

Robert: Great, thanks. Brr. It's very cold outside.

Mark: Come on in. I'm so glad you could make it. *(They enter the living room.)* Grandma, this is Robert. He's our new neighbor. He doesn't have family here, so we've invited him to join us. Robert, this is Brenda.

Robert: Nice to meet you, Brenda.

Grandma: Nice to meet you too. When did you move here?

Mark: *(He shouts across the room)* Jacob, why don't you say hello? You can't spend all your time on your phone.

Jacob: What's up Robert?

Robert: How's it going? Are you enjoying the holiday? Do you like turkey?

Jacob: Not really. I'm a vegetarian, so I won't eat any.

Julia: *(She comes out of the kitchen.)* You always used to eat everything. *(She notices the new guest.)* Oh, hi Robert.

Robert: Hey Julia. Thanks so much for inviting me. Here's a little present. You eat chocolates, don't you? *(He gives her a box as a present.)*

(Mark's phone rings.)

Mark: That's probably Lily. Hello Lily. … Oh, no! *(to the others)* Their plane from Washington, D.C. had troubles and they had to land in New York. *(to Lily)* So when does your plane arrive? … OK. … Will you call again later? I promise we'll save some turkey for you!

CULTURE

Small Talk ist in den USA sehr wichtig. Man unterhält sich über sehr einfache, alltägliche Dinge. Was sind für euch alltägliche Dinge?

3 Find out about the Miller family's Thanksgiving. → M Peer correction, p. 171

a) Who is it? → ○ p. 122

1. Who got stuck in her car last year? That's **Brenda**.
2. Who is the new neighbor?
3. Who doesn't eat turkey any more?
4. Who gets a present?
5. Who talks to Lily on the phone?

b) Find out three things about Lily.

4 (LISTENING) Listen to the conversation.

1,18
37/1

a) Choose the right picture.

b) Listen to the conversation again. Who says it?

1. You've finally made it. **That's Mark.**
2. Everything's fine, thanks.
3. Nice to meet you.
4. How was Thanksgiving?
5. Can I help with anything?

5 (WRITING) Collect small talk phrases.

37/2

a) Match the sentences. → ○ p. 123

1. How's it going?
2. What's up?
3. Sam, this is Beth.
4. Nice to meet you.
5. Do you like turkey?

A Not really.
B Nice to meet you too.
C Not much.
D Great, thanks.
E Beth, this is Sam.

b) Find answers. → V Small talk, p. 192

1. How are things going?
2. Are you enjoying the holiday?
3. Please have a seat.

6 (SPEAKING) Make small talk. → M Milling around, p. 170

Use the sentences from exercise 5.

7 (SOUNDS) Listen, read and say.

1,19

1. Do you like turkey? ↗
2. Yes, I love turkey. ↘
3. I've lived in Boston for five years. ↘

Language → G5, p. 162

Do you like turkey?
Did you have turkey yesterday?
Will you have turkey later?

Wie bildest du Fragen in der Gegenwart, der Vergangenheit und der Zukunft?

38/3-5
53/6

8 Choose the right tense.

Die Signalwörter helfen dir.

1. **Do** • **Did** • **Will** you usually prefer turkey or ham?
2. **Does** • **Did** • **Will** your dad always watch a football game on Thanksgiving?
3. **Do** • **Did** • **Will** you see the heavy storm on the news yesterday?
4. **Do** • **Did** • **Will** you travel by plane last year?
5. **Do** • **Did** • **Will** you teach me how to make a great cake like this tomorrow, please?
6. **Does** • **Did** • **Will** Grandma stay with you next Thanksgiving?

53/7

9 (SPEAKING) Ask questions about holidays.

39/6a)

a) Choose the right question word. Interview your partner. → ○ p. 123

Which ✓ | Where | Who | How many | What

1. Which holidays does your family celebrate?
2. —— do you always eat at Christmas / Easter / Eid / …?
3. —— does your family invite every time?
4. —— guests did your family invite last time?
5. —— will you celebrate next year?

39/6b)

b) Look at the picture. Think of more questions that Grandma asks at the family party.

10 Make a phone call.

a) Complete the phone call between Jacob and his grandma with these questions. → ○ p. 124

39/7a)

Did you have a good trip home? • Will you be there? • Can I bring my new girlfriend? • What about you? • When will you celebrate? • How are you? ✓ • Where will you celebrate?

Jacob:	Grandma:
Hi, Grandma. This is Jacob. (1) How are you?	Hi, Jacob. I'm fine. (2) — How nice of you to call me.
(3) —	Yes, I did. I didn't have any problems with the weather or the traffic. I hope to see you all again on my 65th birthday. I'm planning a big family celebration.
(4) —	I'll celebrate on May 1. (5) —
Yes, I think so. (6) —	Here at my house, in Miami.
That sounds cool. (7) —	Yes, of course. I'd like to meet her.
I'm sure you'll like her.	…

b) Ask two more questions and finish the phone call. You can use these phrases.

39/7b)

How old …? · Where … meet her? · I'm sorry I'll have to … now. · Bye.

11 (YOUR TURN) A holiday dialogue → M Dramatic reading, p. 169

a) Work in groups of five. Each of you chooses a role from the dialogue on page 54.

b) Listen to the dialogue, then practise and read the dialogue.

c) Give feedback to the other groups.

READING SKILLS

Wenn ihr einen Dialog vorlest, achtet auf die richtige Aussprache und lest den Text so oft, bis ihr ihn ohne Stocken lesen könnt. Benutzt eure Stimme, um die Gefühle der Personen gut auszudrücken. Lest z. B. schneller, wenn es aufgeregt klingen soll.

Ich kann einen Text ausdrucksstark vorlesen. ✓

One country, different worlds

1 What have you used electricity for today? → M Round robin, p. 172

This morning I've used the lights, the elevator …

2 (READING) Read the texts about two American teenagers.

1,20

I live in a small Amish community in Pennsylvania. Our lives are simple. We don't have modern devices like a TV, a fridge, a phone or a computer. That means we can concentrate more on our community life. I also cover my hair, wear long dresses, and never use make-up. We grow our own food too. The people in our community look after each other. It doesn't matter what you wear or how you look. It's important who you are and what you do. I really like that. We don't usually have much contact with the outside world. But at 16 we're allowed to go there for some time and do 'forbidden things'. I watched movies, went to parties and drank alcohol. But I felt lonely. Now I have to make the most important decision of my life: Do I join the Amish community or not? Just think: if I didn't go back, I would really miss my family and my community. This is where I belong. I'm sure I'll do the right thing.

I'm an average American girl. I'm interested in fashion and yes … gossip too. I'm always on the phone. I couldn't live without it. My friends and I chat a lot about everyone and everything. My first big decision of the day is: What am I going to wear? At school we usually talk about who's wearing what or who's going out with whom. I often meet my friends. If I had a car, I would drive around town with them. But I don't have one yet. Sometimes we go bowling, watch movies or have something to eat. Some of my friends go to church, but I don't. I wouldn't like to change anything about my life.

CULTURE

Die Amischen sind eine religiöse Gruppe, die im 18. Jahrhundert aus Europa ausgewandert ist. Sie führen in ihren Gemeinschaften ein einfaches Leben und sprechen einen deutschen Dialekt. Welche anderen Lebensstile kennst du?

3 (SPEAKING) Talk to your partner: Which headings would you choose for each text?

A It's all about fashion and people
B Different from others
C Life in a community
D An average teenager

A: I would choose … for text 1 because …

B: I (don't) agree. I would …

4 Compare the girls' lives.

a) What's important in life?

Look at the texts again and find three things for each girl.

b) Do Ruth and Jennifer like the way they live? Find the information in the text.

Ruth likes the way she lives. The text says in lines 20 to 22, "…". Jennifer …

5 (WRITING) Sort the phrases. → M Peer correction, p. 171

40/1a) a) Copy and complete the table. → ○ p. 124

I agree	I disagree
Exactly.	…

Exactly. ✓ · That's true. · I don't think so. · That's for sure. · Absolutely not. · No way!

40/1b) b) Put the phrases into the right list. → V Agreeing and disagreeing, p. 193

- I'm sure: …
- I'm not sure: …

As far as I know, … · I guess … · I'm convinced that … · It's clear to me that …

40/2
41/3

6 (SPEAKING) Talk about devices.

a) Make a list. → ○ p. 125

Rank the devices from the most important to the least important. Talk to your partner.

1
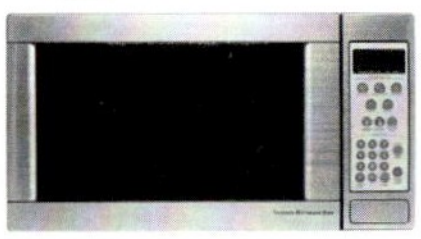
microwave

2

headphones

3

TV

4

phone

5

computer

The most important thing for me **is my phone**. • I don't think **phones** are more important than **computers**. • **TVs** come first/second/third. • **Headphones** are next.

b) Which device could you live without? Talk to other students. → V Devices, p. 193

fan · dishwasher · vacuum cleaner · razor · radiator

Language → G6, p. 163

Jennifer: If I had a car, I would drive around town with my friends.
Ruth: If I didn't go back, I would miss my family.

Wie wahrscheinlich ist es, dass die Bedingung (If-Satz) in Erfüllung geht?
In welchem Teil des Satzes verwendest du would und die Grundform des Verbes, in welchem das simple past?

7 Complete the sentences.

41/4

1. If Jennifer met Ruth, they would compare their different lives. (compare)
2. If Ruth stayed with Jennifer, Jennifer — bowling with her. (go)
3. If Ruth didn't know how to use a computer, Jennifer — her. (help)
4. Ruth — Jennifer how to grow her own food if she visited Ruth's family. (show)
5. Jennifer — about her clothes if she lived with the Amish. (not worry)
6. Jennifer — make-up if she stayed with Ruth's family. (not use)

Erinnerst du dich? Die Verneinung von „would" ist „wouldn't".

8 What would make Jennifer's life easier?

41/5

a) Look at the pictures. Complete the sentences. → ○ p. 126

walk
go
have
not listen
choose ✓

1. Jennifer would be less worried in the morning if she chose her clothes the evening before.

2. She wouldn't get so tired in the morning if she — to bed early.

3. She would hear what her dad said if she — to music.

4. She wouldn't get cold if she — a warm coat.

5. It would be better if she — to school.

42/6

b) What would make your life easier? Make three sentences.

My life would be easier if **I had breakfast in the morning.**

42/7

9 (SPEAKING) What would you do if …? → M Milling around, p. 170

a) Answer the questions. Then ask your partner. → ○ p. 126

What would you do if you …

1. were president of the United States for a day?
2. were a hero?
3. could go back in time?
4. had a million dollars?
5. knew the answers to your next English test before the test?

b) Make more questions for your partner.

be a teacher | meet an alien | have no brothers/sisters | …

If I was a teacher, I would …

10 (YOUR TURN) Giving your opinion → V Giving opinions, p. 196

42/8
43/1-2

Could you live without electricity? Why (not)? Write a short text. Give two reasons.

The question is "Could I live without electricity?"
I could live without electricity
because it would be an adventure.
If I had no lights, I could use candles.
I also think that I would have more time
because I couldn't surf the internet.
So my answer is "yes", I could live without electricity.

couldn't
I would … | I couldn't live without …
phone | fridge | …
couldn't … | would …
"no", I couldn't

WRITING SKILLS

1. Nenne dein Thema. 2. Sage deine Meinung. 3. Begründe deine Aussage.
4. Fasse deine Argumente am Schluss kurz zusammen.

Ich kann meine Meinung sagen und begründen. ✓

The Body by Stephen King, 1982

1 What do you do when you meet your friends?

2 (READING) Read the story.

1,21

In The Body, *Gordie Lachance and his three friends hear that a boy from their area, in the state of Maine, has disappeared and is probably dead. They decide to go on a trip to find the boy's body and here they are preparing for the trip.*

The Gun

My room was on the second floor, and it was really hot up there. I was glad I wasn't sleeping there that night. I was excited about where we were going. I grabbed two blankets and all my money, which was less than a dollar. Then I was ready to go.

I went down the back stairs. I didn't want to meet my dad. I was on my way to the clubhouse when Chris caught up with me. His eyes were shining.

"Gordie! You want to see something?"

"Sure. What?"

Chris put his hand into his backpack and took out a big gun.

"Where did you get that?"

"From my dad's desk."

"Man, your dad's going to beat you when he finds out."

Chris's eyes just went on dancing. "He isn't going to find out. He and his friends have got enough wine to keep them drunk for a week.

I'll put it back before then."
Chris hated alcohol – he'd already seen too much of what it can do.

"Have you got bullets for it?"
"Nine of them."
"Any in it at the moment?"
"No, of course not. What do you think I am?"
I finally took the gun. I liked the heavy way it sat in my hand.
I pointed the gun at a large tin.
KA – BLAM!
The gun jumped in my hand.
Fire shot from the end. It felt as if my wrist was broken. My heart was in my mouth. There was a big hole in the tin.
"Wow!" I screamed.
Chris was laughing wildly; I couldn't tell if he was amused or scared.
"You did it, you did it! Be careful, everyone! Here comes Gordie!"
"Shut up! Let's go!" I screamed, and grabbed him by the shirt.
I gave the gun to Chris.
"Oh, man, that was really great."
"You knew there was a bullet in it, didn't you? That was a mean trick, Chris, really."
"I didn't know, Gordie, honestly. I just took it out of my dad's desk. He always takes the bullets out of it. I think he was too drunk to remember last time."
Chris looked as innocent as a baby, but when we got to the clubhouse we found Vern and Teddy waiting, and he started to laugh again.
He told them the whole story. Everyone laughed. Teddy asked Chris, "What do you think we need a gun for?"
"Nothing, really," Chris said. "But maybe we'll see a wild animal. And anyway, it's scary out in the forest at night." Everyone agreed with that.
Chris was the strongest and bravest guy of us all, and he could say things like that.

"Did you put your tent up in the field?" Teddy asked Vern.

"Yeah, and I put two lamps in it and turned them on, so it'll look as if we're there after dark."

"So let's go," Teddy said. "It's almost twelve already."

Chris stood up and we gathered round him.

"We'll walk across Beeman's field," he said, "and then we'll get to the railway tracks and just walk across the bridge into Harlow."

"Come on, you guys," Chris said, and picked up his backpack, blankets and water bottle.

CULTURE

In den USA sterben jährlich ungefähr 30.000 Menschen durch Schusswaffen. Das Gesetz besagt, dass jeder Amerikaner das Recht hat, eine Waffe zu besitzen. Viele Amerikaner glauben, dass sie eine Waffe brauchen, um sich selbst zu schützen.
Wer darf in Deutschland eine Waffe tragen? Wie findest du das?

3 Do you like the story? Say why or why not.

I (don't) like the story because ... .

funny · boring · exciting · creepy · a mystery story · an adventure · crazy · ...

4 Work with the story.

a) Put the sentences in the right order.

A The boys tell their friends what happened.
B Gordie takes the gun and shoots.
C They leave before twelve.
D Gordie meets Chris.
E Chris shows Gordie his father's gun.
F Gordie gets ready to leave home.

b) Who tells the story? Choose the right answer.

Chris • Gordie • Vern • Teddy • another person

c) Do you think this chapter is near the beginning or the end of the book?

I think this chapter is near the beginning/the end of the book because ... .

5 Find out about Chris and Gordie.

a) Choose the right adjective.

excited ✓ | brave | worried | scared | amused

1. Gordie is excited because he and his friends are going on a trip to find a body.
2. Gordie is — about what Chris's dad would do if he found out.
3. Gordie is — after he shot the gun.
4. Chris is — that Gordie shot the gun.
5. Gordie thinks that Chris is very — .

b) Talk to your partner:

Do you think Chris knew about the bullet in the gun?

I think he knew/didn't know about the bullet in the gun because … .

6 Choose one of these tasks.

44/1-3

a) Find out on the internet how the story *The Body* by Stephen King goes on. Continue the summary. Add five sentences.
→ M Writers' conference, p. 173

The story *The Body* by Stephen King is about the adventures of Gordie Lachance and his three friends. They hear that a boy from their area has disappeared and is probably dead. They decide to go on a trip to find the boy's body …

OR

b) Work in groups of four. Design a cover for the book. → M Gallery walk, p. 169

Take the roles of the four characters and take a photo. Add the title of the book and the writer. Print it and put up your cover in class. Which cover does your class like most?

STUDY SKILLS

Ein Cover sollte neugierig auf das Buch machen und die Atmosphäre des Buches widerspiegeln. Überlegt euch, wie die Charaktere zueinander stehen sollen. Welcher Hintergrund ist geeignet? Welche Schriftart ist für den Titel geeignet? Wo sollte der Titel platziert werden?

Ich kann eine Geschichte über Freunde verstehen. ✓

From Chicago to Boston

INTERNET

A

OUTGOING TRIP		**September 16 (Fri)**			**Price (USD)**
Chicago, IL 08:05 a.m.	>	24h 25m	>	Boston, MA 09:30 a.m. (+ 1 days)	Total fare for 1 Adult $89
RETURN TRIP		**September 18 (Sun)**			
Boston, MA 05:00 p.m.	>	22h 30m	>	Chicago, IL 02:30 p.m. (+ 1 days)	Total fare for 1 Adult $89
				Subtotal	$178
				Taxes and fees	$ 5
				YOUR TOTAL	**$183**

INTERNET

B

Sep 16 (Fri)				
1:39 p.m. Chicago, IL	>	5:05 p.m. Boston, MA	2h 26m	
Sep 18 (Sun)				
5:30 p.m. Boston, MA	>	9:17 p.m. Chicago, IL	4h 47m Philadelphia 1 stop	
			Flight	$141.85
			Tax & Fee	$ 47.35
			Trip total (round trip)	**$189.20**

C

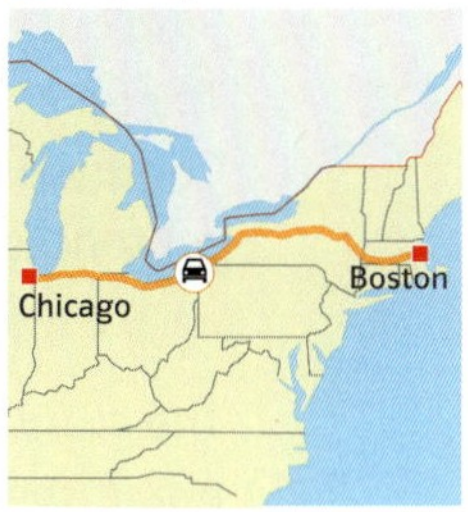

One-way
Time: 14h 46m
Distance: 982 miles
Price of gas:
about $160

1 Beantworte die Fragen.

45/1-2

Welches Verkehrsmittel ist am billigsten? Welches am schnellsten? Erstelle ein Ranking.

CULTURE

In den USA gibt es neun Zeitzonen. In Boston ist es immer eine Stunde später als in Chicago. Wie viele Zeitzonen hat Europa?

2 What do you think?

If you had to go from Berlin to Frankfurt/Main, how would you get there? By train, plane or bus? Say why. Find information on the internet.

Ich kann Informationen über Reisemöglichkeiten weitergeben.

Trouble at Thanksgiving

1 Look at the photo and guess.

a) What is Jessica making?

b) What could the trouble be? Collect ideas in class and vote on the best idea.

Now watch the beginning of the film. Were you right?

2 (VIEWING) Watch the film.

6

a) What else goes wrong that day?

Find out about Amy, Ronan's mum Ella and the turkey.

b) Thanksgiving Day: Which six things do they talk about in the film?

big parade | balloons | turkey dinner | barbecue party | nice presents | football game | special songs | pecan pie | president's pardon | volunteer work | terrible traffic

3 (SPEAKING) Talk about the film.

a) Watch the film from 03:19 again. What activities do people do at Thanksgiving?

b) Which of these activities are most interesting to you? Say why.

I think … is really interesting. I love … .
I like … because … .
… is great because … .

CULTURE

Thanksgiving bedeutet „give thanks" (sich bedanken). In den USA kommt an diesem Tag die Familie zusammen. Mit einem Festessen wird die gute Ernte gefeiert und meistens wird dabei ein Dankgebet gesprochen.
Gibt es bei euch so eine ähnliche Tradition?

VIEWING SKILLS

Filme beinhalten oft Fotos oder Videos mit zusätzlichen Informationen oder Nebenhandlungen.

Ich kann einen Film über Thanksgiving verstehen. ✓

Checklist

Ich kann Informationen über den Nordosten der USA verstehen. ✔

46

Ich kann einen Text ausdrucksstark vorlesen. ✔

What's up? • How's it going? • I'm glad you could make it. • How was …? • Are you enjoying …?

46

Ich kann meine Meinung sagen und begründen. ✔

I really like that. • I wouldn't change … . • I don't think so. • That's for sure. • Absolutely not. • That's true. • I couldn't live without … .

47

Ich kann eine Geschichte über Freunde verstehen. ✔

47

Ich kann Informationen über Reisemöglichkeiten weitergeben. ✔

47

Ich kann einen Film über Thanksgiving verstehen. ✔

(TASK) A talk show

'One day without your phone – piece of cake or total nightmare?' Organize a 5 to 10-minute talk show. At the end make a decision if you want to live without your phone for one day. Do more than one show for practice and for fun.

Step 1

Collect ideas. → M Think-pair-share, p. 173

Collect arguments for both sides:
What's good about a day without a phone? What isn't?

Step 2

Get into groups: 'piece of cake' or 'total nightmare'.

It's always easier to present your own opinion. However, you sometimes have to take a different perspective. Think of that when you make groups.

Step 3

Prepare for the show.

1. Decide on three to four arguments.
2. Explain your arguments, give reasons and examples.
3. Decide who is going to present which argument in the show.
4. Write your arguments on cards (keywords only).
5. Practise your talk.

In my opinion one day without my phone is a piece of cake. I think our parents use our phones to check what we are doing. I'm sure you all know situations like this: You're out with your friends and you have fun. Suddenly your phone rings and your mum asks, "Hi, where are you? Why are you not at home yet?" How embarrassing! That's why I think: If we didn't have any phones, our parents couldn't control us.

Step 4

Set the scene and act the show.

1. Prepare the classroom for the show: Arrange the tables and chairs.
2. Decide which groups are going to be in the first show.
3. Your teacher is the host.
4. Act the show.

SPEAKING SKILLS

Sprich das Publikum direkt an, um dessen Aufmerksamkeit zu gewinnen. Sprich flüssig, aber nicht zu schnell.

Step 5

Make a decision.

What does your class think? Should you live without phones for one day?

Step 6

Do more shows for practice and for fun.

The voyage of the Mayflower

The story of the Mayflower

In September 1620, I sailed from Plymouth, in England, to the New World. On board my sailing ship, the Mayflower, were 102 people who were later to be known as the Pilgrims. They left England because they didn't have religious freedom and they wanted to start a new life.

After two months of heavy storms in the Atlantic Ocean, we landed at Cape Cod where we stayed for the winter. Many people died because of the cold, hard winter, diseases and also of hunger. Thank God, we met Indians who gave us food, showed us how to hunt and to catch fish. Later they showed the Pilgrims how to grow corn. The Pilgrims decided to stay at Cape Cod and founded the colony of Plymouth, named after the starting point of their crossing.

My crew and I left the colony in March. I heard that after the first year in the New World, the Pilgrims invited the Indians for a meal. They celebrated a festival to say thanks for the successful harvest – they called it 'Thanksgiving'.

CULTURE

Viele Städtenamen in den USA kommen ursprünglich aus Europa. Manche Namen sind identisch, wie zum Beispiel „Plymouth“. Oft stellten die Siedler auch ein „New“ vor den ursprünglichen Namen - New York (benannt nach York in England), New Orleans (benannt nach Orléans in Frankreich) … .
Welche deutschen Städtenamen gibt es in den USA?

Build your own Mayflower with recyclable material.

Step 1: Prepare yourself.
You can recycle lots of everyday things to build your own Mayflower: You can choose things from this material list (or your own ideas) in steps 2 to 4 below.

an empty tea light

walnut shells

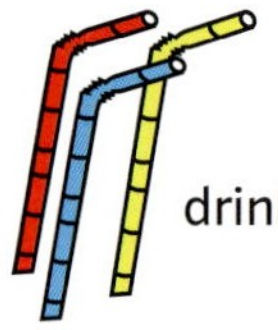
drinking straws

an empty yogurt pot
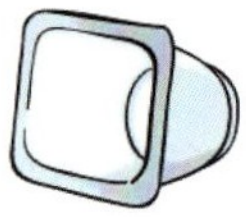

polystyrene

plastic bags
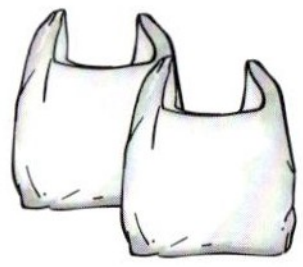

toothpicks

the lid of a jam jar

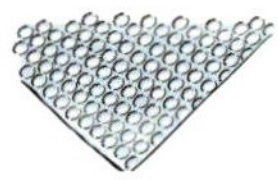
bubble wrap

You also need:

scissors

tape

glue stick

waterproof felt-tips

coloured paper

Step 2: Build and design the body of the ship.
- Choose a material that floats.
- Make the body of the ship.
- Use things like coloured paper and waterproof felt tips to decorate your Mayflower.

Step 3: Make the sails.
- Make the masts and sails and fix them to your Mayflower.

Step 4: Add the crew and passengers.
- Make the Pilgrims, Christopher Jones (Master of the Mayflower) and his crew.
- Put them on your Mayflower.

Welches Schiff kommt zuerst an?

Step 5: Start the journey.
- Fill a big plastic box or a sink with water to make your Atlantic Ocean.
- Put your Mayflower in the water.
- Blow the sails of your Mayflower to make it cross your Atlantic Ocean.

Hier kannst du lernen, wie du eine Zusammenfassung schreibst.

1,22

Healthy and active at Thanksgiving?

headline

written by Pam Warner
(published 07/12/16 in Health & Style)

writer, date, source

introduction

What is your Thanksgiving like? Turkey and pumpkin pie? American football on the sofa? A new trend has become popular in the USA: More people like to eat better quality food and live a more active life.

main part

Fast food is slowly going out of fashion. A number of people shop for organic food at special supermarkets now. In some states farmers' markets sell fresh vegetables and fruit from the region. "There are also other products like bread and meat without chemical additives at these markets. Organic food is much healthier and it tastes a lot better too," explains Emma from Boston. So how about some healthy recipes for Thanksgiving? Pumpkin soup maybe? A roast turkey breast filled with apples and cranberries is delicious too.

But there's more to a healthy lifestyle than just food. A lot of trend sports show that you can have fun, spend time with friends and stay fit at the same time. Have you found the right sport yet? How about standup paddleboarding? If you like water, that's the ideal kind of sport for you. You stand on the board and you use a paddle to move through the water. Don't worry, you don't have to travel to the sea. A lot of clubs offer standup paddleboarding on lakes and rivers.

Of course living healthy also means no alcohol and no drugs. Finn, a fitness instructor from Cleveland, says: "Drinking too much alcohol isn't good for your health. Most alcoholic drinks have a lot of calories and negative effects on your fitness too. So why not try a smoothie instead?" Drugs are even worse. You can easily get addicted, and you often get problems with your family or at school.

conclusion

To sum up, you can say that organic food together with doing sport is a great way to stay fit. You don't have to do without your favorite meals. Just changing your lifestyle a bit will make you a much happier person.

1 Read the text and take notes.

Find the most important keywords in each paragraph and make a list. Look at the examples in the introduction and the first paragraph on the left.

> Notiere keine Beispiele, keine Zahlen, keine Vergleiche, keine Zitate oder direkte Rede. Sie sind für eine Zusammenfassung nicht nötig.

2 Write a summary of the text.

Use your notes to write your summary.

> Normalerweise ist eine Zusammenfassung nicht länger als ein Drittel vom Originaltext. Sie kann natürlich auch kürzer sein. Benutze immer deine eigenen Worte.

1. Start with the introduction. Name the title, the writer and where the text comes from. Don't forget to say what the text is about.

> So kannst du deine Zusammenfassung beginnen:
> The text/article/story "…" was written by … on …. The text/article/story is about ….

2. Now summarise each paragraph of the main part in a few sentences. Use your notes to help you.

> Benutze für die Zusammenfassung das simple present. Verwende verbindende Wörter zwischen den Sätzen oder Abschnitten:
> First … • Then … • After that … • Finally …

Here's an example for the first paragraph:

First Pam Warner writes about organic food. You can get it at special markets. It's without chemical additives and it tastes much better. You can use it for healthy Thanksgiving recipes.

3. Write a conclusion.
   Say what you think about the article.

> So kannst du deine Zusammenfassung beenden:
> I think …. • In my opinion …. •
> To sum up, I can say ….

50/1-2
51/3-5

3 Check your summary.

Read your text again and check:

- Spelling (all words correct?)
- Grammar (correct tense?)
- Style (linking words?)
- Content (the most important information?)

> Wenn du Wörter aus dem Text verwendet hast, kannst du dort nachschauen, ob du sie richtig geschrieben hast. Ansonsten schlag im Wörterbuch nach und kontrolliere deinen Text mit Hilfe der Checkliste auf Seite 175.

He, she, it – das -s muss mit!

Find more online:
i8ce82

Am Ende dieser Unit kann ich ...
- Informationen über Kalifornien und den Westen der USA verstehen.
- eine Werbeanzeige gestalten.
- über Trends sprechen.
- einen Text über den Goldrausch verstehen.
- Informationen über Kinderarbeit weitergeben.
- einen Film über Beruf und Karriere verstehen.

7 2,1

Unit 4
California dreams

With its 840 miles of coast, California has something for everyone – giant redwood trees in the north and sunny beaches in the south. People live a relaxed lifestyle here. They enjoy surfing and beach volleyball.

In San Francisco you can take cable cars which go up and down the hills or visit the largest Chinatown outside of Asia. The Golden Gate Bridge is the city's most famous sight.

1 Look at the photos. → M Think-pair-share, p. 173

a) Use the photos to start a mind map with a partner.

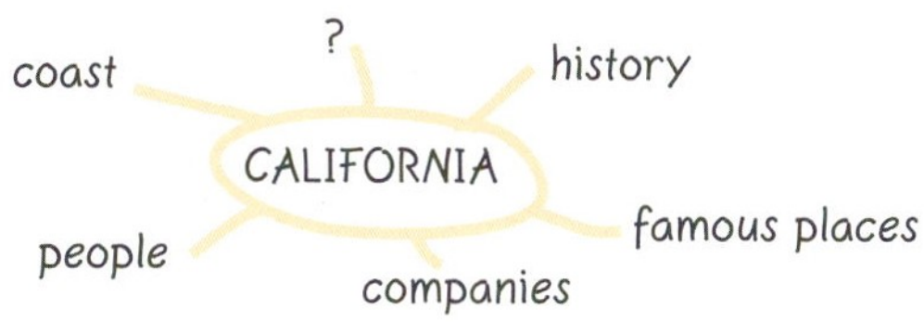

b) Now tell the class what you already know about California.

2 Read the texts and add more information about California to your mind map.

54/1-2

In 1849 the California Gold Rush started. Hundreds of thousands of people moved to the west. They hoped to find gold there and get rich.

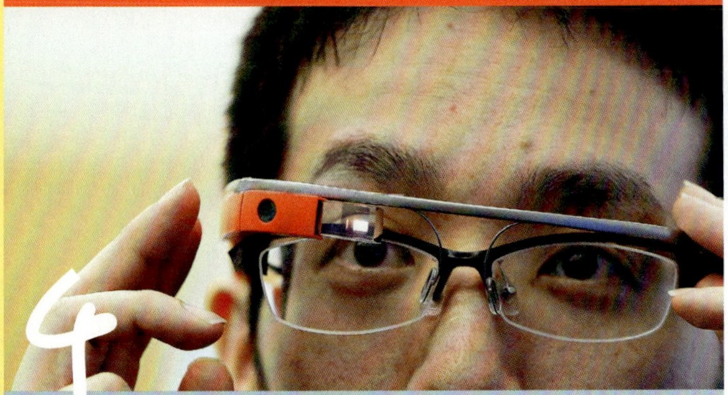

There are a great number of modern high-tech companies in Silicon Valley near San Francisco. You can find the world's largest companies there.

Hollywood is the capital of the world's movie industry. You can visit the movie studios there and see the Walk of Fame.

3 (LISTENING) **Listen to the information about the Golden Gate Bridge.**

2,2

Complete the notes.

The Golden Gate Bridge

1. almost ––– miles long
2. the ––– of the bridge: Joseph Strauss
3. opened in –––
4. safety net saved ––– workers
5. colour of the bridge: –––
6. ––– of San Francisco and California

bay [beɪ] – Bucht
architect ['ɑ:kɪtekt] – Architekt/in
safety net ['seɪfti ˌnet] – Sicherheitsnetz

Ich kann Informationen über Kalifornien und den Westen der USA verstehen. ✓

Enjoy the sunny west!

1 Describe the photos in the ads.

55/1 a) Read the description of photo 1.

In photo 1 I can see a beach.
It's a sunny day.
In the background there is the sea.
In the foreground I can see a man and a bus.
The man is standing next to the bus. He is carrying a surfboard.
He has black hair and he is wearing a top and short trousers. He is smiling.

STUDY SKILLS

Wenn du ein Bild beschreibst, fange mit deinem ersten Eindruck an. Dann beschreibe die Einzelheiten. Sage auch, was die Personen auf dem Bild tun.

b) Describe photos 2 and 3.

1

2

3

2,3 2 (LISTENING) Listen to a conversation about an ad.

a) Answer the questions. → ○ p. 127

1. Emily, Carol and Daniel are talking about one ad from exercise 1. Which one?
2. Who doesn't like the ad?

b) What does Daniel dream about?

Daniel dreams about … .

86/1

3 (SPEAKING) What do you think of the ads?

55/2a)

a) Use these words to talk about the ads. → ○ p. 127

simple | informative | special | clear | spectacular | catchy

I think ad number 1 is/isn't … .

55/2b)

b) Match each word with one of the ads. Does your partner agree? → V Adjectives for ads, p. 197

fascinating | unusual | (un)appealing

4 (SPEAKING) What makes a good ad?

55/3
56/4

a) Rank ads 1–3 from best to worst.

b) Give reasons for your choice.
Say something about …

The layout:
nice/simple/boring/…

The headline:
funny/catchy/too long/…

Text with a message:
informative/too long/clear/…

A: I think the best ad is number … . The layout is very nice.
B: Yes, I agree. And the headline is catchy.
C: I don't think so. I think number … is much better.

5 (SONG) Surfin' U.S.A.

2,4

Listen to the song. What does the song sound like? How does it make you feel?

If everybody had an ocean
Across the U.S.A.
Then everybody'd be surfing
Like Californ-i-a

You'd see 'em wearin' their baggies
Huarache sandals, too
A bushy, bushy blond hairdo
Surfin' U.S.A.

You'd catch 'em surfin' at Del Mar
Ventura County Line
Santa Cruz and Trestles
Australia's Narrabeen

All over Manhattan
And down Doheny way
Everybody's gone surfin'
Surfin' U.S.A.

Language → G7, p. 164

In photo 1 the man is standing next to a bus. He is carrying a surfboard.
He has black hair. The bus looks really old.

Normalerweise verwendest du bei einer Bildbeschreibung das present progressive.
Bei Verben wie have, look (aussehen) und be verwendest du das simple present.
Wie bildest du diese beiden Zeitformen?

56/5

6 (WRITING) What are the people in the ads doing? Write sentences. → M Peer correction, p. 171

1. a boy • ride
   A boy is riding a mountain bike.
2. a man • hold
3. a girl and a boy • carry
4. a man and a woman • sit
5. a girl • walk
6. a woman • run

Manche Verben haben eine besondere Schreibweise:
sit → sitting
run → running
ride → riding

57/6

7 Look at the ads again.

a) Complete the sentences. Use the simple present. → ○ p. 128

1. The mountain bike is $1,500. (be)
2. The helmet —— cool. (look)
3. The backpacks —— $99 each. (be)
4. The camping chairs —— nice. (not look)
5. The girl —— walking. (like)
6. The woman —— an umbrella. (not need)

Für die Verneinung im simple present brauchst du „don't" oder „doesn't".

b) Talk to a partner: Which things would you buy? Say why. Use these verbs.

A: I would buy the helmet. It ... .
B: I need a new ... . This one ... .

look | like | be | have

86/2

8 (WRITING) Simple present or present progressive?

a) Complete Sandy's e-mail. → ○ p. 128

57/7-8a)

E-MAIL

Hi Becky,
At the moment I'm sitting (1, sit) in the sun next to the swimming pool. It's always warm here in California. It —— (2, not rain) often. We usually —— (3, spend) the weekends at the beach.
At the moment I —— (4, learn) how to surf. But lots of other things are the same as in the Midwest.
Every day I —— (5, go) to school, —— (6, do) my homework and —— (7, go) to bed.
What —— you —— (8, do) right now? I miss you.
Sandy

b) Complete the sentences in Becky's e-mail.

57/8b)

E-MAIL

Hi Sandy,
Great to hear from you. I miss you too. (1) Right now I'm waiting for a call from ... . (2) We always ... on Tuesdays. (3) The weather is terrible here. It ... now. Lucky you! I hope I can visit you in summer.
Take care,
Becky

9 (YOUR TURN) Making an ad → V Talking about a region, p. 201

a) Work in groups of four. Make an ad about a state or region in Germany for other students.

1. Decide on a region.
2. Collect ideas. → M Placemat, p. 171
3. Make a quick draft of the layout.
4. Work in pairs:
   - Find pictures or draw your own pictures (two students).
   - Write the text (two students).

Use the ads on page 76 as examples.
Don't write too much! Write a headline plus two or three sentences.

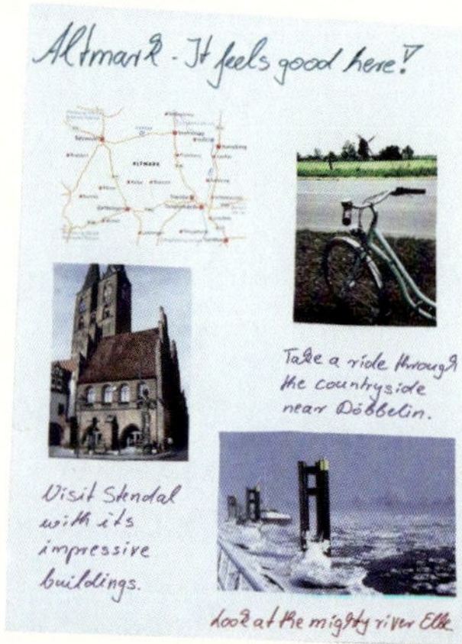

b) Present your work to the class. Which ad is the best? Say why.

STUDY SKILLS

Für welche Zielgruppe ist deine Werbung? Wähle ein Bild aus, das für sich spricht. Der Text sollte kurz und einfach sein und die Botschaft klar. Sprich die Leser direkt an, benutze Fragen und Aufforderungen. Du kannst im Internet auch einen Slogan Maker nutzen.

Ich kann eine Werbeanzeige gestalten. ✓

Hier lerne ich, über Trends zu sprechen.

Made in California

1 How often do you go online? Which websites do you use the most? → M Round robin, p. 172

2 (READING) Read the blog of a Californian teenager.

2,5

BLOG

A quick look back

Thursday, March 16, 2017

California has always welcomed new ideas – just think of the high-tech companies in Silicon Valley or the movie industry.
The internet is one of these ideas. The World Wide Web started in the early 1990s, so it's been around for almost 30 years. And it has really changed the world. Today almost everyone uses social media. I've had an account since I was 13. Why have they been so successful? Well, that's easy: you can post your photos, share your thoughts and keep in touch with friends. Most of the time you don't even have to look for information. It'll find you. We should give that a big 'like'.
Online videos have had a huge impact on our lives too. There are lots of funny videos. I like the tutorials best. You can find anything there from guitar lessons to make-up tips. Nobody watches much TV anymore. People stream their favorite shows instead.
Smartphones and tablets became the next big thing. Most of my friends go online every day, and half of them are online almost all the time. Most use several different social media sites at the same time. Some say it's difficult to stop using social media. They get messages every minute of the day and feel that they have to answer right away. Others are worried about cyberbullying.
If somebody writes bad things about you online, a lot of people can read it. We haven't really found any good answers yet.

Posted by Derek Lee at 8:51 a.m. 2 comments: Links to this post

3 What does the text say?

a) Right or wrong? Correct the wrong sentences. → ○ p. 129

1. The World Wide Web started about 50 years ago.
   That's wrong. The World Wide Web started ….
2. Social media sites are very popular today.
3. Everyone watches TV.
4. Most people are online almost all the time.
5. There are also problems with the internet.

b) What examples does Derek give in the text? Complete the list.

- *Social media:*
  post photos, …
- *Online videos:*
  funny videos, …
- *Problems:*
  too many messages, …

2,6 58/1

4 (LISTENING) Listen to the survey. Choose the right phrase.

1. It's **the latest thing** • **something new**.
2. Didn't it become **a big thing** • **popular** in Europe first?
3. It's **fantastic** • **not really my thing**.
4. **Trends** • **Things** like this come and go.
5. I don't think it will be **boring** • **outdated** so soon.

58/3 86/3

5 Explain the words.

58/2a)

a) Match the words with the definitions. → p. 130

friend · post · like · stream · share

1. You tell people that you agree with them.
2. You watch a movie online.
3. You move a message from your computer or phone to a social media site.
4. You send a message, a photo or a video that you got to others because you like it.
5. You ask someone to connect with you on social media.

58/2b)

b) Explain these words. → V Social media, p. 198

dislike · unfriend · subscribe

1. You tell people … . 2. You tell someone … . 3. When you subscribe to … .

CULTURE

In den USA können sich Kinder ab 13 Jahren in sozialen Netzwerken anmelden, wenn deren Eltern das erlauben. Wie ist das in eurem Land?

6 (SPEAKING) Say what the cartoon is about. → M Think-pair-share, p. 173

In this cartoon you can see … .
The man … .
The cartoon shows …

Language → G8, p. 165

The internet has changed the world.
Online videos have had a huge impact on our lives.
We haven't found answers for these questions yet.

Wie bildest du das present perfect? Welche Signalwörter kennst du für diese Zeitform?

7 What have or haven't they done? → M Bus stop, p. 168

59/4

1. Derek has just made fresh orange juice. (make)

2. Linda — already — her computer. (start)

3. Derek — already — his e-mails. (read)

4. Linda — her blog yet. (not finish)

5. Derek and Linda — each other yet. (not see)

6. They — just — for the first time. (meet)

8 Say for how long or since when.

86/4

a) Choose for or since. → ○ p. 130

59/5

1. I've had my smartphone **for** • **since** three years.
2. I haven't posted a new photo **for** • **since** 10 o'clock.
3. Social media have been popular **for** • **since** 20 years now.
4. Millions of people have seen the cat pictures **for** • **since** Tuesday.
5. More than 5,000 people have watched that tutorial **for** • **since** May.
6. I haven't answered my e-mails **for** • **since** five days.

GRAMMAR → G8, p. 165

since ten o'clock – seit zehn Uhr
for an hour – seit einer Stunde

b) Make sentences with these phrases. Use the present perfect.

59/6

since 7 o'clock | since Monday | for two hours | for three days

I have posted five pictures since 7 o'clock. I haven't been online …

60/7 **9 Complete the survey questions and answers.**

a) Complete the sentences. Use the present perfect. → ○ p. 131

1. Interviewer: — you — a book or a magazine this week? (buy)
   Have you bought a book or a magazine this week?
   Jake: I usually read everything online. I — a book or a magazine for a long time. (not read)
2. Interviewer: — you ever — tutorial videos to learn how to do something? (use)
   Sally: Yes, sure. I — already — to play the guitar that way. (learn)
3. Interviewer: — you — any new music videos that you liked this week? (find)
   Kim: Let me think for a second. Today I — one that I really enjoyed. (see)

b) Make more sentences from the survey. Use the present perfect.

1. I • buy • a book • this morning
2. I • not see • any tutorials • for months
3. I • not think about • that question • yet

10 (YOUR TURN) Talking about trends → V Giving opinions, p. 196

60/8
61/1-2 a) *Hot* or *not?* What do you think? Copy and complete the table.

selfies | torn jeans | veganism

hot	not

b) Think of two more trends and put them in the table.

c) Do you agree with your partner?

A: What do you think about selfies:
Is this trend *hot* or *not?*
B: I think it's hot. / I think it isn't hot.
A: What do you think about this trend?
B: It's cool. / It will be outdated soon. / …
A: Has it had an impact on your life?
B: Yes, (I have lots of funny photos of me and my friends now). /
No, I don't think so.

Ich kann über Trends sprechen.

Gold rush! → M Jigsaw, p. 170

1 (READING) **Home group: Find two partners. Each of you chooses one of the texts (A, B or C).**

a) Read your text.

b) Complete the summary with words from the text.

2 **Expert group: Find students who have read the same text. Compare your results with them.**

STUDY SKILLS

Wenn ihr in Gruppen verschiedene Aufgaben bearbeitet, seid ihr dafür verantwortlich, eure Ergebnisse an die anderen weiterzugeben. Denkt daran, wenn ihr eure Aufgabe löst.

Welche Informationen und welche Vokabeln brauchen die anderen, die den Text nicht gelesen haben, damit sie das Thema verstehen?

2,7 **Text A: A newspaper report**

California Star

December 6, 1848

GOLD! GOLD! GOLD! Found in California

Washington. Yesterday the President of the United States confirmed the discovery of gold in California.

It began in Coloma, a place 40 miles east of Sacramento. In January this year one of Mr. Sutter's workers found gold. Mr. Sutter, a German-Swiss immigrant and businessman, wanted to keep the gold secret. He didn't want to give up his farming plans. He also tried to buy more land and become the official landowner. His workers weren't allowed to talk about the gold, but the news got out slowly. Sutter has to prove now that he officially owns the land.

First, most local people didn't believe it. Then in May people in San Francisco heard the news and half of the city's population decided to look for gold in the American River. Men left everything behind and moved west because they hoped to become rich easily.

Summary

Text A is a n— r— from 1848. It is about the d— of g— in California. W— on a farm in Coloma found g— . They were not allowed to t— about it because their boss, Mr S— , wanted to keep it s— . But the n— got out anyway. Soon a lot of p— went to the American River to l— for g— . They hoped to become r— .

2,8 **Text B: A letter from a gold hunter**

February 15, 1850
San Francisco

Dear Maddy,

It's been weeks since I left you, my dear wife. Finally, I've found the time to send you some news. I arrived safely. There were heavy storms when we crossed the sea to Panama and lots of rain when we went through the jungle. A lot of men got sick, and some died on the journey. Sometimes I wanted to give up, but then I thought of you and our children. Ninety days after I had left you in New York, we arrived in San Francisco Bay.

However, it was more than a week before we arrived at our camp in the wilderness. I've made friends with some of the other men, who came from all over the country. We often sit around the fire at night, telling stories and singing. We all dream about making a lot of money before we return to our families. Sometimes there are fights in the camps. But don't worry, I'm well.

Finding gold isn't easy. Do you know how happy I was when I found my first little piece of gold? Some days are better than others, but my love for you keeps me going. One day I got terribly sick. I hadn't eaten or slept much, and I had worked in very cold water for hours. But I was well after a week.

My thoughts and prayers are with you, Maddy, and our children. Write soon.

Always yours,
Edward

Summary

Text B is a l— from a g— h— to his wife from 1850. His name is E— . He left his family in N— Y— and went on a long and dangerous j— to a camp near S— F— . There he looks for g— . He hopes to become r— and r— to his family soon. But f— g— is very difficult.

2,9

Text C: An encyclopedia entry

A history of California and the Gold Rush

The discovery of gold in California in 1848 made people very excited, not only in America. Thousands of people came from all over the world and in 1849 the Gold Rush started.
By 1852 it had become more and more difficult and expensive to find gold. But many more immigrants arrived. Before the Gold Rush, less than 1,000 non-native people lived in California. Ten years later the population was almost 400,000. San Francisco went from a small village of 500 people to a city of 150,000 in a few years. Many other new towns were also built.
California quickly became the 31st state of the United States in 1850 because of these events. The First Transcontinental Railway to San Francisco opened in 1869. It connected California with the rest of the country.
The impact on the Native American population was terrible. The immigrants killed them or made them their slaves. Before the Gold Rush, there were about 150,000 Native Americans. In 1870 there were only 30,000.
The gold fever did not last long. When there was no more gold, there was no more work. People moved away and left empty towns behind them. Some of the towns are still there today. The town of Bodie, for example, once had 8,000 inhabitants – now it's empty. The houses have not changed since then, and visitors can walk through the town.

Summary

Text C is an encyclopedia e— about the history of the G— R— and its impact on C— . In the middle of the nineteenth century a lot of i— came to C— to find g— . California's p— went from 1,000 to 400,000 within ten y— . However, the i— killed a lot of N— A— . California became the 31st s— of the USA in 1850. When there was no more g— people left. Today there are empty t— like Bodie.

CULTURE

Der Goldrausch wurde zum Symbol des „Kalifornischen Traums". Kalifornien wurde ein Ort des Neuanfangs, wo man mit Glück sehr schnell sehr reich werden konnte.
Würdest du so viele Stunden unter schwierigsten Bedingungen arbeiten wollen, um reich zu werden?

3 Meet your home group again.

a) Read the summary of your text to your group.

b) Write quiz questions: Write one true or false statement about each text. Use your summaries for help.

4 Do a quiz in class.

Read the statements to the class. Are they true or false?

5 Choose one of these tasks.

62/1-2

a) Write an interview and act the role play in class. One of you is a reporter for the *California Star* in 1848. Your partner is a gold hunter who has just found a lot of gold.

Reporter: Prepare questions.

1. Where are you from?
2. When did …?
3. Is it …?
4. How much gold …?
5. What will you …?

SPEAKING SKILLS

Wenn du ein Interview vorbereitest, überlege dir, wie du dein Gegenüber begrüßt. Vergiss nicht, ihm oder ihr am Schluss zu danken.

Gold hunter: Prepare your story and your plans for the future. Make notes to answer the reporter's questions.

1. I'm from … .
2. I … .
3. Yes/No, … .
4. I found … .
5. I think I'll … .

OR

b) Make a timeline about the history of the Gold Rush. Collect information from text C. Present the timeline to the class.

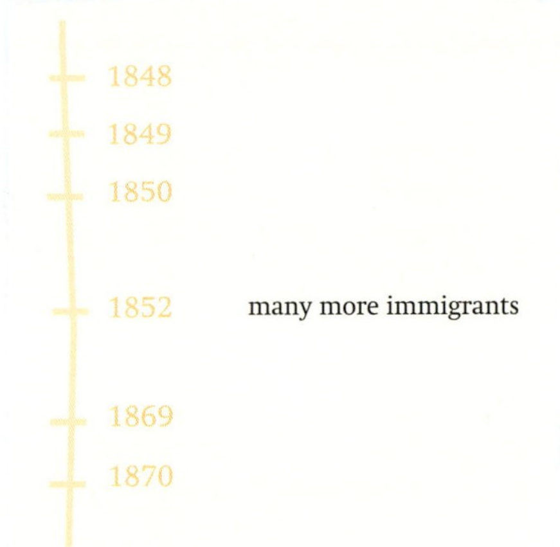

READING SKILLS

Wenn du nach Einzelheiten in einem Text suchst, musst du nicht den ganzen Text lesen. Du kannst ihn überfliegen und nach Stichwörtern oder Zahlen suchen. Lies dann nur die Sätze, in denen das Stichwort oder die Zahl vorkommt.

Ich kann einen Text über den Goldrausch verstehen. ✓

Too young to work?

Many big farms in California employ children, mostly from Latin America, to pick fruit or vegetables. Migrant parents often don't have enough income, so their children have to help them. Many of them don't have many qualifications or can hardly speak English. Some are even in the USA illegally.

Fresno Weekly Magazine talked to Matteo (12) and his brother Ramon (14) from Sacramento, who have been working on different farms.

Fresno Weekly: What can you tell us about the work in the fields?
Matteo: We have to get up at 4:30 in the morning. Buses drive us to the fields, where we work all day in the heat. We sometimes work more than ten hours a day and only earn the minimum wage or even less.
Fresno Weekly: Ramon, how long have you been working in the fields?
Ramon: Since I was ten, just like my dad.
Fresno Weekly: Do you have any health problems?
Ramon: Yes, I always have difficulties breathing because of the pesticides, and I have a constant headache. But that's not all. Some people get injured working with the large machines.

A federal law from 1938 allows farm owners to employ children from the age of twelve on big farms and even younger children on small farms. Officially, they are only allowed to work outside school hours, but some of them don't even finish high school. People have often tried to change the law, but they have never been successful.

1 Beantworte die Fragen.

63/1

1. In welchem Bereich arbeiten Kinder in Kalifornien?
2. Warum müssen Kinder arbeiten?
3. Was sagen Matteo und Ramon über die Arbeitsbedingungen?
4. Wie sind die gesetzlichen Bestimmungen für Kinderarbeit?

CULTURE

Fast die Hälfte des US-amerikanischen Obsts, Gemüses und der Nüsse kommt aus dem Central Valley, Kalifornien. Hohe Temperaturen von 40°C (100°F) und wenig Regen bieten ideale Bedingungen für den Anbau. Aber die Arbeitsbedingungen sind hart.

2 Talk to your class.

What jobs are you allowed to do?

Ich kann Informationen über Kinderarbeit weitergeben.

Talking about jobs

1 Talk about the ad on the right.

a) Which question in the ad is the most important to you?

b) Would the job interest you? Give reasons.

2 (VIEWING) Watch the film.

8 a) Watch the film until 02:08. Jessica, Wesley or Ronan: Who …

1. helps neighbours in their gardens?
2. walks the neighbours' dogs?
3. works as a waitress?
4. helps students with their homework?
5. puts groceries in bags for customers?

b) Watch the film from 02:08 to the end.

1. What does Wesley want to be?
2. What animals would Jessica like to work with?
3. Where would Ronan like to work?

CULTURE

Die Rocky Mountains (the Rockies) liegen im Westen Kanadas und der USA. Sie sind beliebt bei Kletterern, Campern, Wanderern und Skifahrern. Teile der Rockies sind in Nationalparks. Finde die Rockies auf der Karte hinten im Buch.
Welche Gebirge kennst du?

3 (SPEAKING) Talk about the film.

Choose one of the jobs from the film. Find two or three reasons why you'd like this job.

My big dream is to become a … . / I'd like to work with … .

I love … .
I want to … .
I'm good at … .

VIEWING SKILLS

In einem Film bewegen sich die Menschen oder Dinge – oder die Kamera bewegt sich stattdessen (z. B. durch Schwenken oder Näherkommen). Das kann den Film interessanter machen.
Sieh dir die zweite Hälfte des Films erneut an. Wer oder was bewegt sich – die Schauspieler, die Kamera oder beide?

Ich kann einen Film über Beruf und Karriere verstehen. ✓

Checklist

Ich kann Informationen über Kalifornien und den Westen der USA verstehen. ✓

64

Ich kann eine Werbeanzeige gestalten. ✓

The ad looks spectacular. • The layout is simple and … . • The headline is funny. • In the picture there is … .

64

Ich kann über Trends sprechen. ✓

What do you think about this trend? • Almost everyone uses it. • It has had a huge impact. • It's the latest thing/ popular. • It's outdated.

65

Ich kann einen Text über den Goldrausch verstehen. ✓

65

Ich kann Informationen über Kinderarbeit weitergeben. ✓

65

Ich kann einen Film über Beruf und Karriere verstehen. ✓

(TASK) A blog

Write a blog about a trend that you like. Add pictures.
Share your blog with others. Which trends do you find interesting?
Which ones don't you find interesting? Why?

Step 1

Collect ideas.

Work with a partner.
Make a mind map of trends.

trends: fashion, food, technology, entertainment

Step 2

Choose your topic.

Decide which trend you would like to write about.

Step 3

Collect information.

- Say where you learned about the trend.
- Say what you like about it.
- Say where the trend comes from.
- Talk about the trend. What is it? What's special about it?

WRITING SKILLS

In einem Blog schreibst du deine eigene Meinung. Vergiss also nicht zu sagen, was du denkst.

Auf der nächsten Seite findest du ein Beispiel. Welche Formulierungen kannst du für deinen Blog übernehmen?

BLOG

Have you ever heard of bento boxes? No? I didn't know about them either until a friend gave me one. He showed me how to make them.

It's fun to organize food that way. You can use bento boxes for parties and they make nice presents too.

Bento comes from Japan and it's a kind of packed lunch. Bentos have been around since the fifth century. They are made from bamboo. Modern bento boxes are made of plastic or metal. In a traditional box you will find rice, fish or meat and vegetables.

You can make your own bento easily. Just follow these steps:

- Choose food that you can eat with your fingers.
- Cut your food into small pieces.
- Make a nice box or buy one.
- Think of a nice way to put your food into the box.

Here's mine.

Step 4

Write your draft and check it.

Check the content and spelling.

WRITING SKILLS

Überprüft gegenseitig eure Entwürfe:
- Enthält der Text alle wichtigen Informationen?
- Ist der Text verständlich?
- Welche Wörter sind schwierig? Sind sie richtig geschrieben? Kontrolliert mit Hilfe eines Wörterbuchs und der Checkliste auf Seite 175.

Step 5

Share your blog with others. → M Gallery walk, p. 169

Read at least two more blogs.

Step 6

Comment on a blog.

Choose one blog. Write a short comment.

Sounds cool. | Looks awesome! | Not bad. | Sounds boring. | It's not really my thing. | What a great idea! | I think I'll try it. | …

Get to the mountain of nuggets

1 Make a set of cards with your partner.

You need:

paper

scissors

a pen

1. Fold the sheet of paper in half four times.

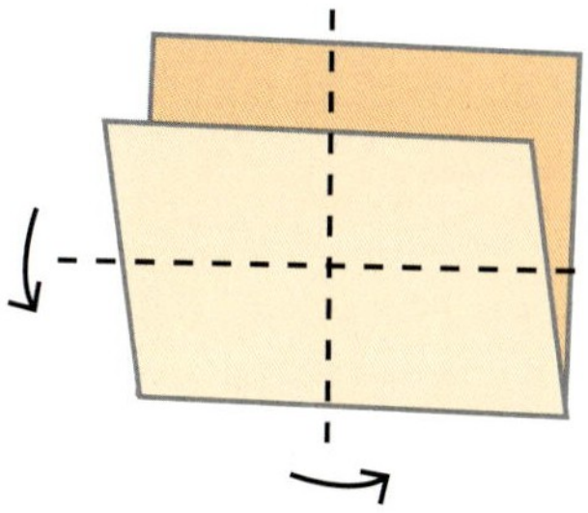

2. Cut along the lines so you have 16 playing cards.

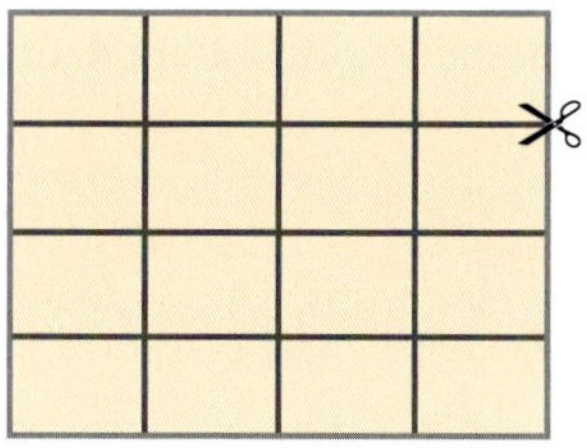

3. Write twelve questions about California on the playing cards. Write the answer in small letters upside down at the bottom of each card.

   Look at Unit 4 for help.

   You need the four empty cards for the next step.

2 Prepare the game.

1. Swap your set of cards with another pair.
2. Put the cards upside down in the middle of the table.
3. Draw a picture of yourself on an empty playing card.
4. Draw a huge mountain of nuggets on another empty card.
5. Put the two cards on the table in front of you.
6. Put the picture of yourself on the left and the mountain of nuggets on the right. Leave enough space for four more cards in between.

3 Play the game.

1. Pick a card from the pile in the middle of the table and read the question to your partner.
2. If your partner answers the question correctly, he or she can put the card next to his or her picture. If he or she is wrong, put the card to one side. It is now out of the game.
3. Take turns.
4. If you answer four questions correctly and get to your mountain of nuggets card, you win and become the richest boy or girl California has ever seen.

Swap your set of cards with another pair and play another round with their set of cards if you finish your game before others in class.

Hier kannst du lernen,
wie du ein Gespräch führst.

2,10

A podcast interview

A

B

Wow, that sounds cool!

Isn't that the same every year?

No way!? That's amazing!

That doesn't sound like much fun.

Tell me more.

Is that really interesting?

Thanks so much.

I can imagine that.

I have to interrupt here.

1 Look at the photos on the left.

a) Talk about the photos with a partner.
Do the people in the photos look interested or bored? Why?

> Wenn ihr herausfinden wollt, wie Menschen sich fühlen, achtet auf den Gesichtsausdruck und die Körperhaltung.

I think the man and the woman in photo 1 look interested/bored because … .

b) Listen to the interviews.
1. Which interview matches which photo?
2. Which interview is the better one?

2 Listen to the interviews again.

Match the sentences from page 94 with the interviews.

> Der Tonfall und die Art, wie Menschen reden, können euch viel über die Situation verraten.

Interview A
- showing interest
- sounding surprised
- saying thank you

Interview B
- sounding bored
- interrupting

68/1
69/2-4

3 Interview your partner about the last movie he or she saw.

a) Answer these questions:

> Beginnt das Interview mit einer Begrüßung:
>
> Hi … . Nice to meet you. We're talking about movies today. What was the last movie you saw?

- What was the last movie you saw?
I saw "…" (title of the movie). It's a(n) action movie/romance/science fiction movie/… .

> Wenn ihr das Interview führt, vergesst nicht, die Sätze aus Interview A zu verwenden.

- What is it about?
- Which actors are in the movie?
- How did you like it?

b) Act the interview with a partner.

> Denkt bei eurem Interview an euren Gesichtsausdruck, eure Körperhaltung und euren Tonfall.

Find more online:
i8ce82

Am Ende dieser Unit kann ich …
- Informationen über die Südstaaten der USA verstehen.
- über Einflüsse verschiedener Kulturen im täglichen Leben sprechen.
- andere über Freizeitaktivitäten informieren.
- einen Bericht über Rassismus verstehen.
- Informationen über Rituale weitergeben.
- einen Film über die Sommerferien verstehen.

9 2,11

Unit 5

Southern life

The Southern Appalachian Mountains, the Gulf Coast beaches, the Florida swamps and the Mississippi River – the South has many exciting places for fans of the outdoors.

Until the 1950s African Americans in the South did not have the same rights as white Americans. The Civil Rights Movement, a peaceful protest movement, changed that.

1 (SPEAKING) Talk about the photos.

Which photo do you like most?
Which photo do you not like? Why?

I like photo 1 most because … .
I don't like photo … because … .

2 Read the texts and find the topics.

72/1-2

a) Which text is it?

A Music is important in the South.
B The nature of the South is great.
C People from Africa had to work as slaves for white people.
D Southern life and culture are different.
E African Americans got more rights.

b) Which topic would you like to know more about?

I'm interested in … . • I like … . •
I'd like to know more about … .

3

In the 18th century, people from France, England, Scotland and Ireland came to the South. Soon they brought in slaves from Africa to work on their plantations.

4

The South has its own lifestyle and culture. People here are proud to be both Americans and Southerners.

5

Some styles of music come from the South like gospel music or rock 'n' roll. New Orleans is the home of jazz, and Nashville is the home of country music.

3 (LISTENING) Listen to the online radio broadcast about Taylor Swift.

2,12

What's special about Taylor Swift? Complete the sentences.

1. She is a ___ singer and a popstar.
2. She writes her own ___ .
3. Since ___ many songs have been at the top of the charts.
4. In 2012 she was the best-paid star under ___ .
5. Her ___ can see themselves in her songs.

charts [tʃɑ:ts] – Charts
best-paid ['best,peɪd] – höchstbezahlt

Ich kann Informationen über die Südstaaten der USA verstehen. ✓

Hier lerne ich, über Einflüsse verschiedener Kulturen im täglichen Leben zu sprechen.

Living together

1 (READING) Read the text.

2,13
73/1

Rich food, rich culture
by Anna Williams

Southern food

The South is famous for its great food. And the food shows the history of the South. I went on a trip there, and here's what I found out.
In the beginning there was the food of the Native Americans. Then European settlers brought new dishes. The slaves from West Africa had a big influence too.
The delicious southern fried chicken is a good example. This dish came from Scotland and some of the spices came from West Africa. First the spices are mixed with flour. The chicken pieces are washed and dried and then covered in the flour. After that, the chicken is fried in oil until it's golden.

The city of New Orleans

In New Orleans different cultures and traditions meet. The French founded the city in 1718; then it became Spanish. New Orleans was the most important cotton and slave market in the South until the middle of the 19th century. Later it became the country's second biggest gateway for immigrants from Europe. In the late 20th century large numbers of Vietnamese people arrived.
When you walk through New Orleans today, you can see that it's a multicultural city. You can be part of it at the famous Mardi Gras carnival and the Jazz Fest.

New Orleans

The Confederate flag

But there are also problems with the different groups. The Confederate flag is one example. It flew over the South Carolina State House for years until 2015. For many white people in the South this flag is a symbol of pride. Others just tolerate it. But for most African Americans it is a symbol of racism.
After nine people had been killed in a black church in Charleston, protests started. The state government had to find a solution. In the end they removed the flag.

CULTURE

Die Südstaaten benutzten eine eigene Fahne im amerikanischen Bürgerkrieg (1861–1865).
Der Norden wollte die Sklaverei abschaffen, der Süden nicht. Heute ist die Fahne im Süden immer noch verbreitet, aber bei vielen umstritten.

The Confederate flag

2 Match the sentence parts.

1. The South is famous for
2. Southern fried chicken is
3. In 1718 French settlers founded
4. Later New Orleans was important as
5. Today New Orleans is
6. The Confederate flag is

A New Orleans.
B a symbol of pride and racism.
C a cotton and slave market.
D its food.
E a famous dish from the South.
F a multicultural city.

73/2

3 What's the nationality?

a) Match the nationalities with the flags. → ○ p. 131

Chinese | Greek | Italian | Russian | Polish | Turkish

1. 中国 2. Россия 3. Polska 4. Ελλάδα 5. Türkiye 6. Italia

b) Do you know the colours of these flags? → V Nationalities, p. 202

Swiss · Spanish · Japanese

Alle Flaggen haben eine Farbe gemeinsam.

74/4

4 Find the words.

a) Find the words with the same meaning. → ○ p. 131

73/3a)

disagreed | made a compromise | tolerated | problems

1. Some people accepted the flag.
2. Others didn't accept it.
3. There were conflicts between the different groups.
4. The different groups found a solution.

STUDY SKILLS

Beim Vokabellernen kann es dir helfen, wenn du Wörter mit gleicher Bedeutung (Synonyme) und Wörter mit gegensätzlicher Bedeutung (Antonyme) zusammen lernst.

b) Find the opposites. → V Conflicts and solutions, p. 203

73/3b)

refuse an idea | break a rule | be happy with a situation | complain about a situation | respect a rule | accept an idea

Language detectives → G9, p. 166

The spices are mixed with flour. The chicken is fried in oil.
It is eaten with the fingers.

Das Passiv verwendest du, wenn der Handelnde („Täter“) unbekannt oder unwichtig ist.
Es kommt häufig in Sachtexten vor. Schau dir die Sätze an: Wie bildest du es?

5 (SPEAKING) Say how southern fried chicken is cooked.

Match the sentences with the pictures.

A The spices and flour are mixed. ✓

B The chicken is fried until it's golden.

C The chicken is covered in flour.

D The chicken pieces are washed.

E The chicken pieces are put in hot oil.

F The chicken pieces are dried.

74/5-6 6 Make passive sentences. → M Bus stop, p. 168

a) Choose the right form. → ○ p. 132

1. Pork is • **are** used in many southern dishes.
2. Southern food **is** • **are** eaten across the USA.
3. Vegetables **is** • **are** kept in the fridge.
4. All these dishes **is** • **are** made with rice.
5. Rice **is** • **are** not grown in many US states.

b) Talk about the food at your school. You can use these words.

sandwiches | cakes | lunch | drinks | ice cream | ...

sold | freshly prepared | offered | ...

87/5

7 Complete the sentences about multicultural schools.

a) Make passive sentences. → ○ p. 132

75/7

1. Many languages are spoken at multicultural schools. (speak)
2. Special lessons —— for people who are new. (organize)
3. Lessons —— in different languages at some schools. (give)
4. Multicultural food —— in the cafeteria. (sell)
5. Special days of different cultures —— at school. (celebrate)
6. Racism —— there. (not accept)

Nutze die Liste der unregelmäßigen Verben (3. Spalte) ab S. 210 als Hilfe!

b) Make passive sentences with these words.

75/8

organize | write | tolerate

1. At multicultural schools different opinions … .
2. Activities against racism … there.
3. Letters to students and parents … in more than one language.

8 (YOUR TURN) Different cultures where I live → V Talking about culture, p. 206

75/9

What is the influence of other cultures where you live? Prepare a short presentation.
→ M Tip top, p. 173

- Say where you live.
- Say what multicultural influences you find in:
  - shops
  - restaurants
  - signs
  - music
- How do you like living there?

I live in … .
There are many Turkish/Chinese/… shops.
People like to buy … there.
When you look around, you see … restaurants.
The signs are written in … .
People like to go there because … .
You can listen to … music at/in … .
I (don't) like living there because … .

STUDY SKILLS

Wenn du ein Wort auf Englisch nicht weißt, schlage im Wörterbuch nach. Manche Wörter lassen sich nicht übersetzen. Diese Wörter kannst du umschreiben, in dem du sie auf Englisch erklärst. Manche kannst du auch mit Hilfe eines Fotos erklären.

So kannst du Wörter umschreiben: 'Ajvar' is a kind of sauce. It's made of peppers. You can eat it with meat, vegetables or bread.

Ich kann über Einflüsse verschiedener Kulturen im täglichen Leben sprechen. ✓

Hier lerne ich, andere über Freizeitaktivitäten zu informieren.

A trip to Florida

1 Look at the websites. Which trip would you like to go on? Why?

I'd like to go to … because … .

INTERNET

Be there for the most important NASCAR race!

Our Daytona 500 race packages:

- Daytona 500 race tickets
- hotel
- transfer to the race track
- a booklet with all details

INTERNET

Go into the Florida Everglades!

Airboat rides, alligators, wildlife show

- hotel pick-up
- exciting 30-minute boat tour
- alligator, snake and wildlife show
- jungle trail through the swamps

2 (READING) Read the friends' dialogue. → M Dramatic reading, p. 169

2,14 76/1

Anna: My dad can take us to Daytona or to the Everglades. He says that he needs an answer today. These are the websites that he's found.

Matt: Well, I know. I'd like to go to the race. It's the biggest NASCAR event of the year.

Anna: That's not my idea of fun. All those noisy people! I prefer the Everglades. I've never seen an alligator in the wild.

Matt: Why do you want to spend the day walking around in the heat?

Anna: What does Ethan think?

Ethan is speech impaired. He can hear, but he uses sign language to speak. Matt understands sign language and translates for Anna.

Matt: Ethan says that he doesn't like crowds much either.

Anna: There you are. He wants to see the alligators too.

Ethan makes more signs.

Matt: I'm sorry, Ethan. Can you repeat it, please? (*Ethan repeats it.*) I see. But he also says that he has always wanted to watch a NASCAR race.

Anna: Oh, no! So we'll go to the NASCAR race.

Ethan makes signs.

Matt: I'm sorry, I didn't get that, Ethan. (*Ethan repeats it.*) Oh, right. He says the jungle trail sounds really interesting too. He'd like to see big snakes. He wants to know if your dad can drive us to the Everglades another time. Maybe next month?

Anna: Yes, I can ask him tonight.

3 (WRITING) Take notes about the places.

a) Where do they want to go?

Matt: …
Anna: …
Ethan: …

b) Copy and complete the table.

	for	against
Daytona	the biggest NASCAR event	
Everglades		

2,15
76/2

4 (LISTENING) Listen to the text about a visit to an alligator farm.

a) Correct the notes. → ○ p. 132

Alligator farm, Florida Everglades
- a slow boat ride
- trainer had fight with snake
- Matt put hand in alligator's mouth
- photo of Ethan with alligator

LISTENING SKILLS

Keine Sorge, wenn du beim ersten Hören nicht alles verstehst. Achte beim zweiten Hören vor allem auf die Sätze in der Aufgabe.

b) What did Matt like most about the visit to the alligator farm? What did Ethan like most?

1 boat ride
2 alligator show
3 snake show

5 (WRITING) How can you say that you (don't) understand? → M Peer correction, p. 171

a) Copy and complete the table. → ○ p. 133

76/3

Could you please explain? ✓ | I get it. | I know what you mean. | Can you repeat it, please? | Excuse me? | I see.

I understand	I don't understand
…	Could you please explain?

b) Match the phrases with the definitions. → V Understanding things, p. 204

I'm sorry, but I didn't catch that. | Absolutely! | What do you mean by '…'?

1. Ask somebody to explain a word.
2. Ask somebody to say something again.
3. Tell somebody that you agree with them.

SPEAKING SKILLS

Wenn du etwas nicht verstehst, sag nicht einfach „Huh?" oder „What?". Das ist unhöflich.

6 Use sign language.

Look at the signs. Then close your books and practise them with a partner.

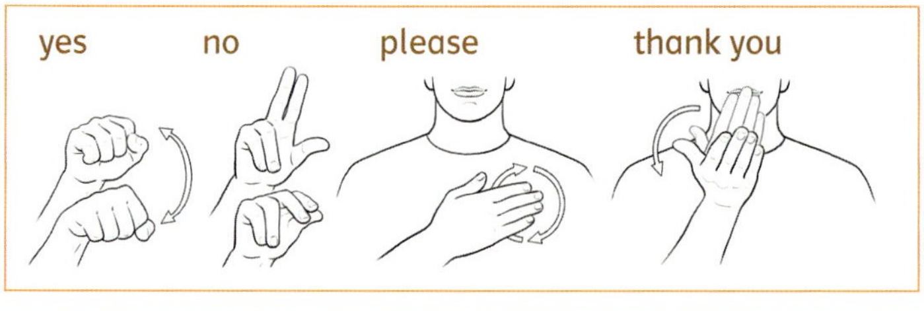

Language detectives → G10, p. 167

Dad: "I need an answer today."
→ Dad says he needs an answer today.

Ethan: "I don't like crowds."
→ Ethan says that he doesn't like crowds.

Diese Sätze geben wieder, was der Vater und Ethan sagen. Sieh dir die Sätze an. Welche Wörter kommen in der indirekten Rede (zweite Zeile) hinzu? Was verändert sich noch?

77/4-6 **7** **Report what other people say.**

a) What did Anna write? → ○ p. 133

Report the underlined sentences from Anna's e-mail from Clearwater, Florida.

E-MAIL

Hi Julie,
(1) I'm at Clearwater right now. (2) I love the the warm weather here. (3) We just wear T-shirts and shorts and (4) we often go to the beach. (5) It's awesome! But (6) I hate the insects.
See you soon,
Anna

Das ändert sich in der indirekten Rede:
I love → he/she loves
we love → they love

1. Anna says (that) she is at Clearwater.
2. She writes (that) she …

b) Play the game.

Your teacher gives a sentence to the first student in your group. He or she whispers the sentence to the next person and so on. Is the sentence still the same at the end?

I want to hold a baby alligator.

Play the game with more sentences.

8 Complete the sentences.

78/7-8
87/6

Report the sentences in the speech bubbles.

I don't like → he/she doesn't like
we don't like → they don't like

1. The girl says (that) she … .
2. The boy says (that) he … .
3. The boy says … .
4. The girl … .
5. …

9 (YOUR TURN) Information for a day trip → V A day trip, p. 207

78/9
79/1-2

Tell an English-speaking friend about Berlin Zoo.

Your friend: Can you tell me where Berlin Zoo is?
You: The website says it's in the centre of Berlin.
Your friend: Which animals can you see there?
You: It says here that you can see … .
Your friend: Which activities can you do there?
You: You can … .
Your friend: When is the zoo open?
You: It's open from … to … .
Your friend: Where can we buy tickets?
You: You can … .

Herzlich willkommen im Zoo Berlin!

Besuchen Sie den ersten Zoo Deutschlands im Zentrum Berlins.
Unter unseren über 17.000 Zoo-Tieren finden Sie Affen, Elefanten, Schlangen, Tiger und viele mehr.

- Erleben Sie die Fütterungen und Tiershows.
- Gehen Sie auf Nachtsafari im Nachttierhaus.
- Feiern Sie Kindergeburtstage bei uns.
- Nehmen Sie am Fotospaziergang teil.

Öffnungszeiten
Heute, 2.6.2018, 9:00 – 18:30 Uhr
Jetzt Online Ticket kaufen!

Was heißt „Nachtsafari im Nachttierhaus" auf Englisch? – You can visit the zoo at night and watch the animals that don't sleep at night.

Ich kann andere über Freizeitaktivitäten informieren. ✓

The girl who fought segregation

1 If you know something is wrong or unfair, what do you do about it?

I talk to .... • I tell .... • I help .... • I don't do anything because ....

2 (READING) Read the report.

2,16

Claudette Colvin was an African-American teenager from Montgomery, Alabama. On March 2, 1955, Claudette was on a bus with three other girls. They were sitting in the middle of the bus. More and more white people got on, and it was soon full. The bus driver told the girls that they had to give up their seats and move to the back. This was the rule. Three of them got up and went to the back. But Claudette didn't move.

The bus driver called the police. A police officer got on the bus, but Claudette still didn't move. She said that she paid her fare like other people. It was her right to sit there. In the end, they dragged her off the bus and arrested her.

Her parents brought her home later that day. Her father was awake all night with his gun because he was afraid of the Ku Klux Klan.

Claudette Colvin, 2016

3 (SPEAKING) Talk to a partner: What is the story about? → M Think-pair-share, p. 173

A Rosa Parks' protest on buses

B the Ku Klux Klan's fight against African Americans

C Claudette Colvin's fight against segregation

I think the story is about ....
The title says '...'. The text says in line(s) ....

READING SKILLS

Die meisten Texte haben ein Hauptthema oder eine Hauptaussage. Es ist wichtig, diese zu finden und zu verstehen. Du findest sie oft in der Überschrift, im ersten Absatz oder am Ende des Textes.

4 Find the information.

1. Where did Claudette sit on the bus?
2. Why did the bus driver tell her to move back?
3. Why was Claudette arrested?
4. Why did Claudette lose a lot of friends?
5. When did segregation on public transport end in Alabama?
6. Why did Claudette move to New York?

The next week Claudette had problems in school too. Some students thought that she was very brave. However, many others thought that she was crazy. They said that she had made things harder for African Americans. Claudette lost a lot of friends.
Claudette's life became very difficult, but her protest was a success. A year later, in 1956, there was a court case and she was the star witness. The case ended segregation on all public transport in Alabama. In that same year Claudette left Montgomery because she couldn't find any work. She moved to New York.
Claudette's story has been forgotten by most people. Instead, Rosa Parks became famous for the fight against segregation on buses. She did exactly the same thing nine months later. For Claudette that was OK.
There were hundreds of brave people like Claudette. You never see their names but they played an important role in the long fight against segregation. Their courage will always be remembered.

CULTURE

Der Ku Klux Klan ist eine geheime Organisation weißer Amerikaner, die sich gegen Menschen anderer Kulturen und Religionen richtet. In den 1950er und -60er Jahren griffen sie Afro-Amerikaner und Mitglieder der Bürgerrechtsbewegung an oder brachten sie um.
Gibt es solche Gruppierungen auch in deinem Land?

5 Choose one of these tasks.

P
80/1-2

a) Search the internet for information about one of these people:

Rosa Parks • Martin Luther King • Malcolm X • Mahatma Gandhi • Malala Yousafzai

Answer these questions and write four to six sentences about your person:
- Who is he or she?
- Where does/did he or she live?
- When?
- What did he or she do to fight for their rights?

Add pictures.

→ M Gallery walk, p. 169

OR

b) Write the court scene with Claudette as the witness.

Here are the questions of the State Attorney:
- What's your name?
- Where are you from?
- Tell the court what happened on the bus on March 2, 1955.
- Do you know the rules on public transport?
- So you broke the rules on purpose. Why did you do that?

Write Claudette's answers. Look at the text for help. Act the scene in class.

→ M Dramatic reading, p. 169

Ich kann einen Bericht über Rassismus verstehen. ✓

Going out in style

INTERNET

The 'jazz funeral' came from Africa with the slaves about 400 years ago. In the beginning it was called 'funeral with music'. People celebrated the end of slavery for the dead person. It was used mainly for poorer African Americans first and later also for musicians. In the mid 20th century it became an accepted funeral.

On the way to the cemetery the brass band plays mostly slow and sad songs. But on the way back you can hear joyful music. One of the most famous songs is 'When the Saints Go Marching In'. At this stage people from the streets are allowed to join in the parade.

One of the biggest jazz funerals in New Orleans took place on August 29, 2006 for the 1,700 victims of Hurricane Katrina. The communities remembered the people who lost their lives the year before. That shows how people here deal with the death of loved ones and still celebrate life.

1 Beantworte die Fragen.

81/1-2

1. Was feierten die Menschen bei einer Jazz-Beerdigung früher?
2. Welche Art Musik wird vor und nach der Beerdigung gespielt?
3. Für wen war die Jazz-Beerdigung am 29. August 2006?

2 Talk to your class.

What do people in your country do after a funeral?

Ich kann Informationen über Rituale weitergeben. ✔

The great outdoors?

1 Talk about the summer holidays.

a) Do you prefer outdoor or indoor activities in your free time?

b) What's your favourite activity? Why?

2 (VIEWING) Watch the film.

10

a) Match the statements with the right scene.

1. "I got the job interview at Silverley!"
2. "That was last year. I'm 16 now!"
3. "That's for really young kids ..."
4. "Very reliable. You can trust her."

b) What are their summer plans? Match each name with the right activity.

Ronan · Amy · Jessica

work at a summer camp

go to a Science camp

stay at home or with grandma

3 (SPEAKING) Talk about the film.

a) Watch from 01:31 to 01:55. Make notes about five of the activities there.

b) Which activity would you like to try? Why?

I would like to .... .
I like .../I'm interested in .... .

CULTURE

In den USA dauern die Sommerferien 8–12 Wochen. Während dieser Zeit besuchen viele Kinder ein Ferienlager. Manche haben Schwerpunkte wie Reiten oder andere Sportarten oder Computerspiele. Gibt es in deiner Nähe ein Ferienlager? Würdest du gerne eins besuchen?

A

B

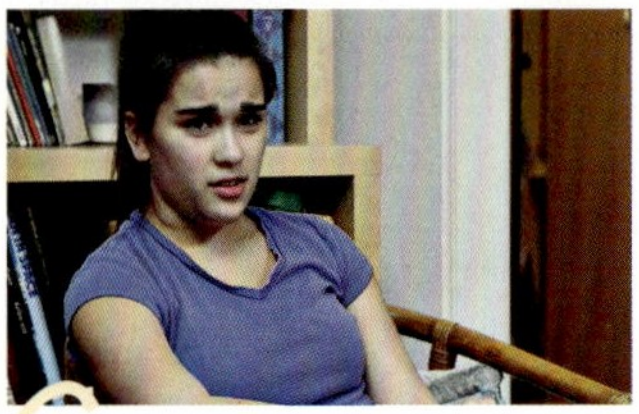
C

D

VIEWING SKILLS

Achte darauf, wie die Person, die das Interview durchführt, auf ihren Gesprächspartner eingeht (indem sie ihn z. B. anlächelt).
Wie kann eine Person in einem Gespräch sonst noch auf ihren Partner eingehen?

Ich kann einen Film über die Sommerferien verstehen. ✓

Checklist

Ich kann Informationen über die Südstaaten der USA verstehen. ✓

82

Ich kann über Einflüsse verschiedener Kulturen im täglichen Leben sprechen. ✓

In … different cultures and traditions meet. • … had a big influence on … . • When you look around, you see … . • There are problems/conflicts … .

82

Ich kann andere über Freizeitaktivitäten informieren. ✓

Here it says that … . • You can … . • I'm sorry I didn't get that. • He wants to know if … .

83

Ich kann einen Bericht über Rassismus verstehen. ✓

83

Ich kann Informationen über Rituale weitergeben. ✓

83

Ich kann einen Film über die Sommerferien verstehen. ✓

(TASK) A feature story

Imagine you are a reporter. Choose a place, watch the people there and take notes. Write a feature story. Make a wall newspaper in class.

Early birds
(by Mika Hensing)
May 13, 2016 — *headline, writer, date*

It's still dark. There are not many people in the street. However, the smell of fresh bread is in the air. At the baker's stall there's a bright light and I can see a crowd of people. — *describing the scene*

They are all waiting in a long queue. Some are looking at their phones. Some are listening to music; others are talking to each other. — *describing details*

Almost everyone looks tired. I feel … . — *describing emotions*

Bakers usually get up at … . — *background information*

"I come here every day," a woman says … . — *direct speech*

Step 1

Look for an interesting place to go.

You can go to the campus, a bus stop, the park or any other place where you can watch other people. Find other students who chose the same place.

Step 2

Take notes about the scene at your place.

What can you see, hear, smell and feel?
What are the people doing?
What are they saying?
What do you think they are thinking?
What is the weather like?
What time of the day is it?

Take photos too. If you take photos of single people or small groups, you have to ask them if that's OK.

Step 3

Find facts about your place.

You can find facts on location or on the internet. If you choose a bus stop, for example, you can find out how many buses stop there every day and where they go.

Step 4

Use your notes to write a draft.

- Find a catchy headline, an interesting opening and a nice photo.
- Describe the scene, the people and the atmosphere.
- Name the place and give interesting facts and details.
- Say what is special about the place or the people.
- Use a computer programme to format your text. You can find help on page 49.

Beschreibe die Atmosphäre mit treffenden Adjektiven: lonely, nervous, in a hurry, busy, … .

Step 5

Check your draft. → M Writers' conference, p. 173

WRITING SKILLS

Prüft eure Entwürfe in der Klasse gegenseitig:
- Sind folgende Dinge vorhanden: Überschrift, Einleitungssatz, Foto, Namen des Autors/der Autorin, Datum? ✓
- Sind der Ort und die Menschen genau beschrieben? ✓
- Habt ihr schwierige Wörter im Wörterbuch nachgeschlagen und anhand der Checkliste auf Seite 175 geprüft? ✓
- Sind die Zeitformen (present progressive und simple present) richtig verwendet? ✓
- Sind die Zeitformen richtig gebildet? ✓

Der Mustertext hilft dabei.

Step 6

Make a wall newspaper in class. Find the most interesting feature story. → M Gallery walk, p. 169

Read the headlines, the first lines and look at the photos. Vote for the best headline, the most interesting first line and the most interesting photo. Read these three feature stories in class.

Recipes from the South

Po Boy Sandwich (serves 4)

The Po Boy Sandwich is a recipe from New Orleans. It's made with fresh French bread and a wide variety of fillings. You can make a perfect Po Boy Sandwich to your own choice and taste!

You need:
1 fresh French baguette bread
(about 14 ounces or 20 inches long)

Filling of your choice

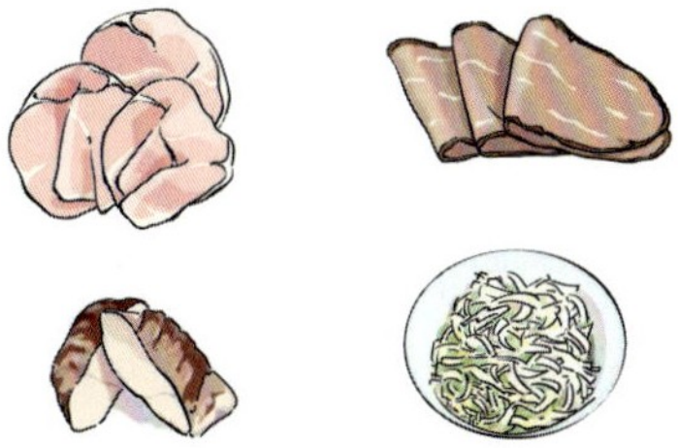

ham, roast beef or chicken breast, coleslaw

smoked tofu, lettuce and tomatoes, onion rings or coleslaw

shrimps in cocktail sauce and tomatoes, shredded lettuce

Sauce

hot BBQ sauce, salsa or mayonnaise

Extras

gherkins or mixed pickles, grated cheese

Serve with

French fries, crisps or nachos

Preparation:

1. Cut the bread into 4 pieces.
2. Cut each piece in half.
3. Spread the sauce on one half.
4. Next choose the fillings of your choice.
5. Add extras to your taste.
6. Put the two halves together.
7. Serve the sandwich with French fries, crisps or nachos.

Guten Appetit!

CULTURE

In den USA benutzt man andere Maßeinheiten für Gewicht, Länge und Volumen als bei uns:
1 ounce = 28,35 g
1 inch = 2,54 cm
1 cup = 24 ml

Louisiana sweet tea (makes 4 glasses)

You need:

4 cups of water

2 breakfast tea bags

1 peppermint tea bag

3–5 tablespoons of sugar

juice of one lemon

crushed ice and slices of lemon

Preparation:

1. Boil the water.

2. Put all the tea bags into the boiling water.
   Brewing time: 5–6 min.

3. Add the sugar and the juice. Stir it well.

4. Cool it down.

5. You can serve it with crushed ice or slices of lemon.

Diff corner

Unit 1, p.15

○ 4 Find the words.

subway · avenue · skyline · playground · rush hour

Choose the right word. The pictures can help you.

1. street • road • 
2. taxis • bus • 

3. park • lake • 
4. traffic jam • roadwork • 
5. skyscraper • tower • 

Unit 1, p.15

○ 5 (SPEAKING) Act as a guide.

Present what is on the map. Look at the numbers for help.

1 Over there you can see ...

2 Don't miss ...

3 You must visit ...

4 Around the corner you can see ...

5 Look, there's ...

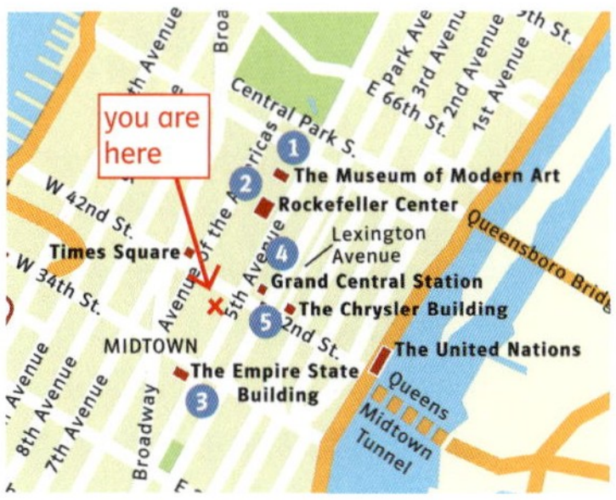

Unit 1, p.16

○ 7 (WRITING) Tell the taxi driver's story.

Make sentences. Use the simple past.

Sieh in der Liste auf S. 210 nach, ob das Verb in Klammern unregelmäßig ist!

1. Last winter I was (be) at the airport. A woman — (get) in my taxi.

2. It — (be) cold and there — (be) heavy snow.

3. Then there — (be) a traffic jam. I — (talk) to the woman.

4. When we — (arrive) at the hotel, she — (forget) her saxophone.

5. I — (run) to the hotel and I — (look) for her.

6. When I — (give) the saxophone back, she was very happy.

Unit 1, p.17

8 (SPEAKING) What did they do at One World Trade Center yesterday?

Look at the people in the picture. Match the questions with the answers.

1. What did Henry eat?
2. Did Susan take a photo?
3. What did Lisa do?
4. What did Frank look at?
5. Where did Linda sit?
6. Did Nancy eat a sandwich?

A He looked at the view.
B She sat next to the window.
C No, she had a drink.
D No, she phoned somebody.
E He ate a sandwich.
F She took a photo of herself.

Unit 1, p.18

2 (WRITING) Collect facts about José and his family. → M Think-pair-share, p.173

1,4

Complete the fact card.

Interviewer: Hello José. Can I ask you a few questions for our magazine, please?
José: Hi. Sure.
Interviewer: You're new on the baseball team. Are you happy?
José: We won the first three matches, so I can't complain.
Interviewer: There are lots of players from Latin America here. When did you immigrate to the United States?
José: That was twelve years ago. I was ten.
Interviewer: That was a big decision for your parents. They left their home and moved to a foreign place.
José: Yes, but they were very poor in Cuba. My father had been unemployed for a long time. My parents wanted to give me and my sisters the best chances. …
Interviewer: What about your plans for the future?
José: I'm a US citizen now and my home is here. But I plan to help people in Cuba.
Interviewer: Thank you for your time.

Name: J— (line 1)
Job: b— p— (lines 4 and 8)
Age: — (line 11)
From: C— (line 15)
Lives in: the U— (lines 9 to 10)
Why they left their country:
p—, u—, get best c— (lines 15 to 18)
Plans: h— p— in C— (line 22)

Unit 1, p. 19

○ 4 Imagine you want to leave your country.

Complete the sentences with these phrases.

chances | get used to | feel foreign | immigrate to ✓ | give up

1. Where could I go? I could immigrate to the USA.
2. It will be hard to g—— my old life.
3. I hope I will have many c—— in the USA.
4. I hope I won't f—— and lonely.
5. I hope I can g—— my new life soon.

Unit 1, p. 20

○ 7 Find out about one of Angela's days.

Welche Puzzleteile gehören zusammen?

Match the sentence parts. The pictures can help you.

After Pablo had invited Angela to his party, …

… she bought a present.

After Angela and Pablo had walked through the park, …

… she had ordered a milkshake.

After they had bought tickets, …

… they took the subway.

Before Angela ate her pizza, …

… they had put on their fan shirts.

Before Angela and Pablo went to the stadium, …

… they visited Ellis Island.

Unit 1, p. 21

○ 8 (WRITING) Write sentences. Use the past perfect.

What had José done before his first important baseball game last summer? What hadn't he done? Look at José's list. Then choose the right word.

José:

1. Before my first big game I had • **hadn't** played every day.
2. I **had** • hadn't bought new sports shoes.
3. I **had** • **hadn't** ordered tickets for my friends.
4. I **had** • **hadn't** watched the other team.
5. I **had** • **hadn't** phoned my dad.
6. I **had** • **hadn't** eaten a big meal.

1. played every day ✓
2. bought new sports shoes ✗
3. ordered tickets for my friends ✓
4. watched the other team ✓
5. phoned my dad ✓
6. eaten a big meal ✗

3 (WRITING) Find out about Luise's exchange year.

1,10

"No! An exchange year in South Dakota? That's in the middle of nowhere," I thought. But after my year there I can say that it was the best time ever.

In the beginning it was like in a movie. I had seen it all on TV. My American school was huge. Teachers usually stay in their classrooms, and students go to them for each class. So we had to put our things into our lockers. After two weeks I got used to it, and I could find the way to the classrooms by myself.

Every day school started at 8:00 with a morning message from the principal. The first class started at 8:30. I had to take Math, English, Science and History. But I could choose subjects like Astronomy and Journalism, for example. We also had six classes a week in the study hall. There we could do our homework or study. You weren't allowed to talk there.

School rules were strict. Much stricter than at home. Another rule was: You weren't allowed to wear short skirts.

Classes finished at 3:30. After that there were many extracurricular activities. I wanted to join the cheerleaders. There was a lot of competition for places. Exchange students were allowed to try too, so I did. And I got a place! Awesome!

My host family was great too. They even took me on a trip to the east coast. My exchange year was fantastic, even in the middle of nowhere.

Make a mind map. Use the underlined phrases from the text for help.

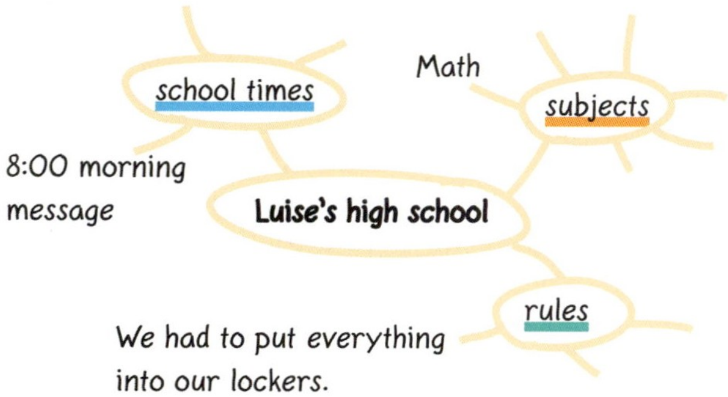

D

Unit 2, p. 35

4 What do these words mean?

Match the words with the definitions. The pictures can help you.

1. where students keep their things
2. the leader of a school
3. where you can do your homework or study
4. a number or letter that tells you how well you did in a test
5. a year with a host family in another country

A 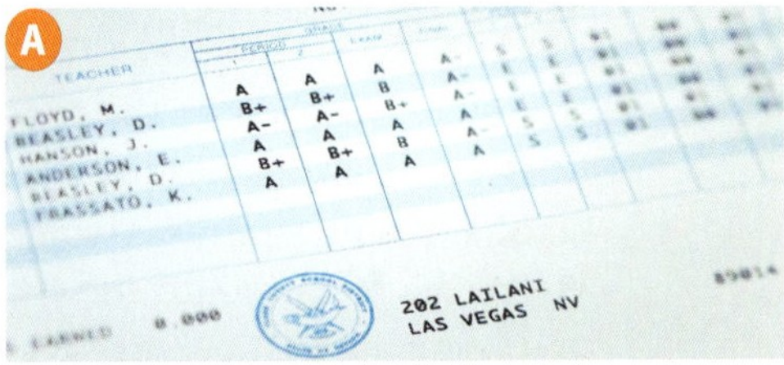

grade

B 

exchange year

C 

locker

D 

study hall

E 

principal

Unit 2, p. 36

○ 8 Complete the sentences.

Complete the sentences about Luise and the cheerleaders with these words.

had to | **musste(n)** | **didn't have to** | **brauchte(n) nicht**

1. Before Luise joined the cheerleaders she (+) get the right clothes.
   Before Luise joined the cheerleaders she had to get the right clothes.
2. She was fit, so she (–) worry.
3. For the first practice she (+) be there 15 minutes early.
4. During her first practice the cheerleaders (+) shout really loudly.
5. Luise learned very quickly, so she (–) do extra practice.

Ob die Aussage stimmt oder nicht, siehst du an den Symbolen (+) und (–).

Unit 2, p. 37

○ 9 Make sentences about Luise's life after her exchange year in the USA.

Say what Luise could (+) or couldn't (–) do after her exchange.

1. Luise (–) get used to her old life easily.
   Luise couldn't get used to her old life easily.
2. She (+) understand English a lot better.
3. She (+) speak English a lot better.
4. She (–) keep in touch with all her American friends.
5. She (+) help other students with English.

Die Verneinung von „could" (konnte) heißt „could not" oder „couldn't".

Unit 2, p. 39

○ 4 (SPEAKING) What do you think?

What should or shouldn't Michael say to the manager?

1. "I'm sorry."
2. "It won't happen again."
3. "But they started it."
4. "It wasn't me."
5. "I don't think you're right."
6. "Next time I'll try to be cooler."

Welche Sätze zeigen, dass er seinen Fehler einsieht? Mit welchen Sätzen gibt er die Schuld anderen?

Unit 2, p. 39

○ 6 (WRITING) Practise words to describe people at work. → M Peer correction, p. 171

Copy and complete the table.

+	–
— ing	lazy
— ful	un —
— ible	un —

lazy ✓ | hard-working | helpful | responsible | unmotivated | unfriendly

Welche bekannten Wörter stecken in den neuen Wörtern drin?

Unit 2, p. 40

○ 9 Complete the sentences.

He, she, it – das -s muss mit!

Use the simple present.

1. If Michael finds a job, he'll earn money. (find a job)

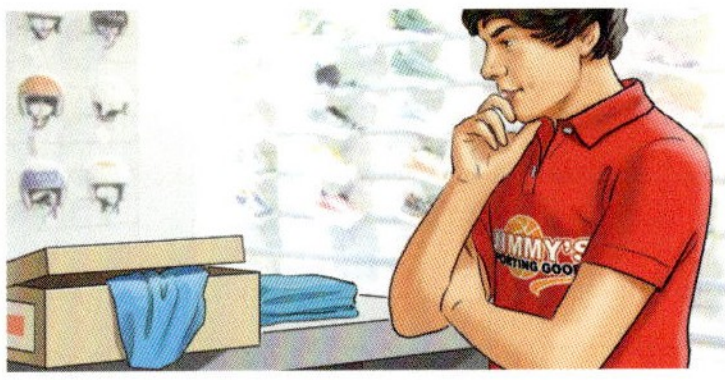

2. If he —, he'll ask his co-workers. (need help)

3. If he —, he'll lose his job. (be late)

4. If the girl —, Michael will catch her. (steal something)

5. If the man —, he'll get a new pullover. (complain)

6. If the woman —, she'll get one free. (buy two)

Unit 2, p. 41

○ 10 (SPEAKING) What will you do if …?

Talk about next weekend. Complete the sentences with these words. I'll | I won't

1. If I get up late, I won't have breakfast.
2. If the weather is fine, — go to the cinema.
3. If it rains, — go cycling.
4. If I don't have any homework, — watch TV.
5. If my parents are away on Saturday evening, — have a party.
6. If I'm too busy, — go shopping.

Unit 3, p. 55

○ 3 Find out about the Miller family's Thanksgiving. → M Peer correction, p. 171

The Millers from Boston are getting ready for Thanksgiving dinner. Julia is in the kitchen. Her husband Mark, their son Jacob and Grandma Brenda are in the living room. Her daughter Lily lives with her boyfriend Evan in Washington D.C. They are not there yet.

Grandma: Last year we had a terrible storm. I got stuck in my car for over two hours. Do you remember?

Mark: Yes, that's right. Did you have a hard time again yesterday?

(The doorbell rings. Mark opens the door. It's their neighbor.)

Robert: Happy Thanksgiving, Mark!

Mark: You too, Robert. How are you doing?

Robert: Great, thanks. Brr. It's very cold outside.

Mark: Come on in. I'm so glad you could make it. *(They enter the living room.)* Grandma, this is Robert. He's our new neighbor. He doesn't have family here, so we've invited him to join us. Robert, this is Brenda.

Robert: Nice to meet you, Brenda.

Grandma: Nice to meet you too. When did you move here?

Mark: *(He shouts across the room)* Jacob, why don't you say hello? You can't spend all your time on your phone.

Jacob: What's up Robert?

Robert: How's it going? Are you enjoying the holiday? Do you like turkey?

Jacob: Not really. I'm a vegetarian, so I won't eat any.

Julia: *(She comes out of the kitchen.)* You always used to eat everything. *(She notices the new guest.)* Oh, hi Robert.

Robert: Hey Julia. Thanks so much for inviting me. Here's a little present. You eat chocolates, don't you? *(He gives her a box as a present.)*

(Mark's phone rings.)

Mark: That's probably Lily. Hello Lily. … Oh, no! *(to the others)* Their plane from Washington, D.C. had troubles and they had to land in New York. *(to Lily)* So when does your plane arrive? … OK. … Will you call again later?
I promise we'll save some turkey for you!

Who is it?

1. Who got stuck in her car last year?
   That's **Brenda**.
2. Who is the new neighbor?
3. Who doesn't eat turkey any more?
4. Who gets a present?
5. Who talks to Lily on the phone?

Unit 3, p. 55

○ 5 (WRITING) Collect small talk phrases.

Choose the right answer.

1. How's it going? – Great, thanks. • Not much.
2. What's up? – Nice to meet you too. • Not much.
3. Sam, this is Beth. – Great, thanks. • Beth, this is Sam.
4. Nice to meet you. – Nice to meet you too. • Not really.
5. Do you like turkey? – Not really. • Great, thanks.

Unit 3, p. 56

○ 9 (SPEAKING) Ask questions about holidays.

Choose the right question word. Interview your partner.

Mit „who" fragt man nach Personen. Es kann „wer" oder „wen" heißen.

What • Where • Who • How many • Which ✓

Partner A:

1. **(Welche)** holidays does your family celebrate?
   Which holidays does your family celebrate?
2. **(Was)** do you always eat at Christmas / Easter / Eid / …?
3. **(Wen)** does your family invite every time?
4. **(Wie viele)** guests did your family invite last time?
5. **(Wo)** will you celebrate next year?

Partner B:

1. We celebrate Christmas / Easter / Eid / … .
2. We always eat … at Christmas / Easter / Eid / … .
3. My family invites my grandparents / uncles / aunts / cousins … every time.
4. Last time my family invited … guests.
5. Next year we'll celebrate at our home / at my …'s home / at a restaurant / … .

Unit 3, p. 57

○ 10 Make a phone call.

Complete the phone call between Jacob and his grandma with these questions.

Did you have a good trip home? • Will you be there? • Can I bring my new girlfriend? • What about you? • When will you celebrate? • How are you? ✓ • Where will you celebrate?

Jacob:	Grandma:
Hi, Grandma. This is Jacob. (1) How are you?	Hi, Jacob. I'm fine. (2) What — How nice of you to call me.
(3) Did —	Yes, I did. I didn't have any problems with the weather or the traffic. I hope to see you all again on my 65th birthday. I'm planning a big family celebration.
(4) When —	I'll celebrate on May 1. (5) Will —
Yes, I think so. (6) Where —	Here at my house, in Miami.
That sounds cool. (7) Can —	Yes, of course. I'd like to meet her.
I'm sure you'll like her.	…

Unit 3, p. 59

○ 5 (WRITING) Sort the phrases. → M Peer correction, p. 171

Copy and complete the table.

I agree 👍	I disagree 👎
Exactly.	— not.
That's —	I —
That's —	No —

Exactly. ✓ · That's true. · I don't think so. · That's for sure. · Absolutely not. · No way!

Unit 3, p. 59

○ 6 (SPEAKING) Talk about devices.

Make a list. Rank the devices from the most important to the least important.
Talk to your partner.

1 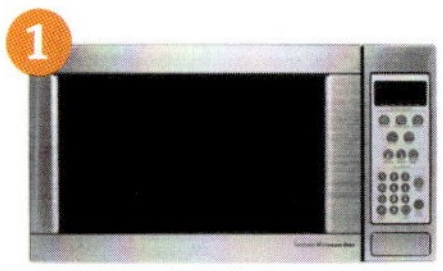
microwave

2 
headphones

3 
TV

4 
phone

5 
computer

Partner A:

The most important thing for me is my phone.

Headphones are second.

——s are third. ——s are next. ——s come last.

Partner B:

I agree.

I don't think so.

I think ——s are more important than ——s.

Achtung, "headphones" ist immer in der Mehrzahl: The most important thing for me are my headphones.

Unit 3, p. 60

○ 8 What would make Jennifer's life easier?

Look at the pictures. Complete the sentences. Use the simple past.

Sieh in der Liste ab S. 210 nach, ob das Verb in Klammern unregelmäßig ist!

1. Jennifer would be less worried in the morning if she chose her clothes the evening before. (choose)

2. She wouldn't feel so tired in the morning if she — to bed early. (go)

3. She would hear what her dad said if she — to music. (not listen)

4. She wouldn't get cold if she — a warm coat. (have)

5. It would be better if she — to school. (walk)

Unit 3, p. 61

○ 9 (SPEAKING) What would you do if ...? → M Milling around, p. 170

Complete the sentences.

1. If I were president of the United States for a day, I would ... .
2. If I were a superhero, I would ... .
3. If I could go back in time, I would ... .
4. If I had a million dollars, I would ... .
5. If I knew the answers to my next English test before the test, I would ... .

Here are some ideas:

- be the best student in class
- buy a big house with a swimming pool
- give all students computers
- always have holidays
- jump from the tallest building
- ...

Now ask your partner. What would you do if you ...

1. were president of the United States for a day?
2. were a superhero?
3. could go back in time?
4. had a million dollars?
5. knew the answers to your next English test before the test?

D

Unit 4, p. 76

○ **2** (LISTENING) **Listen to a conversation about an ad.**

2,3

Choose the right answer.

1

2

3

1. Emily, Carol and Daniel are talking about one ad from exercise one. Which one? **1 • 2 • 3**
2. Who doesn't like the ad? **Emily • Carol • Daniel**

Worüber reden die Jugendlichen? Zu welcher Werbung passt das?

Unit 4, p. 77

○ **3** (SPEAKING) **What do you think of the ads?**

Talk about the ads from exercise 2.

A: I think ad number 1 is spectacular.
I like … .
B: I agree.

2 | 3 | isn't
simple | informative | special | clear | catchy
I don't think so. I think … .

Unit 4, p. 78

○ 7 Look at the ads.

INTERNET

Complete the sentences. Use the simple present.

1. The mountain bike **is** • **are** $1,500.
2. The helmet **looks** • **look** cool.
3. The backpacks **is** • **are** $99 each.
4. The camping chairs **doesn't look** • **don't look** nice.
5. The girl **likes** • **like** walking.
6. The woman **doesn't need** • **don't need** an umbrella.

Unit 4, p. 79

○ 8 (WRITING) Simple present or present progressive?

Choose the right tense. Look at the signal words for help.

E-MAIL

Hi Becky,
At the moment (1) **I sit** • **I'm sitting** in the sun next to the swimming pool. It's always warm here in California. (2) **It doesn't rain** • **It isn't raining** often. (3) We usually **spend** • **are spending** the weekends at the beach. (4) At the moment **I learn** • **I'm learning** how to surf. But lots of other things are the same as in the Midwest. (5) Every day **I go** • **I'm going** to school, (6) **I do** • **I'm doing** my homework and (7) **I go** • **I'm going** to bed.
(8) What **do you do** • **are you doing** right now? I miss you.
Sandy

Unit 4, p. 80

3 What does the text say?

2,5

BLOG

A quick look back

Thursday, March 16, 2017

California has always welcomed new ideas – just think of the high-tech companies in Silicon Valley or the movie industry.

The internet is one of these ideas. The World Wide Web started in the early 1990s, so it's been around for almost 30 years. And it has really changed the world. Today almost everyone uses social media. I've had an account since I was 13. Why have they been so successful? Well, that's easy: you can post your photos, share your thoughts and keep in touch with friends. Most of the time you don't even have to look for information. It'll find you. We should give that a big 'like'.

Online videos have had a huge impact on our lives too. There are lots of funny videos. I like the tutorials best. You can find anything there from guitar lessons to make-up tips. Nobody watches much TV anymore. People stream their favorite shows instead.

Smartphones and tablets became the next big thing. Most of my friends go online every day, and half of them are online almost all the time. Most use several different social media sites at the same time. Some say it's difficult to stop using social media. They get messages every minute of the day and feel that they have to answer right away. Others are worried about cyberbullying.

If somebody writes bad things about you online, a lot of people can read it. We haven't really found any good answers yet.

Posted by Derek Lee at 8:51 a.m. 2 comments: Links to this post

Right or wrong? Correct the wrong sentences.

1. The World Wide Web started about 50 years ago. (lines 3 to 4)
   That's wrong. The World Wide Web started almost 30 years ago.
2. Social media sites are very popular today. (line 5)
3. Everyone watches TV. (line 13)
4. Most people are online almost all the time. (lines 14 to 15)
5. There are also problems with the internet. (lines 16 to 17)

Prüfe, ob die unterstrichenen Satzteile richtig oder falsch sind. Schau im Text in den angegebenen Zeilen nach. Achtung: Die Sätze sind anders formuliert.

Unit 4, p. 81

○ 5 Explain the words.

Find the definitions for these words.

1. You tell people that you agree with them.
2. You watch a movie online.
3. You move a message from your computer or phone to a social media site.

friend | post | like | stream | share

4. You send a message, a photo or a video that you got to others because you like it.
5. You ask someone to connect with you on social media.

Unit 4, p. 82

○ 8 Say for how long or since when.

GRAMMAR → G8, p. 165

since ten o'clock – seit zehn Uhr
for an hour – seit einer Stunde

Choose for or since.

1. I've had my smartphone **for** • **since** three years.
2. I haven't posted a new photo **for** • **since** ten o'clock.
3. Social media have been popular **for** • **since** 20 years now.
4. Millions of people have seen the cat pictures **for** • **since** Tuesday.
5. More than 5,000 people have watched that tutorial **for** • **since** May.
6. I haven't answered my e-mails **for** • **since** five days.

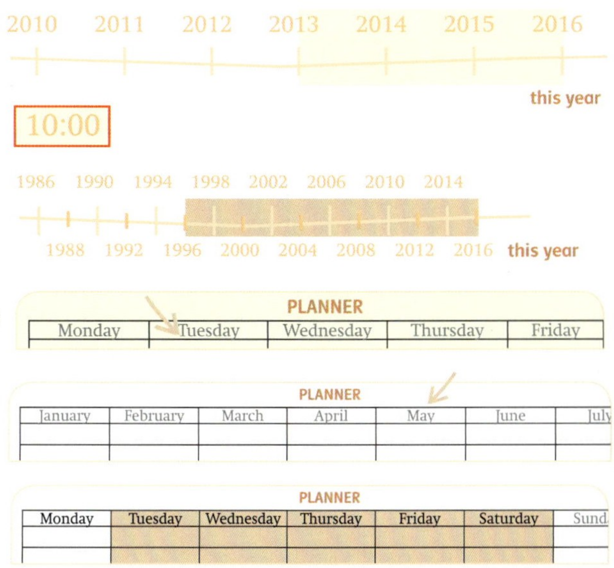

Unit 4, p. 83

○ 9 Complete the survey questions and answers.

Match the questions with the answers.

1. Interviewer: Have you bought a book or a magazine this week?
2. Interviewer: Have you ever used tutorial videos to learn how to do something?
3. Interviewer: Have you found any new music videos that you liked this week?

Kim: Let me think for a second. Today I've seen one that I really enjoyed.

Jake: I usually read everything online. I haven't read a book or a magazine for a long time.

Sally: Yes, sure. I've already learned to play the guitar that way.

Unit 5, p. 99

○ 3 What's the nationality?

Match the nationalities with the flags.

Chinese | Greek | Italian | Russian | Polish | Turkish

1. 中国 (China)

2. Россия (Russia)

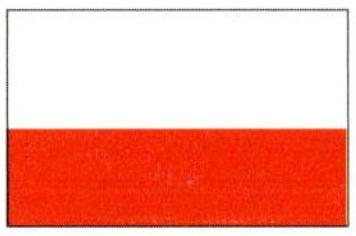

3. Polska (Poland)

4. Ελλάδα (Greece)

5. Türkiye (Turkey)

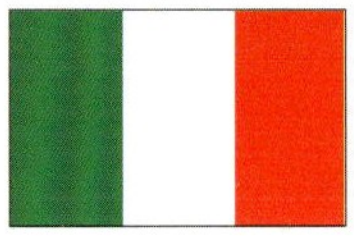

6. Italia (Italy)

Unit 5, p. 99

○ 4 Find the words.

Match the sentences with the same meaning.

1. Some people accepted the flag.
2. Others didn't accept it.
3. There were conflicts between the different groups.
4. The different groups found a solution.

A Others disagreed.
B There were problems between the different groups.
C The different groups made a compromise.
D Some people tolerated the flag.

Unit 5, p.100

○ 6 Make passive sentences. → M Bus stop, p. 168

Choose the right form.

1. Pork **is** • **are** used in many southern dishes.
2. Southern food **is** • **are** eaten across the USA.
3. Vegetables **is** • **are** kept in the fridge.
4. All these dishes **is** • **are** made with rice.
5. Rice **is** • **are** not grown in many US states.

Sieh dir die unterstrichenen Subjekte an:
Einzahl (oder nicht zählbar) → „is"
Mehrzahl (endet meistens auf -s) → „are"

Unit 5, p.101

○ 7 Complete the sentences about multicultural schools.

Make passive sentences.

1. Many languages are spoken at multicultural schools. (speak)
2. Special lessons are —— for people who are new. (organize)
3. Lessons are —— in different languages at some schools. (give)
4. Multicultural food is —— in the cafeteria. (sell)
5. Special days of different cultures are —— at school. (celebrate)
6. Racism isn't —— there. (accept)

„Organize", „celebrate" und „accept" sind regelmäßig. Die anderen Verben kannst du in der Liste der unregelmäßigen Verben (3. Spalte) ab S. 210 nachschauen.

Unit 5, p.103

○ 4 (LISTENING) Listen to the text about a visit to an alligator farm.

2,15

Choose the right word.

Alligator farm, Florida Everglades

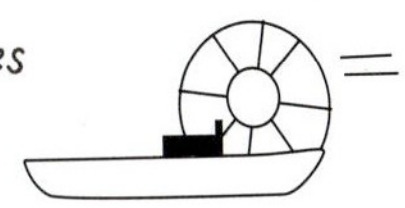

- a fast • slow boat ride
- trainer had fight with snake • alligator
- Matt • trainer put hand in alligator's mouth
- photo of Ethan with snake • alligator

Unit 5, p. 103

○ 5 (WRITING) How can you say that you (don't) understand? → M Peer correction, p. 171

Copy and complete the table.

Could you please explain? ✓ | I get it. | I know what you mean. | Can you repeat it, please? | Excuse me? | I see.

I understand	I don't understand
I —	Could you please explain?
I —	C —
I —	E —

Unit 5, p. 104

○ 7 Report what other people say.

What did Anna write? Read Anna's e-mail from Clearwater, Florida. Then complete the sentences with the right pronoun.

E-MAIL

Hi Julie,
(1) I'm at Clearwater right now. (2) I love the the warm weather here. (3) We just wear T-shirts and shorts and (4) we often go to the beach. (5) It's awesome! But (6) I hate the insects.
See you soon,
Anna

Das ändert sich in der indirekten Rede:
I → he/she
we → they
Diese Pronomen ändern sich nicht: it, they

1. Anna says (that) she is at Clearwater.
2. She writes (that) — loves the warm weather.
3. She writes (that) — just wear T-shirts and shorts.
4. She says (that) — often go to the beach.
5. She says (that) — is awesome.
6. She says (that) — hates the insects.

2,17 Art and culture in NYC

Big city lights

1

New York City has great museums, lots of movie theaters, the finest restaurants, street markets, parades, festivals with free events ...
Walk down Broadway at night, and you'll see the lights of 40 theaters. Watch popular actors in world-class shows, plays and musicals.
There's a great number of things to see and do here ...

Hip hop culture

2

It's the end of the 1960s in the Bronx, at the time a poor part of the city. Here African-American teenagers start a new cultural movement, hip hop.
Rap, DJing, breakdancing and graffiti were the main parts of hip hop culture. DJs took parts of older songs to create a new style of music.

Rappers often rapped about life in street gangs and about social questions. Breakdancers became famous for their robotic moves. Graffiti artists used subway trains and buildings as their canvas. Hip hop has now gone global.

Street art

3

In the past street art meant large murals, often in poorer parts of the city. Today you can go on guided tours to see the best murals. Some think it's art, some don't.

The city in comics

4

Spiderman lives in Queens, Iron Man's company is in Long Island, and Batman's Gotham City is a fictional version of New York. And there are lots of other examples – the city is the home of superheroes.
Comics are an art form that comes from the United States. You can find the biggest comic book companies in New York City, and famous writers too.

1 What's new to you? Tell your partner three things.

I didn't know that … .
It's new to me that … .
I'm surprised to read that … .

movie theater *(AE)* – *Kino;* event – *Ereignis, Veranstaltung;* cultural movement – *kulturelle Bewegung;* social – *gesellschaftlich;* artist – *Künstler/in;* canvas – *Leinwand;* global – *weltweit;* guided tour – *Führung;* fictional – *erfunden*

2,18 Native Americans then and now

Christopher Columbus didn't discover America!

The history of Native Americans in our country is fascinating and tragic. When Europeans made first contact with them around 1500, about ten million Native American people lived in North America. They had come from Siberia to Alaska in about 10,000 BC. They spoke different languages and had many different lifestyles. They were hunters, fishermen, farmers and traders. They lived in houses made of wood and built canoes or they moved from place to place and lived in tepees.

"I was born on the prairie where the wind blew free [...] I want to die there and not within walls. I know every stream and every wood between the Rio Grande and the Arkansas. [...] So, why do you ask us to leave the rivers and the sun and the wind and live in houses?"

Chief Ten Bears in 1867

The Europeans arrive

From the 17th century a large number of European settlers arrived. They brought illnesses which killed thousands of Native Americans. When more people arrived, they wanted land, and the tribes had to leave their traditional farming and hunting lands. The settlers pushed them further away from the coast, until in the 1830s a lot of tribes had to move west of the Mississippi River. On this terrible journey hundreds died of cold, hunger and illness.

Bloody battles

On the Great Plains, however, life was different. The tribes had got horses from the Europeans, so they could hunt buffalo more easily. They didn't want to give up their freedom and their hunting lands, and they often attacked settlers who crossed the plains. Many bloody battles followed. By 1900 most tribes had to go and live on reservations.

Native Americans today

Today Native Americans are full American citizens. Only a minority of the five million Native Americans live on reservations. Some make money from the casino business, but most of them are poor, and they are unemployed. There's a new interest in the Native American culture among younger people today.

"The government took my grandad away from his parents and sent him to boarding school, together with thousands of others. They didn't let him learn about his language or culture there. So my dad never learned anything either. We lost a lot of things.
Even in school today nobody teaches us about the thousands of years of our history before the Europeans arrived. But many of us want to change this situation. My history is part of me. I feel like we Native Americans are picking up the pieces of our culture and moving forward. I want to help rebuild things."
Alaqua, 16, Oklahoma

By Pat Smith
September 15, 2016
Junior History Magazine

1 Choose one paragraph. What did you already know about Native Americans? What didn't you know? Talk in groups.

I already knew that ... .
I didn't know that ... .
It's new to me that ... .

tragic – *tragisch;* BC (= before Christ) – *vor Christus;* hunter – *Jäger/in;* fisherman – *Fischer;* trader – *Händler/in;* illness – *Krankheit;* tribe – *(Volks-)Stamm;* hunting land – *Jagdgebiet;* bloody – *blutig;* Great Plains – *Flachland in den USA;* to attack – *angreifen;* casino business – *Casino-Geschäft;* boarding school – *Internat;* to rebuild – *wiederaufbauen*

2,19 Holidays in the USA

JANUARY Martin Luther King Day

1

I have a dream

This day is the birthday of Martin Luther King. He lived at a time when African Americans did not have the same rights as white Americans. He used peaceful ways to protest against this and to change it. His 'I have a dream' speech is famous. Martin Luther King was assassinated in 1968.

FEBRUARY Presidents' Day

2

This holiday celebrates the birthdays of two great presidents – George Washington and Abraham Lincoln. Washington led the American army which defeated Great Britain. He became the first American president in 1789. In 1865, after the terrible Civil War, Lincoln ended slavery in the United States. He was assassinated in the same year.

JULY Independence Day

3

The Fourth of July celebrates the USA's independence from Great Britain. That is the day in 1776 when the 13 American states signed the Declaration of Independence, now a famous document. People dress in red, white and blue – the color of the flag. They have picnics or barbecues and there are fantastic fireworks across the country.

D

OCTOBER Columbus Day

4

Christopher Columbus first saw America on October 12, 1492. Today there are parades and dinners to celebrate him. However, some people don't like this holiday because Columbus didn't actually discover America. But the day also remembers a man of ideas, dreams and great ambition. That is something most Americans understand very well.

NOVEMBER Thanksgiving

5

The history of Thanksgiving began in 1621 when the Pilgrim settlers celebrated their first year in their new country. They invited some local Native Americans to share their meal. Thanksgiving is a family day. A traditional Thanksgiving dinner has turkey, cranberry sauce, and pumpkin pie for dessert. Football games are usually a big part of the day too.

1 What celebration would you like to take part in? Why? Talk with a partner.

A. I'd like to take part in Independence Day because fireworks are great.
B: I'd like to take part in Independence Day too because I love picnics and barbecues.

rights – *Rechte;* peaceful – *friedlich;* was assassinated – *wurde ermordet;* to defeat – *schlagen, besiegen;* civil war – *Bürgerkrieg;* slavery – *Sklaverei;* to sign – *unterschreiben;* actually – *wirklich;* ambition – *Ehrgeiz;* pumpkin pie – *Kürbiskuchen*

2,20 Hollywood

The movie industry

1

Since the silent movies of the early 20th century, Hollywood has been the center of the movie industry. The sign was originally an ad from 1923 which read HOLLYWOODLAND. They changed it to HOLLYWOOD in 1949. Today the sign is famous all over the world.

"And the Oscar goes to …"

2

The highest honor in the movie business is an Oscar or Academy Award. Millions of people around the world watch the stars arrive and walk along the Red Carpet. There are many different categories of awards, but the most famous are Best Picture, Best Actor and Best Director.

Hollywood Walk of Fame

3

The Walk of Fame remembers famous or important people in the entertainment industry. The names of more than 2,500 actors, musicians, directors, writers and many others from the past and present are written on pink stars. Every year they add new names.

Movie studio tours

4

From the very beginning, big movie companies have had their own production sets and studios. Most of the studios offer tours. At Universal Studios, for example, you can experience a fight between King Kong and a dinosaur.

Hollywood or Bollywood

5

Hollywood may be famous, but the biggest film industry in the world is actually in India. 'Bollywood' is its nickname. Here's the difference:

Bollywood movies	Hollywood movies
- action, drama, romance and comedy all in one movie	- action, drama, romance and comedy in four different movies
- music and dance in every movie	- music and dance in musicals only
- three hours long with a short break in the middle	- usually two hours long

1 What did you find interesting? What did you already know?

I already knew about (the Oscar).
I didn't know about (Bollywood).
It's interesting that … .

silent movie – *Stummfilm;* originally – *ursprünglich;* honor *(AE)* – *Ehre;* movie business – *Filmgeschäft;* the Red Carpet – *der Rote Teppich;* award – *Preis;* fame – *Ruhm;* entertainment – *Unterhaltung;* star – *Stern, Star;* set – *Kulisse;* experience – *erleben;* nickname – *Spitzname*

2,21 Life in the South

Plantation houses

1

In 1803 the United States bought Louisiana and other territories from the French. Rich Anglo-American landowners moved there. They built large houses on their plantations to show their wealth. Many of these houses were destroyed after the American Civil War (1861–1865), but some are still there. Oak Alley Plantation was built by slaves on a sugar plantation. It was completed in 1839. Today the house is open to visitors. It's a popular location for movies and for weddings.

Paddle steamers

2

The Mississippi is almost 4,000 miles long. It's the longest river in the USA. In the 19th century paddle steamers took people and goods up and down the river. Because of their paddlewheels, they could go far up the river, even when the water level was very low. Today there are many modern riverboats for tourists on the Mississippi.

D

Fishing in the Florida Keys

3

In the Florida Keys you can find all kinds of fishing. From fishing for beginners to fishing for experts. If you love the sea and fishing, there's no better place. When you go back to the harbor, take your fish back to one of the local restaurants. They will prepare a great meal for you.

Line dance

4

What is line dance? A group of people who dance in one or more lines. They all face the same direction and they all do the same steps at the same time. Each dance has its own style. People can dance to country and western music but also to rock and pop. Even the internet sensation video 'Gangnam Style' had elements of line dancing in it.

1 Choose one paragraph and tell your group three facts about your topic.

My text is about … • It says that … • Today … • You can also … • However, …

territory – *Gebiet*; Anglo-American – *anglo-amerikanisch (bezieht sich auf Amerikaner mit englischen Wurzeln)*; wealth – *Reichtum*; to destroy – *zerstören*; paddle steamer – *Raddampfer*; fishing – *Angeln*; line – *Reihe*; to face the same direction – *in die gleiche Richtung blicken*

When the earth shakes

1 What's an earthquake?

Every day there are minor or major earthquakes[1] around the world. The ground shakes for seconds or sometimes even minutes. Earthquakes can occur at any time, and we don't notice most of them. You can't tell when or where they will happen. In the USA the West Coast is most at risk[2] because of its special geological structure. However, there can be earthquakes in the Midwest or on the East Coast too.

2 What causes an earthquake?

The earth's crust consists[3] of about 20 different (tectonic) plates which slowly move. The place where two plates meet is called a fault line[4]. One plate rubs[5] against another. This puts both plates under stress. When the force[6] gets too strong, it comes apart with a jerk[7]. The released energy makes the earth move in waves.

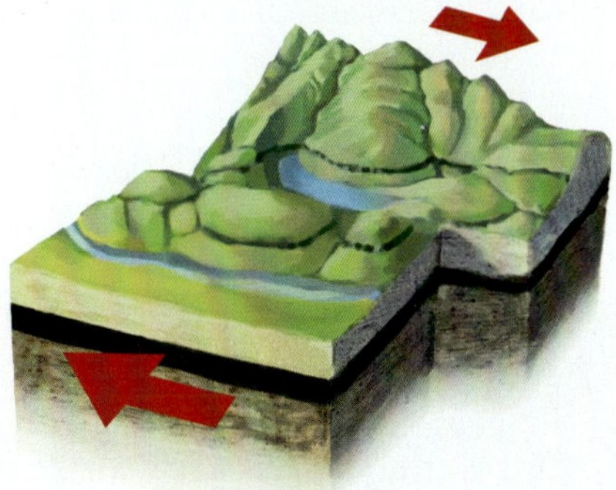

3 What can earthquakes do?

Major earthquakes can cause many problems. Buildings or bridges can collapse[8] or pipelines burst[9]. There can be mudslides[10], fires or tsunamis too. A large number of people can be hurt or even die during an earthquake.

1 earthquake [ˈɜːθkweɪk] – *Erdbeben*; 2 be at risk [rɪsk] – *einem Risiko ausgesetzt sein*; 3 consist of [kənˈsɪst‿əv] – *bestehen aus*; 4 fault line [ˈfɔːltˌlaɪn] – *Verwerfungs-, Bruchlinie*; 5 rub [rʌb] – *reiben*; 6 force [fɔːs] – *Kraft, Stärke*; 7 jerk [dʒɜːk] – *Ruck*; 8 collapse [kəˈlæps] – *zusammenbrechen*; 9 burst [bɜːst] – *platzen*; 10 mudslide [ˈmʌdslaɪd] – *Schlammlawine*

4 How are earthquakes measured?

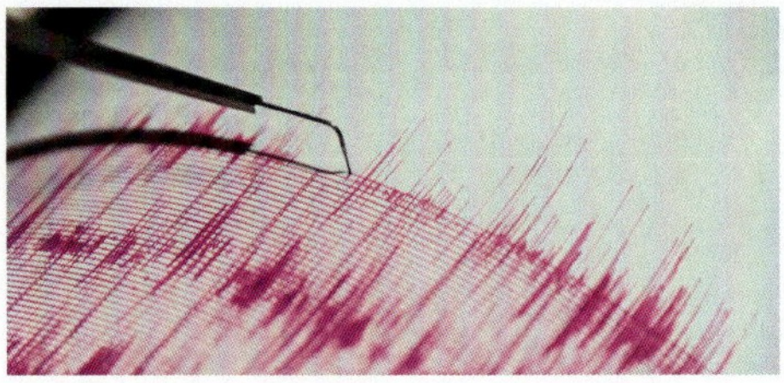

Scientists[1] record earthquakes with the help of a special instrument – the seismograph. It measures[2] the magnitude of an earthquake.
The Richter scale shows how destructive[3] earthquakes can be:

The Richter scale

0 – 1.9	only recorded by seismograph; not felt
2.0 – 2.9	objects may swing; hardly any damage
3.0 – 3.9	comparable to a passing truck
4.0 – 4.9	may break windows; smaller objects may fall
5.0 – 5.9	loose objects may fall from walls; furniture moves
6.0 – 6.9	damage to buildings
7.0 – 7.9	major ground breaks; buildings destroyed in large numbers
8.0 – 8.9	bridges and most houses destroyed
9.0 and over	total devastation

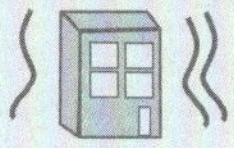

5 Find out about recent earthquakes worldwide.

Search the internet for a 'map of latest earthquakes'. Where did the last earthquakes happen?

6 Earthquake facts – What do you find most interesting?

Animals seem to sense[4] an earthquake is going to happen. No one knows how they do it.

An earthquake on the moon is called a moonquake. But they happen less often and are smaller than earthquakes on earth.

There are about 500,000 earthquakes in the world each year. 100 of them cause heavy damage[5].

Because of the earth's movements, San Francisco and Los Angeles will meet in a few million years.

In Japanese mythology, a giant fish makes the earth move.

1 scientist ['saɪəntɪst] – *Wissenschaftler/-in*; 2 measure ['meʒə] – *messen*; 3 destructive [dɪ'strʌktɪv] – *zerstörerisch*; 4 sense [sens] – *spüren, fühlen*; 5 damage ['dæmɪdʒ] – *Schaden*

Static electricity

1 Are you 'electrified'?

Have you ever …

- ☐ … rubbed[1] a balloon on your hair and made it stand on end[2]?
- ☐ … touched a person or a metal object and felt an electric shock[3]?
- ☐ … taken off a pullover which made your hair crackle[4]?
- ☐ … felt like your clothes were clinging[5] to you?

All of these situations happen because of static[6] electricity. Sometimes your hair does funny things. Sometimes you may feel a small electric shock. It doesn't hurt badly, but it's a strange feeling. The most spectacular example of static electricity is lightning[7].

2 Why does static electricity happen?

Static electricity happens because everything is made of atoms. Atoms are tiny particles that are so small we can't see them. Inside of atoms are protons, neutrons and electrons. Protons, neutrons and electrons are very different from each other. Protons have a positive charge[8] (+). Neutrons have no charge. Electrons have a negative charge (-). Protons and neutrons make the center of the atom, the nucleus. The electrons move around this center.

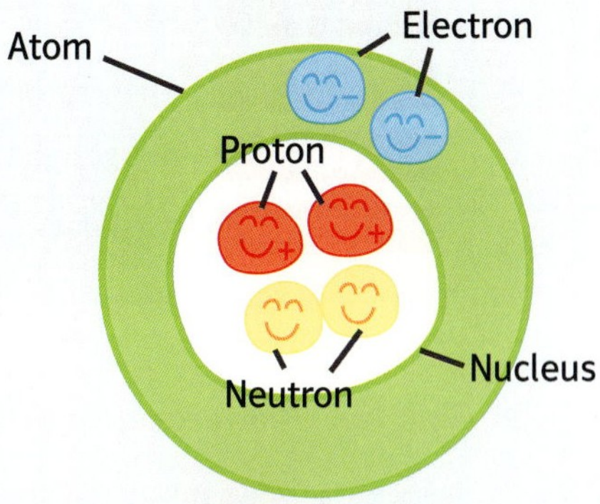

Usually atoms have no charge because there are as many electrons as protons. But some electrons can move between atoms. This happens when two atoms come in contact or rub against each other. If electrons move from one atom to another, the charge of the atom changes. If there are more protons than electrons in an atom, the atom has a positive charge. If there are more electrons than protons, it has a negative charge.

If two atoms meet and they have the same charge, they move away from each other. If two atoms have different charges, they move towards each other.

1 rub [rʌb] – *reiben;* 2 stand on end [stænd‿ɒn‿'end] – *zu Berge stehen lassen;* 3 electric shock [ɪ'lektrɪk ʃɒk] – *elektrischer Schock;* 4 crackle ['krækl] – *knistern;* 5 cling [klɪŋ] – *sich festhalten, klammern, hängenbleiben;* 6 static ['stætɪk] – *statisch;* 7 lightning ['laɪtnɪŋ] – *Blitz;* 8 charge [tʃɑ:dʒ] – *Ladung*

3 Why does your hair stand on end?

When two objects with different charges touch[1] or rub against each other, the charges react and we sometimes see sparks[2] or feel an electric shock. When you rub a balloon on your hair, for example, electrons move from your hair to the balloon. The balloon then has more negative charge and the tips[3] of your hair have more positive charge. That's why your hair moves towards the negative charge of the balloon and away from all the other positively charged hair – suddenly your hair stands on end!

4 Some experiments

a) You need these materials:

balloons

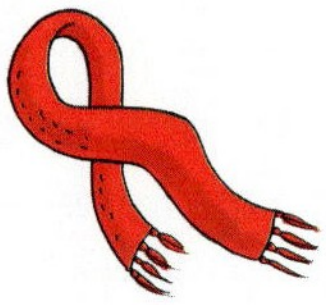

a wool scarf

pieces of paper

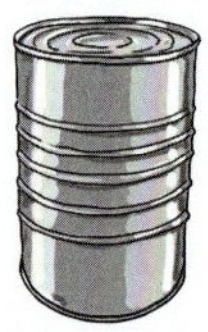

an empty can[4]

a string[5]

b) Try these experiments and write what happens.

1. Rub a balloon on a wool scarf. Hold it against a wall and let go[6].
2. Rub a balloon on a wool scarf. Hold the balloon over some small pieces of paper (e.g. confetti).
3. Put an empty can on the floor or a table. Rub a balloon with a wool scarf. Hold the balloon in front of the can without touching it.
4. Cut a piece of string (~70 cm). Tie a balloon to each end of the string. Rub both balloons with a wool scarf and then hold up the middle of the string so that the balloons hang down.

1 touch [tʌtʃ] – *berühren, antippen;* 2 spark [spɑːk] – *Funke;* 3 tip [tɪp] – *Spitze;* 4 can [kæn] – *Dose, Getränkedose;* 5 string [strɪŋ] – *Schnur, Bindfaden;* 6 let go [let ˈɡəʊ] – *loslassen*

2,22

The Absolutely True Diary of a Part-Time Indian by S. Alexie (2007)

This is the diary of Arnold 'Junior' Spirit. He is small, very skinny[1], wears big glasses and has a stutter[2] and a lisp[3]. He is also really intelligent, and he loves to draw cartoons. This is a cartoon Arnold 'Junior' drew of himself:

Arnold 'Junior' Spirit is a Spokane[4] Indian. He lives in Wellpinit, a small town on an Indian reservation. He calls it the 'rez'. A lot of people there are very poor and never leave the rez.

One day Arnold 'Junior' decides that he has to change his life. He doesn't want to be poor all his life, and he wants to see the world. So Arnold 'Junior' decides to go to school in Reardan, a little town outside the reservation. At Reardan High School, all the kids are white, rich and amazing. Arnold is scared because he will be the only Indian at the school. But he also knows that it is his only chance to make his life better.

That's how Arnold 'Junior' becomes a part-time[5] Indian: He goes to school in Reardan where everyone calls him Arnold, but he lives on the reservation with his family where everyone calls him Junior.

This is his diary entry from his first day at the new school:

The next morning, Dad drove me the twenty-two miles to Reardan.

"I'm scared," I said.

"I'm scared, too," Dad said.

He hugged[6] me. "You don't have to do this," he said. "You can always go back to the rez school."

"No," I said. "I have to do this."

1 skinny ['skɪni] – *dünn, mager*; 2 stutter ['stʌtə] – *Stottern*; 3 lisp [lɪsp] – *Lispeln*; 4 Spokane [spəʊ'kan] – *„Kinder der Sonne" oder „Sonnenvolk", ein Indianerstamm im Nordwesten der USA (Bundesstaat Washington)*; 5 part-time [ˌpɑːt'taɪm] – *Teilzeit-*; 6 hug sb [hʌg] – *jmd. umarmen*

E

"Just remember this," my father said. "Those white people aren't better than you."

But he was so wrong. And he knew he was wrong. He was the loser Indian father of a loser Indian son living in a world built for winners.

But he loved me so much. He hugged me again.

"This is a great thing," he said. "You're so brave. You're a warrior[1]."

It was the best thing he could have said.

"Hey, here's some lunch money," he said and gave me a dollar.

We were poor enough to get free lunch, but I didn't want to be the only Indian and the only one who needed charity[2].

"Thanks, Dad," I said.

"I love you," he said.

"I love you, too."

I felt stronger so I stepped out of the car and walked to the door. It was closed.

I watched my father drive away.

2,23 I stood at the door for a few very long minutes. It was still early.

Then the white kids arrived for school. They surrounded[3] me.

Most of the kids were my size or smaller, but there were ten or twelve monster dudes[4]. Giant white guys. They looked like men, not boys. Some of them looked like they had to shave[5] two or three times a day.

They stared[6] at me, the Indian boy. Those white kids couldn't believe their eyes. They stared at me like I was a UFO. What was I doing at Reardan, whose mascot[7] was an Indian, thereby making me the only other Indian in town?

So what was I doing in racist[8] Reardan, where more than half of every graduating[9] class went to college? Nobody in my family had ever gone near a college.

Reardan was the opposite of the rez. It was the opposite of my family. It was the opposite of me. I didn't deserve to be there. I knew it; all of those kids knew it. Indians don't deserve anything.

So, feeling worthless[10] and stupid[11], I just waited. And pretty soon, a janitor[12] opened the door and all of the other kids strolled inside.

"Okay," I said to myself. "Here I go."

1 warrior ['wɒriə] – *Krieger/-in*; 2 charity ['tʃærɪti] – *Almosen, Wohltätigkeit*; 3 surround [sə'raʊnd] – *umgeben, umringen*; 4 dude [du:d] – *Mann (ugs.)*; 5 shave [ʃeɪv] – *sich rasieren*; 6 stare [steə] – *starren*; 7 mascot ['mæskɒt] – *Maskottchen*; 8 racist ['reɪsɪst] – *rassistisch*; 9 graduating ['grædjueɪtɪŋ] – *Abschluss-*; 10 worthless ['wɜ:θləs] – *wertlos*; 11 stupid ['stju:pɪd] – *blöd, dumm*; 12 janitor ['dʒænɪtə] – *Hausmeister/-in*

I walked into the school, made my way to the office, and told them who I was.

"Oh, you're the one from the reservation," the secretary said.

"Yeah," I said.

I couldn't tell if she thought the reservation was a good or bad thing.

"My name is Melinda," she said. "Welcome to Reardan High School. Here's your schedule and a Student ID. We've got you in Mr. Grant's homeroom[1]. You better walk there quickly. You're late."

"Ah, where is that?" I asked.

"We've only got one hallway[2] here," she said. She had red hair and green eyes. "It's all the way down on the left."

I put the paperwork into my backpack and walked to my homeroom.

I waited a second at the door and then walked inside.

2,24 Everybody, all of the students and the teacher, stopped to stare at me.

They stared hard.

Like I was bad weather.

"Take your seat," the teacher said. He was a muscular[3] guy. He had to be a football coach.

I sat down in the back and tried to ignore[4] all the stares and whispers[5], until a blond girl leaned[6] over toward me.

Penelope!

Yes, there are places left in the world where people are named Penelope!

"What's your name?" Penelope asked.

"Junior," I said.

She laughed and told her girlfriend at the next desk that my name was Junior. They both[7] laughed. Word spread[8] around the

1 homeroom ['həʊmruːm] – *Zimmer des/der Klassenlehrers/-in*; 2 hallway ['hɔːlweɪ] – *Flur*; 3 muscular ['mʌskjələ] – *muskulär*; 4 ignore [ɪg'nɔː] – *ignorieren*; 5 whisper ['wɪspə] – *Geflüster*; 6 lean over toward sb [liːn'əʊvə] – *sich zu jmd. rüberbeugen*; 7 both [bəʊθ] – *beide, beides*; 8 word spread ['wɜːd ˌspred] – *es sprach sich herum*

room and pretty soon everybody was laughing. They were laughing at *my name*. I had no idea that Junior was a weird[1] name. It's a normal name on my rez, on any rez. You walk into any trading post[2] on any rez in the United States and shout, "Hey, Junior!" and seventeen guys will turn around. And three women. But there were no other people named Junior in Reardan, so I was being laughed at because I was the only one who had that silly name.

And then I felt smaller because the teacher was taking roll[3] and he called out my *name* name.

"Arnold Spirit," the teacher said. No, he yelled[4] it.

"Here," I said as quietly as possible.

"Speak up," the teacher said.

"Here," I said.

"My name is Mr. Grant," he said.

"I'm here, Mr. Grant."

He moved on to other students, but Penelope leaned over toward me again, but she wasn't laughing at all. She was very angry now.

"I thought you said your name was Junior," Penelope said.

She *accused*[5] me of telling her my *real* name. Well, okay, it wasn't completely my real name. My full name is Arnold Spirit Jr. But nobody calls me that. Everybody calls me Junior. Well, every other *Indian* calls me Junior.

"My name is Junior," I said. "And my name is Arnold. It's Junior and Arnold. I'm both."

I felt like two people inside of one body. No, I felt like a magician[6] cutting myself in half, with Junior living on the north side of the Spokane River[7] and Arnold living on the south.

"Where are you from?" she asked.

She was so pretty and her eyes were so blue. She was the prettiest girl I had ever seen. She was movie star pretty.

"Hey," she said. "I asked you where you're from."

Wow, she was tough.

"Wellpinit," I said. "Up on the rez, I mean, the reservation."

"Oh," she said. "That's why you talk so funny."

And yes, I had that stutter and lisp, but I also had that singsong reservation accent that made everything I said sound like a bad poem.

Man, I was scared. I didn't say another word for six days.

1 weird [wɪəd] – *komisch*; 2 trading post ['treɪdɪŋ pəʊst] – *Laden, Handelsposten*; 3 take roll [teɪk 'rəʊl] – *die Anwesenheitsliste durchgehen*; 4 yell [jel] – *brüllen, schreien*; 5 accuse sb of sth [ə'kju:z] – *jmd. beschuldigen*; 6 magician [mə'ʤɪʃn] – *Magier, Zauberer*; 7 Spokane River [spəʊˌkæn 'rɪvə] – *Flussname*

2,25

Deep water by C. Gardiner (2009)

Henry Jackson is sixteen years old, and he lives with his grandmother in a small town in Nebraska. Their house is outside of town; near a dam[1] and a lake that were built some years ago. Every day when Henry comes home, his grandmother tells him to not go to The Lake. It is dangerous and people die there. That's why Henry is afraid of deep[2] water, and he still cannot swim. Henry's best friend is Alice. She is a great swimmer, and Henry likes her a lot.

One day Alice tells him that she is going to have a picnic and go swimming with some friends. Henry doesn't go because he hates swimming. But later in the evening he realizes[3] that Alice and the other kids from his class probably went to The Lake. Some strange things have been happening at The Lake and Henry is afraid that something bad will happen, so he quickly leaves the house to go find Alice …

Henry ran into the woods at the back of the house. It was nearly night and the moon was just rising. Now Henry was glad that he was a good runner. No other kid in the school could have got through the woods so fast.

He wished he had Alice's cell phone number. Then he could call her and warn her. But then what could he say – 'don't swim in The Lake! There's something evil[4] there'? She wouldn't believe him and he would just look stupid[5].

He had to go to The Lake. Grandma's worries[6] weren't important. His friend Alice, the girl he liked more than anyone else in the whole school, was in danger[7]. He had to help her.

The moon was up as Henry burst[8] out of the woods. He heard kids laughing. He could see the dam wall not far away. The surface[9] of The Lake was shining in the moonlight. Everything looked calm[10].

The whole class was there with their picnic baskets. But they were over on the other side of The Lake. Henry shouted, "Alice!" She looked up and saw him. She waved to him and shouted something. But she was too far away so he couldn't hear her. He shouted again, "Don't go swimming, it's dangerous!" Alice shook[11] her head to show that she didn't understand what he was saying.

Henry looked around quickly. There was a path all along The Lake. But it was a long way to the other side. Even at his fastest, it'd take time to get to Alice. He was tired from his run through the woods but he had to try.

"Oh, Alice – please, please don't go swimming before I get there," Henry said softly to himself.

1 dam [dæm] – *Damm, Staumauer;* 2 deep [diːp] – *tief;* 3 realize [ˈrɪəlaɪz] – *erkennen, realisieren;* 4 evil [ˈiːvl] – *böse, schlecht;* 5 stupid [ˈstjuːpɪd] – *dumm, blöd;* 6 worry [ˈwʌri] – *Sorge;* 7 danger [ˈdeɪndʒə] – *Gefahr;* 8 burst out of [bɜːst] – *herausstürzen;* 9 surface [ˈsɜːfɪs] – *Oberfläche;* 10 calm [kɑːm] – *ruhig, friedlich;* 11 shake [ʃeɪk] – *schütteln*

Then Matt jumped. Henry heard the splash as Matt went under the water. Henry ran faster. He was afraid that Matt would just disappear, that something would grab his foot and pull him down.

But then Matt's head came up again. He was laughing as he shook the water out of his hair. Henry shouted but the kids paid no attention[1]. He was still a long way away.

Most of the other kids followed Matt into the water. Henry could see their heads as they splashed each other. Alice stood at the waterside. She didn't go in right away. She was watching Henry racing[2] round the path.

Henry ran on although it was getting hard to breathe. He waved and waved, trying to get the kids' attention. Then Alice went into the water. Henry almost fell to the ground. "Alice! No!" Henry was shouting as loudly as he could.

Suddenly something started moving towards the swimmers. It was big and black, like a shadow[3], moving smoothly[4] just under the surface of the water. The kids couldn't see it. They were busy with their game. They were playing with a ball, throwing it and trying to catch[5] it before it hit the water.

1 pay no attention [ˌpeɪ nəʊ‿əˈtenʃn] – *nicht beachten;* 2 race [reɪs] – *(sehr schnell) rennen;* 3 shadow [ˈʃædəʊ] – *Schatten;* 4 smooth [smuːð] – *geschmeidig, gleichmäßig;* 5 catch [kætʃ] – *fangen*

Alice started to swim towards Henry and away from the other kids. Henry could not run another step. He could hardly get his breath.
He fell down onto his knees.

2,26 Then Chet threw the ball up high into the air instead of throwing it to the next kid. He laughed loudly and he looked over at Henry. So Henry could see how surprised Chet was as something pulled him under the water. His head went down so fast that he didn't even have time to shout.
His mouth was wide open as he went under.
The ball that Chet had thrown was still up in the air. At that same moment every other kid disappeared under the water. Every head just went down without making any waves in the water. Except Alice. She was quite a bit away. She was moving fast towards Henry and didn't notice anything behind her.

The surface of the water was smooth again. The Lake was quiet. The black shadow was gone and the kids were gone. It all happened in just a few seconds. The ball landed back on the surface of the water with a splash.

Alice heard the splash. She looked back. The ball floated[1] on the water. There was nothing else, no kids anywhere. She turned round and started to swim faster and faster towards Henry.

Henry stood up again. The dark water of The Lake came right up to the path. He wanted to save Alice. But he was afraid of the black shadow in the water. She was still swimming fast towards him.

Something moved on the other side of The Lake, where the picnic baskets were. Henry didn't want to look but he could not control his eyes. He saw a tall, thin[2] man standing there.

"Henry!" Alice screamed, and he tore[3] his eyes away from the man. She was much nearer Henry now but still too far for him to reach[4] her. He put one foot into the water. It was very cold. It was like putting his foot into ice. He stepped in a bit deeper. Alice swam closer[5]. Behind her Henry saw the black shadow in the water again. It was coming very close to her. Henry went into the water as fast as he could. The water was up to his knees. The black shadow was right at Alice's feet. Her hand came towards him, her fingers just touched[6] his fingers – then a shout came from the other side of The Lake.

"Henry! Henry!" That was Grandma's voice!

Henry automatically looked up towards her.

And then suddenly he couldn't feel Alice's hand any more.

He looked back at the Lake.

Alice was gone.

What happened? Will Henry be able to save Alice?

1 float [fləʊt] – *gleiten, treiben;* 2 thin [θɪn] – *dünn;* 3 tear one's eyes away [teə] – *die Augen losreißen;* 4 reach [ri:tʃ] – *erreichen, greifen;* 5 close [kləʊs] – *nah;* 6 touch [tʌtʃ] – *berühren, antippen*

Grammar

G2

Mit G sind die Grammatikkapitel gekennzeichnet und der Reihe nach durchnummeriert. Eine Übersicht über alle Themen in diesem Band findest du auf der nächsten Seite.

Hier stehen Besonderheiten und Tipps.

(TEST YOURSELF)

Hier kannst du üben.
Die Lösungen findest du auf S. 282.

(FÜR PROFIS)

Hier findest du knifflige Extras zum Thema.

R = Revision (Wiederholung)

Unit 1

G1 R: Die einfache Vergangenheit

Revision: The simple past

Um über Dinge zu sprechen, die in der Vergangenheit passiert und vorbei sind, verwendest du die einfache Vergangenheit (**simple past**).

Signalwörter

yesterday	gestern
last year	letztes Jahr
a week ago	vor einer Woche
in 2015	(im Jahr) 2015

Das **simple past** bildest du so:
Hänge die Endung **-ed** an das Verb.
Achte auf unregelmäßige Verben, z. B. have → **had**; do → **did**; get → **got**; build → **built**; go → **went** etc.

Eine Liste der unregelmäßigen Verben findest du ab Seite 210.

They **started** roadwork last Monday.	Sie begannen am letzten Montag mit Straßenarbeiten.
Two years ago they **had** a lot of snow in New York.	Vor zwei Jahren hatten sie in New York viel Schnee.

Um zu sagen, was in der Vergangenheit nicht passiert ist, setzt du **didn't** (= did not) vor das Verb.

David **didn't get** into the city.	David kam nicht in die Stadt.

Und so kannst du im **simple past** Fragen stellen:

Did you **have** a good time in New York?	Yes, I **did**.	No, I **didn't**.
When **did** your friend **visit** Manhattan?	Last weekend.	

Aussagen und Verneinungen mit **be** bildest du so:

I **was** in New York.	Ich war in New York.
I **wasn't** in Washington.	Ich war nicht in Washington.
The Statue of Liberty **was** a present from France. It **wasn't** a present from Germany.	Die Freiheitsstatue war ein Geschenk von Frankreich. Sie war kein Geschenk von Deutschland.
We **were** in New York, but we **weren't** in Brooklyn.	Wir waren in New York, aber wir waren nicht in Brooklyn.

Fragen mit **be** bildest du so:

Were you at the zoo in Central Park?	Yes, I **was**.	No, I **wasn't**.
What **was** special in New York?	The Brooklyn Bridge.	

(TEST YOURSELF) Put the verbs in the simple past.

1. Tom — (have) a great time in NYC last summer.
2. He — (like) the New York skyline.
3. We — (not take) a taxi.
4. What — you — (do) in Manhattan?
5. — (be) you in the USA last year?
6. I — (not be) in Chicago.

G2 Die Vorvergangenheit

The past perfect

After I had built my new house, I felt much better.

Um über Ereignisse zu sprechen, die noch **vor** einem vergangenen Ereignis stattfanden, verwendest du die Vorvergangenheit, das **past perfect: had / hadn't + 3. Form** des Verbs (past participle).

Signalwörter	
after	nachdem
before	bevor

Bei den meisten Verben hängst du für die 3. Form ein **-ed** an das Verb: visit → visit**ed**
Achte auf unregelmäßige Verben, z. B. go → **gone**; see → **seen**; be → **been** etc.

Eine Liste der unregelmäßigen Verben findest du ab Seite 210.

Was in der Vergangenheit weiter zurückliegt, wird mit dem **past perfect** ausgedrückt!

She wasn't at home. She **had gone** to Tim's (house).	Sie war nicht zu Hause. Sie war zu Tim gegangen.
After I **had been** in NYC for two months, I moved to Chicago.	Nachdem ich zwei Monate in NYC gewesen war, zog ich nach Chicago um.
I **hadn't seen** skyscrapers before I went to New York.	Ich hatte noch keine Wolkenkratzer gesehen, bevor ich nach New York ging.

Aufgepasst! Im Nebensatz mit **after** steht **past perfect**, dann folgt **simple past**.
Im Nebensatz mit **before** steht **simple past**, dann folgt **past perfect**.

(TEST YOURSELF) Put the verbs in the past perfect.

1. After I — (leave) the shop, I lost my shopping bag.
2. I couldn't go to the swimming pool because I — (not do) my homework.
3. When I arrived, the concert — already — (start).
4. I — (watch) a TV show before you phoned me.
5. My grandad didn't want to move because he — (live) in Cuba all his life.
6. Yesterday I saw an animal which I — (not see) before.

Unit 2

G3 Modale Hilfsverben und ihre Ersatzformen

Modal auxiliaries and their substitutes

I'm lucky. I didn't have to book a holiday. I only had to swim to this lovely rock.

Modale Hilfsverben kannst du nur im **simple present** verwenden. Für alle anderen Zeiten benötigst du **Ersatzformen**. Ausnahme **can**: Für **can** kannst du im **simple past** auch **could** verwenden.

Mit **can** und **could** sagst du, was du tun **kannst** (Fähigkeit).

Simple present	Simple past
Kim **can** speak English. Kim **kann** Englisch sprechen. **Can** your friend speak English? **Kann** dein Freund Englisch sprechen?	Kim **could** understand it. Kim **konnte** es verstehen. **Could** he speak English? **Konnte** er Englisch sprechen?

Mit **can/could** und der Ersatzform **be allowed to** sagst du, was du tun **darfst** (Erlaubnis).

She **can't/isn't allowed to** use her phone. Sie **darf** ihr Handy **nicht** benutzen. **Can** you/**Are** you **allowed to** wear jeans? **Darfst** du Jeans tragen?	She **couldn't/wasn't allowed to** use it. Sie **durfte** es **nicht** benutzen. **Could** you/**Were** you **allowed to** wear jeans? **Durftest** du Jeans tragen?

Mit **must** und der Ersatzform **have to** sagst du, was du tun **musst** (Verpflichtung).

Sarah **must** take English and History. Sarah **muss** Englisch und Geschichte nehmen. We **don't have to** worry. Wir **müssen** uns **keine** Sorgen machen. **Must** you help your parents? **Musst** du deinen Eltern helfen?	Sarah **had to** take Biology too. Sarah **musste** auch Biologie nehmen. We **didn't have to** worry. Wir **mussten** uns **keine** Sorgen machen. **Did** you **have to** help in the house? **Musstest** du im Haus helfen?

Bei **must** musst du die Ersatzform schon in **verneinten Sätzen** im **simple present** benutzen!

(TEST YOURSELF) Use the correct forms in the simple past.

1. When Luise was in the USA, she — (not can) keep her things in the classrooms.
2. She — (must) put her books into lockers.
3. She — (can) travel around the USA.
4. She — (not must) take lessons in basketball.
5. The students — (can) wear jeans.
6. When she was ten, she — (not can) dance like she dances today.

G4 R: Bedingungssätze Typ I

Revision: If-clauses type I

Um Bedingungen und Folgen auszudrücken, benutzt man **if**-Sätze.
Dabei steht im **if-Satz** das **simple present**, im Hauptsatz das **will-future**.
Geht der **if**-Satz voran, steht am Ende des **if**-Satzes ein Komma.

Bedingung (condition)	Folge (consequence)	
If Michael **finds** a job,	he **will earn** some money.	Wenn Michael einen Job findet, wird er etwas Geld verdienen.
If you **don't work** well,	you **won't get** extra money.	Wenn du nicht gut arbeitest, bekommst du nicht mehr Geld.

Bedingungssätze können auch mit dem Hauptsatz beginnen. Dann entfällt das Komma.

Folge (consequence)	Bedingung (condition)	
You **will be** late	if you **walk.**	Du wirst zu spät kommen, wenn du zu Fuß gehst.
You **won't be** successful	if you **don't work** more carefully.	Du wirst nicht erfolgreich sein, wenn du nicht sorgfältiger arbeitest.

Das **will-future** drückt allgemein Zukünftiges aus. Im **if**-Satz steht nie **will** oder **won't**!

Für das **will-future** kannst du im Deutschen die Zukunft oder die Gegenwart benutzen. Beides ist richtig. Vergleiche:

He will earn some money.	Er wird etwas Geld verdienen. Er verdient etwas Geld.

(TEST YOURSELF) Complete the sentences.

1. If you need me, I — (help) you.
2. If you don't phone me, I — (be) sad.
3. If she — (not come) on time, she will lose her job.
4. Matt — (not find) a job if he doesn't read the adverts.
5. I will talk to Sue if I — (meet) her.
6. You won't sleep well if you always — (read) scary stories.

(FÜR PROFIS)

Im Deutschen können **if** (falls, wenn) und **when** (dann, wenn) mit wenn übersetzt werden.
Im Englischen kommt es darauf an, welche **Absicht** du ausdrücken möchtest.

If I go shopping, I'll get you a T-shirt.
(Ich weiß noch nicht, **ob** ich einkaufen gehe. Aber **falls** ich gehe, dann kaufe ich dir ein T-Shirt. Es ist nicht sicher und nur eine Möglichkeit.)

When I go shopping, I'll get you a T-shirt.
(Ich gehe auf jeden Fall einkaufen. Das weiß ich schon sicher. Ich weiß nur noch nicht, **wann**. Aber dann kaufe ich dir ein T-Shirt. Es ist sicher und nur eine Frage des Zeitpunkts.)

Unit 3

G5 R: Fragen

Revision: Questions / questions with who

So bildest du unterschiedliche Fragen mit Vollverben, z. B. like, go etc.:

Fragen, auf die man mit yes oder no antwortet (Ja/Nein-Fragen)
– Fragen im **simple present** beginnst du mit **do** oder **does** (he, she, it).

Do you **like** turkey?	Magst du Truthahn?
Does Jacob **like** chocolate?	Mag Jacob Schokolade?

– Fragen im **simple past** beginnst du mit **did** für alle Personen.

Did you **travel** by car last year?	Bist du letztes Jahr mit dem Auto verreist?
Did it **rain** last December?	Hat es im letzten Dezember geregnet?

– Fragen im **will-future** beginnst du mit **will** für alle Personen.

Will you **call** us again tomorrow?	Wirst du uns morgen nochmal anrufen?

Fragen mit Fragewörtern

What do you **like**?	Was magst du gerne?
Where did you **spend** your summer?	Wo hast du deinen Sommer verbracht?
When will you **go** to Boston?	Wann wirst du nach Boston fahren?

Fragen mit who
– Das Fragewort **who?** kann **verschiedene Bedeutungen haben:**
– Heißt es **Wer?** wird **keine Form von do** verwendet.
– Heißt es **Wen?** oder **Wem?** muss **eine Form von do** verwendet werden.

Who lives in Boston?	**Wer** lebt in Boston?
Who do you **like**?	**Wen** magst du?
Who did you **help** last week?	**Wem** hast du letzte Woche geholfen?

(TEST YOURSELF) Put in do, does, did, will – if necessary.

1. —— you often have a turkey dinner?
2. Where —— your uncle live?
3. Who —— you invite next Friday?
4. —— you see the heavy storm on TV last Sunday?
5. Who —— got stuck in his car last night?
6. Who —— Mark meet yesterday?

G6 R: Bedingungssätze Typ II

Revision: If-clauses type II

Bei den Bedingungssätzen Typ II ist eine Bedingung unwahrscheinlich oder nicht erfüllbar. Du verwendest im **if-Satz simple past**. Im Hauptsatz steht **would / wouldn't + Grundform des Verbs**.

Bedingung (condition)	Folge (consequence)	
If it **rained**,	I **would stay** at home.	Wenn es regnen würde, würde ich zu Hause bleiben (aber es regnet nicht).
If you **didn't call**,	I **would be** very sad.	Wenn du nicht anrufen würdest, wäre ich sehr traurig (aber du rufst bestimmt an).

Bedingungssätze können auch mit dem Hauptsatz beginnen. Dann entfällt das Komma.

Folge (consequence)	Bedingung (condition)	
I **would buy** new clothes	if I **had** more money.	Ich würde mir neue Kleidung kaufen, wenn ich genug Geld hätte (aber ich habe nicht genug Geld).
I **wouldn't have** problems with my clothes,	if I **lived** in the Amish community.	Ich hätte keine Kleidungsprobleme, wenn ich in der Gemeinschaft der Amish leben würde (aber ich lebe dort nicht).

Statt **If I was** … wird oft **If I were** … gebraucht.

If I **were** a film star,	I **would live** in Beverly Hills.	Wenn ich ein Filmstar wäre, würde ich in Beverly Hills wohnen.

Im **if**-Satz steht nie **would / wouldn't**!

Im Deutschen verwendet man in beiden Satzteilen **würde**, **wäre** oder **hätte (Konjunktiv)**.

(TEST YOURSELF) Complete the sentences.

1. If you visited your grandma on Sundays, she — (be) very glad.
2. If she had less time, she — (not meet) her friends every week.
3. If I — (be) in Pennsylvania, I would like to see the Amish community.
4. I would really miss you if you — (not come) back.
5. Jennifer — (not worry) about clothes if she lived with the Amish community.
6. Maybe it — (be) better if you didn't phone me every day.

Unit 4

G7 R: Gegenüberstellung: Simple present – present progressive

Revision: Simple present – present progressive

Du kennst schon die Zeiten **simple present** und **present progressive**. Hier findest du noch einmal die Situationen, in denen du sie benutzen kannst und siehst, wie sie gebildet werden.

Simple present

Das **simple present** verwendest du, wenn du sagen willst, dass jemand etwas häufig oder regelmäßig tut.

Signalwörter: always, never, sometimes, often, usually, every …

Aussagen bildest du mit der Grundform des Verbs.

I **work** every day. You never **listen**.

Achtung: **He**, **she**, **it** – das **s** muss mit:
He work**s**. She talk**s**. It rain**s**. Aber: He go**es**.

Sätze mit Vollverben verneinst du mit **don't** und **doesn't**:

I **don't play** football.

Bei Fragen mit Vollverben musst du mit **do** oder **does** beginnen:

Do you **eat** fish? **Does** he **like** games?

Present progressive

Mit dem **present progressive** kannst du sagen, was jemand gerade tut oder was im Augenblick passiert.

Signalwörter: now, at the moment

Aussagen bildest du so:
am / are / is + Verb + -ing

I**'m working** at the moment. It **is raining** now.

Achtung Schreibweise: make → mak**ing**; write → writ**ing**; run → run**ning**; sit → sit**ting**

So verneinst du Sätze:
am / are / is not + Verb + -ing:

He **isn't eating** at the moment.

Bei Fragen stellst du **am / are / is** an den Satzanfang:

Are you **listening**? **Is** she **dancing**?

Simple present und present progressive kannst du auch einsetzen, um ein **Bild** zu beschreiben. Zunächst sagst du, wen oder was du siehst. Dann beschreibst du, was jemand tut.

Simple present

Du benutzt es, um zu sagen, wer oder was auf dem Bild zu sehen ist, oder in welchem Zustand etwas ist.

There is a boy in the picture.
There are a man and a woman.
She **looks** happy.
She **has** two dogs.
The weather **is** nice. It **is** warm.

Present progressive

Du benutzt es für alle Handlungen, die im Bild zu sehen sind und für alles, was jemand tut.

The boy **is riding** a mountain bike.
They**'re sitting** in camping chairs.
She**'s wearing** boots.
They **are playing** with a ball.
The sun **is shining**. It **isn't raining**.

(TEST YOURSELF) Use present progressive or simple present.

1. Sandy often — (go) surfing.
2. But at the moment she — (not surf).
3. "— you really — (listen), Sandy?"
4. Students — (not like) tests.
5. What — you usually — (do) after school?
6. We sometimes — (meet) some friends.

G8 R: Das Perfekt

Revision: The present perfect

Wenn eine Handlung in der Vergangenheit beginnt und in der Gegenwart zu einem Ergebnis führt, verwendest du das **present perfect**:
have/has + 3. Form des Verbs (past participle).
Bei den meisten Verben hängst du ein **-ed** an das Verb: help → help**ed**

Signalwörter	
already	schon
just	gerade
not ... yet	noch ... nicht
never	noch nie
ever (in Fragen)	jemals (in Fragen)
since	seit (Zeitpunkt)
for	seit (Zeitspanne)

Eine Liste der unregelmäßigen Verben findest du ab Seite 210.

Einige Verben haben unregelmäßige 3. Formen: z. B. be → **been**; write → **written**

I **have** just **posted** a photo.	Ich habe gerade ein Foto verschickt.
She **has** already **written** ten text messages.	Sie hat schon zehn SMS geschrieben.

Um Sätze zu verneinen, benutzt du **haven't** oder **hasn't** (bei he, she, it):

I **haven't been** to California yet.	Ich bin noch nicht in Kalifornien gewesen.
She **hasn't seen** Los Angeles yet.	Sie hat Los Angeles noch nicht gesehen.

Fragen und Kurzantworten bildest du so:

Have you ever **been** to San Francisco?	Yes, I **have**.	No, I **haven't**.
Has your sister ever **met** a famous star?	Yes, she **has**.	No, she **hasn't**.

Present perfect mit **for** und **since**
since (**seit**) verwendest du vor einem **Zeitpunkt**, z. B. **since** 5 o'clock, **since** July, **since** 2013.
for (**seit**) verwendest du vor einer **Zeitspanne**, z. B. **for** five hours, **for** three years, **for** a long time.

I haven't seen Lara **since** Monday.	Ich habe Lara **seit** Montag nicht gesehen.
I haven't seen Lara **for** a week.	Ich habe Lara **seit** einer Woche nicht gesehen.

Im Deutschen verwendet man oft die **Gegenwart**, wenn man sagen will, seit wann oder wie lange etwas schon andauert. Vergleiche:

I **have lived** in Los Angeles for two years.	Ich **lebe seit** zwei Jahren in Los Angeles.
She **has had** a smartphone since last year.	Sie **hat seit** letztem Jahr ein Smartphone.

(TEST YOURSELF) Put the verbs in the present perfect.

1. Linda — never — (meet) a Hollywood star.
2. I — (not see) you for two months.
3. Why — your sister — (not call) yet?
4. — you — (forget) your homework again?
5. We — (not be) on holiday since 2010.
6. — you ever — (watch) funny videos?

Unit 5

G9 Das Passiv

Passive voice (simple present)

English is important.
It is spoken all over the world.

Mit dem Passiv kannst du über eine Handlung Auskunft geben, ohne zu sagen, wer die Handlung ausführt. Im Vordergrund steht die Handlung.

So bildest du das **Passiv** im **simple present: am / are / is + 3. Form des Verbs** (past participle)

English **is spoken** in a lot of countries.	Englisch **wird** in vielen Ländern **gesprochen**.
Racism **isn't accepted**.	Rassismus **wird nicht akzeptiert**.
Spices and flour **are mixed**.	Gewürze und Mehl **werden gemischt**.
Tickets **aren't sold** here.	Karten **werden** hier **nicht verkauft**.

(TEST YOURSELF) Use the passive voice.

1. Southern fried chicken —— (cook) all over the USA.
2. This dish —— (make) with flour and spices.
3. The chicken and the rice —— (not cook) for a long time.
4. Language courses —— (organize) for people who are new.
5. Chewing gum —— (not accept) at school.
6. Bananas and pineapples —— (not grow) in Germany.

G10 Indirekte Rede (ohne Zeitverschiebung)

Reported speech (without backshift)

Oh no!
Dad says we have to take a shower now.

Mit der indirekten Rede kannst du über das berichten, was jemand anderes **gerade gesagt hat**. Du beginnst mit **He says that ... / She says that ...** usw. Das Wort **that** kann man auch weglassen.

Positive Aussagen und verneinte Sätze in der indirekten Rede bildest du so:

Direkte Rede	Indirekte Rede
Anna says, "**I like** Florida."	Anna says (that) **she likes** Florida.
Anna says, "**We want** to see the alligators."	Anna says (that) **they want** to see the alligators.
Anna says, "**I don't need** a hotel."	Anna says (that) **she doesn't need** a hotel.
Anna says, "**We don't need** a sweatshirt."	Anna says (that) **they don't need** a sweatshirt.
Anna says, "**I can see** a snake over there."	Anna says (that) **she can see** a snake over there.
Anna says, "**We can't visit** the animal show."	Anna says (that) **they can't visit** the animal show.

Beachte die Änderungen:

I	→ **he/she**	**my**	→ **his/her**
we	→ **they**	**our**	→ **their**
(I) **like**	→ (he/she) **likes**		
(I) **don't ...**	→ (he/she) **doesn't ...**		

(TEST YOURSELF) Report what Anna says.

1. "We prefer the Everglades."
2. "I want to go on a boat tour."
3. "I don't like all those crowds."
4. "I don't want to feed the alligators."
5. "I know Florida."
6. "We can't visit the zoo at night."

Methods

1-minute-presentation

Step 1
Nimm ein Blatt DIN A4-Papier quer und falte es so, dass das untere Drittel nach hinten wegknickt.

Step 2
Schreibe den Vortragstext auf die oberen zwei Drittel.

Step 3
Streiche nun die wichtigsten Stichpunkte im Text an. Notiere sie noch einmal auf dem unteren Drittel. Das ist dein Spickzettel.

Step 4
In deiner Präsentation verwendest du nur den Spickzettel. Wenn du steckenbleibst, darfst du ihn umknicken und kurz auf den Text oben schauen.

Bus stop

(Lerntempoduett)

Step 1
Bearbeite die Aufgabe zunächst allein. Schreibe deine Lösungen auf.

Step 2
Wenn du fertig bist, gehe zum „bus stop". Warte dort auf die nächste Person bzw. triff die Person, die dort schon wartet. Vergleicht und korrigiert eure Ergebnisse.

Step 3
Gehe danach wieder zu deinem Platz zurück. Bearbeite die nächste Aufgabe.

Dramatic reading

(Szenisches Lesen)

Step 1

Verteilt die Rollen innerhalb eurer Gruppe.

Step 2

Lies dir deinen Text lautlos oder ganz leise immer wieder vor, bis du ihn gut kennst.

Step 3

Übt euren Text in der Gruppe mit der Methode „Read and look up“ (Seite 172).

Step 4

Überlegt euch, wie ihr euch in der Rolle fühlt und wie ihr euch bewegen würdet. Tragt euren Text so frei wie möglich vor.

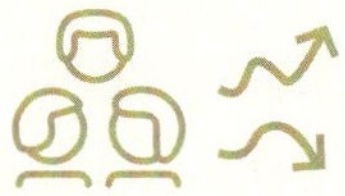

Gallery walk

Step 1

Hängt nach eurer Gruppenarbeit euer Produkt gut sichtbar im Klassenzimmer auf.

Step 2

Einer von euch, der „Experte“, bleibt bei eurem Produkt stehen und erklärt es den anderen. Die anderen gehen herum. Nach jedem Durchgang wechselt der Experte.

Step 3

Seht euch die Produkte der anderen an und bewertet sie.

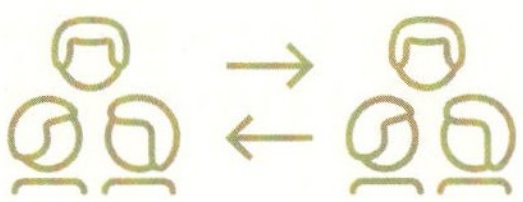

Step 4

Wertet im Anschluss eure Ergebnisse in der Klasse aus.

Jigsaw
(Gruppenpuzzle)

Step 1
Bildet Stammgruppen („home groups").
Jedes Gruppenmitglied wählt einen Text aus, liest ihn und bearbeitet ihn. Macht euch Notizen dazu.

Step 2
Trefft euch in Expertengruppen („expert groups") mit den Mitgliedern der anderen Stammgruppen, die denselben Text wie ihr bearbeitet haben. Vergleicht eure Notizen, besprecht sie gemeinsam und ergänzt sie.

Step 3
Geht zurück in eure Stammgruppe. Präsentiert dort die Informationen aus eurem Text. Macht euch Notizen zu den Texten der anderen, so dass am Ende jeder die Informationen aus allen Texten hat.

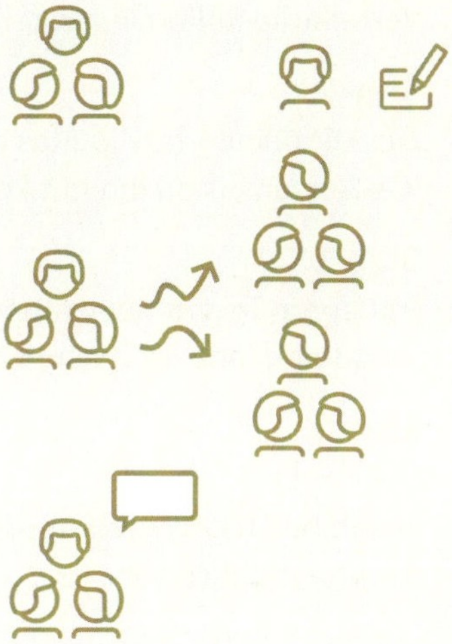

Milling around
(Marktplatz)

Step 1
Bearbeite die Aufgabe zunächst allein.
Auf ein Zeichen vom Lehrer oder der Lehrerin steht ihr auf und geht durch den Raum.
Nimm die Aufgabe und einen Stift mit.

Step 2
Wenn ein Signal ertönt, bleibt ihr stehen.
Besprecht mit der Person die Aufgabe, die euch am nächsten steht.

Step 3
Beim nächsten Signal trennt ihr euch und geht weiter durch den Raum. Wiederholt den Vorgang.

Peer correction

(Partnerkontrolle)

Step 1

Bearbeite die Aufgabe zunächst selbstständig.

Step 2

Tausche deine Lösungen mit einem Partner/einer Partnerin. Kontrolliere seine oder ihre Lösungen.

Step 3

Tauscht euch danach zu der Aufgabe aus und korrigiert den Text.

Placemat

(Platzdeckchen)

Step 1

Bildet Vierergruppen.

Step 2

Teilt ein großes Blatt Papier in fünf Bereiche ein.

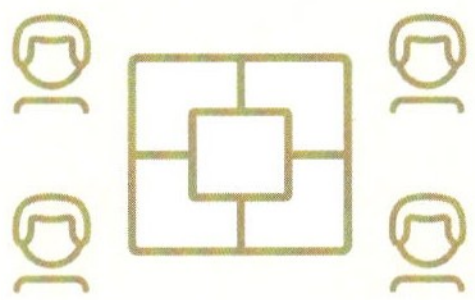

Step 3

Setzt euch so hin, dass alle in eine Ecke des Blattes schreiben können.

Step 4

Jedes Gruppenmitglied denkt allein über das Thema nach und schreibt Ideen auf seinen Teil des Blattes.

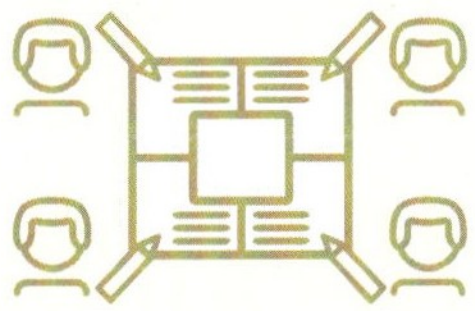

Step 5

Tauscht euch über die Ideen aus. Einigt euch auf die besten Ideen und schreibt diese in die Mitte des Blattes.

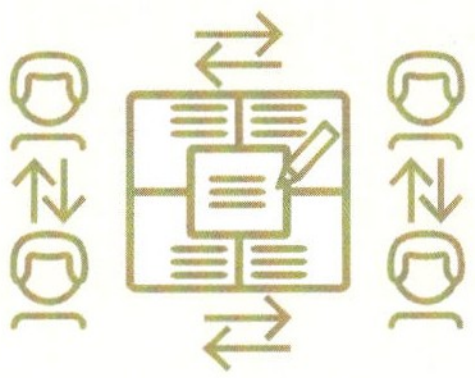

Read and look up

(Lesen und Aufschauen)

Step 1

Schaue auf deinen Text und präge dir die erste Zeile oder den ersten Satz ein. Schaue hoch und sprich deine Zeile/deinen Satz lautlos oder leise vor dich hin. Nimm dir die nächste Zeile/den nächsten Satz vor.

Step 2

Übe nun mit einer Partnerin/einem Partner. Erzähle deinen Text, Zeile für Zeile oder Satz für Satz. Dazwischen schaust du immer wieder nach unten auf deinen Text.

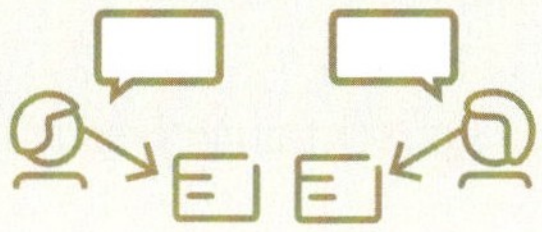

Step 3

Wiederhole alles, bis es gut klappt. Überlege dir, wo du stehen und wie du dich bewegen willst.

Round robin

(Blitzlicht)

Step 1

Bildet Gruppen und setzt euch in einen Kreis.

Step 2

Jedes Gruppenmitglied überlegt sich kurz einen Satz, der seine persönliche Meinung zum Thema ausdrückt.

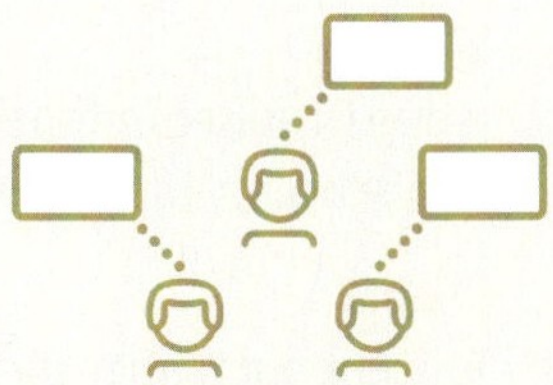

Step 3

Wenn alle bereit sind, sagen die Gruppenmitglieder der Reihe nach ihre Meinung.

Step 4

Die anderen Gruppenmitglieder dürfen die Sätze nicht kommentieren.

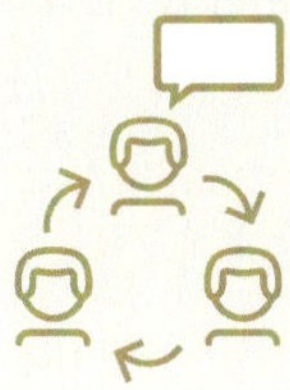

Think – pair – share

Step 1

Schreibe deine Ideen, Gedanken oder Lösungen zur Aufgabe auf.

Step 2

Tauscht eure Notizen zu zweit aus und besprecht sie.

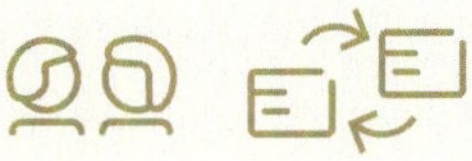

Step 3

Präsentiert euer Ergebnis anderen Paaren oder der gesamten Klasse.

Tip top

Step 1

Sage zunächst, was dir gut gefallen hat – was „top“ war.

Step 2

Sage nun, was noch nicht so gut war, und gib einen Tipp, was man noch verbessern könnte.

Writers' conference

(Schreibwerkstatt)

Step 1

Bildet Vierergruppen.

Step 2

Lest euch eure Sätze/Texte gegenseitig vor.

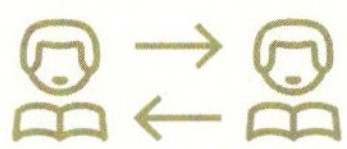

Step 3

Die anderen sagen, was ihnen gefallen hat.

Step 4

Die Zuhörer machen Verbesserungsvorschläge.

Step 5

Jede Gruppe wählt den besten Text aus und liest ihn der Klasse vor.

Du kennst schon einige Tipps und
Tricks zum Vokabellernen.
Erinnerst du dich?
Hier gibt es weitere Tipps.

Vocabulary

Vocabulary tips

Lerntipp: Englisch im Alltag

Achte während des Tages auf alle englischen Wörter, die dir begegnen. Ob im Supermarkt, im Fernsehen, in Büchern, auf Werbeplakaten oder Schildern am Bahnhof, Flughafen etc.: Du wirst erstaunt sein, wie oft man im Alltag auf die englische Sprache stößt. Das ist ein gutes Training, um auf noch unbekannte Vokabeln aufmerksam zu werden. Deinen Sprachschatz erweiterst du ganz leicht, indem du dir ein schönes Heft oder Notizbuch kaufst, das speziell für solche Vokabeln da ist. Nimm es so oft wie möglich mit, vor allem, wenn du verreist! Die noch unbekannten Wörter kannst du dann zu Hause in einem Wörterbuch nachschlagen. Da du mit jedem Wort eine kleine Geschichte oder bestimmte besondere Umstände verbindest (zum Beispiel: „Ach ja! Dieses Wort habe ich am Bahnhof gesehen, im Kino gehört“ etc.), wirst du es dir sehr leicht merken können!

Wortbildung

Es gibt verschiedene Möglichkeiten, um aus einem Verb ein Nomen abzuleiten.

1. Du kannst die Endung *-ing* anhängen:
   to build → a building
   to meet → a meeting
2. Manche Nomen werden mit der Endung *-er* oder *-or* gebildet.
   Solche Nomen bezeichnen meistens eine Person:
   to ride → a rider
   to visit → a visitor
3. Es gibt auch die Endung *-ion:*
   to define → a definition
   to invent → an invention
4. Sehr oft haben auch Verb und Nomen dieselbe Form:
   to call → a call
   to dream → a dream

Diese Checkliste kann dir helfen, Fehler zu vermeiden und deine Rechtschreibung zu verbessern. Prüfe alle deine Texte damit.

- **Schreibung:**
  - ☐ *gh* wird meist nicht gesprochen. Vergiss es beim Schreiben nicht.
  - ☐ *k* kommt vor *t* so gut wie nie vor, z. B. action – Aktion, October – Oktober
- **Gleiche Aussprache, unterschiedliche Schreibung:**
  - ☐ [iː] z. B. teacher, meeting, media, magazine, people, field
  - ☐ [uː] z. B. food, route, to do, swimsuit, supermarket, true, crew
- **Gleiche Aussprache, unterschiedliche Schreibung und Bedeutung:**
  - ☐ [iː] z. B. see – sehen, sea – Meer; meet – treffen, meat – Fleisch
  - ☐ [uː] z. B. two – zwei, too – auch
- **Verdoppelung der Endkonsonanten:**
  - ☐ to stop – stopping, stopped
  - ☐ to plan – planning, planned
- ***y* wird zu *ie*:**
  - ☐ in der 3. Person Singular: z. B. to carry – he carries; aber: to buy – she buys
  - ☐ im Plural: z. B. city – cities, party – parties; aber: boy – boys
  - ☐ bei der Steigerung von Adjektiven: z. B. happy – happier – (the) happiest; easy – easier – (the) easiest
- **Ähnlich und doch anders:**
  - ☐ Wortendung *le:* z. B. engl. title – dt. Titel; engl. middle – dt. Mittel
  - ☐ *ph* statt *f:* z. B. engl. phone – dt. Telefon; engl. photo – dt. Foto
- **Großschreibung:**
  - ☐ Monatsnamen: z. B. January, July, December
  - ☐ Wochentage: z. B. Monday, Wednesday, Saturday
  - ☐ Eigennamen: z. B. Tom, Lisa, the Brooks, the London Eye, the Thames
  - ☐ geografische Namen: Bristol, Greenwich, Germany, Italy
- **Plural:**
  - ☐ Der Plural bekommt normalerweise ein *-s:* z. B. friend – friends, chair – chairs, film – films
  - ☐ Endet ein Wort auf *s* oder *x*, wird *-es* angehängt: z. B. bus – buses, box – boxes
  - ☐ Manche Wörter haben einen unregelmäßigen Plural: z. B. man – men, child – children, shelf – shelves, mouse – mice
- **Apostroph:**
  - ☐ bei Kurzformen: z. B. she is → she's; they are → they're
  - ☐ beim Genitiv-s: z. B. Sam's bike, Emma's family, the Jacksons' house, the children's games
- **Wörterbuch:**
  - ☐ Prüfe die Schreibung aller Wörter, bei denen du dir nicht ganz sicher bist, indem du sie im Wörterbuch nachschlägst.

Vocabulary

Das Vocabulary enthält alle neuen Wörter und Wendungen. Sie stehen in der Reihenfolge, wie sie im Buch vorkommen.

Die Wortliste ist in drei Spalten aufgeteilt:

Links findest du das englische Wort mit der Lautschrift in Klammern. (Die Lautschrift wird ganz unten auf jeder Seite im *Dictionary* erklärt.)

In der mittleren Spalte steht die deutsche Übersetzung.

Rechts findest du Beispielsätze, Hinweise und Tipps, die dir beim Lernen helfen.

Die **fett** gedruckten Wörter musst du lernen.
Die blau gedruckten Wörter kannst du lernen, musst du aber nicht.
Die Wörter aus den Checkpoints musst du nicht lernen.

Symbole und Abkürzungen:

👄	Achte auf die Aussprache!	=	entspricht
✏	Achte auf die Schreibung!	*(sg)*	Einzahl (Singular)
↔	ist das Gegenteil von	*(pl)*	Mehrzahl (Plural)
→	ist verwandt mit	[R]	ähnlich wie im Russischen
sth	something	[T]	ähnlich wie im Türkischen
sb	somebody		

Die *Word bank*-Seiten helfen dir, die *Your turn*-Aufgaben in den *Units* zu bearbeiten.
Du findest dort nützlichen individuellen Wortschatz zum Thema der *Unit*, der dir hilft, über deine eigene Situation zu sprechen oder zu schreiben. Diese Wörter findest du auch im *Dictionary*.

Wenn du ein Wort nicht weißt und im Wörterbuch nachschlagen willst, schau auf den *Dictionary*-Seiten ab S. 213 nach. Oder bei den *Instructions* auf S. 208.

Zoom in – The USA

p. 8	**fall** *(AE)* [fɔ:l]	Herbst	AE: **fall** BE: autumn
	state [steɪt]	Staat; Bundesstaat; Land	There are 50 **states** in the USA.
	to shine [ʃaɪn], **shone** [ʃɒn], **shone** [ʃɒn]	scheinen; glänzen	The sun is **shining** today.
	bright [braɪt]	hell; leuchtend; strahlend	**bright** ↔ dark
	color *(AE)* ['kʌlə]	Farbe	AE: **color** BE: colour
p. 9	**huge** [hju:dʒ]	riesig; riesengroß	**huge** = very big
	area ['eəriə]	Fläche; Gegend; Gebiet; Areal	The USA has an **area** of over 9,000,000 km².
	corn [kɔ:n]	Korn; Mais; Getreide	

	soy bean ['sɔɪ ˌbi:n]	Sojabohne	You can see **soy beans** in the Midwest.
	field [fi:ld]	Feld; Wiese; Weide	There are corn **fields** in the Midwest.
	surfer ['sɜ:fə]	Wellenreiter; Wellenreiterin; Surfer; Surferin	T sörfçü 
	paradise ['pærədaɪs]	Paradies	Hawaii is a surfer's **paradise**.
	perfect ['pɜ:fɪkt]	perfekt; vollkommen	Today is the **perfect** weather for a picnic.
	wave [weɪv]	Welle	
p. 8	**North America** [ˌnɔ:θ‿ə'merɪkə]	Nordamerika	Denali is the highest mountain in **North America**.
p. 9	**landscape** ['lændskeɪp]	Landschaft	Tourists enjoy the beautiful **landscape**.
	American [ə'merɪkən]	amerikanisch; Amerikanisch; aus Amerika; Amerikaner; Amerikanerin	**American** → America
	swamp [swɒmp]	Sumpf	There are **swamps** in the American south.
	alligator ['ælɪgeɪtə]	Alligator	R аллигатор T alligator 
p. 8	**rose** [rəʊz]	Rose	R роза 
	bald eagle [ˌbɔ:ld 'i:gl]	Weißkopfseeadler	The **bald eagle** is an American symbol.
	population [ˌpɒpjə'leɪʃn]	Einwohner; Einwohnerzahl; Bevölkerung	What's the **population** of the United States?
	total ['təʊtl]	Gesamt-; gesamt	The **total** area is all of the area.
	square mile (= sq. mi.) [ˌskweə 'maɪl]	Quadratmeile	The United States' total area is about 3,600,000 **square miles**.
	currency ['kʌrnsi]	Währung	The **currency** in Germany is the euro.
	dollar ['dɒlə]	Dollar *(amer. Währungseinheit)*	R доллар T dolar
	time zone ['taɪm ˌzəʊn]	Zeitzone	There are nine **time zones** in the USA.
	major ['meɪdʒə]	Haupt-; wichtig; bedeutend	There are three **major** rivers in the USA.
p. 9	**to name** [neɪm]	benennen	to **name** → name
	north of ['nɔ:θ‿əv]	nördlich von	Denmark is **north of** Germany.
	south of ['saʊθ‿əv]	südlich von	Italy is **south of** Germany.
	ocean ['əʊʃn]	Ozean; Meer	R океан T okyanus
	east of ['i:st‿əv]	östlich von	Poland is **east of** Germany.
	west of ['west‿əv]	westlich von	France is **west of** Germany.
	distance ['dɪstns]	Entfernung; Distanz	Find out the **distance** from A to B.

Unit 1 Gateway NYC

p. 12	**gateway** ['geɪtweɪ]	Tor; Eingangstor	NYC is the **gateway** to America.

Way in

	over ['əʊvə]	über	**Over** eight million people live in NYC.
	borough ['bʌrə]	Stadtteil; Bezirk	NYC has five **boroughs**.
	skyline ['skaɪlaɪn]	Skyline	
	to **replace** [rɪ'pleɪs]	ersetzen	I **replaced** my old car.
	attack [ə'tæk]	Angriff; Attacke	There were **attacks** on September 11, 2001.
p. 13	**baseball** ['beɪsbɔ:l]	Baseball	R бейсбол T beyzbol 
	New Yorker [ˌnju: 'jɔ:kə]	New Yorker; New Yorkerin	**New Yorkers** live in New York City.
	center *(AE)* ['sentə]	Zentrum; Mitte; Center	AE: **center** BE: centre
	culture ['kʌltʃə]	Kultur	It is a center for American **culture**.
	theater *(AE)* ['θɪətə]	Theater	AE: **theater** BE: theatre
	street art ['stri:t ɑ:t]	Straßenkunst	**Street art** started in New York.
	independence [ˌɪndɪ'pendəns]	Unabhängigkeit	They celebrated 100 years of **independence**.
	immigrant ['ɪmɪgrənt]	Immigrant; Immigrantin; Einwanderer; Einwanderin	A lot of **immigrants** went to America.
	symbol ['sɪmbl]	Symbol	R символ T sembol
	hope [həʊp]	Hoffnung	**hope** → to hope
	on TV [ɒn ˌti:'vi:]	im Fernsehen	You could see everything **on TV**.
	billion ['bɪliən]	Milliarde	R биллион
	top [tɒp]	Spitze	It took 30 seconds to travel to the **top**.
	elevator *(AE)* ['elɪveɪtə]	Aufzug; Lift	AE: **elevator** BE: lift
	light [laɪt]	Licht	

Station 1

City words

traffic jam ['træfɪk ˌdʒæm]	Stau	**avenue** ['ævənju:]	Allee; Boulevard
rush hour ['rʌʃ ˌaʊə]	Hauptverkehrszeit	**lights** [laɪts]	Ampel
roadwork *(AE)* ['rəʊdwɜ:k]	Straßenbauarbeiten	**sidewalk** *(AE)* ['saɪdwɔ:k]	Gehweg; Bürgersteig
downtown *(AE)* [ˌdaʊn'taʊn]	im Stadtzentrum	**suburb** ['sʌbɜ:b]	Vorort
skyscraper ['skaɪskreɪpə]	Wolkenkratzer	**construction site** [kən'strʌkʃn ˌsaɪt]	Baustelle
subway *(AE)* ['sʌbweɪ]	U-Bahn	**parking lot** *(AE)* ['pɑ:kɪŋ ˌlɒt]	Parkplatz

p. 14	**ride** [raɪd]	Fahrt; Ritt	A taxi **ride** in NYC is very interesting.
	snow [snəʊ]	Schnee	
	to get into [ˌget‿'ɪntə]	hineingelangen; hineinkommen	I usually **get into** town by bus.
	look [lʊk]	Blick; Anblick; Sicht	**look** → to look
	to get tired of sth [ˌget 'taɪəd‿əv]	etw. sattbekommen; etw. satthaben	I never **get tired of** it.
	financial [faɪ'nænʃl]	finanziell; Finanz-	Where is the **financial** centre of the world?
	view [vju:]	Aussicht; Sicht; Ausblick; Blick	The **view** from the top is amazing.
	anyway ['eniweɪ]	eigentlich	How long are you here for, **anyway**?
	around [ə'raʊnd]	um … herum	The café is **around** the corner.
	hot dog ['hɒt ˌdɒg]	Hot Dog *(Würstchen im Brötchen)*	R хот-дог T hot dog 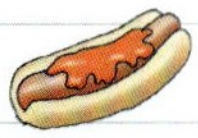
p. 15	**in the distance** [ˌɪn ðə 'dɪstns]	in der Ferne	I can see the bridge **in the distance**.
	right ahead [ˌraɪt ə'hed]	geradeaus	Look, the museum is **right ahead**.

Station 2

Going to a new country

to **immigrate** ['ɪmɪgreɪt]	einwandern; immigrieren
decision [dɪ'sɪʒn]	Entscheidung
foreign ['fɒrɪn]	fremd; ausländisch
unemployed [ˌʌnɪm'plɔɪd]	arbeitslos
chance [tʃɑ:ns]	Möglichkeit
community [kə'mju:nəti]	Gemeinde; Gemeinschaft
to **get used to (sth)** [ˌget 'ju:zd tə]	sich an (etw.) gewöhnen
career [kə'rɪə]	Beruf; Laufbahn; Karriere
citizen ['sɪtɪzn]	Staatsbürger; Staatsbürgerin; Staatsangehöriger; Staatsangehörige
papers *(pl)* [ˌpeɪpəz]	Unterlagen; Papiere
to **emigrate** ['emɪgreɪt]	auswandern; emigrieren
support [sə'pɔ:t]	Unterstützung; Hilfe
to **fail (at)** [feɪl (ət)]	versagen (in/bei); ausfallen; fehlschlagen

p. 18	**interviewer** ['ɪntəvju:ə]	Interviewer; Interviewerin; Befrager; Befragerin	**interviewer** → interview → to interview
	to **complain** [kəm'pleɪn]	sich beschweren; sich beklagen	Don't **complain** and think positive.
	Latin America [ˌlætɪn ə'merɪkə]	Lateinamerika	In **Latin America** the first language isn't English.
	poor [pɔ:]	arm	**poor** ↔ rich
	Cuba ['kju:bə]	Kuba	[R] Куба [T] Küba
	Cuban ['kju:bən]	kubanisch; aus Kuba; Kubaner; Kubanerin	**Cuban** → Cuba
	to **give up** [ˌgɪv‿'ʌp]	aufgeben	The spider never **gives up**.
	to **begin** [bɪ'gɪn], **began** [bɪ'gæn], **begun** [bɪ'gʌn]	beginnen; anfangen	**to begin** ↔ to finish
	to **take sth seriously** [ˌteɪk 'sɪəriəsli]	etw. ernst nehmen	I don't **take sport seriously**, I do it for fun.
	high school ['haɪ ˌsku:l]	Highschool *(weiterführende Schule, Oberstufe)*	I worked hard at **high school**.
	future ['fju:tʃə]	Zukunft	I had a better **future** in the USA.
	US [ju:'es]	US-amerikanisch	It is a **US** school, not a British one.
p. 19	**The Philippines** [ˌðə 'fɪlɪpi:nz]	die Philippinen	Angela is from **the Philippines**.
	college ['kɒlɪdʒ]	College; Institut	Angela goes to **college** too.

V

Reading corner

p. 22	**immigration** [ˌɪmɪ'greɪʃn]	Immigration; Zuwanderung	**immigration** → to immigrate → immigrant
	condition [kən'dɪʃn]	Bedingung; Zustand	The **conditions** were very hard.
	crowded ['kraʊdɪd]	überfüllt	**crowded** → crowd
	air [eə]	Luft	You have to put **air** in the tyres.
	to **move** [mu:v]	(sich) bewegen	I **moved** slowly aound the ship.
	harbor *(AE)* ['hɑ:bə]	Hafen	AE: **harbor** BE: harbour
	powerful ['paʊəfl]	stark; mächtig; bedeutend; beeindruckend	America is a **powerful** country.
	check [tʃek]	Kontrolle	**check** → to check
	disease [dɪ'zi:z]	Krankheit	Doctors checked for **diseases**.
	minority [maɪ'nɒrəti]	Minderheit	The **minority** of the people were OK.
p. 23	**percent (%)** [pə'sent]	Prozent	50 **percent** of ten is five.
	the rest [ðə 'rest]	der Rest	**The rest** of us left for our new life.
	Ireland ['aɪələnd]	Irland	Immigrants came from **Ireland**.
	Scandinavia [ˌskændɪ'neɪviə]	Skandinavien	Denmark is in **Scandinavia**.
	majority [mə'dʒɒrəti]	Mehrheit	**majority** ↔ minority
	Greece [gri:s]	Griechenland	**Greece** is in the south of Europe.
	Eastern Europe ['i:stn ˌjʊərəp]	Osteuropa	Poland is in **Eastern Europe**.
	Russia ['rʌʃə]	Russland	**Russia** is to the east of Germany.
	freedom *(no pl)* ['fri:dəm]	Freiheit; Unabhängigkeit	**Freedom** hat keine Mehrzahl.
	Mexico ['meksɪkəʊ]	Mexiko	R Мексика T Meksika
	China ['tʃaɪnə]	China	Achtung Aussprache!
	The Dominican Republic [ðə dəˌmɪnɪkn rɪ'pʌblɪk]	Dominikanische Republik	**The Dominican Republic** is to the east of Cuba.
	Vietnam [ˌvjet'næm]	Vietnam	**Vietnam** is south of China.

Film corner

p. 25	**once** [wʌns]	einst; einmal	at a time in the past
	honor *(AE)* ['ɒnə]	Ehre	There's a Wall of **Honor** on Ellis Island.
	great-grandparents [ˌgreɪt'grænˌpeərənts]	Urgroßeltern	My **great-grandparents** are my grandparents' parents.
	inside [ˌɪn'saɪd]	innen; drinnen	In summer it can get hot **inside**.

Checkpoint

Spanish ['spænɪʃ]	spanisch; Spanisch; aus Spanien	**ethnic** ['eθnɪk]	ethnisch; Volks-

Word bank: City guide

skyscraper

cathedral

tower

museum

gallery

station

bridge

building

monument

Over there you can see …
Don't miss …
Around this corner we'll come to …
Right/Straight ahead are …
You must visit …
In the distance you can see …
Have a look at/Look at …

Make sure you visit …
I'd like to point out …
Down there/Over there is …
From here …
… built it in …
It opened in …
It is special because …

Word bank: Presenting personal information

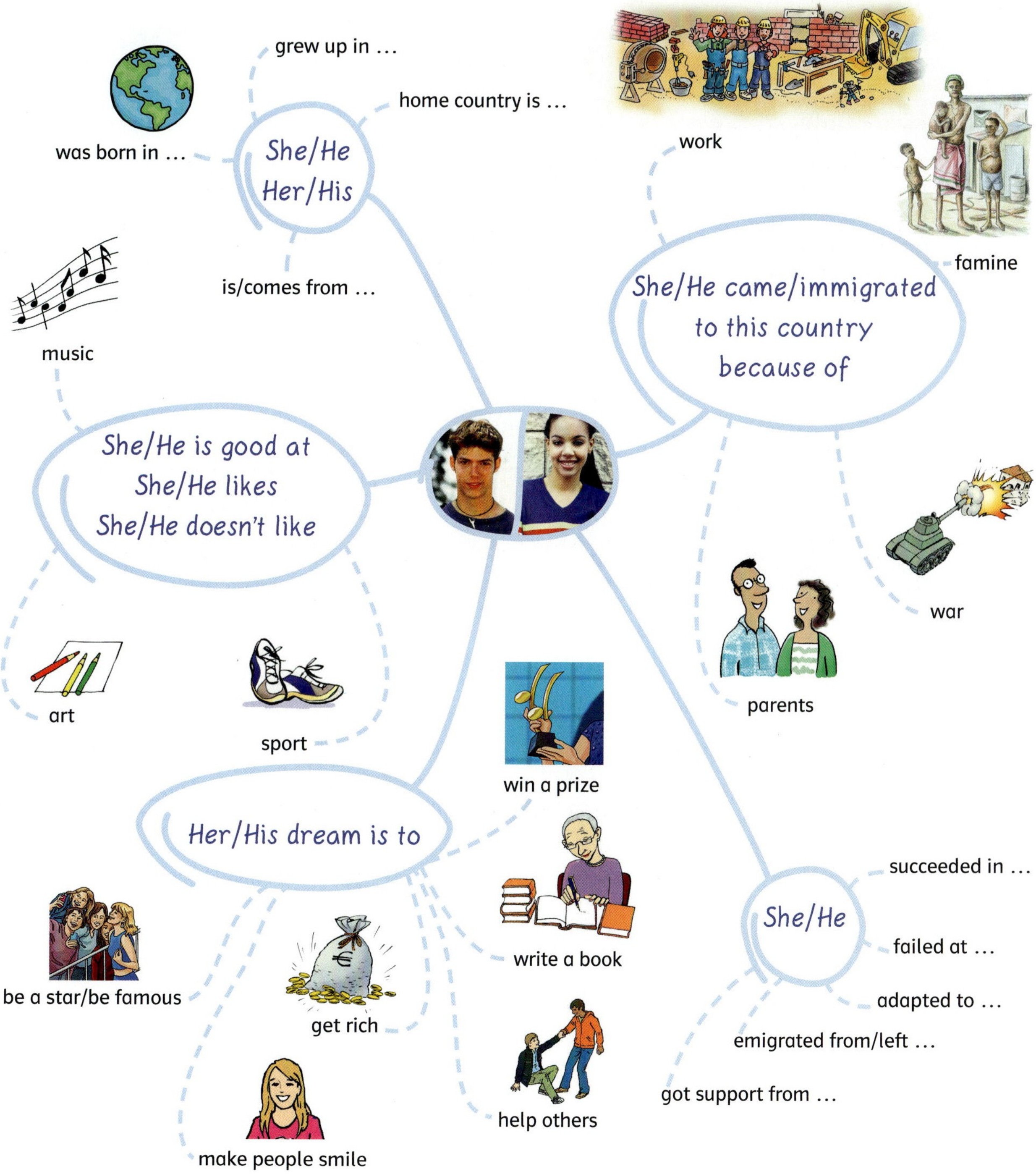

Unit 2 Teens in the Midwest

Way in

p. 32	**farmland** ['fɑ:mlænd]	Ackerland; Ackerboden; Landwirtschaftsflächen	You can see corn on **farmland** in the Midwest.
	storm [stɔ:m]	Sturm	The **storm** was awful. I was sick.
	European [ˌjʊərə'pi:ən]	europäisch; Europäisch; aus Europa; Europäer; Europäerin	T Avrupalı
	settler ['setlə]	Siedler; Siedlerin	Thousands of **settlers** came to the West.
	Native American [ˌneɪtɪv‿ə'merɪkən]	Ureinwohner Amerikas; Ureinwohnerin Amerikas; Indianer; Indianerin; indianisch	**Native Americans** live in the USA.
	reservation [ˌrezə'veɪʃn]	Reservat	We had to live on **reservations**.
p. 33	**store** *(AE)* [stɔ:]	Laden; Geschäft	AE: **store** BE: shop
	to clear [klɪə]	abräumen; ausräumen	I **clear** the tables in a café on Fridays.
	to serve [sɜ:v]	servieren	Sarah **serves** ice cream in the new café.
	grade *(AE)* [greɪd]	Note; Klasse	AE: **grade** BE: mark; class
	schedule *(AE)* ['skedʒu:l]	Stundenplan; Fahrplan	AE: **schedule** BE: timetable
	Homecoming *(AE)* ['həʊmˌkʌmɪŋ]	Ehemaligentreffen	The **Homecoming** Dance is always fun.
	to vote for ['vəʊt fə]	abstimmen über; wählen	
	tornado [tɔ:'neɪdəʊ]	Tornado; Wirbelsturm	R торнадо
	cloud [klaʊd]	Wolke	
	chaser ['tʃeɪsə]	Jäger; Jägerin; Verfolger; Verfolgerin	Warren is a storm **chaser**.
	warning ['wɔ:nɪŋ]	Warnung	There was a **warning** on the radio.

Station 1

At American schools

locker ['lɒkə]	Schließfach; Spind
morning message ['mɔ:nɪŋ ˌmesɪdʒ]	morgendliche Ansprache
principal *(AE)* ['prɪnsɪpl]	Schulleiter; Schulleiterin
class [klɑ:s]	Unterrichtsstunde; Kurs
Math *(AE)* [mæθ]	Mathematik; Mathe
study hall period ['stʌdi hɔ:l ˌpɪəriəd]	Freistunde
extracurricular [ˌekstrəkə'rɪkjələ]	außerhalb des Lehrplans; außerunterrichtlich *(Zusatzunterricht)*
cheerleader ['tʃɪəˌli:də]	Cheerleader *(Mädchen, das in einer Gruppe eine Sportmannschaft anfeuert)*
elective [ɪ'lektɪv]	Wahlfach
detention [dɪ'tenʃn]	Nachsitzen
core subject [ˌkɔ: 'sʌbdʒɪkt]	Pflichtfach
dress code ['dres ˌkəʊd]	Kleiderordnung; Bekleidungsvorschriften

p. 34	**exchange** [ɪks'tʃeɪndʒ]	Austausch	Luise did a student **exchange** in the USA.
	nowhere ['nəʊweə]	nirgendwo; nirgendwohin	We live in the middle of **nowhere**.
	way [weɪ]	Weg	I couldn't find the **way** to school.
	astronomy [ə'strɒnəmi]	Astronomie	R астрономия T astronomi
	journalism ['dʒɜ:nlɪzm]	Journalistik; Journalismus	R журналистика
	for example [fər‿ ɪg'zɑ:mpl]	zum Beispiel	I like fruit, **for example** apples.
	to **be allowed to (do sth)** [bi: ə'laʊd tə]	(etw.) dürfen	We **were allowed to** talk in class.
	strict [strɪkt]	streng; strikt	The school rules are very **strict**.
	competition [ˌkɒmpə'tɪʃn]	Konkurrenz	There was lots of **competition** for places.
	awesome ['ɔ:səm]	super; spitze	**awesome** = amazing, great
	host family ['həʊst ˌfæmli]	Gastfamilie	I really liked my **host family**.

V

Station 2

Describing people

helpful ['helpfl]	hilfsbereit	**generous** ['dʒenrəs]	großzügig
responsible [rɪs'pɒnsəbl]	verantwortlich; verantwortungsvoll	**rude** [ru:d]	unhöflich; unverschämt
hard-working [ˌhɑ:d'wɜ:kɪŋ]	fleißig	**selfish** ['selfɪʃ]	selbstsüchtig
unmotivated [ˌʌn'məʊtɪveɪtɪd]	unmotiviert	**shy** [ʃaɪ]	schüchtern

p. 38	**outside** [ˌaʊt'saɪd]	außerhalb	Extracurricular activites are **outside** school.
	to earn [ɜ:n]	verdienen	I have a job and **earn** money.
	driver's license *(AE)* ['draɪvəz ˌlaɪsns]	Führerschein	AE: **driver's license** BE: driving licence
	girlfriend ['gɜ:lfrend]	Freundin *(in einer Paarbeziehung)*	Sarah is Michael's **girlfriend**.
	job title ['dʒɒb ˌtaɪtl]	Stellenbezeichnung; Berufsbezeichnung	What is the **job title** of your new job?
	sales associate *(AE)* [ˌseɪlz ə'səʊʃiət]	Verkäufer; Verkäuferin	AE: **sales associate** BE: sales assistant
	education [ˌedʒʊ'keɪʃn]	Ausbildung; Erziehung; Bildung	My **education** was at the local school.
	to apply (for) [ə'plaɪ (fə)]	sich bewerben (für/um)	He **applied for** the student job.
	interview ['ɪntəvju:]	Vorstellungsgespräch	He had an **interview** on Thursday.
	manager ['mænɪdʒə]	Manager; Managerin; Geschäftsführer; Geschäftsführerin	R менеджер
	somebody ['sʌmbədi]	jemand	**somebody** ↔ nobody
	to steal [sti:l], **stole** [stəʊl], **stolen** ['stəʊlən]	stehlen	I saw the boy **steal** a T-shirt.
	to offer ['ɒfə]	anbieten	The manager **offered** Michael the job.
	minimum ['mɪnɪməm]	Minimum; minimal; Mindest-	T minimum
	wage [weɪdʒ]	Lohn	He earned the minimum **wage**.
	co-worker ['kəʊˌwɜ:kə]	Arbeitskollege; Arbeitskollegin	My **co-workers** are friendly.
	to tease [ti:z]	hänseln; sticheln; reizen	People came in and **teased** Michael.
	to throw [θrəʊ], **threw** [θru:], **thrown** [θrəʊn]	werfen	He **threw** them out of the store.
p. 39	**working hours** *(pl)* ['wɜ:kɪŋ ˌaʊəz]	Arbeitszeit	9:00 to 5:00 are my **working hours**.

	feedback ['fi:dbæk]	Feedback; Rückmeldung	She got good **feedback**.
	best-paying [ˌbest'peɪɪŋ]	bestbezahlt	This is the **best-paying** job I've ever had.
p. 41	**dog walker** ['dɒg ˌwɔ:kə]	Hundeausführer; Hundeausführerin	a person who takes dogs for a walk
	per [pɜ:]	pro	I earn $40 **per** week.
	babysitter ['beɪbɪˌsɪtə]	Babysitter; Babysitterin	a person who looks after children
	paperboy ['peɪpəˌbɔɪ]	Zeitungsausträger	I'm Dave, I'm a **paperboy**.
	papergirl ['peɪpəˌgɜ:l]	Zeitungsausträgerin	A paperboy or **papergirl** works every day.

Reading corner

p. 42	**date** [deɪt]	Verabredung; Date	They went on their first **date**.
	boyfriend ['bɔɪfrend]	Freund *(in einer Paarbeziehung)*	**boyfriend** ↔ girlfriend
	shy [ʃaɪ]	schüchtern	I like her, but I'm too **shy** to tell her.
	to **ask sb out** [ˌɑ:sk … 'aʊt]	sich mit jmdm. verabreden	Dylan **asked Abby out** on a date.
	guy [gaɪ]	Typ; Kerl	Who is the **guy** in the hall?
	to **fall out of** [ˌfɔ:l‿'aʊt‿əv]	herausfallen aus	All my books **fell out of** my locker.
	right [raɪt]	gerade; genau; in dem Moment als	It happened **right** when he walked past.
	to **show up** [ˌʃəʊ‿'ʌp]	auftauchen; erscheinen	He **showed up** late for school.
	embarrassing [ɪm'bærəsɪŋ]	peinlich	It was so **embarrassing**, I went red.
	gym(nasium) [dʒɪm (dʒɪm'neɪziəm)]	Turnhalle	the room in a school where PE lessons are
	to **attack** [ə'tæk]	angreifen	The boys **attacked** him in the gym.
p. 43	to **pick up** [ˌpɪk‿'ʌp]	abholen	Dylan **picked** Abby **up** at seven o'clock.
	everybody ['evribɒdi]	jeder; alle	**everybody** = everyone
	dancing ['dɑ:nsɪŋ]	Tanzen; Tanz-	T dans
	to **take** [teɪk]	bringen; hinbringen	Dylan **took** Abby home.
	stereotype ['steriəʊtaɪp]	Stereotyp; Klischee	Which **stereotypes** do you know from movies?

Film corner

p. 45	**buddy** *(infml)* ['bʌdi]	Kumpel	David is my best **buddy**.
	homeroom ['həʊmru:m]	erste Stunde *(in der Schule)*	We are in the same **homeroom**.
	detention [dɪ'tenʃn]	Nachsitzen	I haven't had **detention** this year.

pledge of allegiance [ˌpledʒ‿əv‿əˈliːdʒns]	Treueeid	We say the **pledge of allegiance** every morning.

Checkpoint

to interest [ˈɪntrəst]	interessieren	to elect [ɪˈlekt]	wählen

Presentation skills

p. 51 **presentation** [ˌpreznˈteɪʃn]	Präsentation; Vortrag	My **presentation** is about cats.
topic [ˈtɒpɪk]	Thema	My next **topic** is the rules of the game.

Word bank: Comparing schools

dress code

cheerleading

marching band

pledge of allegiance

school bus

locker

Homecoming Dance

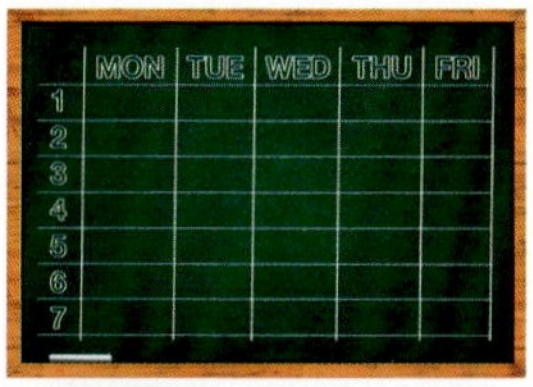

schedule

grade

hall pass

class

I would like to compare …
In/At American high schools …
In/At German schools …
Both countries have detention/principals/…

In America there is … but not in Germany.
… is the same.
… is different.

Word bank: Jobs

waitress

waiter

serve ice cream

work on a market stall

shop assistant

wash up in a café/
restaurant

babysitter

dog walker

paperboy/girl

help in the garden/
mow the lawn

do the shopping for
people

I earn …
I work inside/outside.
I work every day/at the weekends/in the holidays/on …
I work in the mornings/afternoons/evenings.
I start work at …

I like it/don't like it because …
I'm a … person.
It's hard/easy work.
It's fun/boring.
I work with nice/interesting/fun/strange/quiet/… people.

Unit 3 In the Northeast

Way in

p. 52	**border** ['bɔ:də]	Grenze	There is a **border** between two countries.
	to **drive** [draɪv], **drove** [drəʊv], **driven** ['drɪvn]	fahren; treiben	You can **drive** through the beautiful woods.
	celebration [ˌseləˈbreɪʃn]	Feier	**celebration** → to celebrate
p. 53	**Thanksgiving** [ˌθæŋksˈgɪvɪŋ]	Erntedankfest	**Thanksgiving** is the 4th Thursday in November.
	turkey ['tɜ:ki]	Truthahn; Pute	
	dinner ['dɪnə]	Essen	meals: breakfast, lunch, **dinner**
	president ['prezɪdnt]	Präsident; Präsidentin	R президент
	to **pardon** ['pɑ:dn]	begnadigen; entschuldigen; verzeihen	The President **pardons** a turkey.
	favorite *(AE)* ['feɪvrɪt]	Lieblings-	AE: **favorite** BE: favourite
	creepy ['kri:pi]	gruselig	**Creepy** films are often made in Maine.
	forest ['fɒrɪst]	Wald	
	land of the free [ˌlænd‿əv ðə 'fri:]	Land der Freien	The USA is called the **land of the free**.
	the Amish [ði 'ɑ:mɪʃ]	die Amischen	**The Amish** don't have mobile phones.
	Christian ['krɪstʃn]	christlich	T Hıristiyan
	daredevil ['deəˌdevl]	Draufgänger; Draufgängerin	The **daredevil** did dangerous tricks.
	stuntman ['stʌntmæn]	Stuntman	**Stuntmen** work in films.
	close [kləʊs]	in der Nähe; nahe	It's **close**, not far from here.
	barrel ['bærl]	Fass; Tonne	
	to **sign autographs** [ˌsaɪn 'ɔ:təgrɑ:fs]	Autogramme geben	The actor **signed autographs** for us.

Station 1

Small talk

What's up? [ˌwɒts‿'ʌp]	Wie geht's?	How are things going? [ˌhaʊ ɑ: θɪŋz 'gəʊɪŋ]	Wie läuft's?; Wie geht's?
How's it going? [ˌhaʊz‿ɪt 'gəʊɪŋ]	Wie geht's?; Wie läuft's?		

V

p. 54	to **get ready** [ˌget ˈredi]	sich vorbereiten; sich fertig machen	We have to **get ready** for the party.
	husband [ˈhʌzbənd]	Ehemann	My **husband** is in the kitchen.
	to **get stuck** [ˌget ˈstʌk]	stecken bleiben	I **got stuck** in the snow for two hours.
	doorbell [ˈdɔːbel]	Türklingel	
	neighbor *(AE)* [ˈneɪbə]	Nachbar; Nachbarin	AE: **neighbor** BE: neighbour
	glad [glæd]	froh	We were **glad** you liked the flowers.
	make it [ˈmeɪk‿ɪt]	es schaffen	I'm glad you could **make it**.
	to **enter** [ˈentə]	hineingehen; hereinkommen; betreten; eintreten	**to enter** ↔ to leave
	across [əˈkrɒs]	über; hinüber; herüber; quer durch	He looked **across** the room at me.
	chocolate [ˈtʃɒklət]	Praline	T çikolata 
	to **land** [lænd]	landen	Our plane **lands** at seven o'clock.
	to **promise** [ˈprɒmɪs]	versprechen	I **promise** we will wait for you.
	to **save** [seɪv]	aufheben	We will **save** you some turkey.
p. 55	**Please have a seat.** [ˌpliːz hæv‿ə‿ˈsiːt]	Bitte Platz nehmen.	Come in. **Please have a seat.**

Station 2

Agreeing and disagreeing

Exactly. [ɪgˈzæktli]	Genau.	I guess ... [aɪ ˈges]	Ich nehme an, dass ...
Absolutely not. [ˌæbsəˈluːtli nɒt]	Ganz und gar nicht.; Auf keinen Fall!	I'm convinced that ... [ˌaɪm kənˈvɪnst ðət]	Ich bin überzeugt, dass ...
As far as I know, ... [ˌəz ˈfɑːr‿əz‿aɪ nəʊ]	Soweit ich weiß, ...	It's clear to me that ... [ɪts ˈklɪə tə ˌmiː ðæt]	Mir ist klar, dass ...

Devices

device [dɪˈvaɪs]	Gerät; Vorrichtung	dishwasher [ˈdɪʃˌwɒʃə]	Spülmaschine
microwave [ˈmaɪkrəweɪv]	Mikrowelle	vacuum cleaner [ˈvækjuːm ˌkliːnə]	Staubsauger
headphones *(pl)* [ˈhedfəʊnz]	Kopfhörer	razor [ˈreɪzə]	Rasierer; Rasierapparat
fan [fæn]	Ventilator	radiator [ˈreɪdieɪtə]	Heizkörper

p. 58	**Amish** ['ɑːmɪʃ]	amisch	We live in an **Amish** community.
	to **concentrate** ['kɒnsntreɪt]	(sich) konzentrieren	This is hard. I have to **concentrate**.
	to **cover** ['kʌvə]	bedecken; abdecken	Amish girls often **cover** their hair. 
	make-up ['meɪkʌp]	Make-up; Schminke	T makyaj
	to **grow** [grəʊ], **grew** [gruː], **grown** [grəʊn]	anbauen; züchten; ziehen; wachsen	We **grow** our own vegetables.
	forbidden [fə'bɪdn]	verboten	I never do **forbidden** things. 
	alcohol *(no pl)* ['ælkəhɒl]	Alkohol	R алкоголь T alkol
	average ['ævrɪdʒ]	durchschnittlich	I'm an **average** American teenager.
	fashion *(no pl)* ['fæʃn]	Mode	I love clothes and the newest **fashion**.
	gossip ['gɒsɪp]	Klatsch; Tratsch; Gerede	I read the **gossip** about the stars too.
	to **go out with** [ˌgəʊ‿'aʊt wɪð]	(aus)gehen mit	She's **going out with** him.
	whom [huːm]	wem; wen	They ask who has a date with **whom**. 
	bowling ['bəʊlɪŋ]	Bowlen	R боулинг T bowling
p. 59	**electric** [ɪ'lektrɪk]	elektrisch	T elektrik
p. 61	**before** [bɪ'fɔː]	vor	**before** ↔ after 
	alien ['eɪliən]	Außerirdischer; Außerirdische	

Reading corner

p. 62	**body** ['bɒdi]	Leiche	There was a man's **body** on the beach.
	to **disappear** [ˌdɪsə'pɪə]	verschwinden	The man **disappeared** two weeks ago.
	gun [gʌn]	Schusswaffe	He had a **gun** in his hand. 
	blanket ['blæŋkɪt]	Decke; Bettdecke; Wolldecke	
	back [bæk]	Hinter-	We went in the **back** door.
	clubhouse ['klʌbhaʊs]	Klubhaus; Vereinsheim	We meet at the **clubhouse** on Tuesdays.
	backpack ['bækpæk]	Rucksack	  
	desk [desk]	Schreibtisch	
	wine [waɪn]	Wein	
	drunk [drʌŋk]	betrunken	After one glass of wine he was **drunk**.
p. 63	**bullet** ['bʊlɪt]	Kugel; Geschoss	There are no **bullets** in the gun.
	sat [sæt]	simple past, past participle von *to sit* (sitzen)	I **sat** = ich saß/ich habe gesessen

	tin [tɪn]	Dose; Büchse; *hier:* Mülleimer	
	to jump [dʒʌmp]	springen	
	to shoot (at) [ʃuːt (ət)], **shot (at)** [ʃɒt (ət)], **shot (at)** [ʃɒt (ət)]	schießen (auf)	He **shot** at the bottles on the wall.
	wrist [rɪst]	Handgelenk	It is between your hand and your arm.
	to scream [skriːm]	schreien; kreischen	Don't **scream**. I can hear you.
	wild [waɪld]	wild	There are **wild** animals at the zoo.
	amused [ə'mjuːzd]	amüsiert; vergnügt	Was Chris **amused** or scared?
	to shut up [ˌʃʌt‿'ʌp]	die Klappe halten	**Shut up** and listen to me!
	by [baɪ]	an	He grabbed me **by** the shirt.
	mean [miːn]	gemein	He was really **mean** to us.
	honestly ['ɒnɪstli]	ehrlich	**Honestly**, I didn't know it was broken.
	innocent ['ɪnəsnt]	unschuldig	He didn't do it, he is **innocent**.
	whole [həʊl]	ganz	We spent the **whole** week there.
	nothing ['nʌθɪŋ]	nichts	**nothing** ↔ something
	to stand up [ˌstænd‿'ʌp]	aufstehen; stehen	He **stood up** and left the room.
p. 64	to gather ['gæðə]	(sich) sammeln	We **gathered** round him and listened.
	railway track ['reɪlweɪ ˌtræk]	Gleis	We went across the bridge on the **railway tracks**.
	scared [skeəd]	verängstigt	I was **scared** in the dark.

Film corner

p. 67	**pecan** ['piːkæn]	Pekannuss	**Pecan** pie is my favourite pie.
	pardon ['pɑːdn]	Begnadigung; Entschuldigung; Verzeihung	The President's **pardon** is for a turkey.

Checkpoint

out [aʊt]	aus; draußen; außerhalb	to control [kən'trəʊl]	kontrollieren

Writing skills

p. 73	**to sum up** [ˌsʌm‿'ʌp]	zusammenfassen	To **sum up** you can say this food is better.

Word bank: **Giving opinions**

- I agree with the statement …
- I agree with you.
- I think you're right (there).
- That's true.
- I think so because …
- In my opinion …
- I think …

- I also think that … because …
- So my answer is …
- I tried it when I was …
- One reason is …
- Another reason is …
- To conclude I would like to say …
- It had an impact on my life because …

- I don't agree/disagree with the statement …
- I don't agree/disagree with you.
- That's false.
- I don't think so because …
- In my opinion …
- I think …

- You can't be serious!
- I think you're wrong (there).
- I tried it when I was …
- Another reason is …
- One reason is …
- To conclude I would like to say …
- It had an impact/influence on my life because …

Unit 4 California dreams

Way in

p. 74	**giant** [dʒaɪənt]	Riesen-; riesig	Look at the **giant** sandwiches.
	redwood (tree) ['redwʊd (tri:)]	Mammutbaum	
	relaxed [rɪ'lækst]	entspannt; locker; gelassen	People are very **relaxed** in California.
	lifestyle ['laɪfstaɪl]	Lebensart; Lifestyle	the way you live your life
	surfing ['sɜ:fɪŋ]	Wellenreiten; Surfen	I love **surfing** in the summer.
	volleyball ['vɒlibɔ:l]	Volleyball	R волейбол T voleybol
	cable car ['keɪbl ˌkɑ:]	Seilbahn	
	hill [hɪl]	Berg; Hügel	
	Asia ['eɪʒə]	Asien	R азия T Asya
p. 75	**number** ['nʌmbə]	Anzahl	There are a **number** of big museums.
	high-tech [ˌhaɪ'tek]	Hightech-	I work for a **high-tech** company.
	studio ['stju:diəʊ]	Studio	They make movies in **studios**.
	safety net ['seɪfti ˌnet]	Sicherheitsnetz	There's a **safety net** to catch you.
	bay [beɪ]	Bucht	
	architect ['ɑ:kɪtekt]	Architekt; Architektin	R архитектор

Station 1

Adjectives for ads

informative [ɪn'fɔ:mətɪv]	informativ	**fascinating** ['fæsɪneɪtɪŋ]	faszinierend
clear [klɪə]	klar; eindeutig; deutlich	**unusual** [ʌn'ju:ʒl]	ungewöhnlich; außergewöhnlich
spectacular [spek'tækjələ]	spektakulär	**appealing** [ə'pi:lɪŋ]	ansprechend
catchy ['kætʃi]	eingängig; einprägsam	**unappealing** [ˌʌnə'pi:lɪŋ]	uninteressant

p. 76	**ad(vert) (advertisement)** ['æd(vɜ:t) (əd'vɜ:tɪsmənt)]	Annonce; Werbespot	I saw an **advert** for a student job.
	surfboard ['sɜ:fbɔ:d]	Surfbrett	I have a new **surfboard**. Let's go surfing!
	to chill out [ˌtʃɪl‿'aʊt]	chillen; sich entspannen	**Chill out** in sunny California.

	reservation [ˌrezəˈveɪʃn]	Reservierung	T rezervasyon
	to **book** [bʊk]	buchen; reservieren	We booked our **flights** yesterday.
	lifetime [ˈlaɪftaɪm]	Leben; Lebenszeit	It will be the holiday of a **lifetime**.
	tour [tʊə]	Tour; Fahrt; Reise	We went on the Grand Canyon **tour**.
p. 77	**layout** [ˈleɪaʊt]	Layout; Anordnung	Look at the **layout** of this ad.
	headline [ˈhedlaɪn]	Überschrift; Schlagzeile	We need a good **headline** for our ad.

Station 2

Social media

social media [ˌsəʊʃl ˈmiːdiə]	soziale Medien
account [əˈkaʊnt]	Konto
to **post** [pəʊst]	online stellen; posten
video [ˈvɪdiəʊ]	Video
tutorial [tjuːˈtɔːriəl]	Anleitung; Tutorial
to **stream** [striːm]	*hier:* streamen *(im Internet)*
smartphone [ˈsmɑːtˌfəʊn]	Smartphone
site [saɪt]	*hier:* Seite *(im Internet)*
cyberbullying [ˈsaɪbəˌbʊliŋ]	Cyber-Mobbing
to **dislike** [dɪˈslaɪk]	nicht mögen
to **friend** [frend]	befreunden *(jmdn. zu seiner Freundesliste hinzufügen)*
to **unfriend** [ʌnˈfrend]	entfreunden *(jmdn. von seiner Freundesliste streichen)*
to **subscribe** [səbˈskraɪb]	abonnieren
to **update** [ˈʌpdeɪt]	updaten; auf den neuesten Stand bringen
status [ˈsteɪtəs]	Status
selfie [ˈselfi]	Selfie *(Schnappschuss von sich selbst)*

p. 80	to **welcome** [ˈwelkəm]	willkommen heißen	California **welcomes** new ideas.
	for [fɔː]	seit	I have lived here **for** two months.
	to **be around** [biː əˈraʊnd]	geben; existieren	The WWW has **been around** for 30 years.
	since [sɪns]	seit; seitdem	I have lived here **since** March.
	trend [trend]	Trend; Entwicklung; Richtung	There are always new **trends** to follow.
	impact [ˈɪmpækt]	Einfluss; Auswirkung	Social media had a big **impact** on us.
	instead [ɪnˈsted]	stattdessen; anstelle von	I don't like ham, let's have cheese **instead**.
	half *(sg)* [hɑːf], **halves** *(pl)* [hɑːvz]	(die) Hälfte	**half** a lemon 
	several [ˈsevrl]	einige; mehrere; verschiedene	**several** = three or more, but not many
	right away [ˌraɪt‿əˈweɪ]	sofort; gleich	I answer my messages **right away**.

p. 81	**jumping fitness** ['dʒʌmpɪŋ ˌfɪtnəs]	Jumping Fitness *(Trendsportart)*	**Jumping fitness** is a new sport.
	outdated [ˌaʊt'deɪtɪd]	veraltet	Listening to CDs is very **outdated.**
	cartoon [kɑ:'tu:n]	Cartoon; Zeichentrickfilm	The **cartoon** was so funny, wasn't it?
p. 83	**torn** [tɔ:n]	zerrissen; aufgerissen	The jeans are **torn.** 
	veganism *(no pl)* ['vi:gənɪzm]	Veganismus	T veganizm

Reading corner

p. 84	**gold rush** ['gəʊld ˌrʌʃ]	Goldrausch	Everyone wanted gold in the **gold rush.**
	report [rɪ'pɔ:t]	Bericht	T rapor
	to confirm [kən'fɜ:m]	bestätigen; bekräftigen	Can you **confirm** when you arrive?
	discovery [dɪ'skʌvri]	Entdeckung	I made an awesome **discovery** – gold!
	Swiss [swɪs]	schweizerisch; aus der Schweiz; Schweizer; Schweizerin	He was a **Swiss** immigrant.
	businessman ['bɪznɪsmæn]	Geschäftsmann	R бизнесмен
	official [ə'fɪʃl]	offiziell	It was his **official** name.
	landowner ['lændˌəʊnə]	Grundbesitzer; Grundbesitzerin	He owns the land, he's the **landowner.**
	to allow [ə'laʊ]	erlauben; gestatten	He didn't **allow** us to say anything.
	to prove [pru:v]	beweisen	He has to **prove** he owns the land.
p. 85	**hunter** ['hʌntə]	Jäger; Jägerin	Gold **hunters** came to California.
	rain [reɪn]	Regen	**rain** → to rain 
	jungle ['dʒʌŋgl]	Dschungel	
	wilderness ['wɪldənəs]	Wildnis	Our camp was in the **wilderness.**
	all over [ˌɔ:l‿'əʊvə]	überall	There's food **all over** the floor.
	to return [rɪ'tɜ:n]	zurückkehren	My friends had to **return** home.
	love [lʌv]	Liebe	**love** → to love
	to keep going [ki:p 'gəʊɪŋ]	weitergehen; weitermachen	I will **keep going** until I find more gold.
	prayer [preə]	Gebet	Say a **prayer** for me on Sunday.
	wife *(sg)* [waɪf], **wives** *(pl)* [waɪvz]	Ehefrau	**wife** ↔ husband
p. 86	**encyclopedia** *(AE)* [ɪnˌsaɪklə'pi:diə]	Enzyklopädie; Lexikon	✎ Achtung Schreibweise! en<u>cyc</u>lop<u>edia</u>
	entry ['entri]	Eintrag	What does the **entry** for Gold Rush say?
	event [ɪ'vent]	Ereignis; Veranstaltung	Many people watched the **events.**

transcontinental [ˌtrænsˌkɒntɪ'nentl]	transkontinental *(über den Kontinent hinweg)*	**Transcontinental** trains make long journeys.
railway ['reɪlweɪ]	Eisenbahn	
slave [sleɪv]	Sklave; Sklavin	There were **slaves** before the Civil War.
fever ['fi:və]	Fieber	The gold rush is also called gold **fever**.
to last [lɑ:st]	dauern; andauern; anhalten	My headache **lasted** for hours.
empty ['emti]	leer	**empty** ↔ full

Film corner

p. 89 **helper** ['helpə]	Helfer; Helferin	**helper** → to help → help
as soon as [əz 'su:n‿əz]	sobald	**as soon as** → soon
regular ['regjələ]	regelmäßig; normal; üblich; gleichmäßig	I work **regular** hours in my job.
to **respect** [rɪ'spekt]	respektieren	I love and **respect** animals.
energetic [ˌenə'dʒetɪk]	tatkräftig	I am **energetic** and fit for the job.
practical ['præktɪkl]	praktisch	I like making things, I'm **practical**.
attitude ['ætɪtju:d]	Einstellung; Haltung	I have a practical **attitude** to work.
waitress ['weɪtrəs]	Kellnerin; Bedienung	She is a **waitress** in the new café.
groceries *(pl)* ['grəʊsriz]	Lebensmittel	We buy our **groceries** at the supermarket.

Checkpoint

technology [tek'nɒlədʒi]	Technologie	Japan [dʒə'pæn]	Japan
entertainment *(no pl)* [ˌentə'teɪnmənt]	Unterhaltung	bamboo [ˌbæm'bu:]	Bambus

Communication skills

p. 94 **podcast** ['pɒdkɑ:st]	Podcast	I got the new **podcast** last night.
Thanks so much. [ˌθæŋk‿səʊ 'mʌtʃ]	Vielen Dank.; Herzlichen Dank.	**Thanks so much** for your help!
to **interrupt** [ˌɪntə'rʌpt]	unterbrechen	I have to **interrupt** here.

Word bank: Talking about a region

Which region?

north

west  east

south

How many people live in the region/visit the region?

thousands millions billions

What does it look like?

mountains

beach

countryside

town

city

coastline

What can you do there?

museum

amusement park

zoo

church

skiing

shopping

hiking

sightseeing

It's in the … of …
It's near the …
There are …
There is …

… people live in the region/visit the region.
I like it because …
It's nice/quiet/busy/beautiful/…

Unit 5 Southern Life

p. 96	**southern** ['sʌðən]	südlich	**northern** ↔ southern

Way in

	African American [ˌæfrɪkən əˈmerɪkən]	Afroamerikaner; Afroamerikanerin	There were lots of **African Americans** in the South.
	right [raɪt]	Recht	African Americans wanted the same **rights**.
	civil rights *(pl)* [ˌsɪvl 'raɪts]	Bürgerrechte	They fought for **civil rights** in the 1950s.
	movement ['mu:vmənt]	Bewegung	The Civil Rights **Movement** changed people's rights.
	peaceful ['pi:sfl]	friedlich	Protests aren't always **peaceful**.
	protest ['prəʊtest]	Protest; Demonstration	R протест
p. 97	**plantation** [plæn'teɪʃn]	Plantage	People had to work on the **plantations**.
	Southerner ['sʌðnə]	Südstaatler; Südstaatlerin	**Southern** → south → southern
	charts *(pl only)* [tʃɑ:ts]	*hier:* Hitparade	There are **charts** for different types of music.
	best-paid ['bestˌpeɪd]	bestbezahlt	He is the **best-paid** actor.

Station 1

Nationalities

the **French** *(pl)* [ðə 'frenʃ]	die Franzosen	**Russian** ['rʌʃn]	russisch; Russisch; aus Russland; Russe; Russin
Spanish ['spænɪʃ]	spanisch; Spanisch; aus Spanien	**Polish** ['pəʊlɪʃ]	polnisch; Polnisch; aus Polen
Vietnamese [ˌvjetnə'mi:z]	vietnamesisch; Vietnamesisch; aus Vietnam; Vietnamese; Vietnamesin	**Turkish** ['tɜ:kɪʃ]	türkisch; Türkisch; aus der Türkei
Chinese [tʃaɪ'ni:z]	chinesisch; Chinesisch; aus China; Chinese; Chinesin	**Japanese** [ˌdʒæpən'i:z]	japanisch; Japanisch; aus Japan; Japaner; Japanerin
Greek [gri:k]	griechisch; Griechisch; aus Griechenland		

Conflicts and solutions

to **tolerate** ['tɒlreɪt]	tolerieren; dulden	to **accept** [ək'sept]	akzeptieren; annehmen; hinnehmen
solution [sə'lu:ʃn]	Lösung	**conflict** ['kɒnflɪkt]	Konflikt; Auseinandersetzung
compromise ['kɒmprəmaɪz]	Kompromiss	to **refuse** [rɪ'fju:z]	ablehnen; sich weigern

p. 98	**influence** ['ɪnfluəns]	Einfluss	He is a bad **influence** on her.
	example [ɪg'zɑ:mpl]	Beispiel	Give me an **example** of a good book.
	to **mix** [mɪks]	mischen; vermischen; mixen	If you **mix** blue and yellow, you get green.
	to **dry** [draɪ]	trocknen	**to dry** → dry
	to **cover in flour** [ˌkʌvər‿ɪn 'flaʊə]	in Mehl wenden	First **cover** the chicken **in flour**.
	to **fry** [fraɪ]	braten; frittieren	
	oil [ɔɪl]	Öl	
	golden ['gəʊldn]	golden; Gold-	California is called 'The **Golden** State'.
	to **found** [faʊnd]	gründen	They **founded** the city in 1718.
	multicultural [ˌmʌlti'kʌltʃrl]	multikulturell	The south is a **multicultural** area.
	carnival ['kɑ:nɪvl]	Karneval; Fasching	R карнавал T karnaval
	State House *(AE)* ['steɪt ˌhaʊs]	Regierungsgebäude	The US flag flies over the **State House**.
	pride [praɪd]	Stolz	This flag is a symbol of **pride**.
	racism ['reɪsɪzm]	Rassismus	Some say the flag is a symbol of **racism**.
	state government ['steɪt ˌgʌvnmənt]	Landesregierung	Protesters confronted the **state government**.
	to **remove** [rɪ'mu:v]	entfernen	I **removed** the plaster from my knee.

Station 2

Understanding things

I didn't get that. [aɪ ˌdɪdnt 'get ðæt]	Ich habe es nicht verstanden.	**I didn't catch that.** [aɪ ˌdɪdnt 'kætʃ ðæt]	Das habe ich nicht verstanden.; Das habe ich nicht gehört.
I know what you mean. [aɪ ˌnəʊ wɒt jə 'mi:n]	Ich verstehe, was du meinst.	**Absolutely!** [ˌæbsə'lu:tli]	Auf jeden Fall!
I see. [aɪ 'si:]	Ich verstehe.		

p. 102	**package** ['pækɪdʒ]	Paket	T paket 
	transfer [træns'fɜ:]	Transport; Transfer	There is a free **transfer** by bus.
	track [træk]	Strecke	The race **track** isn't far away. 
	booklet ['bʊklət]	Broschüre; Heft	
	detail ['di:teɪl]	Detail; Einzelheit	T detay
	airboat ['eəbəʊt]	Propellerboot	We can go on an **airboat** there.
	wildlife ['waɪldlaɪf]	Tierwelt *(in freier Wildbahn)*	There is lots of **wildlife** in Florida.
	show [ʃəʊ]	Show; Schau; Aufführung	There is a **show** every 30 minutes.
	pick-up ['pɪkʌp]	Abholung; Pick-up	Look, there is a free hotel **pick-up** too.
	trail [treɪl]	Wanderweg; Spur	There is a **trail** through the swamps.
	the wild [ðə 'waɪld]	Wildnis; freie Wildbahn	I've never seen a cat in **the wild**.
	heat [hi:t]	Hitze	This **heat** is too much for me.
	speech impaired ['spi:tʃ ɪmˌpeərd]	sprachbehindert	He can't speak, he's **speech impaired**.
	to **translate** [trænz'leɪt]	übersetzen	I can **translate** the text for you.
p. 103	**trainer** ['treɪnə]	Trainer; Trainerin	The **trainer** fed the alligators.

Reading corner

p. 106	**segregation** [ˌsegrɪ'geɪʃn]	Rassentrennung; Trennung	Not everyone believed in **segregation**.
	African-American [ˌæfrɪkənə'merɪkən]	afroamerikanisch	Obama was the first **African-American** president of the USA.
	to **get on (the bus)** [ˌget‿'ɒn]	einsteigen (in den Bus)	A police officer **got on** the bus.
	full [fʊl]	voll	**full** ↔ empty
	seat [si:t]	Sitz; Sitzplatz	If we book early, we'll get good seats.
	back [bæk]	Hinterteil	We moved to the **back** of the bus.

V

p. 107	to **drag** [dræg]	schleppen; schleifen; ziehen	They **dragged** him away from the dog.
	off [ɒf]	von … weg	They pulled the dog **off** the man.
	to **arrest** [ə'rest]	festnehmen; verhaften	She was **arrested** by the police.
	success [sək'ses]	Erfolg	**success** → successful
	court case ['kɔːt ˌkeɪs]	Gerichtsverhandlung; Rechtsfall	The **court case** ended segregation.
	witness ['wɪtnəs]	Zeuge; Zeugin	She saw it, she was a **witness**.
	to **end** [end]	enden	The court case **ended** segregation.
	role [rəʊl]	Rolle	I played an important **role** in the fight.
	courage ['kʌrɪdʒ]	Mut; Tapferkeit; Courage	She showed a lot of **courage** on the bus.

Film corner

p. 109	**reliable** [rɪ'laɪəbl]	verlässlich; zuverlässig; vertrauenswürdig	She's very **reliable**. She's always on time.
	to **trust** [trʌst]	vertrauen	She's reliable and you can **trust** her.

Checkpoint

feature story ['fiːtʃə ˌstɔːri]	Leitartikel; Sonderbericht

Word bank: Talking about culture

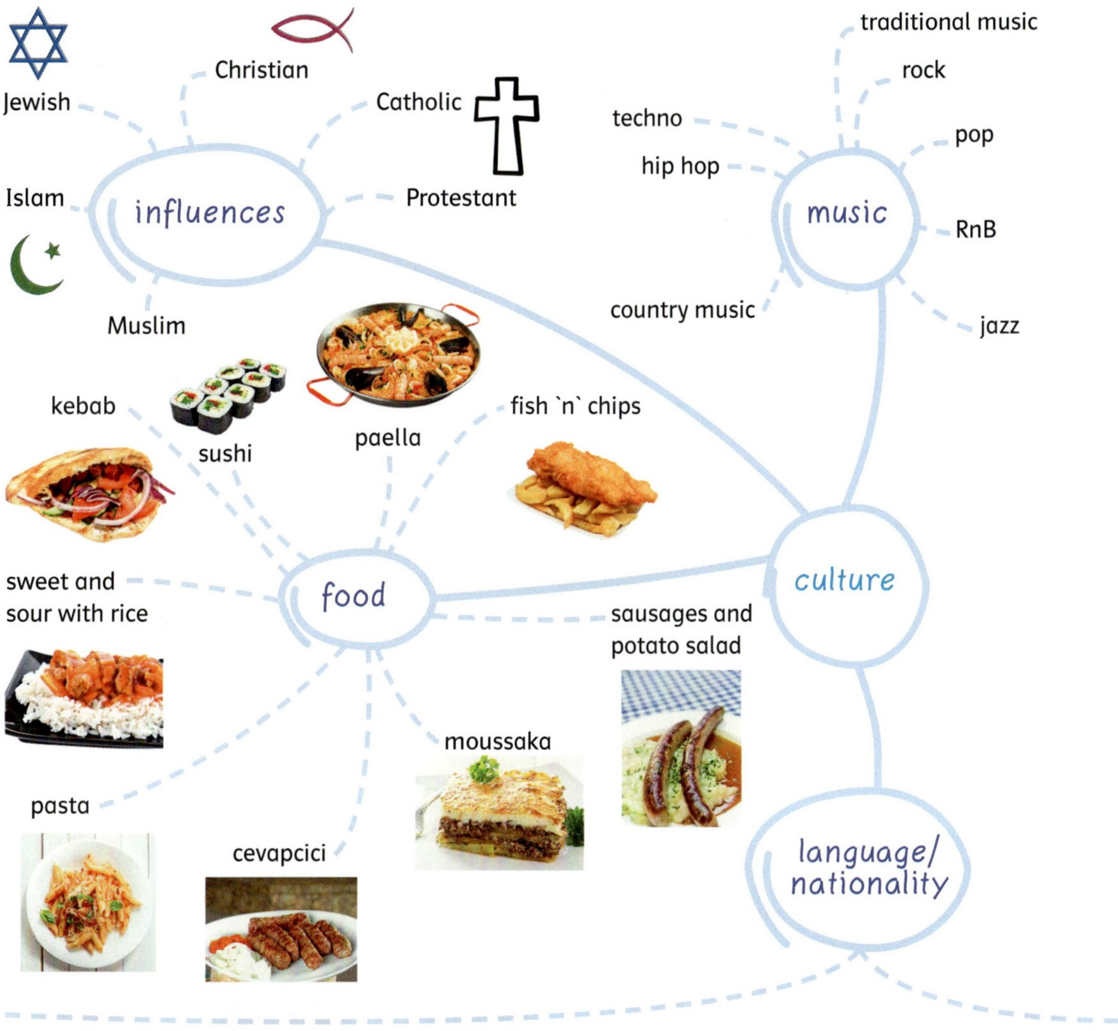

V

Word bank: A day trip

opening times

all day   half day
from 9:00 a.m. until 5:00 p.m.
weekends only
last entry one hour before closing time
afternoons/morning only
closed on Mondays

tickets

adults	£ 10.00
children (under 14)	£ 5.00
senior citizens/OAPs	£ 5.00
students	£ 5.00
family (2 adults + 2 children)	£ 17.50

places

museum

zoo

amusement/
theme park

city

beach

transport

coach

train

tram

car

bike

boat

activities

hiking

sightseeing

fishing

a guided tour

cycling

Instructions

Arbeitsanweisungen mit Operatoren

Act the dialogue • the role play.	**Spielt** den Dialog • das Rollenspiel.
Add more words.	**Ergänze** mehr Wörter.
Answer the questions.	**Beantworte** die Fragen.
Ask a partner.	**Frage** eine Partnerin / einen Partner.
Check the sentences.	**Überprüfe** die Sätze.
Choose one of the tasks • the right answer.	**Wähle** eine der Aufgaben • die richtige Antwort **aus**.
Collect ideas.	**Sammle** Ideen.
Compare with your partner.	**Vergleicht** zu zweit.
Complete the sentences • the dialogue.	**Vervollständige** die Sätze • den Dialog.
Copy the list.	**Schreibe** die Liste **ab**.
Correct the wrong sentences.	**Verbessere** die falschen Sätze.
Decide on the best order.	**Entscheide dich für** die beste Reihenfolge.
Describe the picture.	**Beschreibe** das Bild.
Discuss in groups.	**Besprecht euch** in Gruppen.
Draw a picture.	**Zeichne** ein Bild.
Exchange your lists.	**Tauscht** eure Listen aus.
Explain the rules.	**Erkläre** die Regeln.
Finish the sentences.	**Vervollständige** die Sätze.
Give feedback.	**Gib** Rückmeldung.
Give reasons.	**Gib Gründe an.**
Guess.	**Überlege.**
Interview your partner.	**Interviewe** deine Partnerin / deinen Partner.
Label the picture.	**Beschrifte** das Bild.
Listen to the dialogue.	**Höre** dir den Dialog **an**.
Look at the photos • pictures (again).	**Schau** dir die Fotos • Bilder (noch einmal) **an**.
Make a list • a chart • a mind map.	**Erstelle** eine Liste • eine Tabelle • ein Wörternetz.
Make notes.	**Mache** dir **Stichpunkte.**
Make up more verses.	**Denke dir** weitere Strophen **aus.**
Match the sentences with the pictures.	**Ordne** den Bildern die richtigen Sätze **zu**.
Name the place.	**Nenne** den Ort.
Plan your role play.	**Plant** euer Rollenspiel.
Practise with a partner.	**Übe** mit einer Partnerin / einem Partner.
Present your profile to the class.	**Stelle** dein Profil deiner Klasse **vor**.
Put in the right verbs.	**Setze** die richtigen Verben **ein**.
Put the words **in the right order.**	**Bringe** die Wörter **in die richtige Reihenfolge.**
Read the story **again.**	**Lies** die Geschichte **noch einmal.**
Record your dialogue.	**Nehmt** euren Dialog **auf**.

Rewrite the sentences.	**Schreibe** die Sätze **um**.
Say how you feel.	**Sage**, wie du dich fühlst.
Show your text to a partner.	**Zeige** deinen Text einer Partnerin / einem Partner.
Sort the words **into groups**.	**Sortiere** die Wörter **in Gruppen**.
Take notes.	**Mache dir Notizen.**
Talk about the photos.	**Rede** über die Fotos.
Tell the class.	**Erzähle** es der Klasse.
Think about the story.	**Denke über** die Geschichte **nach**.
Think of a number.	**Denke** dir eine Nummer **aus.**
Use your own ideas.	**Benutze** deine eigenen Ideen.
Watch the film.	**Schau** den Film **an**.
Write a poem • a heading • a draft.	**Schreibe** ein Gedicht • einen Titel • einen Entwurf.

Classroom phrases

You and your teacher

I'm sorry I'm late.	Tut mir leid, dass ich mich verspätet habe.
I'm sorry I don't have my exercise book.	Tut mir leid, ich habe mein Heft nicht dabei.
What's the homework?	Was haben wir als Hausaufgabe auf?
Can you help me, please?	Können Sie / Kannst du mir bitte helfen?
Can you say that again, please?	Können Sie / Kannst du das bitte wiederholen?
Can I go to the toilet, please?	Kann ich bitte auf Toilette gehen?
Mr / Mrs / Miss …, I don't feel well.	Herr / Frau …, mir geht es nicht gut.
What page is it, please?	Auf welcher Seite ist das?
What's the German / English word for …?	Was ist das deutsche / englische Wort für …?
How do you spell …?	Wie schreibt man …?
What does that mean?	Was heißt / bedeutet das?
Sorry, I don't understand / I don't know.	Tut mir leid, ich verstehe das nicht / ich weiß es nicht.

Working together

Can we work in pairs / groups?	Können wir zu zweit / in Gruppen arbeiten?
Do you want to work with me / us?	Willst du / Wollt ihr mit mir / uns arbeiten?
Let's make a / draw a …	Lass(t) uns ein … machen / zeichnen.
Whose turn is it? – It's my / your turn.	Wer ist dran? – Ich bin dran. / Du bist dran.

Your teacher can say …

Turn to page …	Schlagt Seite … auf.
Look at the board.	Schaut an die Tafel.
Put your hands up, please!	Meldet euch, bitte!
Try again!	Versuche es noch einmal.

List of irregular verbs

Hier findest du alle unregelmäßigen Verben, die im Buch vorkommen. Die Liste enthält jeweils alle drei Formen, auch wenn sie noch nicht alle in den Units vorgekommen sind.

infinitive	simple past	past participle	German
be [bi:]	was, were [wɒz, wɜ:]	been [bi:n]	sein
beat [bi:t]	beat [bi:t]	beaten ['bi:tn]	schlagen; besiegen
become [bɪ'kʌm]	became [bɪ'keɪm]	become [bɪ'kʌm]	werden
begin [bɪ'gɪn]	began [bɪ'gæn]	begun [bɪ'gʌn]	beginnen; anfangen
bleed [bli:d]	bled [bled]	bled [bled]	bluten
break [breɪk]	broke [brəʊk]	broken ['brəʊkn]	brechen
bring [brɪŋ]	brought [brɔ:t]	brought [brɔ:t]	bringen; mitbringen
build [bɪld]	built [bɪlt]	built [bɪlt]	bauen
burn [bɜ:n]	burned/burnt [bɜ:nt]	burned/burnt [bɜ:nt]	brennen
buy [baɪ]	bought [bɔ:t]	bought [bɔ:t]	kaufen
choose [tʃu:z]	chose [tʃəʊz]	chosen ['tʃəʊzn]	auswählen; wählen
come [kʌm]	came [keɪm]	come [kʌm]	kommen
cost [kɒst]	cost [kɒst]	cost [kɒst]	kosten
cut [kʌt]	cut [kʌt]	cut [kʌt]	(sich) schneiden
do [du:]	did [dɪd]	done [dʌn]	machen; tun
draw [drɔ:]	drew [dru:]	drawn [drɔ:n]	zeichnen
dream [dri:m]	dreamed/dreamt [dremt]	dreamed/dreamt [dremt]	träumen
drink [drɪŋk]	drank [dræŋk]	drunk [drʌŋk]	trinken
drive [draɪv]	drove [drəʊv]	driven ['drɪvn]	fahren; treiben
eat [i:t]	ate [eɪt]	eaten ['i:tn]	essen
fall [fɔ:l]	fell [fel]	fallen ['fɔ:ln]	fallen; hinfallen
feed [fi:d]	fed [fed]	fed [fed]	füttern; ernähren
feel [fi:l]	felt [felt]	felt [felt]	(sich) fühlen
fight [faɪt]	fought [fɔ:t]	fought [fɔ:t]	kämpfen; streiten
find [faɪnd]	found [faʊnd]	found [faʊnd]	finden
fly [flaɪ]	flew [flu:]	flown [fləʊn]	fliegen
forget [fə'get]	forgot [fə'gɒt]	forgotten [fə'gɒtn]	vergessen
freeze [fri:z]	froze [frəʊz]	frozen ['frəʊzn]	frieren; gefrieren
get [get]	got [gɒt]	got [gɒt]	bekommen; werden
give [gɪv]	gave [geɪv]	given ['gɪvn]	geben
go [gəʊ]	went [went]	gone [gɒn]	gehen; fahren
grow [grəʊ]	grew [gru:]	grown [grəʊn]	anbauen; züchten; ziehen; wachsen
grow up [ˌgrəʊ‿'ʌp]	grew up [ˌgru:‿'ʌp]	grown up [ˌgrəʊn‿'ʌp]	aufwachsen
hang [hæŋ]	hung [hʌŋ]	hung [hʌŋ]	hängen
have [hæv]	had [hæd]	had [hæd]	haben; besitzen
hear [hɪə]	heard [hɜ:d]	heard [hɜ:d]	hören
hide [haɪd]	hid [hɪd]	hidden ['hɪdn]	verstecken

infinitive	simple past	past participle	German
hit [hɪt]	hit [hɪt]	hit [hɪt]	schlagen; treffen
hold [həʊld]	held [held]	held [held]	halten; festhalten
hurt [hɜːt]	hurt [hɜːt]	hurt [hɜːt]	verletzen; weh tun
keep [kiːp]	kept [kept]	kept [kept]	halten
know [nəʊ]	knew [njuː]	known [nəʊn]	wissen; kennen
know [nəʊ]	knew [njuː]	known [nəʊn]	wissen; kennen
lay [leɪ]	laid [leɪd]	laid [leɪd]	legen; (den Tisch) decken
leave [liːv]	left [left]	left [left]	verlassen; lassen; abfahren
lend [lend]	lent [lent]	lent [lent]	leihen; verleihen
lose [luːz]	lost [lɒst]	lost [lɒst]	verlieren
make [meɪk]	made [meɪd]	made [meɪd]	machen; tun; bilden
mean [miːn]	meant [ment]	meant [ment]	bedeuten; meinen
meet [miːt]	met [met]	met [met]	kennen lernen; (sich) treffen
pay [peɪ]	paid [peɪd]	paid [peɪd]	bezahlen
put [pʊt]	put [pʊt]	put [pʊt]	setzen; legen; stellen
read [riːd]	read [red]	read [red]	lesen
ride [raɪd]	rode [rəʊd]	ridden ['rɪdn]	fahren; reiten
ring [rɪŋ]	rang [ræŋ]	rung [rʌŋ]	klingeln; läuten
run [rʌn]	ran [ræn]	run [rʌn]	laufen; rennen
say [seɪ]	said [sed]	said [sed]	sagen; sprechen
see [siː]	saw [sɔː]	seen [siːn]	sehen
sell [sel]	sold [səʊld]	sold [səʊld]	verkaufen
send [send]	sent [sent]	sent [sent]	schicken; senden
shine [ʃaɪn]	shone [ʃɒn]	shone [ʃɒn]	glänzen; scheinen
shoot [ʃuːt]	shot [ʃɒt]	shot [ʃɒt]	schießen
show [ʃəʊ]	showed [ʃəʊd]	shown [ʃəʊn]	zeigen
sing [sɪŋ]	sang [sæŋ]	sung [sʌŋ]	singen
sink [sɪŋk]	sank [sæŋk]	sunk [sʌŋk]	untergehen; sinken
sit [sɪt]	sat [sæt]	sat [sæt]	sitzen
sleep [sliːp]	slept [slept]	slept [slept]	schlafen
smell [smel]	smelled/smelt [smelt]	smelled/smelt [smelt]	riechen
speak [spiːk]	spoke [spəʊk]	spoken ['spəʊkn]	sprechen
spell [spel]	spelled/spelt [spelt]	spelled/spelt [spelt]	buchstabieren
spend [spend]	spent [spent]	spent [spent]	ausgeben; verbringen
stand [stænd]	stood [stʊd]	stood [stʊd]	stehen
steal [stiːl]	stole [stəʊl]	stolen ['stəʊlən]	stehlen
sweep [swiːp]	swept [swept]	swept [swept]	fegen
swim [swɪm]	swam [swæm]	swum [swʌm]	schwimmen

infinitive	simple past	past participle	German
take [teɪk]	took [tʊk]	taken ['teɪkn]	nehmen; mitnehmen
tell [tel]	told [təʊld]	told [təʊld]	erzählen; sagen
think [θɪŋk]	thought [θɔ:t]	thought [θɔ:t]	denken; glauben
throw [θrəʊ]	threw [θru:]	thrown [θrəʊn]	werfen
understand [ˌʌndə'stænd]	understood [ˌʌndə'stʊd]	understood [ˌʌndə'stʊd]	verstehen
wake up [weɪk‿'ʌp]	woke up [wəʊk‿'ʌp]	woken up [ˌwəʊkn‿'ʌp]	aufwachen
wear [weə]	wore [wɔ:]	worn [wɔ:n]	tragen
win [wɪn]	won [wʌn]	won [wʌn]	gewinnen; siegen
write [raɪt]	wrote [rəʊt]	written ['rɪtn]	schreiben

Dictionary

Im *Dictionary* sind alle wichtigen Wörter aus deinem Buch enthalten. Die Wörter stehen in alphabetischer Reihenfolge. Englische Wörter schlägst du ab S. 213 nach, deutsche Wörter ab S. 257.

Die Abkürzungen geben an, wo das Wort zum ersten Mal im Buch erscheint.

account	[əˈkaʊnt]	Konto	IV	U4	80
englisches Wort	Aussprache	deutsche Übersetzung	Band 4	Unit 4	Seite 80

Die mit einem Sternchen (*) gekennzeichneten Verben sind unregelmäßige Verben (→ *List of irregular verbs*, S. 210 – 212).

Manche Wörter haben verschiedene Bedeutungen. Am besten liest du alle, bevor du dich für eine entscheidest.

practice [ˈpræktɪs] Training; Übung I[1]
addicted [əˈdɪktɪd] süchtig <IV U3, 73>[3]
*to **spend** [spend] ausgeben *(Geld)*; verbringen *(Zeit)* II[1]
accident [ˈæksɪdnt] Unfall III[1]
appealing [əˈpiːlɪŋ] ansprechend IV U4, 77[2]
address [əˈdres] Adresse II[2]

1 Lernwortschatz für alle: schwarz; 2 Differenzierungswortschatz: blau; 3 kein Lernwortschatz: < >

A

a [ə] ein, eine I
  a bit [ə ˈbɪt] ein bisschen; ein wenig II
  a few [ə ˈfjuː] ein paar; wenige; einige III
  a five minute walk [ə ˈfaɪv mɪnɪt ˌwɔːk] fünf Minuten zu Fuß III
  a little [ə ˈlɪtl] ein bisschen II
  a lot [ə ˈlɒt] viel I; sehr II
  a lot of [ə ˈlɒt‿əv] viel(e); eine Menge I
  a pair of [ə ˈpeər‿əv] ein Paar II
  a/one hundred [ˈhʌndrəd] einhundert; hundert I
  a/one thousand [ə/wʌn ˈθaʊznd] eintausend; tausend II
a.m. [ˌeɪˈem] vormittags *(Uhrzeit)* II
*to be **able** [biː ˈeɪbl] fähig sein; können; dürfen <IV U1, 24>
about [əˈbaʊt] über I; ungefähr; circa; etwa II
  to be about [biː əˈbaʊt] gehen um; handeln von III
  out and about [ˌaʊt‿ən‿əˈbaʊt] unterwegs I
to **abseil** [ˈæbseɪl] sich abseilen II
absolutely [ˌæbsəˈluːtli] absolut; völlig IV U3, 59
to **accept** [əkˈsept] akzeptieren; annehmen; hinnehmen IV U5, 99
accident [ˈæksɪdnt] Unfall III
account [əˈkaʊnt] Konto IV U4, 80
stomach **ache** [ˈstʌmək ˌeɪk] Bauchweh; Bauchschmerzen II
across [əˈkrɒs] über; hinüber; herüber; quer durch IV U3, 54
to **act** [ækt] spielen II
acting [ˈæktɪŋ] Schauspielen; Schauspielerei III
  acting workshop [ˈæktɪŋ ˌwɜːkʃɒp] Schauspielworkshop II
Action! [ˈækʃn] Achtung, Aufnahme <III>
active [ˈæktɪv] aktiv <IV U3, 72>
activity [ækˈtɪvəti] Aktivität I
  activity centre [ækˈtɪvəti ˌsentə] Jugendzentrum III
actor [ˈæktə] Schauspieler; Schauspielerin II
actually [ˈæktʃuəli] tatsächlich; wirklich; eigentlich III
adaptor [əˈdæptə] Adapter III
to **add** [æd] hinzufügen II
addicted [əˈdɪktɪd] süchtig <IV U3, 72>
chemical **additive** [ˌkemɪkl ˈædətɪv] chemischer Zusatzstoff <IV U3, 72>
address [əˈdres] Adresse II
adjective [ˈædʒɪktɪv] Adjektiv; Eigenschaftswort III
adult [ˈædʌlt] Erwachsene; Erwachsener III
adventure [ədˈventʃə] Abenteuer I
adverb [ˈædvɜːb] Adverb <III>

ad(vert) (= advertisement) ['æd(vɜ:t) (əd'vɜ:tɪsmənt)] Annonce; Werbespot IV U4, 76
advertisement [əd'vɜ:tɪsmənt] Anzeige; Werbespot II
advice [əd'vaɪs] Rat; Ratschlag III
afraid [ə'freɪd] ängstlich II
to be afraid [bi: ə'freɪd] sich fürchten; Angst haben II
African American [ˌæfrɪkən ə'merɪkən] Afroamerikaner; Afroamerikanerin IV U5, 96
African-American [ˌæfrɪkənə'merɪkən] afroamerikanisch IV U5, 106
after ['ɑ:ftə] nach I; danach; später III
after that ['ɑ:ftə ðət] danach I
afternoon [ˌɑ:ftə'nu:n] Nachmittag I
in the afternoon [ˌɪn ði ˌɑ:ftə'nu:n] nachmittags I
again [ə'gen] wieder; noch einmal II
against [ə'genst] gegen II
age [eɪdʒ] Alter I
ago [ə'gəʊ] vor II
to **agree** [ə'gri:] zustimmen II
to agree (on) [ə'gri: (ɒn)] sich einigen (auf) <III>
to agree (with) [ə'gri: (wɪð)] einer Meinung sein (mit); zustimmen III
right **ahead** [ˌraɪt‿ə'hed] geradeaus IV U1, 15
ain't (= isn't/aren't) [eɪnt] ist nicht; sind nicht <IV U1, 19>
air [eə] Luft IV U1, 22
airboat ['eəbəʊt] Propellerboot IV U5, 102
airport ['eəpɔ:t] Flughafen II
alarm clock [ə'lɑ:m ˌklɒk] Wecker I
Alaskan [ə'læskən] Alaska-; alaskisch <IV U1, 30>
alcohol *(no pl)* ['ælkəhɒl] Alkohol IV U3, 58
alcoholic [ˌælkə'hɒlɪk] alkoholisch; Alkohol- <IV U3, 72>
alert [ə'lɜ:t] Alarm <IV U1, 30>
algebra ['ældʒɪbrə] Algebra <IV U2, 48>
alien ['eɪliən] Außerirdischer; Außerirdische I
alive [ə'laɪv] am Leben III
all [ɔ:l] alle I; ganz II
all alone [ˌɔ:l‿ə'ləʊn] ganz allein I
all day [ˌɔ:l 'deɪ] den ganzen Tag III
all over [ˌɔ:l‿'əʊvə] überall IV U4, 85
all right [ˌɔ:l 'raɪt] in Ordnung; alles klar II
allegiance [ə'li:dʒns] Treue IV U2, 45
pledge of allegiance [ˌpledʒ‿əv‿ə'li:dʒns] Treueeid IV U2, 45
allergic to [ə'lɜ:dʒɪk tə] allergisch gegen II
allergy ['ælədʒi] Allergie II
alligator ['ælɪgeɪtə] Alligator IV ZI, 9
to **allow** [ə'laʊ] erlauben; gestatten IV U4, 84
to be allowed to (do sth) [bi: ə'laʊd tə] (etw.) dürfen IV U2, 34
almost ['ɔ:lməʊst] fast; beinahe III
alone [ə'ləʊn] allein I
all alone [ˌɔ:l‿ə'ləʊn] ganz allein I
along [ə'lɒŋ] entlang I
alphabet ['ælfəbet] Alphabet I
already [ɔ:l'redi] schon; bereits II
also ['ɔ:lsəʊ] auch I
always ['ɔ:lweɪz] immer I
amazing [ə'meɪzɪŋ] unglaublich; toll; erstaunlich II
ambition [æm'bɪʃn] Ziel II; Ehrgeiz; Streben; Ambitionen <IV U3, 139>
ambulance ['æmbjələns] Krankenwagen III
American [ə'merɪkən] amerikanisch; Amerikanisch; aus Amerika; Amerikaner; Amerikanerin IV ZI, 9
Native American [ˌneɪtɪv‿ə'merɪkən] Ureinwohner Amerikas; Ureinwohnerin Amerikas; Indianer; Indianerin; indianisch IV U2, 32
the **Amish** [ði 'ɑ:mɪʃ] die Amischen IV U3, 53
Amish ['ɑ:mɪʃ] amisch IV U3, 58
amount (of) [ə'maʊnt (əv)] Menge; Summe <IV U1, 24>
amused [ə'mju:zd] amüsiert; vergnügt IV U3, 63
amusement park [ə'mju:zmənt ˌpɑ:k] Freizeitpark <IV U4, 201>
an [ən] ein, eine I
and [ænd] und I
Anglo-American [ˌæŋgləʊə'merɪkən] anglo-amerikanisch <IV U5, 142>
angry ['æŋgri] wütend; zornig; verärgert; böse II
animal ['ænɪml] Tier I
animal rescue shelter [ˌænɪml 'reskju: ˌʃeltə] Tierheim I
ankle ['æŋkl] Fußgelenk; Fußknöchel II
announcement [ə'naʊnsmənt] Durchsage; Ankündigung II
annoyed [ə'nɔɪd] verärgert III
another [ə'nʌðə] ein anderer; noch ein II
answer ['ɑ:nsə] Antwort II
to **answer** ['ɑ:nsə] antworten; beantworten I
to answer the phone [ˌɑ:nsə ðə 'fəʊn] ans Telefon gehen III
antenna [æn'tenə] Antenne III
any ['eni] irgendein; irgendwelche II
not … any [ˌnɒt … eni] kein II
anything ['eniθɪŋ] irgendetwas II
Anything else? ['eniθɪŋ ˌels] Darf es sonst noch etwas sein? I
anything to drink ['eniθɪŋ tə 'drɪŋk] etwas zu trinken II
anyway ['eniweɪ] eigentlich IV U1, 14
anywhere ['eniweə] überall; irgendwo <IV U1, 19>
appealing [ə'pi:lɪŋ] ansprechend IV U4, 77
apple crumble [ˌæpl 'krʌmbl] Apfelauflauf *(mit Streuseln bedeckt)* II
to **apply** (for) [ə'plaɪ (fə)] sich bewerben (für/um) IV U2, 38
approval form [ə'pru:vl ˌfɔ:m] Einverständnisformular <IV U2, 44>
April ['eɪprl] April I
Arabic ['ærəbɪk] arabisch; Arabisch <IV U5, 206>
architect ['ɑ:kɪtekt] Architekt; Architektin IV U4, 75
archive ['ɑ:kaɪv] Archiv II
are [ɑ:] bist; sind I

are required [rɪ'kwaɪəd] werden gebeten <IV U2, 48>

Are you serious? [ˌɑ: ju 'sɪəriəs] Im Ernst? III

... are 99p. [ɑ: 'naɪntinaɪn ˌpens] ... kosten 99 Pence. I

area ['eəriə] Fläche; Gegend; Gebiet; Areal IV ZI, 9

argument ['ɑ:gjəmənt] Auseinandersetzung; Streit II; Argument <IV U3, 68>

arm [ɑ:m] Arm I

armour ['ɑ:mə] Rüstung III

army ['ɑ:mi] Armee; Heer III

around [ə'raʊnd] herum; umher I; gegen; ungefähr um III; um ... herum IV U1, 14

around the house [ə'raʊnd ðə haʊs] im Haus I

to be around [bi: ə'raʊnd] geben; existieren IV U4, 80

to get around [ˌget ə'raʊnd] herumkommen III

to **arrange** [ə'reɪndʒ] ausmachen; arrangieren <IV U1, 27>

to **arrest** [ə'rest] festnehmen; verhaften IV U5, 107

to **arrive** [ə'raɪv] ankommen II

Art [ɑ:t] Kunst I

street art ['stri:t ɑ:t] Straßenkunst IV U1, 13

article ['ɑ:tɪkl] Artikel; Bericht *(in einer Zeitung)* <IV U1, 21>

artist ['ɑ:tɪst] Künstler; Künstlerin <IV U1, 134>

as [æz] als II; wie II

as ... as [əz ... əz] so ... wie II

as far as [ˌəz 'fɑ:r‿əz] soweit IV U3, 59

as soon as [əz 'su:n‿əz] sobald IV U4, 89

to **ask** [ɑ:sk] fragen I

to ask about ['ɑ:sk‿əˌbaʊt] sich erkundigen nach; fragen nach II

to ask for ['ɑ:sk fɔ:] bitten um II

to ask sb out [ˌɑ:sk ... 'aʊt] sich mit jmdm. verabreden IV U2, 42

asking the way ['ɑ:skɪŋ ðə ˌweɪ] nach dem Weg fragen I

*to be **asleep** [bi: ə'sli:p] schlafen III

to fall asleep [ˌfɔ:l‿ə'sli:p] einschlafen III

aspect ['æspekt] Aspekt; Gesichtspunkt; Blickwinkel <IV U1, 29>

to **assassinate** [ə'sæsɪneɪt] ermorden <IV U3, 138>

assistant [ə'sɪstnt] Verkäufer; Verkäuferin III

shop assistant ['ʃɒp‿əˌsɪstnt] Verkäufer; Verkäuferin II

sales **associate** *(AE)* [ˌseɪlz ə'səʊʃiət] Verkäufer; Verkäuferin IV U2, 38

astronomy [ə'strɒnəmi] Astronomie IV U2, 34

at [æt] an; in; um; bei; auf I

at break [ət 'breɪk] in der Pause I

at home [ət 'həʊm] zu Hause I

at last [ət 'lɑ:st] endlich; zu guter Letzt II

at school [ət 'sku:l] in der Schule I

at the back [ət ðə 'bæk] hinten; am Ende; im hinteren Teil <IV ZI, 9>

at the front of [ət ðə 'frʌnt‿əv] an der Spitze (von); im vorderen Bereich II

at the seaside [ət ðə 'si:saɪd] am Meer I

at the weekend [ˌət ðə 'wi:kend] am Wochenende I

at this stage [æt ðɪs 'steɪdʒ] zu diesem Zeitpunkt <IV U5, 108>

ate [eɪt] simple past von *to eat* II

atmosphere ['ætməsfɪə] Atmosphäre; Stimmung <IV U5, 111>

to **attach** [ə'tætʃ] verbinden III

attack [ə'tæk] Angriff; Attacke IV U1, 12

to **attack** [ə'tæk] angreifen IV U2, 42

to **attend** [ə'tend] teilnehmen; anwesend sein; besuchen <IV U2, 48>

attic ['ætɪk] Dachboden I

attitude ['ætɪtju:d] Einstellung; Haltung IV U4, 89

attorney [ə'tɜ:ni] Anwalt; Anwältin; Staatsanwalt; Staatsanwältin <IV U5, 108>

audition [ɔ:'dɪʃn] Vorspielen; Vorsprechen; Vorsingen; Vortanzen II

August ['ɔ:gəst] August I

in August [in 'ɔ:gəst] im August I

aunt [ɑ:nt] Tante II

autograph ['ɔ:təgrɑ:f] Autogramm IV U3, 53

to sign autographs [ˌsaɪn 'ɔ:təgrɑ:fs] Autogramme geben IV U3, 53

avenue ['ævənju:] Allee; Boulevard IV U1, 14

average ['ævrɪdʒ] durchschnittlich IV U3, 58

awake [ə'weɪk] bei Bewusstsein; wach III

away [ə'weɪ] weg; entfernt II

right away [ˌraɪt‿ə'weɪ] sofort; gleich IV U4, 80

awesome ['ɔ:səm] super; spitze IV U2, 34

awful ['ɔ:fl] schrecklich; furchtbar I

B

baby ['beɪbi] Baby II

babysitter ['beɪbɪˌsɪtə] Babysitter; Babysitterin IV U2, 41

back [bæk] Rückseite <III>; Hinterteil IV U5, 106

at the back [ət ðə 'bæk] hinten; am Ende; im hinteren Teil <IV ZI, 9>

back [bæk] Hinter- IV U3, 62

back [bæk] zurück I

back home [bæk 'həʊm] zu Hause II

background ['bækgraʊnd] Hintergrund III

in the background [ɪn ðə 'bækgraʊnd] im Hintergrund III

backpack ['bækpæk] Rucksack IV U3, 62

bad [bæd] schlecht I

bag [bæg] Tasche; Tüte; Sack I

tea bag ['ti: ˌbæg] Teebeutel <IV U5, 113>

baggies *(pl) (coll)* ['bægiz] kurze Hosen *(ugs.)* <IV U4, 77>

bagpipes *(pl)* ['bægpaɪps] Dudelsack III

baguette [bæg'et] **Baguette** ***(Stangenweißbrot)*** <IV U5, 112>

pasta **bake** [ˌpæstə 'beɪk] Nudelauflauf II

baker ['beɪkə] Bäcker; Bäckerin III

baker's ['beɪkəz] Bäckerei III

bald eagle [ˌbɔ:ld 'i:gl] Weißkopfseeadler IV ZI, 8

ball [bɔ:l] Ball II

cannon ball ['kænən ˌbɔ:l] Kanonenkugel II

balloon [bə'lu:n] Luftballon I

bamboo [bæm'bu:] Bambus <IV U4, 90>

banana [bə'nɑ:nə] Banane I

band [bænd] Band; Musikgruppe II

brass band [ˌbrɑ:s 'bænd] Blaskapelle; Blasensemble <IV U5, 108>

marching band ['mɑ:tʃɪŋ ˌbænd] Marschkapelle <IV U2, 190>

to start a band [ˌstɑ:t‿ə 'bænd] eine Band gründen II

bandage ['bændɪdʒ] Verband III

bar chart ['bɑ: ˌtʃɑ:t] Balkendiagramm; Säulendiagramm <IV U1, 27>

bar of chocolate [bɑ:r‿əv 'tʃɒklət] Tafel Schokolade I

barbecue ['bɑ:bɪkju:] Grill; Grillparty I

bargain ['bɑ:gɪn] Schnäppchen II

barrel ['bærl] Fass; Tonne IV U3, 53

baseball ['beɪsbɔ:l] Baseball IV U1, 13

basic ['beɪsɪk] grundlegend; einfach <IV U1, 24>

basketball ['bɑ:skɪtbɔ:l] Basketball II

bat [bæt] Fledermaus I

bathroom ['bɑ:θrʊm] Badezimmer; Bad I

battle ['bætl] Kampf; Schlacht III

bay [beɪ] Bucht IV U4, 75

BC (= before Christ) [ˌbi:'si:] vor Christus <IV U2, 136>

*to **be** [bi:] sein I

to be able [bi: 'eɪbl] fähig sein; können; dürfen <IV U1, 24>

to be about [bi: ə'baʊt] gehen um; handeln von III

to be afraid [bi: ə'freɪd] sich fürchten; Angst haben II

to be allowed to (do sth) [bi: ə'laʊd tə] (etw.) dürfen IV U2, 34

to be around [bi: ə'raʊnd] geben; existieren IV U4, 80

to be asleep [bi: ə'sli:p] schlafen III

to be born [bi: 'bɔ:n] geboren werden III

to be called [bi: 'kɔ:ld] heißen; genannt werden II

to be fed up (with) [bi: fed‿'ʌp (wɪð)] die Nase voll haben (von); sauer sein III

to be good at [bi: 'gʊd‿ət] gut sein in/bei I

to be homesick [bi: 'həʊmsɪk] Heimweh haben III

to be interested in [bi: 'ɪntrəstɪd‿ɪn] sich interessieren für; interessiert sein an III

to be known as [bi: 'nəʊn‿əz] bekannt sein als <IV U3, 70>

to be lucky [bi: 'lʌki] Glück haben III

to be made of [bi: 'meɪd‿əv] hergestellt sein aus III

to be on fire [bi: ɒn 'faɪə] brennen II

to be right [bi: 'raɪt] recht haben II

to be scared [bi: 'skeəd] Angst haben; erschrocken sein II

to be sick [bi: 'sɪk] sich übergeben I

to be sorry [bi: 'sɒri] leidtun III

to be stuck [bi: 'stʌk] feststecken; nicht weg können I

to be up to [bi: 'ʌp tə] vorhaben III

Be careful! [bi: 'keəfl] Sei vorsichtig! I

beach [bi:tʃ] Strand I

to go beach combing [gəʊ 'bi:tʃ ˌkəʊmɪŋ] den Strand nach Strandgut absuchen II

kidney **bean** ['kɪdni ˌbi:n] Kidneybohne II

soy **bean** ['sɔɪ ˌbi:n] Sojabohne IV ZI, 9

bear [beə] Bär I

grizzly bear ['grɪzli ˌbeə] Grizzlybär <IV U1, 30>

*to **beat** [bi:t] besiegen; schlagen III

beat [bi:t] simple past von *to beat* III

beaten ['bi:tn] past participle von *to beat* III

beautiful ['bju:tɪfl] schön; hübsch I

became [bɪ'keɪm] simple past von *to become* II

because [bɪ'kɒz] weil; da I

because of [bɪ'kɒz‿əv] wegen III

*to **become** [bɪ'kʌm] werden II

become [bɪ'kʌm] past participle von *to become* II

bed [bed] Bett I

bed and breakfast (B & B) [ˌbed‿ən 'brekfəst] Frühstückspension III

to go to bed [ˌgəʊ tə 'bed] ins Bett gehen I

bedroom ['bedrʊm] Schlafzimmer; Kinderzimmer I

beef [bi:f] Rindfleisch II

roast beef [ˌrəʊst 'bi:f] Roastbeef; Rinderbraten <IV U5, 112>

been [bi:n] past particple von *to be* II

before [bɪ'fɔ:] vorher; zuvor II; bevor; bis zu II; vor IV U3, 61

began [bɪ'gæn] simple past von *to begin* IV U1, 18

*to **begin** [bɪ'gɪn] beginnen; anfangen IV U1, 18

beginner [bɪ'gɪnə] Anfänger; Anfängerin <IV U5, 143>

beginning [bɪ'gɪnɪŋ] Anfang; Beginn III

begun [bɪ'gʌn] past participle von *to begin* IV U1, 18

behind [bɪ'haɪnd] hinter II

from behind [ˌfrəm bɪ'haɪnd] von hinten I

to **believe** [bɪ'li:v] glauben II

bell [bel] Glocke II

bench [benʃ] Bank; Sitzbank III

best [best] beste II

to like … best [ˌlaɪk ˈbest] am meisten mögen; am liebsten mögen I
Best wishes, [ˌbest ˈwɪʃɪz] Viele Grüße, I
the best [ðə ˈbest] die besten II
best-paid [ˈbestˌpeɪd] bestbezahlt IV U5, 97
best-paying [ˌbestˈpeɪɪŋ] bestbezahlt IV U2, 39
better [ˈbetə] besser I
better quality food [ˌbetə ˈkwɒləti ˌfu:d] qualitativ besseres Essen <IV U3, 72>
between [bɪˈtwi:n] zwischen II
in between [ˌɪn bɪˈtwi:n] dazwischen <IV U4, 92>
big [bɪg] groß I
big wheel [ˌbɪg ˈwi:l] Riesenrad II
bike [baɪk] Fahrrad I
bill [bɪl] Rechnung III
to pay the bill [ˌpeɪ ðə ˈbɪl] die Rechnung bezahlen III
billion [ˈbɪliən] Milliarde IV U1, 13
biography [baɪˈɒgrəfi] Biografie <III>
Biology [baɪˈɒlədʒi] Biologie I
bird [bɜ:d] Vogel I
bird watching [ˈbɜ:d ˌwɒtʃɪŋ] Vogelbeobachtung III
birthday [ˈbɜ:θdeɪ] Geburtstag I
Happy birthday! [ˌhæpi ˈbɜ:θdeɪ] Alles Gute zum Geburtstag! I
biscuit [ˈbɪskɪt] Keks II
dog biscuit [ˈdɒg ˌbɪskɪt] Hundekeks II
a **bit** [ə ˈbɪt] ein bisschen; ein wenig II
black [blæk] schwarz I
blanket [ˈblæŋkɪt] Decke; Bettdecke; Wolldecke IV U3, 62
bled [bled] simple past, past participle von *to bleed* III
*to **bleed** [bli:d] bluten III
blog [blɒg] Blog; Internettagebuch II
blond [blɒnd] blond <IV U4, 77>
bloody [ˈblʌdi] blutig <IV U2, 136>
blouse [blaʊz] Bluse I
*to **blow** [bləʊ] wehen; blasen; pusten <IV U3, 71>
blue [blu:] blau I
blue cheese [ˌblu: ˈtʃi:s] Schimmelkäse II
board [bɔ:d] Tafel I; Brett <IV U3, 72>
on board [ˈɒn bɔ:d] an Bord III
boarding school [ˈbɔ:dɪŋ ˌsku:l] Internat <IV U2, 137>
boat [bəʊt] Boot II
boat trip [ˈbəʊt ˌtrɪp] Bootsfahrt; Schiffsfahrt II
body [ˈbɒdi] Körper III; Leiche IV U3, 62
body lotion [ˈbɒdi ˌləʊʃn] Körperlotion III
to **boil** [bɔɪl] kochen <IV U5, 113>
boiling [bɔɪlɪŋ] kochend <IV U5, 113>
book [bʊk] Buch; Heft I
exercise book [ˈeksəsaɪz ˌbʊk] Übungsheft I
to **book** [bʊk] buchen; reservieren IV U4, 76
booklet [ˈbʊklət] Broschüre; Heft IV U5, 102
to **bookmark** [ˈbʊkmɑ:k] zu … hinzufügen II
boot [bu:t] Stiefel II; Schuh <IV U2, 50>
border [ˈbɔ:də] Grenze IV U3, 52
boring [ˈbɔ:rɪŋ] langweilig I
*to be **born** [bi: ˈbɔ:n] geboren werden III
borough [ˈbʌrə] Stadtteil; Bezirk IV U1, 12
to **borrow** [ˈbɒrəʊ] ausleihen II
boss [bɒs] Boss; Chef; Chefin II
both [bəʊθ] beide <IV U3, 68>
bottle [ˈbɒtl] Flasche I
bottle bank [ˈbɒtl bæŋk] Altglascontainer II
bought [bɔ:t] simple past von *to buy* I; past participle von *to buy* II
bowl [bəʊl] Schale; Schälchen; Schüssel II
bowling [ˈbəʊlɪŋ] Bowlen IV U3, 58
box [bɒks] Box; Kiste; Schachtel I
telephone box [ˈtelɪfəʊn ˌbɒks] Telefonzelle II
boy [bɔɪ] Junge I
boyfriend [ˈbɔɪfrend] Freund *(in einer Paarbeziehung)* IV U2, 42
brand [brænd] Marke III
brass band [ˌbrɑ:s ˈbænd] Blaskapelle; Blasensemble <IV U5, 108>
brave [breɪv] tapfer; mutig III
bread [bred] Brot II
sliced bread [ˌslaɪst ˈbred] in Scheiben geschnittenes Brot III
break [breɪk] Pause I
at break [ət ˈbreɪk] in der Pause I
to take a break [ˌteɪk‿ə ˈbreɪk] Pause machen II
*to **break** [breɪk] brechen; zerbrechen II
breakdancing [ˈbreɪkdɑ:nsɪŋ] Breakdance <IV U1, 134>
breakfast [ˈbrekfəst] Frühstück I
bed and breakfast (B & B) [ˌbed‿ən ˈbrekfəst] Frühstückspension III
to have breakfast [ˌhæv ˈbrekfəst] frühstücken I
breast [brest] Brust <IV U3, 72>
to **breathe** [bri:ð] atmen III
breathing [ˈbri:ðɪŋ] Atmung <IV U4, 88>
brewing time [ˈbru:ɪŋ ˌtaɪm] Brühzeit <IV U5, 113>
brick [brɪk] Stein; Ziegelstein II
bridge [brɪdʒ] Brücke II
briefcase [ˈbri:fkeɪs] Aktenkoffer; Aktentasche III
bright [braɪt] hell; leuchtend; strahlend IV ZI, 8
brilliant [ˈbrɪliənt] toll I
*to **bring** [brɪŋ] bringen; mitbringen II
to bring down [ˌbrɪŋ ˈdaʊn] herunterbringen <IV U2, 35>
British [ˈbrɪtɪʃ] britisch II
broadcast [ˈbrɔ:dkɑ:st] Sendung; Ausstrahlung; Übertragung <IV U5, 97>
brochure [ˈbrəʊʃə] Broschüre; Prospekt III
broke [brəʊk] simple past von *to break* II
broken [ˈbrəʊkn] past participle von *to break* II

brother ['brʌðə] Bruder I
brought [brɔ:t] simple past von *to bring* II
brown [braʊn] braun I
bubble wrap ['bʌbl ˌræp] Luftpolsterfolie <IV U3, 71>
speech **bubble** ['spi:tʃ ˌbʌbl] Sprechblase <III>
bucket of water ['bʌkɪt‿əv ˌwɔ:tə] Eimer Wasser I
buddy *(infml)* ['bʌdi] Kumpel IV U2, 45
buffalo ['bʌfləʊ] Büffel <IV U2, 136>
buffet ['bʊfeɪ] Büfett III
*to **build** [bɪld] bauen II
builder ['bɪldə] Bauarbeiter; Bauarbeiterin II
ship builder ['ʃɪp ˌbɪldə] Schiffsbauer; Schiffsbauerin III
building ['bɪldɪŋ] Gebäude II
built [bɪlt] simple past, past participle von *to build* II
light **bulb** ['laɪt ˌbʌlb] Glühbirne III
bullet ['bʊlɪt] Kugel; Geschoss IV U3, 63
burger ['bɜ:gə] Hamburger II
burglar ['bɜ:glə] Einbrecher; Einbrecherin I
*to **burn** [bɜ:n] verbrennen; brennen III
to burn down [bɜ:n 'daʊn] niederbrennen; verbrennen II
burnt [bɜ:nt] simple past, past participle von *to burn* III
bus [bʌs] Bus I
bus stop ['bʌs ˌstɒp] Bushaltestelle II
on the bus [ˌɒn ðə 'bʌs] im Bus II
bushy ['bʊʃi] buschig <IV U4, 77>
business ['bɪznɪs] Geschäft; Branche <IV U2, 137>
businessman ['bɪznɪsmæn] Geschäftsmann IV U4, 84
busy ['bɪzi] beschäftigt; arbeitsreich I
a busy day [ə ˌbɪzi 'deɪ] ein ausgefüllter Tag I
but [bʌt] aber I
butcher's ['bʊtʃəz] Metzgerei III
butter ['bʌtə] Butter I
peanut butter [ˌpi:nʌt 'bʌtə] Erdnussbutter III
*to **buy** [baɪ] kaufen I
by [baɪ] von II; bis (spätestens) III; an IV U3, 63
by *(train)* [baɪ] mit *(dem Zug)* I
by the end [ˌbaɪ ði 'end] am Schluss II
by yourself [baɪ 'jɔ:self] allein II
Bye. [baɪ] Tschüss. I

C

cabbage ['kæbɪdʒ] Kohl; Kraut II
cable car ['keɪbl ˌkɑ:] Seilbahn IV U4, 74
café ['kæfeɪ] Café I
cafeteria [kæfə'tɪəriə] Cafeteria; Mensa I
cage [keɪdʒ] Käfig I
cake [keɪk] Kuchen I
to make a cake [ˌmeɪk‿ə 'keɪk] einen Kuchen backen I
piece of cake ['pi:s‿əv keɪk] einfach <IV U3, 68>
calculator ['kælkjəleɪtə] Rechner; Taschenrechner I
call [kɔ:l] Anruf; Ruf III
phone call ['fəʊn ˌkɔ:l] Telefonanruf I
to **call** [kɔ:l] rufen; anrufen I
to be called [bi: 'kɔ:ld] heißen; genannt werden II
caller ['kɔ:lə] Anrufer; Anruferin II
calorie ['kælri] Kalorie <IV U3, 72>
came [keɪm] simple past von *to come* I
camel ['kæml] Kamel I
camera ['kæmrə] Fotoapparat; Kamera <III>
camp [kæmp] Camp; Lager II
camping ['kæmpɪŋ] Camping; Zelten III
to go camping [ˌgəʊ 'kæmpɪŋ] campen gehen; zelten II
campsite ['kæmpsaɪt] Campingplatz; Zeltplatz III
campus ['kæmpəs] Campus; Hochschulgelände <IV U5, 110>
can [kæn] Dose I
can [kæn; kən] können I
can't [kɑ:nt] nicht können I
canary [kə'neəri] Kanarienvogel III
candle ['kændl] Kerze I
cannon ['kænən] Kanone II
cannon ball ['kænən ˌbɔ:l] Kanonenkugel II
cannot ['kænɒt] nicht können III
canoe [kə'nu:] Kanu <IV U2, 136>
canoeing [kə'nu:ɪŋ] Kanufahren I
canvas ['kænvəs] Leinwand <IV U1, 134>
cap [kæp] Kappe; Mütze I
capital (city) ['kæpɪtl (ˌsɪti)] Hauptstadt III
captain ['kæptɪn] Kapitän; Kapitänin I
caption ['kæpʃn] Untertitel; Bildunterschrift <II>
car [kɑ:] Auto I
caravan ['kærəvæn] Wohnwagen III
card [kɑ:d] Karte; Spielkarte I
playing card ['pleɪɪŋ ˌkɑ:d] Spielkarte <IV U4, 92>
prompt card ['prɒmt ˌkɑ:d] Stichwortkarte <IV U2, 51>
cardboard ['kɑ:dbɔ:d] Pappe; Karton III
to **care** (for) ['keə (fə)] sich kümmern (um) III
career [kə'rɪə] Beruf; Laufbahn; Karriere IV U1, 18
careful ['keəfl] vorsichtig; sorgfältig II
Be careful! [bi: 'keəfl] Sei vorsichtig! I
caretaker ['keəˌteɪkə] Hausmeister; Hausmeisterin I
carnival ['kɑ:nɪvl] Karneval; Fasching IV U5, 98
carpenter ['kɑ:pəntə] Zimmermann; Zimmerin; Tischler; Tischlerin II
carpet ['kɑ:pɪt] Teppich I
carrot ['kærət] Karotte II
to **carry** ['kæri] tragen; befördern II

cartoon [kɑ:'tu:n] Cartoon; Zeichentrickfilm IV U4, 81
case [keɪs] Fall IV U5, 107
court case ['kɔ:t ˌkeɪs] Gerichtsverhandlung; Rechtsfall IV U5, 107
pencil case ['pensl ˌkeɪs] Federmäppchen I
cash [kæʃ] (mit) Bargeld II
casino [kə'si:nəʊ] Kasino; Spielkasino <IV U2, 137>
cast [kɑ:st] Gips III
castle ['kɑ:sl] Schloss; Burg II
cat [kæt] Katze I
*to **catch** [kætʃ] fangen II; finden <IV U4, 77>
catchy ['kætʃi] eingängig; einprägsam IV U4, 77
category ['kætəgri] Kategorie <IV U4, 140>
catering college ['keɪtərɪŋ ˌkɒlɪdʒ] Hotelfachschule II
cathedral [kə'θi:drl] Dom; Kathedrale <IV U1, 183>
Catholic ['kæθlɪk] Katholik; Katholikin; katholisch III
caught [kɔ:t] simple past, past participle von *to catch* II
'cause (= because) [kɒz] weil <IV U2, 35>
cave [keɪv] Höhle II
ceiling ['si:lɪŋ] Zimmerdecke I
to **celebrate** ['seləbreɪt] feiern I
celebration [ˌselə'breɪʃn] Feier IV U3, 52
cemetery ['semətri] Friedhof <IV U5, 108>
center *(AE)* ['sentə] Zentrum; Mitte; Center IV U1, 13
centimetre (cm) ['sentɪˌmi:tə] Zentimeter (cm) I
centre ['sentə] Zentrum; Mitte; Center III
activity centre [æk'tɪvəti ˌsentə] Jugendzentrum III
city centre [ˌsɪti 'sentə] Stadtzentrum; Stadtmitte III
shopping centre ['ʃɒpɪŋ ˌsentə] Einkaufszentrum I
town centre [ˌtaʊn 'sentə] Stadtzentrum; Stadtmitte <IV U1, 15>
in the centre of [ˌɪn ðə 'sentər‿əv] in der Mitte III
century ['senʃri] Jahrhundert III
cereal ['sɪəriəl] Müsli; Cornflakes III
certain ['sɜ:tn] bestimmte <IV U1, 24>
cevapcici [səvæp'tʃətʃi] Cevapcici <IV U5, 206>
chair [tʃeə] Stuhl I
chalk [tʃɔ:k] Kreide <IV U1, 28>
chance [tʃɑ:ns] Chance; Gelegenheit II; Möglichkeit IV U1, 18
change [tʃeɪndʒ] Münzgeld; Wechselgeld II
to **change** [tʃeɪndʒ] wechseln II; verändern; (sich) ändern; umsteigen III
to change one's mind [ˌtʃeɪndʒ wʌnz 'maɪnd] seine Meinung ändern III
chant [tʃɑ:nt] Sprechgesang <I>
character ['kærəktə] Charakter; Figur <IV U1, 24>
charades [ʃə'rɑ:dz] Scharaden <II>
charger ['tʃɑ:dʒə] Ladegerät III
chart [tʃɑ:t] Diagramm; Tabelle <I>
bar chart ['bɑ: ˌtʃɑ:t] Balkendiagramm; Säulendiagramm <IV U1, 27>
pie chart ['paɪ ˌtʃɑ:t] Kuchendiagramm; Tortendiagramm <IV U1, 26>
charts *(pl only)* [tʃɑ:ts] Hitparade IV U5, 97
chaser ['tʃeɪsə] Jäger; Jägerin; Verfolger; Verfolgerin IV U2, 33
video **chat** ['vɪdiəʊ ˌtʃæt] Video-Chat III
to **chat** [tʃæt] chatten; plaudern II
cheap [tʃi:p] billig II
check [tʃek] Kontrolle IV U1, 22
to **check** [tʃek] überprüfen; kontrollieren III
to check in [ˌtʃek‿'ɪn] einchecken III
to check out [ˌtʃek‿'aʊt] auschecken III
checklist ['tʃeklɪst] Checkliste <I>
cheeky ['tʃi:ki] frech III
to **cheer** sb up [ˌtʃɪər‿'ʌp] jmdn. aufheitern; jmdn. aufmuntern III
cheerleader ['tʃɪəˌli:də] Cheerleader *(Mädchen, das in einer Gruppe eine Sportmannschaft anfeuert)* IV U2, 34
cheese [tʃi:z] Käse I
blue cheese [ˌblu: 'tʃi:s] Schimmelkäse II
cheesecake ['tʃi:skeɪk] Käsekuchen II
chef [ʃef] Koch; Köchin II
head chef ['hed ʃef] Chefkoch II
chemical additive [ˌkemɪkl 'ædətɪv] chemischer Zusatzstoff <IV U3, 72>
chewing gum ['tʃu:ɪŋ ˌgʌm] Kaugummi I
chic [ʃɪk] schick; elegant I
chicken ['tʃɪkɪn] Huhn I
child [tʃaɪld] Kind II
children *(pl)* ['tʃɪldrn] Kinder II
to **chill** out [ˌtʃɪl‿'aʊt] chillen; sich entspannen IV U4, 76
chilli ['tʃɪli] Chili II
Chinese [tʃaɪ'ni:z] chinesisch; Chinesisch; aus China; Chinese; Chinesin IV U5, 99
chips *(pl)* [tʃɪps] Pommes frites I
chocolate ['tʃɒklət] Schokolade I; Praline IV U3, 54
choice [tʃɔɪs] Auswahl; Wahl <IV U4, 77>
*to **choose** [tʃu:z] auswählen; wählen II
chorus ['kɔ:rəs] Refrain <I>
chose [tʃəʊz] simple past von *to choose* II
chosen ['tʃəʊzn] past participle von *to choose* II
Christian ['krɪstʃn] christlich IV U3, 53
Christmas ['krɪsməs] Weihnachten I
church [tʃɜ:tʃ] Kirche II
cinema ['sɪnəmə] Kino I
circle ['sɜ:kl] Kreis; Ring III
citizen ['sɪtɪzn] Staatsbürger; Staatsbürgerin; Staatsangehöriger; Staatsangehörige IV U1, 18

citizenship [ˈsɪtɪznʃɪp] Staatsangehörigkeit; Staatsbürgerschaft <IV U1, 24>
city [ˈsɪti] Stadt; Großstadt II
city centre [ˌsɪti ˈsentə] Stadtzentrum; Stadtmitte III
civil rights *(pl)* [ˌsɪvl ˈraɪts] Bürgerrechte IV U5, 96
Civil War [ˌsɪvl ˈwɔː] Bürgerkrieg <IV U3, 138>
to **clap** [klæp] klatschen <I>
class [klɑːs] Unterricht I; Klasse III; Unterrichtsstunde; Kurs IV U2, 34
classmate [ˈklɑːsmeɪt] Klassenkamerad; Klassenkameradin; Mitschüler; Mitschülerin <II>
classroom [ˈklɑːsrʊm] Klassenzimmer I
to **clean** [kliːn] sauber machen; putzen I
clean [kliːn] sauber I
vacuum **cleaner** [ˈvækjuːm ˌkliːnə] Staubsauger IV U3, 59
to **clear** [klɪə] abräumen; ausräumen IV U2, 33
to clear the table [ˌklɪə ðə ˈteɪbl] den Tisch abräumen II
clear [klɪə] klar; eindeutig; deutlich IV U4, 77
clever [ˈklevə] schlau; klug; intelligent I
to **click** [klɪk] klicken I
to **climb** [klaɪm] besteigen; steigen; klettern III
rock **climbing** [ˈrɒk ˌklaɪmɪŋ] Klettern I
clock [klɒk] Uhr II
alarm clock [əˈlɑːm ˌklɒk] Wecker I
clock tower [ˈklɒk ˌtaʊə] Uhrenturm II
o'clock [əˈklɒk] Uhr *(Zeitangabe bei vollen Stunden)* I
to **close** [kləʊz] schließen; zumachen I
close [kləʊs] in der Nähe; nahe IV U3, 53

clothes *(pl)* [kləʊðz] Kleider *(Pl.)*; Kleidung I
cloud [klaʊd] Wolke IV U2, 33
cloudy [ˈklaʊdi] wolkig I
club [klʌb] Klub; Verein II
clubhouse [ˈklʌbhaʊs] Klubhaus; Vereinsheim IV U3, 62
clue [kluː] Hinweis; Spur I
coach [kəʊtʃ] Trainer; Trainerin <III>; Reisebus <IV U5, 207>
coal [kəʊl] Kohle III
coast [kəʊst] Küste III
on the coast [ˌɒn ðə ˈkəʊst] an der Küste III
roller **coaster** [ˈrəʊlə ˌkəʊstə] Achterbahn II
coastline [ˈkəʊstlaɪn] Küste <IV U4, 201>
coat [kəʊt] Jacke I
cocktail sauce [ˈkɒkteɪl ˌsɔːs] Cocktailsoße <IV U5, 112>
coconut [ˈkəʊkənʌt] Kokosnuss II
dress **code** [ˈdres ˌkəʊd] Kleiderordnung; Bekleidungsvorschriften IV U2, 36
coin [kɔɪn] Münze III
coke [kəʊk] Cola I
cold [kəʊld] Kälte <IV U2, 136>
cold [kəʊld] kalt I
to get cold [ˌget ˈkəʊld] frieren III
coleslaw [ˈkəʊlslɔː] Krautsalat <IV U5, 112>
collar [ˈkɒlə] Halsband I
to **collect** [kəˈlekt] sammeln I
college [ˈkɒlɪdʒ] College; Institut IV U1, 19
catering college [ˈkeɪtərɪŋ ˌkɒlɪdʒ] Hotelfachschule II
colonist [ˈkɒlənɪst] Kolonist; Kolonistin; Siedler; Siedlerin <IV U1, 24>
colony [ˈkɒləni] Kolonie <IV U3, 70>
color *(AE)* [ˈkʌlə] Farbe IV ZI, 8
colour [ˈkʌlə] Farbe I
coloured [ˈkʌləd] buntes <IV U3, 71>
colourful [ˈkʌləfl] bunt II
comb [ˈkəʊm] Kamm III
combination [ˌkɒmbɪˈneɪʃn] Kombination II

*to **come** [kʌm] kommen I
Come on! [ˌkʌm‿ˈɒn] Komm jetzt! I
comedy [ˈkɒmədi] Komödie III
comfortable [ˈkʌmftəbl] bequem; angenehm II
comic [ˈkɒmɪk] Comic(heft) II
comic strip [ˈkɒmɪk strɪp] Comicstrip <IV U2, 42>
comment [ˈkɒment] Kommentar IV U4, 80
to put a comment [ˌpʊt‿ə ˈkɒment] einen Kommentar schreiben <I>
community [kəˈmjuːnəti] Gemeinde; Gemeinschaft IV U1, 18
company [ˈkʌmpəni] Gesellschaft; Firma II
to **compare** [kəmˈpeə] vergleichen I
comparison [kəmˈpærɪsn] Vergleich <IV U2, 37>
competition [ˌkɒmpəˈtɪʃn] Wettbewerb II; Konkurrenz IV U2, 34
to **complain** [kəmˈpleɪn] sich beschweren; sich beklagen IV U1, 18
to **complete** [kəmˈpliːt] vervollständigen I; absolvieren; abschließen <IV U2, 44>
complete [kəmˈpliːt] vollständig <IV U2, 48>
compromise [ˈkɒmprəmaɪz] Kompromiss IV U5, 99
computer [ˌkəmˈpjuːtə] Computer I
to **concentrate** [ˈkɒnsntreɪt] (sich) konzentrieren IV U3, 58
concert [ˈkɒnsət] Konzert II
to **conclude** [kənˈkluːd] schließen; zusammenfassen <IV U3, 196>
conclusion [kənˈkluːʒn] Schlussfolgerung; Schluss III
concrete [ˈkɒŋkriːt] Beton III
condition [kənˈdɪʃn] Bedingung; Zustand IV U1, 22
confident [ˈkɒnfɪdnt] selbstsicher; selbstbewusst III
to **confirm** [kənˈfɜːm] bestätigen; bekräftigen IV U4, 84

conflict ['kɒnflɪkt] Konflikt; Auseinandersetzung IV U5, 99
confused [kən'fju:zd] verwirrt; wirr III
Congratulations! [ˌkɒŋgrætʃʊ'leɪʃnz] Glückwunsch! II
to connect [kə'nekt] verbinden III
connecting [kə'nektɪŋ] verbindend <II>
constant ['kɒnstənt] ständig; konstant <IV U4, 88>
construction site [kən'strʌkʃn ˌsaɪt] Baustelle IV U1, 15
contact ['kɒntækt] Kontakt <IV U2, 136>
eye contact [aɪ 'kɒntækt] Augenkontakt <IV U2, 47>
to contact ['kɒntækt] sich in Verbindung setzen; kontaktieren <IV U2, 44>
content ['kɒntent] Inhalt III
to continue [kən'tɪnju:] weitermachen <IV U3, 65>
to contribute [kən'trɪbju:t] beitragen; mitwirken <IV U2, 49>
to control [kən'trəʊl] kontrollieren <IV U3, 68>
conversation [ˌkɒnvə'seɪʃn] Konversation; Gespräch; Unterhaltung <IV U3, 55>
convinced [kən'vɪnst] überzeugt IV U3, 59
to cook [kʊk] kochen II
cooking ['kʊkɪŋ] Kochen II
to cool [ku:l] kühlen III; abkühlen lassen <IV U5, 113>
cool [ku:l] cool; super; kühl I
to keep cool [ˌki:p 'ku:l] Ruhe bewahren <III>
copy ['kɒpi] Kopie II; Abschrift <III>
to copy ['kɒpi] kopieren II; abschreiben <III>
core subject [ˌkɔ: 'sʌbdʒɪkt] Pflichtfach IV U2, 35
corn [kɔ:n] Korn; Mais; Getreide IV ZI, 9
corner ['kɔ:nə] Ecke III
corner shop ['kɔ:nə ˌʃɒp] Tante-Emma-Laden I
Cornish ['kɔ:nɪʃ] Cornish; aus Cornwall II
to correct [kə'rekt] verbessern I
correct [kə'rekt] richtig; korrekt <III>
corridor ['kɒrɪdɔ:] Gang; Flur II
*__to cost__ [kɒst] kosten III
cost [kɒst] simple past, past participle von *to cost* III
costume ['kɒstju:m] Kostüm I
cosy ['kəʊzi] gemütlich III
cottage ['kɒtɪdʒ] Häuschen III
cotton ['kɒtn] Baumwolle III
to cough [kɒf] husten III
could [kʊd] konnte; könnte III
countdown ['kaʊntdaʊn] Countdown <I>
country ['kʌntri] ländliche Gegend; Land I; Country *(Musikrichtung)* IV U5, 97
country and western music [ˌkʌntri ənd 'westən ˌmju:zɪk] Country-musik <IV U5, 143>
in the country [ɪn ðə 'kʌntri] auf dem Land I
countryside ['kʌntrɪsaɪd] Landschaft; Land III
a **couple of** [ə 'kʌpl əv] ein paar Mal <IV U2, 47>
courage ['kʌrɪdʒ] Mut; Tapferkeit; Courage IV U5, 107
course [kɔ:s] Kurs III
main course [ˌmeɪn 'kɔ:s] Hauptgericht II
of **course** [əv 'kɔ:s] natürlich; selbstverständlich I
court [kɔ:t] Spielfeld III; Gericht IV U5, 107
court case ['kɔ:t ˌkeɪs] Gerichtsverhandlung; Rechtsfall IV U5, 107
cousin ['kʌzn] Cousin; Cousine II
cover ['kʌvə] Cover; Titelblatt <IV U3, 65>
to cover ['kʌvə] bedecken; abdecken IV U3, 58
to cover in flour [ˌkʌvər‿ɪn 'flaʊə] in Mehl wenden IV U5, 98
cow [kaʊ] Kuh III
co-worker ['kəʊˌwɜ:kə] Arbeitskollege; Arbeitskollegin IV U2, 38
cranberry ['krænbri] Cranberry; Preiselbeer- <IV U3, 72>
crazy ['kreɪzi] verrückt I
to drive sb crazy [ˌdraɪv … 'kreɪzi] jmdn. verrückt machen III
ice cream [ˌaɪs 'kri:m] Eiscreme; Eis I
to create [kri'eɪt] machen <IV U2, 48>
credit ['kredɪt] Schein <IV U2, 48>
creepy ['kri:pi] gruselig IV U3, 53
crew [kru:] Crew; Besatzung; Mannschaft III
cricket ['krɪkɪt] Kricket II
crisp [krɪsp] Kartoffelchip I
critic ['krɪtɪk] Kritiker; Kritikerin <IV U1, 28>
Croatian [krəʊ'eɪʃn] kroatisch; Kroatisch; aus Kroatien; Kroate; Kroatin <IV U5, 206>
crocodile ['krɒkədaɪl] Krokodil I
to cross [krɒs] überqueren III
crowd [kraʊd] Menschenmenge II
crowded ['kraʊdɪd] überfüllt IV U1, 22
crushed ice ['krʌʃt ˌaɪs] zerstoßenes Eis <IV U5, 113>
Cuban ['kju:bən] kubanisch; aus Kuba; Kubaner; Kubanerin IV U1, 18
cuddly ['kʌdli] knuddelig III
cuddly toy ['kʌdli ˌtɔɪ] Kuscheltier III
cultural ['kʌltʃrl] kulturell <IV U1, 134>
culture ['kʌltʃə] Kultur IV U1, 13
cup [kʌp] Tasse II
cupboard ['kʌbəd] Schrank III
currency ['kʌrnsi] Währung IV ZI, 8
curry ['kʌri] Curry II
custard ['kʌstəd] Vanillesauce II
customer ['kʌstəmə] Kunde; Kundin III
*__to cut__ [kʌt] (sich) schneiden II
cut [kʌt] simple past, past participle von *to cut* II
cute [kju:t] niedlich; süß I
CV (= Curriculum Vitae) [ˌsi:'vi:] Lebenslauf <IV U2, 48>

cyberbullying ['saɪbəˌbʊliɪŋ] Cyber-Mobbing IV U4, 80
cycling ['saɪklɪŋ] Radfahren III

D

dad [dæd] Papa I
daily ['deɪli] täglich III
dance [dɑ:ns] Tanz III
line dance ['laɪn ˌdɑ:ns] Line Dance *(alle tanzen zusammen in einer Reihe)* <IV U5, 143>
to **dance** [dɑ:ns] tanzen I
dancer ['dɑ:nsə] Tänzer; Tänzerin I
dancing ['dɑ:nsɪŋ] Tanzen; Tanz- IV U2, 43
dangerous ['deɪndʒrəs] gefährlich III
daredevil ['deəˌdevl] Draufgänger; Draufgängerin IV U3, 53
the **dark** [ðə 'dɑ:k] Dunkelheit III
dark [dɑ:k] dunkel I
date [deɪt] Datum I; Verabredung; Date IV U2, 42
daughter ['dɔ:tə] Tochter I
day [deɪ] Tag I
all day [ˌɔ:l 'deɪ] den ganzen Tag III
lucky day [ˌlʌki 'deɪ] Glückstag II
one day [wʌn 'deɪ] eines Tages III
a busy day [ə ˌbɪzi 'deɪ] ein ausgefüllter Tag I
four hours a day [ˌaʊəz‿ə 'deɪ] vier Stunden täglich I
dead [ded] tot III
deadline ['dedlaɪn] Termin; Abgabetermin <IV U2, 49>
deadly ['dedli] tod-; tödlich III
deaf [def] gehörlos; schwerhörig; taub III
Dear ..., [dɪə] Liebe/Lieber ..., *(Anrede in Briefen)* I
death [deθ] Tod <IV U5, 108>
December [dɪ'sembə] Dezember I
to **decide** [dɪ'saɪd] (sich) entscheiden III
decision [dɪ'sɪʒn] Entscheidung IV U1, 18
to **decorate** ['dekreɪt] dekorieren; verzieren; schmücken <IV U3, 71>
to **defeat** [dɪ'fi:t] besiegen <IV U3, 138>
definition [ˌdefɪ'nɪʃn] Definition <III>
delicious [dɪ'lɪʃəs] köstlich II
department [dɪ'pɑ:tmənt] Abteilung II
department store [dɪ'pɑ:tmənt ˌstɔ:] Kaufhaus II
to **depend** (on) [dɪ'pend (ɒn)] abhängen (von) <IV U2, 48>
to **describe** [dɪ'skraɪb] beschreiben <I>
description [dɪ'skrɪpʃn] Beschreibung <IV U2, 49>
Design Technology (DT) [dɪˌzaɪn tek'nɒlədʒi, ˌdi:'ti:] Technik I
graphic **design** [ˌgræfɪk dɪ'zaɪn] Grafikdesign; grafische Gestaltung <IV U2, 49>
to **design** [dɪ'zaɪn] entwerfen; gestalten <III>
desk [desk] Schreibtisch IV U3, 62
information desk [ɪnfə'meɪʃn ˌdesk] Information II
dessert [dɪ'zɜ:t] Nachspeise II
to **destroy** [dɪ'strɔɪ] zerstören <IV U5, 142>
detail ['di:teɪl] Detail; Einzelheit IV U5, 102
language **detectives** ['læŋgwɪdʒ ˌdɪtektɪvz] Sprachdetektive <I>
detention [dɪ'tenʃn] Nachsitzen IV U2, 45
device [dɪ'vaɪs] Gerät; Vorrichtung IV U3, 58
dialogue ['daɪəlɒg] Dialog; Gespräch <III>
diamond ['daɪəmənd] Diamant <II>
diary ['daɪəri] Tagebuch I
dictionary ['dɪkʃnri] Wörterbuch <III>
did [dɪd] simple past von *to do* I
to **die** [daɪ] sterben III
difference ['dɪfrns] Unterschied <IV U4, 141>
different ['dɪfrnt] anders; unterschiedlich I
difficult ['dɪfɪklt] schwierig III
difficulty ['dɪfɪklti] Schwierigkeit <IV U4, 88>
dining room ['daɪnɪŋ ˌrʊm] Esszimmer I
dinner ['dɪnə] Abendessen II; Essen IV U3, 53
dinosaur ['daɪnəsɔ:] Dinosaurier <IV U4, 141>
direct speech [dɪˌrekt 'spi:tʃ] direkte Rede <IV U5, 110>
direction [dɪ'rekʃn] Richtung <IV U5, 143>
directions [dɪ'rekʃnz] Anweisungen; Wegbeschreibung <III>
director [dɪ'rektə] Regisseur; Regisseurin II
dirty ['dɜ:ti] dreckig; schmutzig I
to **disagree** [ˌdɪsə'gri:] anderer Meinung sein; nicht einverstanden sein II
to **disappear** [ˌdɪsə'pɪə] verschwinden IV U3, 62
disaster [dɪ'zɑ:stə] Katastrophe; Desaster; Unglück III
to **discover** [dɪ'skʌvə] entdecken <IV U2, 136>
discovery [dɪ'skʌvri] Entdeckung IV U4, 84
disease [dɪ'zi:z] Krankheit IV U1, 22
dish [dɪʃ] Gericht; Speise II
dishwasher ['dɪʃˌwɒʃə] Spülmaschine IV U3, 59
to **dislike** [dɪ'slaɪk] nicht mögen IV U4, 81
distance ['dɪstns] Entfernung; Distanz IV ZI, 9
in the distance [ˌɪn ðə 'dɪstns] in der Ferne IV U1, 15
DJing [ˌdi:'dʒeɪɪŋ] Musikauflegen <IV U1, 134>
*to **do** [du:] machen; tun I
to do homework [ˌdu: 'həʊmwɜ:k] Hausaufgabe(n) machen I
to do the right thing [ˌdu: ðə 'raɪt θɪŋ] das Richtige tun III
to do the shopping [ˌdu: ðə 'ʃɒpɪŋ] Einkäufe machen; Besorgungen machen II
to do the washing up [ˌdu: ðə 'wɒʃɪŋ‿ʌp] abspülen II

doctor ['dɒktə] Arzt; Ärztin II
document ['dɒkjəmənt] Dokument <IV U3, 138>
dog [dɒg] Hund I
dog biscuit ['dɒg ˌbɪskɪt] Hundekeks II
dog walker ['dɒg ˌwɔ:kə] Hundeausführer; Hundeausführerin IV U2, 41
dollar ['dɒlə] Dollar *(amer. Währungseinheit)* IV ZI, 8
dome [dəʊm] Kuppel II
done [dʌn] past participle von *to do* II
door [dɔ:] Tür I
doorbell ['dɔ:bel] Türklingel IV U3, 54
down [daʊn] entlang; herunter; hinunter; deprimiert III
down there [ˌdaʊn 'ðeə] dahin; da unten <IV U1, 183>
to **download** [ˌdaʊn'ləʊd] herunterladen II
downtown *(AE)* [ˌdaʊn'taʊn] im Stadtzentrum IV U1, 14
Dr ['dɒktə] Dr. *(Anrede)* III
draft [drɑ:ft] Entwurf <II>
to **drag** [dræg] schleppen; schleifen; ziehen IV U5, 107
drama ['drɑ:mə] Theater II; Drama III
drank [dræŋk] simple past von *to drink* II
*to **draw** [drɔ:] zeichnen II
drawn [drɔ:n] past participle von *to draw* II
dreadful ['dredfl] furchtbar III
dream [dri:m] Traum I
*to **dream** [dri:m] träumen III
dreamt [dremt] simple past, past participle von *to dream* III
dress [dres] Kleid I
dress code ['dres ˌkəʊd] Kleiderordnung; Bekleidungsvorschriften IV U2, 36
fancy dress [ˌfænsi 'dres] Verkleidung; Kostüm I
dressed [drest] angezogen (wie); verkleidet (als) III
to get dressed [ˌget 'drest] sich anziehen II
drew [dru:] simple past von *to draw* II
drink [drɪŋk] Getränk II
*to **drink** [drɪŋk] trinken II
anything to drink ['eniθɪŋ tə 'drɪŋk] etwas zu trinken II
drinking straw ['drɪŋkɪŋ ˌstrɔ:] Trinkhalm <IV U3, 71>
drive [draɪv] Fahrt; Autofahrt III
*to **drive** [draɪv] fahren; treiben IV U3, 52
to drive sb crazy [ˌdraɪv … 'kreɪzi] jmdn. verrückt machen III
driven ['drɪvn] past participle von *to drive* IV U3, 52
driver ['draɪvə] Fahrer; Fahrerin III
driver's license *(AE)* ['draɪvəz ˌlaɪsns] Führerschein IV U2, 38
lorry driver ['lɒri ˌdraɪvə] LKW-Fahrer; LKW-Fahrerin II
driving ['draɪvɪŋ] Fahren; Fahr- <IV U2, 44>
driving school ['draɪvɪŋ ˌsku:l] Fahrschule <IV U2, 44>
drove [drəʊv] past simple von *to drive* IV U3, 52
drug [drʌg] Droge <IV U3, 72>
drumming ['drʌmɪŋ] Trommel- III
drunk [drʌŋk] past participle von *to drink* II; betrunken IV U3, 62
to **dry** [draɪ] trocknen IV U5, 98
dry [draɪ] trocken III
dumpling ['dʌmplɪŋ] Kloß II
during ['djʊərɪŋ] während III

E

each [i:tʃ] jeder <I>
each other [i:tʃ_'ʌðə] einander; sich; sich gegenseitig III
each [i:tʃ] pro Stück II
bald eagle [ˌbɔ:ld 'i:gl] Weißkopfseeadler IV ZI, 8
ear [ɪə] Ohr II
early ['ɜ:li] früh I
earlier ['ɜ:liə] früher I
to **earn** [ɜ:n] verdienen IV U2, 38
east [i:st] Osten III
east of ['i:st_əv] östlich von IV ZI, 9
easy ['i:zi] einfach; leicht I
*to **eat** [i:t] essen I
eaten ['i:tn] past participle von *to eat* II
editing ['edɪtɪŋ] Bearbeitung; Redaktion <IV U2, 49>
education [ˌedʒʊ'keɪʃn] Ausbildung; Erziehung; Bildung IV U2, 38
effect [ɪ'fekt] Effekt; Wirkung <IV U3, 72>
egg [eg] Ei I
scrambled egg [ˌskræmbld_'eg] Rührei II
eight [eɪt] acht I
eighteen [ˌeɪ'ti:n] achtzehn I
eighty ['eɪti] achtzig I
not … **either** [nɒt … 'aɪðə] auch nicht III
to **elect** [ɪ'lekt] wählen <IV U2, 46>
elective [ɪ'lektɪv] Wahlfach IV U2, 34
electric [ɪ'lektrɪk] elektrisch IV U3, 59
electricity [ˌelɪk'trɪsəti] Strom; Elektrizität III
element ['elɪmənt] Element <IV U5, 139>
elephant ['elɪfənt] Elefant I
elevator *(AE)* ['elɪveɪtə] Aufzug; Lift IV U1, 13
eleven [ɪ'levn] elf I
e-mail ['i:meɪl] E-Mail I
embarrassed [ɪm'bærəst] verlegen II
embarrassing [ɪm'bærəsɪŋ] peinlich IV U2, 42
emergency [ɪ'mɜ:dʒnsi] Notfall III
emergency call [ɪ'mɜ:dʒnsi ˌkɔ:l] Notruf III
emergency service [ɪ'mɜ:dʒnsi ˌsɜ:vɪs] Notdienst; Rettungsdienst III
to **emigrate** ['emɪgreɪt] auswandern; emigrieren IV U1, 19
to **emphasize** ['emfəsaɪz] betonen <IV U2, 51>
to **employ** [ɪm'plɔɪ] einstellen; anstellen; beschäftigen <IV U4, 88>

empty ['emti] leer IV U4, 86
encyclopedia [ɪnˌsaɪklə'pi:diə] Enzyklopädie; Lexikon IV U4, 86
end [end] Ende; Schluss II
by the end [ˌbaɪ ði 'end] am Schluss II
in the end [ɪn ði 'end] schließlich; zum Schluss II
to **end** [end] enden IV U5, 107
ending ['endɪŋ] Schluss; Ende III
enemy ['enəmi] Feind; Feindin III
energetic [ˌenə'dʒetɪk] tatkräftig IV U4, 89
fire **engine** ['faɪər‿ˌendʒɪn] Feuerwehrauto II
steam **engine** ['sti:m‿ˌendʒɪn] Dampfmaschine III
engineer [ˌendʒɪ'nɪə] Ingenieur; Ingenieurin; Techniker; Technikerin II
English ['ɪŋglɪʃ] englisch; Englisch; aus England I
the **English** [ði 'ɪŋglɪʃ] die Engländer III
to **enjoy** [ɪn'dʒɔɪ] genießen II; mögen III
enough [ɪ'nʌf] genug; genügend III
to **enter** ['entə] hineingehen; hereinkommen; betreten; eintreten IV U3, 54
entertainment *(no pl)* [ˌentə'teɪnmənt] Unterhaltung <IV U4, 90>
entry ['entri] Eintrag IV U4, 86; Einlass <IV U5, 207>
entry form ['entri ˌfɔ:m] Anmeldeformular II
equipment [ɪ'kwɪpmənt] Ausrüstung III
Victorian **era** [vɪkˌtɔ:riən 'ɪərə] viktorianisches Zeitalter III
eraser [ɪ'reɪzə] Radiergummi I
escalator ['eskəleɪtə] Rolltreppe II
especially [ɪ'speʃli] besonders; vor allem II
ethnic ['eθnɪk] ethnisch; Volks- <IV U1, 26>
euro ['jʊərəʊ] Euro *(Währung)* III
European [ˌjʊərə'pi:ən] europäisch; Europäisch; aus Europa; Europäer; Europäerin IV U2, 32
even ['i:vn] noch; sogar II
evening ['i:vnɪŋ] Abend I
in the **evenings** [ɪn ði 'i:vnɪŋz] abends III
event [ɪ'vent] Ereignis; Veranstaltung IV U4, 86
sporting event ['spɔ:tɪŋ ɪˌvent] Sportereignis; Sportveranstaltung <IV U2, 50>
ever ['evə] jemals II
every ['evri] jeder I; alle III
everybody ['evribɒdi] jeder; alle IV U2, 43
everyone ['evriwʌn] jeder I; zusammen; alle II
everything ['evriθɪŋ] alles II
exact [ɪg'zækt] exakt; genau III
Exactly. [ɪg'zæktli] Genau. IV U3, 59
example [ɪg'za:mpl] Beispiel IV U5, 98
for example [fər‿ɪg'za:mpl] zum Beispiel IV U2, 34
except [ɪk'sept] außer III
exchange [ɪks'tʃeɪndʒ] Austausch IV U2, 34
to **exchange** [ɪks'tʃeɪndʒ] tauschen; austauschen <III>
excited [ɪk'saɪtɪd] aufgeregt; begeistert II
exciting [ɪk'saɪtɪŋ] spannend; aufregend I
Excuse me! [ɪk'skju:z mi] Entschuldigung! I
exercise ['eksəsaɪz] Übung I
exercise book ['eksəsaɪz ˌbʊk] Übungsheft I
exhausted [ɪg'zɔ:stɪd] erschöpft III
to **exist** [ɪg'zɪst] existieren; bestehen <IV U1, 28>
to **expect** [ɪk'spekt] erwarten III
expensive [ɪk'spensɪv] teuer II
to **experience** [ɪk'spɪəriəns] erleben; erfahren <IV U4, 141>
experiment [ɪk'sperɪmənt] Versuch II
expert ['ekspɜ:t] Experte; Expertin <IV U4, 80>
to **explain** [ɪk'spleɪn] erklären III
to **explode** [ɪk'spləʊd] explodieren III
to **explore** [ɪk'splɔ:] erkunden; erforschen II
explosion [ɪk'spləʊʒn] Explosion III
extra ['ekstrə] Extra; Zusatz <IV U5, 112>
extra ['ekstrə] zusätzlich; Zusatz- II
extra activities ['ekstrə ˌæktɪvətiz] Zusatzaktivitäten <I>
extracurricular [ˌekstrəkə'rɪkjələ] außerhalb des Lehrplans; außerunterrichtlich *(Zusatzunterricht)* IV U2, 34
extreme [ɪk'stri:m] Extreme <IV U1, 30>
eye [aɪ] Auge II
eye contact [aɪ 'kɒntækt] Augenkontakt <IV U2, 47>

F

fable ['feɪbl] Fabel; Märchen III
to **face** [feɪs] schauen <IV U5, 143>
fact [fækt] Fakt; Tatsache II
factory ['fæktri] Fabrik; Werk III
to **fail** (at) [feɪl (ət)] versagen (in/bei); ausfallen; fehlschlagen IV U1, 19
fall *(AE)* [fɔ:l] Herbst IV ZI, 8
*to **fall** [fɔ:l] fallen I
to fall (over) [ˌfɔ:l‿'əʊvə] fallen; hinfallen; umfallen III
to fall asleep [ˌfɔ:l‿ə'sli:p] einschlafen III
to fall behind [ˌfɔ:l bɪ'haɪnd] zurückfallen <IV U2, 35>
to fall in love (with) [ˌfɔ:l‿ɪn 'lʌv] sich verlieben (in) III
to fall out of [ˌfɔ:l‿'aʊt‿əv] herausfallen aus IV U2, 42
false [fɔ:ls] falsch <II>
family ['fæmli] Familie I
host family ['həʊst ˌfæmli] Gastfamilie IV U2, 34
famine ['fæmɪn] Hungersnot <IV U1, 184>
famous ['feɪməs] berühmt I

fan [fæn] Fan I; Ventilator IV U3, 59
fancy dress [ˌfænsi ˈdres] Verkleidung; Kostüm I
fantastic [fænˈtæstɪk] fantastisch; großartig II
fantasy [ˈfæntəsi] Fantasie; Fantasy II
FAQ (= frequently asked questions) [ˌefeɪˈkjuː (ˌfriːkwəntli ˌɑːskt ˈkwestʃənz)] häufig gestellte Fragen <IV U1, 30>
far [fɑː] weit III
as far as [ˌəz ˈfɑːr͜ əz] soweit IV U3, 59
fare [feə] Fahrpreis III
farewell speech [feəˈwel spiːtʃ] Abschiedsrede II
farm [fɑːm] Bauernhof I
wind farm [ˈwɪnd fɑːm] Windpark III
farmer [ˈfɑːmə] Landwirt; Landwirtin; Bauer; Bäuerin I
farmers' market [ˌfɑːməz ˈmɑːkɪt] Bauernmarkt <IV U3, 72>
farming [ˈfɑːmɪŋ] Landwirtschaft; Ackerbau <IV U2, 136>
farmland [ˈfɑːmlænd] Ackerland; Ackerboden; Landwirtschaftsflächen IV U2, 32
fascinating [ˈfæsɪneɪtɪŋ] faszinierend IV U4, 77
fashion *(no pl)* [ˈfæʃn] Mode IV U3, 58
out of fashion [ˌaʊt͜ əv ˈfæʃn] altmodisch; nicht mehr aktuell <IV U3, 72>
fashionable [ˈfæʃnəbl] modisch II
fast [fɑːst] schnell II
fast food [ˌfɑːst ˈfuːd] Fastfood I
fast food restaurant [ˌfɑːst fuːd ˈrestrɒnt] Fastfood-Restaurant I
the fastest [ðə ˈfɑːstɪst] der/die/das schnellste I
father [ˈfɑːðə] Vater I
favorite *(AE)* [ˈfeɪvrɪt] Lieblings- IV U3, 53
favourite [ˈfeɪvrɪt] Lieblings- I
feature [ˈfiːtʃə] Merkmal <III>; Feature; Artikel <IV U2, 49>
feature story [ˈfiːtʃə ˌstɔːri] Leitartikel; Sonderbericht <IV U5, 110>
February [ˈfebruri] Februar I
fed [fed] simple past von *to feed* I; past participle von *to feed* II
*to be **fed** up (with) [biː fed͜ ˈʌp (wɪð)] die Nase voll haben (von); sauer sein III
federal [ˈfedrl] Bundes-; föderalistisch <IV U4, 88>
fee [fiː] Gebühr <IV U3, 66>
*to **feed** [fiːd] füttern I
feedback [ˈfiːdbæk] Feedback; Rückmeldung IV U2, 39
*to **feel** [fiːl] (sich) fühlen II
to feel sorry for [ˌfiːl ˈsɒri] Mitleid haben mit; bedauern III
to make sb feel like sth [ˌmeɪk … ˈfiːl laɪk] jmdm. das Gefühl geben, etw. zu sein III
feeling [ˈfiːlɪŋ] Gefühl <III>
fell [fel] simple past von *to fall* I
felt [felt] simple past von *to feel* II
felt-tip [ˌfeltˈtɪp] Filzstift I
fever [ˈfiːvə] Fieber IV U4, 86
a **few** [ə ˈfjuː] ein paar; wenige; einige III
science **fiction** [ˌsaɪəns ˈfɪkʃn] Science-Fiction I
fictional [ˈfɪkʃnl] fiktiv <IV U1, 135>
field [fiːld] Feld; Wiese; Weide IV ZI, 9
field goal [ˈfiːld ˌɡəʊl] Feldtor <IV U2, 50>
fifteen [ˌfɪfˈtiːn] fünfzehn I
fifty [ˈfɪfti] fünfzig I
fight [faɪt] Kampf; Streit III
*to **fight** [faɪt] kämpfen; (sich) streiten III
file [faɪl] Datei II
to **fill** [fɪl] befüllen <IV U3, 71>
filled with [ˈfɪld ˌwɪð] gefüllt mit <IV U3, 72>
filling [ˈfɪlɪŋ] Füllung <IV U5, 112>
film [fɪlm] Film I
film maker [ˈfɪlm ˌmeɪkə] Filmemacher; Filmemacherin <III>
to **film** [fɪlm] filmen; drehen <III>
final match [ˌfaɪnl ˈmætʃ] Endspiel <IV U2, 50>
finally [ˈfaɪnli] schließlich; zum Schluss II
financial [faɪˈnænʃl] finanziell; Finanz- IV U1, 14
*to **find** [faɪnd] finden; herausfinden I
to find out [ˌfaɪnd͜ ˈaʊt] herausfinden I
fine [faɪn] schön; gut; in Ordnung II
finger [ˈfɪŋɡə] Finger III
fingerprint [ˈfɪŋɡəprɪnt] Fingerabdruck II
to **finish** [ˈfɪnɪʃ] beenden; enden; aufhören; fertigstellen; vervollständigen II
fire [faɪə] Feuer I
to be on fire [biː ɒn ˈfaɪə] brennen II
fire engine [ˈfaɪər͜ˌendʒɪn] Feuerwehrauto II
firework [ˈfaɪəwɜːk] Feuerwerk <IV U3, 138>
first [fɜːst] zuerst; als Erstes; erste I
fish *(sg)* [fɪʃ], **fish** *(pl)* [fɪʃ] Fisch I
fisherman [ˈfɪʃəmən] Fischer <IV U2, 136>
fishing [ˈfɪʃɪŋ] Angeln; Fischen <IV U5, 143>
to **fit** [fɪt] passen II
to fit (in) [fɪt (ɪn)] hineinpassen (in) <IV U2, 35>
fit [fɪt] fit; in Form III
fitness [ˈfɪtnəs] Fitness <IV U3, 72>
fitness instructor [ˈfɪtnəs ɪnˌstrʌktə] Fitnesstrainer; Fitnesstrainerin <IV U3, 72>
jumping fitness [ˈdʒʌmpɪŋ ˌfɪtnəs] Jumping Fitness *(Trendsportart)* IV U4, 81
five [faɪv] fünf I
to **fix** [fɪks] fixieren; befestigen <IV U3, 71>
flag [flæɡ] Flagge; Fahne II
flamingo [fləˈmɪŋɡəʊ] Flamingo I
flat [flæt] Wohnung I
flew [fluː] simple past von *to fly* II

flight [flaɪt] Flug II
to **float** [fləʊt] treiben <IV U3, 71>
floor [flɔː] Fußboden I; Stockwerk II
flour [flaʊə] Mehl II
to cover in flour [ˌkʌvər‿ɪn ˈflaʊə] in Mehl wenden IV U5, 98
flower [ˈflaʊə] Blume III
flown [fləʊn] past participle von *to fly* II
fluent [ˈfluːənt] fließend; flüssig III
*to **fly** [flaɪ] fliegen II
flyer [ˈflaɪə] Flyer; Faltblatt II
foggy [ˈfɒgi] neblig I
to **fold** in half [ˌfəʊld‿ɪn ˈhɑːf] in der Mitte falten <IV U4, 92>
to **follow** [ˈfɒləʊ] befolgen; folgen III
food [fuːd] Essen; Nahrung; Lebensmittel I
food stall [ˈfuːd ˌstɔːl] Essensstand II
better quality food [ˌbetə ˈkwɒləti ˌfuːd] qualitativ besseres Essen <IV U3, 72>
foot *(sg)* [fʊt], **feet** *(pl)* [fiːt] Fuß I
on foot [ɒn ˈfʊt] zu Fuß I
football [ˈfʊtbɔːl] Fußball I
for [fɔː] für I; seit IV U4, 80
for five months [fə ˈfaɪv ˌmʌnθs] fünf Monate lang I
for fun [fə ˈfʌn] zum Spaß III
forbidden [fəˈbɪdn] verboten IV U3, 58
foreground [ˈfɔːgraʊnd] Vordergrund III
in the foreground [ɪn ðə ˈfɔːgraʊnd] im Vordergrund III
foreign [ˈfɒrɪn] fremd; ausländisch IV U1, 18
forest [ˈfɒrɪst] Wald IV U3, 53
*to **foretell** [fɔːˈtel] vorhersagen III
forever [fəˈrevə] für immer; ewig II
*to **forget** [fəˈget] vergessen I
forgot [fəˈgɒt] simple past von *to forget* I
forgotten [fəˈgɒtn] past participle von *to forget* II
fork [fɔːk] Gabel II
form [fɔːm] Form <III>; Art <IV U2, 48>
approval form [əˈpruːvl ˌfɔːm] Einverständnisformular <IV U2, 44>
entry form [ˈentri ˌfɔːm] Anmeldeformular II
forty [ˈfɔːti] vierzig I
forward [ˈfɔːwəd] vorwärts <IV U2, 137>
fought [fɔːt] simple past, past participle von *to fight* III
to **found** [faʊnd] gründen IV U5, 98
found [faʊnd] simple past von *to find* I
four [fɔː] vier I
fourteen [ˌfɔːˈtiːn] vierzehn I
fourth [fɔːθ] vierte I
land of the **free** [ˌlænd‿əv ðə ˈfriː] Land der Freien IV U3, 53
free [friː] kostenlos III
free range [ˌfriː ˈreɪndʒ] Freiland- II
free time [ˌfriː ˈtaɪm] Freizeit I
freedom *(no pl)* [ˈfriːdəm] Freiheit; Unabhängigkeit IV U1, 23
religious freedom [ˌrɪlɪdʒəs ˈfriːdəm] Religionsfreiheit <IV U3, 70>
*to **freeze** [friːz] frieren; gefrieren III
freeze frame [ˈfriːz ˌfreɪm] Standbild <I>
freezing [ˈfriːzɪŋ] eiskalt; gefrierend <IV U1, 30>
French [frentʃ] Französisch I
the **French** *(pl)* [ðə ˈfrenʃ] die Franzosen IV U5, 98
fresh [freʃ] frisch II
Friday [ˈfraɪdeɪ] Freitag I
fridge [frɪdʒ] Kühlschrank III
fried [fraɪd] (in der Pfanne) gebraten II
friend [frend] Freund; Freundin I
to make friends [ˌmeɪk ˈfrendz] Freundschaften schließen I
to see friends [siː ˈfrendz] Freunde treffen I
to **friend** [frend] befreunden *(jmdn. zu seiner Freundesliste hinzufügen)* IV U4, 81
friendly [ˈfrendli] freundlich; nett III
frisbee [ˈfrɪzbi] Frisbee; Frisbeescheibe I
from [frɒm] aus; von I
from behind [ˌfrəm bɪˈhaɪnd] von hinten I
front [frʌnt] Vorderseite; Front-; Vorder- <IV U1,
at the front of [ət ðə ˈfrʌnt‿əv] an der Spitze (von); im vorderen Bereich II
in front of [ɪn ˈfrʌnt‿əv] vor; davor II
froze [frəʊz] simple past von *to freeze* III
frozen [ˈfrəʊzn] past participle von *to freeze* III
fruit [fruːt] Frucht; Obst I
to **fry** [fraɪ] braten; frittieren IV U5, 98
full [fʊl] vollwertig <IV U2, 137>; voll IV U5, 106
fun [fʌn] Freude; Spaß I
for fun [fə ˈfʌn] zum Spaß III
fundamental [ˌfʌndəˈmentl] Grundlage <IV U2, 49>
funeral [ˈfjuːnrəl] Beerdigung; Begräbnis <IV U5, 108>
funny [ˈfʌni] lustig; witzig I; merkwürdig; seltsam II
furious [ˈfjʊəriəs] wütend III
further [ˈfɜːðə] weiter <IV U2, 136>
future [ˈfjuːtʃə] Zukunft IV U1, 18

G

galaxy [ˈgæləksi] Galaxie; Galaxis <IV U2, 48>
gallery [ˈgælri] Galerie <IV U1, 28>
game [geɪm] Spiel I
gamer [ˈgeɪmə] Spieler *(Computer)*; Spielerin *(Computer)* II
street **gang** [ˈstriːt ˌgæŋ] Straßengang <IV U1, 134>
garden [ˈgɑːdn] Garten I
garlic [ˈgɑːlɪk] Knoblauch II
gas [gæs] Gas III
gas *(AE)* [gæs] Benzin <IV U3, 66>
gateway [ˈgeɪtweɪ] Tor; Eingangstor IV U1, 12
to **gather** [ˈgæðə] (sich) sammeln IV U3, 64

gave [geɪv] simple past von *to give* II
gel [dʒel] Gel III
 hair gel ['heə ˌdʒel] Haargel III
 shower gel ['ʃaʊə ˌdʒel] Duschgel III
generous ['dʒenrəs] großzügig IV U2, 39
geocaching ['dʒiəʊkæʃɪŋ] Geocaching I
Geography [dʒi'ɒgrəfi] Geografie; Erdkunde I
German ['dʒɜ:mən] Deutsch I; deutsch; aus Deutschland III
***to get** [get] bekommen; werden I; holen II; verstehen III
 to get around [ˌget ə'raʊnd] herumkommen III
 to get cold [ˌget 'kəʊld] frieren III
 to get dressed [ˌget 'drest] sich anziehen II
 to get in ['get‿ɪn] hereinkommen I
 to get into [ˌget‿'ɪntə] hineingelangen; hineinkommen IV U1, 14
 to get lost [get lɒst] sich verirren I
 to get married [ˌget 'mærɪd] heiraten II
 to get off [ˌget‿'ɒf] aussteigen II
 to get on (the bus) [ˌget‿'ɒn] einsteigen (in den Bus) IV U5, 106
 to get out [ˌget 'aʊt] herauskommen III
 to get ready [ˌget 'redi] sich vorbereiten; sich fertig machen IV U3, 54
 to get started [ˌget 'stɑ:tɪd] anfangen <III>
 to get sth [get] etw. verstehen IV U5, 102
 to get stuck [ˌget 'stʌk] stecken bleiben IV U3, 54
 to get tired of sth [ˌget 'taɪəd‿əv] etw. sattbekommen; etw. satthaben IV U1, 14
 to get to know [ˌget tə 'nəʊ] kennen lernen II
 to get up [ˌget‿'ʌp] aufstehen I
 to get used to (sth) [ˌget 'ju:zd tə] sich an (etw.) gewöhnen IV U1, 18
gherkin ['gɜ:kɪn] Essiggurke <IV U5, 112>
ghost [gəʊst] Geist II
giant [dʒaɪənt] Riese III
giant [dʒaɪənt] Riesen-; riesig IV U4, 74
giraffe [dʒɪ'rɑ:f] Giraffe I
girl [gɜ:l] Mädchen I
girlfriend ['gɜ:lfrend] Freundin *(in einer Paarbeziehung)* IV U2, 38
***to give** [gɪv] geben I
 to give a talk [ˌgɪv‿ə 'tɔ:k] einen Vortrag halten <III>
 to give reasons [ˌgɪv 'ri:znz] Gründe nennen; Gründe angeben III
 to give sth a miss [ˌgɪv sʌmθɪŋ‿ə 'mɪs] auf etw. verzichten; etw. bleiben lassen III
 to give up [ˌgɪv‿'ʌp] aufgeben IV U1, 18
glad [glæd] froh IV U3, 54
glass [glɑ:s] Glas II
global ['gləʊbl] global; weltweit <IV U1, 134>
glove [glʌv] Handschuh <IV U2, 50>
glue [glu:] Klebstoff I
 glue stick ['glu: ˌstɪk] Klebestift <IV U3, 71>
***to go** [gəʊ] gehen; fahren I
 to go beach combing [gəʊ 'bi:tʃ ˌkəʊmɪŋ] den Strand nach Strandgut absuchen II
 to go camping [ˌgəʊ 'kæmpɪŋ] campen gehen; zelten II
 to go on [ˌgəʊ‿'ɒn] hineingehen II; weitermachen <IV U2, 37>
 to go out with [ˌgəʊ‿'aʊt wɪð] (aus)gehen mit IV U3, 58
 to go shopping [ˌgəʊ 'ʃɒpɪŋ] einkaufen gehen II
 to go sightseeing [gəʊ 'saɪtsi:ɪŋ] eine Besichtigungstour machen II
 to go swimming [ˌgəʊ 'swɪmɪŋ] schwimmen gehen I
 to go to bed [ˌgəʊ tə 'bed] ins Bett gehen I
field goal ['fi:ld ˌgəʊl] Feldtor <IV U2, 50>
goat [gəʊt] Ziege III
thank God [ˌθæŋk‿'gɒd] Gott sei Dank <IV U3, 70>
gold [gəʊld] Gold III
gold [gəʊld] golden; Gold- III
 gold rush ['gəʊld ˌrʌʃ] Goldrausch IV U4, 84
golden ['gəʊldn] golden; Gold- IV U5, 98
gone [gɒn] past participle von *to go* II
good [gʊd] gut I
 to be good at [bi: 'gʊd‿ət] gut sein in/bei I
 Good morning. [ˌgʊd 'mɔ:nɪŋ] Guten Morgen. II
 good luck [ˌgʊd 'lʌk] viel Glück II
Goodbye. [gʊd'baɪ] Auf Wiedersehen. I
gospel ['gɒspl] Gospel *(Musikrichtung)* IV U5, 97
gossip ['gɒsɪp] Klatsch; Tratsch; Gerede IV U3, 58
got [gɒt] simple past von *to get* I
government ['gʌvnmənt] Regierung <IV U1, 24>
 state government ['steɪt ˌgʌvnmənt] Landesregierung IV U5, 98
GPS *(Global Positioning System)* [ˌdʒi:pi:'es] GPS I
to grab [græb] schnappen; greifen; ergreifen III
grade *(AE)* [greɪd] Note; Klasse IV U2, 33
graduation [ˌgrædʒu'eɪʃn] Schulabschluss <IV U2, 48>
graffiti [grə'fi:ti] Graffiti <IV U1, 134>
grammar ['græmə] Grammatik <I>
grandad ['grændæd] Opa III
 great-great-grandad [ˌgreɪtgreɪt 'grændæd] Ururopa I
grandfather ['grænˌfɑ:ðə] Großvater II
grandma ['grænmɑ:] Oma II
grandmother ['grænˌmʌðə] Großmutter III

grandparents *(pl)* ['græn,peərənts] Großeltern II
graphic design [,græfɪk dɪ'zaɪn] Grafikdesign; grafische Gestaltung <IV U2, 49>
grass [grɑ:s] Gras I
grated ['greɪtɪd] gerieben <IV U5, 112>
grave [greɪv] Grab III
great [greɪt] großartig; toll I
great-grandparents [,greɪt'græn,peərənts] Urgroßeltern IV U1, 25
Greek [gri:k] griechisch; Griechisch; aus Griechenland IV U5, 99
green [gri:n] grün I
greengrocer's ['gri:n,grəʊsəz] Obst- und Gemüseladen III
grew [gru:] simple past von *to grow* IV U3, 58
grey [greɪ] grau I
grizzly bear ['grɪzli ,beə] Grizzlybär <IV U1, 30>
groceries *(pl)* ['grəʊsriz] Lebensmittel IV U4, 89
ground [graʊnd] Boden; Erdboden III
group [gru:p] Gruppe I
tutor group ['tju:tə ,gru:p] Klasse *(in einer englischen Schule)* I
*to **grow** [grəʊ] anbauen; züchten; ziehen; wachsen IV U3, 58
to grow up [,grəʊ‿'ʌp] aufwachsen III
grown [grəʊn] past participle von *to grow* IV U3, 58
to **guess** [ges] erraten; raten; überlegen II; schätzen; vermuten IV U3, 59
guest [gest] Gast III
guestbook ['gestbʊk] Gästebuch <I>
guide [gaɪd] Führer; Führerin II
guided tour ['gaɪdɪd ,tɔ:] Führung <IV U1, 13>
guinea pig ['gɪni ,pɪg] Meerschweinchen I
guitar [gɪ'tɑ:] Gitarre III
gun [gʌn] Schusswaffe IV U3, 62
guy [gaɪ] Typ; Kerl IV U2, 42
guys *(pl)* [gaɪz] Leute II
gym(nasium) [dʒɪm (dʒɪm'neɪziəm)] Turnhalle IV U2, 42
gymnasium [dʒɪm'neɪziəm] Fitnessraum III

H

had [hæd] simple past von *to have* I; past participle von *to have* II
haggis ['hægɪs] Haggis *(schottisches Gericht aus Schafsinnereien)* III
hair [heə] Haar; Haare III
hair gel ['heə ,dʒel] Haargel III
hair straightener ['heə ,streɪtnə] Haarglätter I
haircut ['heəkʌt] Haarschnitt II
to have a haircut ['heəkʌt] sich die Haare schneiden lassen II
hairdo ['heədu:] Frisur <IV U4, 77>
hairdresser ['heə,dresə] Friseur; Friseurin II
hairdryer ['heə,draɪə] Fön III
half *(sg)* [hɑ:f], **halves** *(pl)* [hɑ:vz] (die) Hälfte IV U4, 80
to fold in half [,fəʊld‿ɪn 'hɑ:f] in der Mitte falten <IV U4, 92>
half [hɑ:f] halb III
half a million [,hɑ:f‿ə 'mɪljən] eine halbe Million III
half past (two) [,hɑ:f 'pɑ:st] halb (drei) I
hall [hɔ:l] Flur; Diele; Korridor II
town hall [,taʊn 'hɔ:l] Rathaus II
ham [hæm] Schinken II
hand [hænd] Hand I
*to **hang** [hæŋ] hängen II
to **happen** ['hæpn] geschehen; passieren II
That's what happened. [,ðæts wɒt 'hæpnd] Das ist passiert. II
happy ['hæpi] glücklich I
Happy birthday! [,hæpi 'bɜ:θdeɪ] Alles Gute zum Geburtstag! I
harbor *(AE)* ['hɑ:bə] Hafen IV U1, 22
harbour ['hɑ:bə] Hafen II
hard [hɑ:d] hart; schwer; schwierig II
hardly ['hɑ:dli] kaum <IV U4, 88>
hard-working [,hɑ:d'wɜ:kɪŋ] fleißig IV U2, 39
harvest ['hɑ:vɪst] Ernte <IV U3, 70>
hat [hæt] Hut II
to **hate** [heɪt] hassen; nicht mögen I
*to **have** [hæv] haben I; essen II
to have a haircut ['heəkʌt] sich die Haare schneiden lassen II
to have a look [,hæv‿ə 'lʊk] anschauen II
to have breakfast [,hæv 'brekfəst] frühstücken I
to have got [hæv 'gɒt] besitzen; haben II
to have to ['hæv tə] müssen II
Please have a seat. [,pli:z hæv‿ə‿'si:t] Bitte Platz nehmen. IV U3, 55
he [hi:] er I
head [hed] Kopf II
head chef ['hed ʃef] Chefkoch II
head first ['hed fɜ:st] kopfüber III
headache ['hedeɪk] Kopfschmerzen; Kopfweh II
heading ['hedɪŋ] Überschrift; Titel <III>
headline ['hedlaɪn] Schlagzeile; Überschrift IV U4, 77
headphones *(pl)* ['hedfəʊnz] Kopfhörer IV U3, 59
health [helθ] Gesundheits-; gesundheitlich <IV U4, 88>
*to **hear** [hɪə] hören I
heard [hɜ:d] simple past von *to hear* I; past participle von *to hear* II
heartbeat ['hɑ:tbi:t] Herzschlag <IV U2, 35>
heat [hi:t] Hitze IV U5, 102
heavy ['hevi] schwer; stark II
height [haɪt] Höhe II
held [held] simple past, past participle von *to hold* III
helicopter ['helɪkɒptə] Helikopter; Hubschrauber I
Hello. [hə'ləʊ] Hallo. I
Hello there. [hə'ləʊ ,ðeə] Hallo.; Grüß dich. I
helmet ['helmət] Helm III
help [help] Hilfe II

to **help** [help] helfen I
to help oneself [ˌhelp wʌn'self] sich bedienen III
I couldn't help but … [ˌaɪ kʊdnt 'help bʌt] Ich konnte nicht anders als … III
helper ['helpə] Helfer; Helferin IV U4, 89
helpful ['helpfl] hilfsbereit; hilfreich; nützlich IV U2, 38
her [hɜː] ihr, ihre; sie I
here [hɪə] hier I
Here you are. [ˌhɪə ju‿'ɑː] Bitte schön. I
hero *(sg)* ['hɪərəʊ], **heroes** *(pl)* ['hɪərəʊz] Held III
hers [hɜːz] ihre II
herself [hɜː'self] sie selbst; sich selbst III
Hi. [haɪ] Hi.; Hallo. I
to say hi to [ˌseɪ 'haɪ tə] grüßen; Grüße ausrichten I
hid [hɪd] simple past von *to hide* III
hidden ['hɪdn] past participle von *to hide* III
*to **hide** [haɪd] (sich) verstecken III
high [haɪ] hoch; groß I
high school ['haɪ ˌskuːl] Highschool *(weiterführende Schule, Oberstufe)* IV U1, 18
highlighted ['haɪlaɪtɪd] markiert <III>
high-tech [ˌhaɪ'tek] Hightech- IV U4, 75
to **hike** [haɪk] wandern II
hiking ['haɪkɪŋ] Wandern III
hill [hɪl] Berg; Hügel IV U4, 74
him [hɪm] ihm; ihn I
himself [hɪm'self] sich (selbst); er selbst III
hip hop ['hɪphɒp] Hip-Hop *(Musik)* III
his [hɪz] sein I; seins; seiner II
History ['hɪstrɪ] Geschichte I
history ['hɪstri] Geschichte III
*to **hit** [hɪt] treffen; schlagen II; (sich) stoßen; anstoßen; gegen etw. fahren III
hit [hɪt] simple past, past participle von *to hit* II
hobby ['hɒbi] Hobby III

*to **hold** [həʊld] halten; festhalten III
hole [həʊl] Loch I
holiday ['hɒlədeɪ] Ferien; Urlaub I
national holiday [ˌnæʃnl 'hɒlədeɪ] Nationalfeiertag <IV U1, 24>
home [həʊm] Zuhause; Heim; nach Hause I
at home [ət 'həʊm] zu Hause I
back home [bæk 'həʊm] zu Hause II
Homecoming *(AE)* ['həʊmˌkʌmɪŋ] Ehemaligentreffen IV U2, 33
homepage ['həʊmpeɪdʒ] Homepage <I>
homeroom ['həʊmruːm] erste Stunde *(in der Schule)* IV U2, 45
homeschooling ['həʊmˌskuːlɪŋ] Hausunterricht <IV U2, 34>
*to be **homesick** [biː 'həʊmsɪk] Heimweh haben III
homework ['həʊmwɜːk] Hausaufgabe(n) I
to do homework [ˌduː 'həʊmwɜːk] Hausaufgabe(n) machen I
honestly ['ɒnɪstli] ehrlich IV U3, 63
honor *(AE)* ['ɒnə] Ehre IV U1, 25
to **hoover** ['huːvə] staubsaugen II
hope [həʊp] Hoffnung IV U1, 13
to **hope** [həʊp] hoffen I
hopeful ['həʊpfl] hoffnungsvoll III
horrible ['hɒrəbl] schrecklich; furchtbar III
horse [hɔːs] Pferd I
horse riding ['hɔːs ˌraɪdɪŋ] Reiten I
hospital ['hɒspɪtl] Hospital; Krankenhaus I
host [həʊst] Talkmaster; Gastgeber; Gastgeberin <IV U3, 69>
host family ['həʊst ˌfæmli] Gastfamilie IV U2, 34
hostel ['hɒstl] Herberge III
hot [hɒt] heiß I
hot BBQ sauce [hɒt 'bɑːbɪkjuː ˌsɔːs] scharfe Grillsoße <IV U5, 112>
hot dog ['hɒt ˌdɒg] Hot Dog *(Würstchen im Brötchen)* IV U1, 14
hotel [həʊ'tel] Hotel II
hour [aʊə] Stunde I

rush hour ['rʌʃ ˌaʊə] Hauptverkehrszeit IV U1, 14
working hours *(pl)* ['wɜːkɪŋ ˌaʊəz] Arbeitszeit IV U2, 39
40 kilometres an hour [kɪ'lɒmɪtəz‿ən‿'aʊə] 40 Kilometer pro Stunde I
house [haʊs] Haus I
around the house [ə'raʊnd ðə haʊs] im Haus I
State House *(AE)* ['steɪt ˌhaʊs] Regierungsgebäude IV U5, 98
how [haʊ] wie I
How about …? [ˌhaʊ‿ə'baʊt] Wie wäre es mit …? II
how are things going [ˌhaʊ ɑː θɪŋz 'gəʊɪŋ] wie läuft's; wie geht's IV U3, 55
How are you? [ˌhaʊ‿'ɑː jə] Wie geht es dir? I
How are you doing? [ˌhaʊ‿ə jə 'duːɪŋ] Wie geht es dir? IV U3, 54
how do I get there [ˌhaʊ du aɪ 'get ðeə] wie komme ich dahin III
how many [ˌhaʊ 'meni] wie viele II
How much (is/are) …? [ˌhaʊ 'mʌtʃ‿ɪz/ɑː] Wie viel (kostet/kosten) …? I
How old are you? [haʊ‿'əʊld‿ə juː] Wie alt bist du? I
How to … ['haʊ tə] Wie man … II
How's it going? [ˌhaʊz‿ɪt 'gəʊɪŋ] Wie geht's?; Wie läuft's? IV U3, 54
however [haʊ'evə] jedoch III
huge [hjuːdʒ] riesig; riesengroß IV ZI, 9
a/one **hundred** ['hʌndrəd] einhundert; hundert I
hung [hʌŋ] simple past, past participle von *to hang* II
hunger ['hʌŋgə] Hunger <IV U2, 136>
hungry ['hʌŋgri] hungrig I
to **hunt** [hʌnt] jagen <IV U2, 136>
hunter ['hʌntə] Jäger; Jägerin IV U4, 85
to **hurry** ['hʌri] sich beeilen II
*to **hurt** [hɜːt] weh tun; verletzen II
hurt [hɜːt] simple past, past participle von *to hurt* II; verletzt II
husband ['hʌzbənd] Ehemann IV U3, 54

husky ['hʌski] Husky *(Schlittenhunderasse)* <IV U1, 30>

I

I [aɪ] ich I
  I don't know! [ˌaɪ ˌdəʊnt 'nəʊ] Ich weiß (es) nicht! I
  I see. [aɪ 'si:] Ich verstehe. IV U5, 103
  I wouldn't like (to) … [aɪ 'wʊdnt laɪk (tə)] Ich möchte nicht …; Ich würde nicht gerne … I
  I'd like (to) … (= I would like to) [aɪd 'laɪk (tə)] Ich möchte …; Ich würde gerne … I
  I'd rather [aɪd 'rɑ:ðə] ich würde lieber III
  I'm from … ['aɪm ˌfrɒm] Ich komme aus … I
  I'm sorry. [aɪm 'sɒrɪ] Es tut mir leid.; Entschuldigung. I
crushed **ice** ['krʌʃt ˌaɪs] zerstoßenes Eis <IV U5, 113>
ice cream [ˌaɪs 'kri:m] Eiscreme; Eis I
iceberg ['aɪsbɜ:g] Eisberg III
ID [ˌaɪ'di:] Ausweis; Personalausweis III
idea [aɪ'dɪə] Idee; Ahnung I
ideal [aɪ'dɪəl] ideal; optimal <IV U3, 72>
if [ɪf] wenn; falls II
ill [ɪl] krank; schlecht II
illegally [ɪ'li:gli] illegal; unrechtmäßig; rechtswidrig <IV U4, 88>
illness ['ɪlnəs] Krankheit <IV U2, 136>
to **imagine** [ɪ'mædʒɪn] sich vorstellen <IV U2, 39>
immigrant ['ɪmɪgrənt] Immigrant; Immigrantin; Einwanderer; Einwandererin IV U1, 13
to **immigrate** ['ɪmɪgreɪt] einwandern; immigrieren IV U1, 18
immigration [ˌɪmɪ'greɪʃn] Immigration; Zuwanderung IV U1, 22
impact ['ɪmpækt] Einfluss; Auswirkung IV U4, 80
speech **impaired** ['spi:tʃ ɪmˌpeərd] sprachbehindert IV U5, 102
important [ɪm'pɔ:tnt] wichtig; einflussreich II
impossible [ɪm'pɒsəbl] unmöglich III
to **impress** [ɪm'pres] beeindrucken III
in [ɪn] in I; drinnen II
  in August [ɪn 'ɔ:gəst] im August I
  in between [ˌɪn bɪ'twi:n] dazwischen <IV U4, 92>
  in front of [ɪn 'frʌnt‿əv] vor; davor II
  in the afternoon [ˌɪn ði ˌɑ:ftə'nu:n] nachmittags I
  in the background [ɪn ðə 'bækgraʊnd] im Hintergrund III
  in the centre of [ˌɪn ðə 'sentər‿əv] in der Mitte III
  in the country [ɪn ðə 'kʌntri] auf dem Land I
  in the distance [ˌɪn ðə 'dɪstns] in der Ferne IV U1, 15
  in the end [ɪn ði 'end] schließlich; zum Schluss II
  in the evenings [ɪn ði 'i:vnɪŋz] abends III
  in the foreground [ɪn ðə 'fɔ:graʊnd] im Vordergrund III
  in the middle [ɪn ðə 'mɪdl] in der Mitte III
  in the south of [ˌɪn ðə 'saʊθ‿əv] im Süden von III
  in the world [ɪn ðə 'wɜ:ld] auf der Welt II
  in time [ɪn 'taɪm] rechtzeitig I
inch [ɪnʃ] Zoll (Längenmaß: 2, 54 cm) <IV U5, 112>
to **include** [ɪn'klu:d] beinhalten; einschließen <IV U2, 48>
income ['ɪnkʌm] Einkommen <IV U4, 88>
independence [ˌɪndɪ'pendəns] Unabhängigkeit IV U1, 13
Indian ['ɪndiən] indisch I; indisch II; Indianer; Indianerin <IV U3, 70>
individual [ˌɪndɪ'vɪdʒuəl] individuell; einzeln <IV U2, 48>
indoor [ˌɪn'dɔ:] Hallen-; Innen- III
Industrial Revolution [ɪnˌdʌstriəl revl'u:ʃn] industrielle Revolution III
industry ['ɪndəstri] Industrie III
influence ['ɪnfluəns] Einfluss IV U5, 98
information *(no pl)* [ˌɪnfə'meɪʃn] Information; Informationen I
  information desk [ɪnfə'meɪʃn ˌdesk] Information II
informative [ɪn'fɔ:mətɪv] informativ IV U4, 77
ingredient [ɪn'gri:diənt] Zutat II
inhabitant [ɪn'hæbɪtnt] Einwohner; Einwohnerin; Bewohner; Bewohnerin III
injection [ɪn'dʒekʃn] Spritze III
injured ['ɪndʒəd] verletzt <IV U4, 88>
innocent ['ɪnəsnt] unschuldig IV U3, 63
insect ['ɪnsekt] Insekt III
inside [ˌɪn'saɪd] in … hinein II; in; innen in; im Innern III; innen; drinnen IV U1, 25
instead [ɪn'sted] stattdessen; anstelle von IV U4, 80
instruction [ɪn'strʌkʃn] Unterricht; Anweisung <IV U2, 44>
instructor [ɪn'strʌktə] Lehrer; Lehrerin III
  fitness instructor ['fɪtnəs ɪnˌstrʌktə] Fitnesstrainer; Fitnesstrainerin <IV U3, 72>
intelligent [ɪn'telɪdʒnt] intelligent; klug; vernünftig III
interest ['ɪntrəst] Interesse <IV U2, 137>
to **interest** ['ɪntrəst] interessieren <IV U4, 89>
*to be **interested** in [bi: 'ɪntrəstɪd‿ɪn] sich interessieren für; interessiert sein an III
interesting ['ɪntrəstɪŋ] interessant I
internet ['ɪntənet] Internet II
  to surf the internet [ˌsɜ:f ði 'ɪntənet] im Internet surfen II
to **interrupt** [ˌɪntə'rʌpt] unterbrechen IV U4, 94
interview ['ɪntəvju:] Interview; Befragung II; Vorstellungsgespräch IV U2, 38
to **interview** ['ɪntəvju:] interviewen; befragen I

interviewer [ˈɪntəvjuːə] Interviewer; Interviewerin; Befrager; Befragerin IV U1, 18
to **introduce** [ˌɪntrəˈdjuːs] einführen; einleiten <IV U2, 44>; zeigen <IV U2, 48>
introduction [ˌɪntrəˈdʌkʃn] Einleitung; Einführung III
to **invade** [ɪnˈveɪd] einmarschieren (in); eindringen (in) III
to **invent** [ɪnˈvent] erfinden III
invention [ɪnˈvenʃn] Erfindung III
inventor [ɪnˈventə] Erfinder; Erfinderin III
invincible [ɪnˈvɪnsəbl] unschlagbar; unbesiegbar <IV U2, 35>
invitation [ˌɪnvɪˈteɪʃn] Einladung I
to **invite** [ɪnˈvaɪt] einladen I
Irish [ˈaɪrɪʃ] irisch; Irisch III
is [ɪz] ist I
 ... is £1.25. [ɪz ˈwʌn paʊnd twentiˌfaɪv] ... kostet ein Pfund fünfundzwanzig. I
Islam [ˈɪzlɑːm] Islam <IV U5, 206>
island [ˈaɪlənd] Insel II
isn't it? [ˈɪznt‿ɪt] nicht wahr?; stimmt's? II
it [ɪt] es I
IT (Information Technology) [ˌaɪˈtiː, ɪnfəˌmeɪʃn tekˈnɒlədʒi] Informatik; Informationstechnik I
Italian [ɪˈtæliən] italienisch; Italienisch; Italiener; Italienerin II
its [ɪts] sein; ihr III
itself [ɪtˈself] (sich) selbst III

J

jacket [ˈdʒækɪt] Jacke II
 jacket potato [ˌdʒækɪt pəˈteɪtəʊ] Ofenkartoffel II
jam [dʒæm] Marmelade; Konfitüre III
 traffic jam [ˈtræfɪk ˌdʒæm] Stau IV U1, 14
Jamaican [dʒəˈmeɪkən] jamaikanisch II
January [ˈdʒænjuri] Januar I
Japanese [ˌdʒæpənˈiːz] japanisch; Japanisch; aus Japan; Japaner; Japanerin IV U5, 99
jar [dʒɑː] Glas III
jazz [dʒæz] Jazz *(Musikrichtung)* IV U5, 97
jealous [ˈdʒeləs] eifersüchtig; neidisch II
jeans *(pl)* [dʒiːnz] Jeans I
jersey [ˈdʒɜːzi] Trikot <IV U2, 50>
jewellery [ˈdʒuːəlri] Schmuck II
Jewish [ˈdʒuːɪʃ] jüdisch <IV U5, 206>
job [dʒɒb] Job I; Aufgabe; Tätigkeit; Arbeit; Beruf II
 job title [ˈdʒɒb ˌtaɪtl] Stellenbezeichnung; Berufsbezeichnung IV U2, 38
to **join** [dʒɔɪn] sich anschließen III; verbinden <IV U2, 48>
joke [dʒəʊk] Witz I
journalism [ˈdʒɜːnlɪzm] Journalistik; Journalismus IV U2, 34
journalistic [ˈdʒɜːnlɪstɪk] journalistisch <IV U2, 49>
journey [ˈdʒɜːni] Fahrt; Reise III
to **joust** [dʒaʊst] einen Turnierzweikampf austragen; turnieren III
jousting [ˈdʒaʊstɪŋ] Turnierzweikampf III
joyful [ˈdʒɔɪfl] freudig <IV U5, 108>
judge [dʒʌdʒ] Juror; Jurorin II
juice [dʒuːs] Saft II
July [dʒʊˈlaɪ] Juli I
jumble sale [ˈdʒʌmbl ˌseɪl] Flohmarkt II
to **jump** [dʒʌmp] zusammenzucken; erschrecken III; springen IV U3, 63
 jumping fitness [ˈdʒʌmpɪŋ ˌfɪtnəs] Jumping Fitness *(Trendsportart)* IV U4, 81
June [dʒuːn] Juni I
jungle [ˈdʒʌŋgl] Dschungel IV U4, 85
junior [ˈdʒuːniə] Nachwuchs- <IV U2, 137>
just [dʒʌst] gerade (eben); soeben; nur II

K

karate [kəˈrɑːti] Karate III
kebab [kɪˈbæb] Döner <IV U5, 206>
*to **keep** [kiːp] halten II
 to keep cool [ˌkiːp ˈkuːl] Ruhe bewahren <III>
 to keep going [kiːp ˈgəʊɪŋ] weitergehen; weitermachen IV U4, 85
 to keep in touch [ˌkiːp ɪn ˈtʌtʃ] in Verbindung bleiben II
 to keep out [ˌkiːp‿ˈaʊt] draußen halten III
kept [kept] simple past, past participle von *to keep* II
ketchup [ˈketʃʌp] Ketchup II
key word [ˈkiː ˌwɜːd] Stichwort; Schlüsselbegriff <IV U3, 68>
keyword [ˈkiːwɜːd] Schlüsselwort <IV U1, 31>
kid [kɪd] Kind II
kidney bean [ˈkɪdni ˌbiːn] Kidneybohne II
to **kill** [kɪl] töten III
kilogram (kg) [ˈkɪləgræm] Kilogramm (kg) I
 7 kilograms a day [ˌkɪləgræmz‿ə ˈdeɪ] sieben Kilogramm täglich I
kilometre (km) [kɪˈlɒmɪtə] Kilometer (km) I
 40 kilometres an hour [kɪˈlɒmɪtəz‿ən‿ˈaʊə] 40 Kilometer pro Stunde I
kilt [kɪlt] Schottenrock; Kilt III
kind [kaɪnd] freundlich; nett II
king [kɪŋ] König III
kiss [kɪs] Kuss II
kitchen [ˈkɪtʃɪn] Küche I
knee [niː] Knie III
knife *(sg)* [naɪf], **knives** *(pl)* [naɪvz] Messer II
knight [naɪt] Ritter III
*to **know** [nəʊ] wissen; kennen I; verstehen IV U5, 103
 to get to know [ˌget tə ˈnəʊ] kennen lernen II
 I don't know! [ˌaɪ ˌdəʊnt ˈnəʊ] Ich weiß (es) nicht! I

knowledge *(no pl)* ['nɒlɪdʒ] Wissen; Kenntnisse <IV U1, 24>
*to be **known** as [bi: 'nəʊn‿əz] bekannt sein als <IV U3, 70>

L

lab fee ['læb ˌfi:] Laborgebühr <IV U2, 48>
label ['leɪbl] Etikett; Beschriftung <IV U1, 27>
to **label** ['leɪbl] beschriften <III>
ladder ['lædə] Leiter I
lady ['leɪdi] Dame; Frau II
laid [leɪd] simple past, past participle von *to lay* II
lake [leɪk] See III
lamb [læm] Lamm II
lamp [læmp] Lampe I
land [lænd] Land II
land of the free [ˌlænd‿əv ðə 'fri:] Land der Freien IV U3, 53
to **land** [lænd] landen IV U3, 54
landlord ['lændlɔ:d] Eigentümer II
landowner ['lændˌəʊnə] Grundbesitzer; Grundbesitzerin IV U4, 84
landscape ['lændskeɪp] Landschaft IV ZI, 9
language ['læŋgwɪdʒ] Sprache II
language detectives ['læŋgwɪdʒ ˌdɪtektɪvz] Sprachdetektive <I>
language tip [ˌlæŋgwɪdʒ 'tɪp] Grammatikhinweis <I>
sign language ['saɪn ˌlæŋgwɪdʒ] Gebärdensprache; Zeichensprache III
laptop ['læptɒp] Laptop I
large [lɑ:dʒ] groß II
lasagne [lə'zænjə] Lasagne II
to **last** [lɑ:st] dauern; andauern; anhalten IV U4, 86
last [lɑ:st] letzte I
at last [ət 'lɑ:st] endlich; zu guter Letzt II
late [leɪt] (zu) spät I
later ['leɪtə] später I
to **laugh** [lɑ:f] lachen II
to mow the **lawn** [ˌməʊ ðə 'lɔ:n] den Rasen mähen <IV U2, 191>
*to **lay** [leɪ] legen; decken II
to lay the table [ˌleɪ ðə 'teɪbl] den Tisch decken II
layout ['leɪaʊt] Layout; Anordnung IV U4, 77
lead [li:d] Leine I
leader ['li:də] Führer; Führerin; Anführer; Anführerin III
to **learn** [lɜ:n] lernen II
to learn about sth [ˌlɜ:n ə'baʊt] etwas erfahren über III
least [li:st] geringste; am wenigsten <IV U3, 59>
leather ['leðə] Leder III
leave [li:v] lassen; verlassen; abfahren II
leaving ['li:vɪŋ] Abschieds- II
left [left] simple past, past participle von *to leave* II
left [left] links III
to turn left [ˌtɜ:n 'left] (nach) links abbiegen I
on the left [ɒn ðə 'left] auf der linken Seite; links I
leg [leg] Bein II
lemon ['lemən] Zitrone II
lemonade [ˌlemə'neɪd] Limonade II
*to **lend** [lend] leihen; verleihen II
length *(no pl)* [leŋθ] Dauer; Länge <IV U2, 44>
lent [lent] simple past von *to lend* II
less [les] weniger III
lesson ['lesn] Schulstunde; Unterricht I
let's [lets] lass uns I
Let's see ... [ˌlets 'si:] Lass mal sehen ...; Also ... I
letter ['letə] Buchstabe; Brief III
lettuce ['letɪs] Kopfsalat II
water **level** ['wɔ:tə ˌlevl] Wasserpegel; Wasserstand <IV U5, 142>
library ['laɪbri] Bibliothek; Bücherei III
driver's **license** *(AE)* ['draɪvəz ˌlaɪsns] Führerschein IV U2, 38
lid [lɪd] Deckel <IV U3, 71>
life *(sg)* [laɪf], **lives** *(pl)* [laɪvz] Leben I
lifeboat ['laɪfbəʊt] Rettungsboot III
lifestyle ['laɪfstaɪl] Lebensart; Lifestyle IV U4, 74
lifetime ['laɪftaɪm] Leben; Lebenszeit IV U4, 76
lift [lɪft] Aufzug; Lift <IV U1, 15>
light [laɪt] Licht IV U1, 13
light bulb ['laɪt ˌbʌlb] Glühbirne III
tea light ['ti: ˌlaɪt] Teelicht <IV U3, 71>
lights [laɪts] Ampel IV U1, 14
to **like** [laɪk] mögen I
to like ... best [ˌlaɪk 'best] am meisten mögen; am liebsten mögen I
would like [wʊd 'laɪk] würde(n) gern; hätte(n) gern II
I wouldn't like (to) ... [aɪ 'wʊdnt laɪk (tə)] Ich möchte nicht ...; Ich würde nicht gerne ... I
I'd like (to) ... (= I would like to) [aɪd 'laɪk (tə)] Ich möchte ...; Ich würde gerne ... I
Would you like (to) ...? [ˌwʊd jə 'laɪk (tə)] Möchtest du? I
like [laɪk] wie I
like this [laɪk 'ðɪs] so; auf diese Weise I
line [laɪn] Zeile; Linie II
line dance ['laɪn ˌdɑ:ns] Line Dance *(alle tanzen zusammen in einer Reihe)* <IV U5, 143>
lines *(pl)* [laɪnz] Text II
link [lɪŋk] Link; Verbindung IV U4, 80
linking word [ˌlɪŋkɪŋ 'wɜ:d] Verbindungswort <IV U3, 73>
lion ['laɪən] Löwe I
list [lɪst] Liste II
ranking list ['ræŋkɪŋ lɪst] Rangliste; Rangfolge <IV U3, 59>
shopping list ['ʃɒpɪŋ ˌlɪst] Einkaufszettel I
to **listen** (to) ['lɪsn] zuhören; anhören; hören I
listener ['lɪsənə] Zuhörer; Zuhörerin II
listening ['lɪsnɪŋ] Hörverstehen <I>
little ['lɪtl] klein II

a little [ə 'lɪtl] ein bisschen II
to **live** [lɪv] wohnen; leben I
living room ['lɪvɪŋ ˌrʊm] Wohnzimmer I
loaf *(sg)* [ləʊf], **loaves** *(pl)* [ləʊvz] Brotlaib III
local ['ləʊkl] hiesig; örtlich; lokal III
to **locate** [ləʊ'keɪt] finden <IV U2, 48>
location [ləʊ'keɪʃn] Drehort; Lage III; Aufenthaltsort; Standort <IV U5, 111>
to **lock** [lɒk] abschließen I
locker ['lɒkə] Schließfach; Spind IV U2, 34
lonely ['ləʊnli] einsam III
long [lɒŋ] lang I
look [lʊk] Blick; Anblick; Sicht IV U1, 14
to have a look [ˌhæv‿ə 'lʊk] anschauen II
to **look** [lʊk] schauen; nachschauen I; aussehen; sehen II
to look after [ˌlʊk‿'ɑ:ftə] aufpassen; hüten II
to look at ['lʊk‿ət] anschauen I
to look for ['lʊk fə] suchen nach II
to look up [ˌlʊk‿'ʌp] aufschauen; nachschauen II
Look ... [lʊk] Schau mal ...; Schau ... nach. I
lookout point ['lʊkaʊt ˌpɔɪnt] Aussichtspunkt II
loose [lu:s] locker; lose II
lorry driver ['lɒri ˌdraɪvə] LKW-Fahrer; LKW-Fahrerin II
*to **lose** [lu:z] verlieren II
lost [lɒst] simple past von *to lose* II; past participle von *to lose* III
to get lost [get lɒst] sich verirren I
a **lot** [ə 'lɒt] viel I; sehr II
a lot of [ə 'lɒt‿əv] viel(e); eine Menge I
parking **lot** *(AE)* ['pɑ:kɪŋ ˌlɒt] Parkplatz IV U1, 15
body **lotion** ['bɒdi ˌləʊʃn] Körperlotion III
lots [lɒts] viel; jede Menge III
lots of ['lɒts‿əv] viel; jede Menge I
loud [laʊd] laut III
love [lʌv] Liebe IV U4, 85
*to fall in **love** (with) [ˌfɔ:l‿ɪn 'lʌv] sich verlieben (in) III
to **love** [lʌv] lieben; gern mögen I
loved ones ['lʌvd ˌwʌnz] Angehörige; Nahestehende <IV U5, 108>
lovely ['lʌvli] schön; herrlich; hübsch II
low [ləʊ] niedrig II
lower ['ləʊə] untere III
good **luck** [ˌgʊd 'lʌk] viel Glück II
luckily ['lʌkɪli] glücklicherweise II
*to be **lucky** [bi: 'lʌki] Glück haben III
lucky day [ˌlʌki 'deɪ] Glückstag II
lucky number [ˌlʌki 'nʌmbə] Glückszahl I
lunch [lʌnʃ] Mittagessen I
packed lunch [ˌpækt 'lʌnʃ] Lunchpaket; Vesper II
lunchtime ['lʌnʃtaɪm] Mittagszeit; Mittagspause I
lyrics *(pl)* ['lɪrɪks] Liedtext <II>

M

machine [mə'ʃi:n] Automat; Maschine II
payment machine ['peɪmənt ˌməʃi:n] Bezahlautomat II
made [meɪd] simple past von *to make* I; past participle von *to make* II
to be made of [bi: 'meɪd‿əv] hergestellt sein aus III
magazine [ˌmægə'zi:n] Zeitschrift I
magic ['mædʒɪk] Magie; Zauberei II
magic ['mædʒɪk] magisch; Zauber- II
main course [ˌmeɪn 'kɔ:s] Hauptgericht II
major ['meɪdʒə] Haupt-; wichtig; bedeutend IV ZI, 8
majority [mə'dʒɒrəti] Mehrheit IV U1, 23
*to **make** [meɪk] erstellen; machen; tun; bilden I
to make a cake [ˌmeɪk‿ə 'keɪk] einen Kuchen backen I
to make a reservation [ˌmeɪk‿ə 'rezəveɪʃn] reservieren III
to make friends [ˌmeɪk 'frendz] Freundschaften schließen I
to make it ['meɪk‿ɪt] es schaffen IV U3, 54
to make sb feel like sth [ˌmeɪk ... 'fi:l laɪk] jmdm. das Gefühl geben, etw. zu sein III
film **maker** ['fɪlm ˌmeɪkə] Filmemacher; Filmemacherin <III>
make-up ['meɪkʌp] Make-up; Schminke IV U3, 58
mama ['mæmə] Mama II
man *(sg)* [mæn], **men** *(pl)* [men] Mann I
manager ['mænɪdʒə] Manager; Managerin; Geschäftsführer; Geschäftsführerin IV U2, 38
many ['meni] viele II
how many [ˌhaʊ 'meni] wie viele II
map [mæp] Stadtplan; Landkarte III
mind map ['maɪnd ˌmæp] Wörternetz <I>
March [mɑ:tʃ] März I
to **march** [mɑ:tʃ] marschieren <IV U5, 108>
marching band ['mɑ:tʃɪŋ ˌbænd] Marschkapelle <IV U2, 190>
market ['mɑ:kɪt] Markt II
farmers' market [ˌfɑ:məz 'mɑ:kɪt] Bauernmarkt <IV U3, 72>
market stall ['mɑ:kɪt ˌstɔ:l] Marktstand; Marktbude <IV U2, 191>
marquee [mɑ:'ki:] Partyzelt; Festzelt <IV U1, 19>
*to get **married** [ˌget 'mærɪd] heiraten II
mashed potatoes [ˌmæʃt pə'teɪtəʊz] Kartoffelbrei II
mast [mɑ:st] Mast <IV U3, 71>
master ['mɑ:stə] Herr; Meister <IV U3, 71>
match [mætʃ] Spiel I
final match [ˌfaɪnl 'mætʃ] Endspiel <IV U2, 50>
to **match** [mætʃ] zuordnen I; zusammenpassen <IV U4, 95>

material [mə'tɪəriəl] Material; Stoff <III>
Math *(AE)* [mæθ] Mathematik; Mathe IV U2, 34
Maths [mæθs] Mathematik; Mathe I
It doesn't **matter.** [ɪt ˌdʌznt 'mætə] Es ist egal. II
May [meɪ] Mai I
may [meɪ] vielleicht; können; dürfen II
maybe ['meɪbi] vielleicht I
mayonnaise [ˌmeɪə'neɪz] Mayonnaise II
me [mi:] mich; ich; mir I
meal [mi:l] Essen; Mahlzeit II
*to **mean** [mi:n] bedeuten; meinen III
mean [mi:n] gemein IV U3, 63
meaning ['mi:nɪŋ] Bedeutung; Sinn <III>
meant [ment] simple past, past participle von *to mean* III
meat [mi:t] Fleisch I
social **media** [ˌsəʊʃl 'mi:diə] soziale Medien IV U4, 80
mediation [ˌmi:'di'eɪʃn] Sprachmittlung <I>
medicine ['medsn] Medikamente; Medizin III
*to **meet** [mi:t] kennen lernen; treffen I
menu ['menju:] Speisekarte II
mess [mes] Unordnung; Durcheinander I
message ['mesɪdʒ] Botschaft; Nachricht; SMS II
morning message ['mɔ:nɪŋ ˌmesɪdʒ] morgendliche Ansprache IV U2, 34
text message ['tekst ˌmesɪdʒ] SMS II
met [met] simple past von *to meet* I
metal ['metl] Metall III
method ['meθəd] Methode II
metre ['mi:tə] Meter I
microwave ['maɪkrəweɪv] Mikrowelle IV U3, 59
middle ['mɪdl] Mitte III
in the middle [ɪn ðə 'mɪdl] in der Mitte III
midnight ['mɪdnaɪt] Mitternacht III
migrant ['maɪgrnt] Migrant; Migrantin <IV U4, 88>
mild [maɪld] mild I
mile [maɪl] Meile II
square mile (= sq. mi.) [ˌskweə 'maɪl] Quadratmeile IV ZI, 8
milk [mɪlk] Milch I
milkshake ['mɪlkˌʃeɪk] Milchmischgetränk; Milchshake III
million ['mɪljən] Million III
half a million [ˌhɑ:f‿ə 'mɪljən] eine halbe Million III
mind map ['maɪnd ˌmæp] Wörternetz <I>
Never **mind.** [ˌnevə 'maɪnd] Macht nichts.; Schon gut.; Mach dir nichts draus. II
mine [maɪn] Bergwerk III
mine [maɪn] meins; meine II
of mine [əv 'maɪn] von mir II
miner ['maɪnə] Bergarbeiter; Bergarbeiterin III
mineral water ['mɪnrl ˌwɔ:tə] Mineralwasser III
minimum ['mɪnɪməm] Minimum; minimal; Mindest- IV U2, 38
minority [maɪ'nɒrəti] Minderheit IV U1, 22
minute ['mɪnɪt] Minute II
mirror ['mɪrə] Spiegel III
miserable ['mɪzrəbl] elend; armselig; jämmerlich III
*to give sth a **miss** [ˌgɪv sʌmθɪŋ‿ə 'mɪs] auf etw. verzichten; etw. bleiben lassen III
to **miss** [mɪs] verpassen; vermissen II
to **mix** [mɪks] mischen; vermischen; mixen IV U5, 98
mixed pickles [ˌmɪkst 'pɪklz] gemischtes Essiggemüse <IV U5, 112>
mobile (phone) ['məʊbaɪl (ˌfəʊn)] Handy; Mobiltelefon I
modern ['mɒdn] modern I
moment ['məʊmənt] Moment; Augenblick II
Monday ['mʌndeɪ] Montag I
money ['mʌni] Geld I
monkey ['mʌŋki] Affe I
monster ['mɒnstə] Ungeheuer; Monster III
month [mʌnθ] Monat I
monthly ['mʌnθli] monatlich III
monument ['mɒnjəmənt] Denkmal II
moral ['mɒrl] moralisch <IV U1, 24>
more [mɔ:] mehr I
morning ['mɔ:nɪŋ] Morgen; Vormittag I
Good morning. [ˌgʊd 'mɔ:nɪŋ] Guten Morgen. II
morning message ['mɔ:nɪŋ ˌmesɪdʒ] morgendliche Ansprache IV U2, 34
mosque [mɒsk] Moschee II
most [məʊst] die meisten; die Mehrheit I; am meisten II
mostly ['məʊstli] hauptsächlich <IV U5, 108>
mother ['mʌðə] Mutter I
to **motivate** ['məʊtɪveɪt] motivieren <IV U2, 50>
motorbike ['məʊtəbaɪk] Motorrad I
mountain ['maʊntɪn] Berg III
mouse *(sg)* [maʊs], **mice** *(pl)* [maɪs] Maus I
moussaka [mu'sɑ:kə] Moussaka II
mouth [maʊθ] Mund II
move [mu:v] Bewegung III
to **move** [mu:v] (sich) bewegen IV U1, 22
to move (house) [mu:v] umziehen II
movement ['mu:vmənt] Bewegung IV U5, 96
movie ['mu:vi] Film I
movie theater *(AE)* ['mu:vi ˌθi:ətə] Kino <IV U1, 134>
to **mow** the lawn [ˌməʊ ðə 'lɔ:n] den Rasen mähen <IV U2, 191>
Mr ['mɪstə] Herr *(Anrede)* I
Mrs ['mɪsɪz] Frau *(Anrede)* I
Ms [mɪz] Frau *(Anrede)* I
much [mʌtʃ] viel I
so much [ˌsəʊ 'mʌtʃ] so sehr III
too much [ˌtu: 'mʌtʃ] zu sehr II
mud [mʌd] Schlamm; Matsch III

muddy [ˈmʌdi] schlammig I
multicultural [ˌmʌltiˈkʌltʃrl] multikulturell IV U5, 98
mum [mʌm] Mama I
mural [ˈmjʊərəl] Wandgemälde III
murderer [ˈmɜːdrə] Mörder; Mörderin III
museum [mjuːˈziːəm] Museum II
music [ˈmjuːzɪk] Musik I
country and western music [ˌkʌntri ənd ˈwestən ˌmjuːzɪk] Countrymusik <IV U5, 143>
musical [ˈmjuːzɪkl] Musical <IV U1, 134>
musical [ˈmjuːzɪkl] Musik-; musikalisch III
musician [mjuːˈzɪʃn] Musiker; Musikerin <IV U4, 140>
Muslim [ˈmʊzlɪm] Muslim; Muslimin I; muslimisch <IV U5, 206>
must [mʌst] müssen I
must not/never [ˌmʌst ˈnɒt/ˈnevə] nicht/nie dürfen III
mustn't [ˈmʌsnt] nicht dürfen III
mustard [ˈmʌstəd] Senf II
my [maɪ] mein, meine I
My name is … [maɪ ˈneɪm‿ɪz] Ich heiße … I
myself [maɪˈself] selbst; selber III
mystery [ˈmɪstri] Rätsel; Geheimnis I

N

nacho [ˈnɑːtʃəʊ] Nacho <IV U5, 112>
to **nag** [næg] nörgeln; meckern III
nail [neɪl] Nagel III
nail scissors [ˈneɪl ˌsɪzəz] Nagelschere III
name [neɪm] Name I
to **name** [neɪm] benennen IV ZI, 9
named after [ˈneɪmd ˌɑːftə] benannt nach <IV U3, 70>
napkin [ˈnæpkɪn] Serviette II
narrator [nəˈreɪtə] Erzähler; Erzählerin I
national [ˈnæʃnl] National-; national III
national holiday [ˌnæʃnl ˈhɒlədeɪ] Nationalfeiertag <IV U1, 24>
national park [ˌnæʃnl ˈpɑːk] Nationalpark; Naturpark <IV U1, 30>
nationality [ˌnæʃnˈæləti] Nationalität; Staatsangehörigkeit <IV U5, 99>
Native American [ˌneɪtɪv‿əˈmerɪkən] Ureinwohner Amerikas; Ureinwohnerin Amerikas; Indianer; Indianerin; indianisch IV U2, 32
nature [ˈneɪtʃə] Natur III
naughty [ˈnɔːti] frech; böse III
near [nɪə] in der Nähe von I; nah III
to **need** [niːd] brauchen I
needn't [ˈniːdnt] nicht brauchen; nicht müssen I
with special **needs** [wɪð ˌspeʃl ˈniːdz] mit Behinderung; mit besonderen Bedürfnissen III
neighbor *(AE)* [ˈneɪbə] Nachbar; Nachbarin IV U3, 54
neighbour [ˈneɪbə] Nachbar; Nachbarin III
nervous [ˈnɜːvəs] nervös; aufgeregt II
net [net] Netz IV U4, 75
safety net [ˈseɪfti ˌnet] Sicherheitsnetz IV U4, 75
netball [ˈnetbɔːl] Korbball I
never [ˈnevə] nie; niemals I
Never mind. [ˌnevə ˈmaɪnd] Macht nichts.; Schon gut.; Mach dir nichts draus. II
new [njuː] neu I
New Yorker [ˌnjuː ˈjɔːkə] New Yorker; New Yorkerin IV U1, 13
news [njuːz] Neuigkeit(en); Nachricht(en) II
newsagent's [ˈnjuːzˌeɪdʒnts] Zeitschriftenladen III
newspaper [ˈnjuːsˌpeɪpə] Zeitung II
next [nekst] nächste I; als Nächstes II
next to [ˈnekst tə] neben I
nice [naɪs] schön; nett I; lecker; gut III
nickname [ˈnɪkneɪm] Spitzname <IV U4, 141>
niece [niːs] Nichte III
night [naɪt] Nacht I
night walk [ˌnaɪt ˈwɔːk] Nachtwanderung I
that night [ˌðæt ˈnaɪt] an jenem Abend; in jener Nacht II
nightmare [ˈnaɪtmeə] Alptraum <IV U3, 68>
nine [naɪn] neun I
nineteen [ˌnaɪnˈtiːn] neunzehn I
ninety [ˈnaɪnti] neunzig I
no [nəʊ] kein; keine; nein I
no one [ˈnəʊ wʌn] niemand I
No way! [ˌnəʊ ˈweɪ] Auf keinen Fall!; Was?!; Echt?! III
nobody [ˈnəʊbədi] niemand III
noise [nɔɪz] Geräusch I
noisy [ˈnɔɪzi] laut III
Norman [ˈnɔːmən] Normanne; Normannin III
the **Normans** [ðə ˈnɔːmənz] die Normannen III
north [nɔːθ] Norden III
north of [ˈnɔːθ‿əv] nördlich von IV ZI, 9
northwest [ˌnɔːθˈwest] Nordwesten III
northwest of [ˌnɔːθˈwest‿əv] nordwestlich III
nose [nəʊz] Nase I
not [nɒt] nicht I
not at all [ˌnɒt‿ət‿ˈɔːl] überhaupt nicht; gar nicht II
not … any [ˌnɒt … eni] kein II
not … any more [ˌnɒt … eni ˈmɔː] nicht mehr III
not … either [nɒt … ˈaɪðə] auch nicht III
not … yet [nɒt … ˈjet] noch nicht II
note [nəʊt] Geldschein II
notes [ˈnəʊts] Notizen <IV U2, 37>
nothing [ˈnʌθɪŋ] nichts IV U3, 63
noun [naʊn] Nomen; Hauptwort <I>
November [nəˈvembə] November I
now [naʊ] jetzt; nun I; heutzutage II
right now [ˌraɪt ˈnaʊ] gerade; jetzt gleich; sofort III
nowhere [ˈnəʊweə] nirgendwo; nirgendwohin IV U2, 34

nugget ['nʌgɪt] Klumpen; Nugget <IV U4, 92>
number ['nʌmbə] Nummer; Zahl I; Anzahl IV U4, 75
lucky number [ˌlʌki 'nʌmbə] Glückszahl I
ordinal number [ˌɔ:dɪnəl 'nʌmbə] Ordinalzahl <I>
phone number ['fəʊn ˌnʌmbə] Telefonnummer III
nurse [nɜ:s] Krankenschwester; Krankenpfleger II
nut [nʌt] Nuss I

O

o'clock [ə'klɒk] Uhr *(Zeitangabe bei vollen Stunden)* I
oak [əʊk] Eiche <IV U5, 142>
OAP [ˌəʊeɪ'pi:] Rentner; Rentnerin <IV U5, 207>
oat [əʊt] Hafer III
object ['ɒbdʒɪkt] Objekt; Gegenstand <III>
observation [ˌɒbzə'veɪʃn] Beobachtung <IV U2, 48>
ocean ['əʊʃn] Ozean; Meer IV ZI, 9
October [ɒk'təʊbə] Oktober I
the **odd** one out [ˌɒd wʌn‿'aʊt] das Wort, das nicht in die Gruppe passt <III>
of [ɒv] von I
of course [əv 'kɔ:s] natürlich; selbstverständlich I
of mine [əv 'maɪn] von mir II
off [ɒf] abseits von <IV U1, 134>; von … weg IV U5, 107
special **offer** [ˌspeʃl‿'ɒfə] Sonderangebot III
to **offer** ['ɒfə] anbieten IV U2, 38
office ['ɒfɪs] Büro II
post office ['pəʊst‿ˌɒfɪs] Postamt I
police officer [pə'li:s‿ɒfɪsə] Polizeibeamter; Polizeibeamtin I
official [ə'fɪʃl] offiziell IV U4, 84
often ['ɒfn] oft; häufig I
oh [əʊ] null *(bei Uhrzeiten und Telefonnummern)* I
oil [ɔɪl] Öl IV U5, 98
OK [əʊ'keɪ] okay I
old [əʊld] alt I
on [ɒn] auf; an I
to get on (the bus) [ˌget‿'ɒn] einsteigen (in den Bus) IV U5, 106
to try on [ˌtraɪ‿'ɒn] anprobieren II
on board ['ɒn bɔ:d] an Bord III
on foot [ɒn 'fʊt] zu Fuß I
on purpose [ɒn 'pɜ:pəs] absichtlich II
on 7th July [ɒn ðə 'sevnθ əv ˌdʒʊlaɪ] am 7. Juli I
on the bus [ˌɒn ðə 'bʌs] im Bus II
on the left [ɒn ðə 'left] auf der linken Seite; links I
on the right [ɒn ðə 'raɪt] auf der rechten Seite; rechts I
on the way [ˌɒn ðə ˌ'weɪ] auf dem Weg; unterwegs I
on time [ɒn 'taɪm] pünktlich III
on Tuesday [ˌɒn 'tju:zdeɪ] am Dienstag I
on TV [ɒn ˌti:'vi:] im Fernsehen IV U1, 13
on Wednesdays [ɒn 'wenzdeɪz] mittwochs I
on weekdays [ɒn 'wi:kdeɪz] unter der Woche; an Werktagen III
once [wʌns] einst; einmal IV U1, 25
once more ['wʌns ˌmɔ:] noch einmal II
one [wʌn] eins I
a/one hundred ['hʌndrəd] einhundert; hundert I
one day [wʌn 'deɪ] eines Tages III
one stop [ˌwʌn 'stɒp] einmal Umsteigen <IV U3, 66>
one(s) [wʌn(z)] *Platzhalter für ein Nomen* III
loved ones ['lʌvd ˌwʌnz] Angehörige; Nahestehende <IV U5, 108>
one-way ['wʌnweɪ] einfach <IV U3, 66>
onion ['ʌnjən] Zwiebel II
onion rings ['ʌnjən ˌrɪŋz] Zwiebelringe <IV U5, 112>
online [ˌɒn'laɪn] online II
only ['əʊnli] nur I; einzige II
to **open** ['əʊpn] öffnen; aufmachen I
opening ['əʊpnɪŋ] Anfang; Eröffnung <IV U5, 111>
opening times ['əʊpnɪŋ ˌtaɪmz] Öffnungszeiten <IV U5, 207>
operation [ˌɒpr'eɪʃn] Operation III
operator ['ɒpreɪtə] Vermittlung III
opinion [ə'pɪnjən] Meinung III
opposite ['ɒpəzɪt] Gegenteil <II>
opposite ['ɒpəzɪt] gegenüber I
optimistic [ˌɒptɪ'mɪstɪk] optimistisch III
or [ɔ:] oder I
orange ['ɒrɪndʒ] Orange I
orange ['ɒrɪndʒ] orange I
orchestra ['ɔ:kɪstrə] Orchester III
order ['ɔ:də] Reihenfolge <III>
to **order** ['ɔ:də] bestellen II
ordinal number [ˌɔ:dɪnəl 'nʌmbə] Ordinalzahl <I>
organic [ɔ:'gænɪk] Bio-; organisch <IV U3, 72>
to **organize** ['ɔ:gənaɪz] organisieren II
original [ə'rɪdʒnl] original; ursprünglich <IV U1, 24>
other ['ʌðə] andere; weitere I
each other [ˌi:tʃ‿'ʌðə] einander; sich; sich gegenseitig III
others ['ʌðəz] andere II
the others [ðiˌ'ʌðəz] die anderen I
ounce [aʊns] Unze (Maßeinheit: 28,35 Gramm) <IV U5, 112>
our [aʊə] unser, unsere I
ours [aʊəz] unsere III
ourselves [ˌaʊə'selvz] selber; selbst III
out [aʊt] heraus II; aus; draußen; außerhalb <IV U3, 68>
to ask sb out [ˌɑ:sk … 'aʊt] sich mit jmdm. verabreden IV U2, 42
to fall out of [ˌfɔ:l‿'aʊt‿əv] herausfallen aus IV U2, 42
to go out with [ˌgəʊ‿'aʊt wɪð] (aus) gehen mit IV U3, 58
to keep out [ˌki:p‿'aʊt] draußen halten III
to point out [ˌpɔɪnt‿'aʊt] hinweisen auf <IV U1, 183>

out and about [ˌaʊt‿ən‿əˈbaʊt] unterwegs I
out of [ˈaʊt‿əv] aus … heraus II; von <IV U2, 44>
out of fashion [ˌaʊt‿əv ˈfæʃn] altmodisch; nicht mehr aktuell <IV U3, 72>
outdated [ˌaʊtˈdeɪtɪd] veraltet IV U4, 81
outdoor [ˌaʊtˈdɔː] Freiluft-; Outdoor- III
outfit [ˈaʊtfɪt] Outfit; Kleidung III
outline [ˈaʊtlaɪn] Skizze; Kontur; Überblick <III>
outside [ˌaʊtˈsaɪd] draußen; im Freien II; außerhalb IV U2, 38
oven [ˈʌvn] Backofen II
over [ˈəʊvə] über IV U1, 12
over there [ˌəʊvə ˈðeə] da drüben; dort drüben II
to **own** [əʊn] besitzen II
own [əʊn] eigene II

P

p.m. [ˌpiːˈem] nachmittags *(Uhrzeit)* II
to **pack** [pæk] packen; einpacken II
to pack up [ˈpæk‿ʌp] packen; einpacken II
package [ˈpækɪdʒ] Paket IV U5, 102
packed lunch [ˌpækt ˈlʌnʃ] Lunchpaket; Vesper II
packet [ˈpækɪt] Packung; Tüte I
pad [pæd] Polster; Schutz <IV U2, 50>
paddle [ˈpædl] Paddel <IV U3, 72>
paddle steamer [ˈpædl ˌstiːmə] Raddampfer <IV U5, 142>
standup **paddleboarding** [ˈstændʌp ˌpædlbɔːdɪŋ] Stehpaddeln <IV U3, 72>
paddlewheel [ˈpædlˌwiːl] Schaufelrad <IV U5, 142>
page [peɪdʒ] Seite I
paid [peɪd] simple past, past participle von *to pay* II
to **paint** [peɪnt] streichen; anmalen; malen II

pair [peə] Paar <III>
a pair of [ə ˈpeər‿əv] ein Paar II
pancake [ˈpænkeɪk] Pfannkuchen II
to **panic** [ˈpænɪk] panisch werden II
pantomime [ˈpæntəmaɪm] Weihnachtstheaterstück II
paper [ˈpeɪpə] Papier III
paperboy [ˈpeɪpəˌbɔɪ] Zeitungsausträger IV U2, 41
papergirl [ˈpeɪpəˌɡɜːl] Zeitungsausträgerin IV U2, 41
papers *(pl)* [ˈpeɪpəz] Unterlagen; Papiere IV U1, 19
parade [pəˈreɪd] Parade; Umzug III
paradise [ˈpærədaɪs] Paradies IV ZI, 9
paragraph [ˈpærəɡrɑːf] Paragraf; Absatz <IV U2, 43>
pardon [ˈpɑːdn] Begnadigung; Entschuldigung; Verzeihung IV U3, 67
Pardon? [ˈpɑːdn] Wie bitte? I
to **pardon** [ˈpɑːdn] begnadigen; entschuldigen; verzeihen IV U3, 53
parent [ˈpeərnt] Elternteil <IV U1, 184>
parents *(pl)* [ˈpeərnts] Eltern II
park [pɑːk] Park I
amusement park [əˈmjuːzmənt ˌpɑːk] Freizeitpark <IV U4, 201>
national park [ˌnæʃnl ˈpɑːk] Nationalpark; Naturpark <IV U1, 30>
theme park [ˈθiːm ˌpɑːk] Freizeitpark I; Themenpark II
parking lot *(AE)* [ˈpɑːkɪŋ ˌlɒt] Parkplatz IV U1, 15
parrot [ˈpærət] Papagei I
part [pɑːt] Rolle; Teil II
to take part (in) [ˌteɪk ˈpɑːt] teilnehmen (an) II
partner [ˈpɑːtnə] Partnerin; Partner III
party [ˈpɑːti] Party; Feier I
to **pass** [pɑːs] reichen II
passenger [ˈpæsndʒə] Passagier; Passagierin II
passive [ˈpæsɪv] Passiv; Passiv- <IV U5, 100>
past [pɑːst] Vergangenheit III
past perfect [ˌpɑːst ˈpɜːfɪkt] Plusquamperfekt <IV U1, 21>

past [pɑːst] nach *(bei Uhrzeitangaben)* II; vorbei III
half past (two) [ˌhɑːf ˈpɑːst] halb (drei) I
pasta [ˈpæstə] Pasta; Nudeln II
pasta bake [ˌpæstə ˈbeɪk] Nudelauflauf II
to **paste** [peɪst] einfügen II
pasty [ˈpæsti] Pastete II
patient [ˈpeɪʃnt] Patient; Patientin II
patient [ˈpeɪʃnt] geduldig III
patterned [ˈpætənd] gemustert II
*to **pay** [peɪ] bezahlen II
to pay back [ˌpeɪ ˈbæk] zurückzahlen II
to pay the bill [ˌpeɪ ðə ˈbɪl] die Rechnung bezahlen III
pay phone [ˈpeɪ fəʊn] Münztelefon III
payment machine [ˈpeɪmənt ˌməʃiːn] Bezahlautomat II
PE (Physical Education) [ˌpiːˈiː, ˌfɪzɪkl edʒʊˈkeɪʃn] Sportunterricht I
peace [piːs] Frieden III
peaceful [ˈpiːsfl] friedlich IV U5, 96
peach [piːtʃ] Pfirsich I
peanut butter [ˌpiːnʌt ˈbʌtə] Erdnussbutter III
pecan [ˈpiːkæn] Pekannuss IV U3, 67
pen [pen] Füller; Stift I
pence *(pl)* [pens], **penny** *(sg)* [ˈpeni] Pence *(brit. Währungseinheit)* I
… are 99p. [ɑː ˈnaɪntinaɪn ˌpens] … kosten 99 Pence. I
pencil [ˈpensl] Bleistift; Buntstift I
pencil case [ˈpensl ˌkeɪs] Federmäppchen I
pencil sharpener [ˈpensl ˌʃɑːpnə] Anspitzer I
penguin [ˈpeŋɡwɪn] Pinguin I
people *(pl)* [ˈpiːpl] Leute; Menschen I
pepper [ˈpepə] Pfeffer II
peppermint [ˈpepəmɪnt] Pfefferminz <IV U5, 113>
per [pɜː] pro IV U2, 41
percent (%) [pəˈsent] Prozent IV U1, 23
past **perfect** [ˌpɑːst ˈpɜːfɪkt] Plusquamperfekt <IV U1, 21>

present **perfect** [ˌpreznt 'pɜːfɪkt] das Perfekt <III>
perfect ['pɜːfɪkt] perfekt; vollkommen IV ZI, 9
performance [pə'fɔːməns] Aufführung; Vorstellung <IV U2, 50>
perfume ['pɜːfjuːm] Parfüm III
period ['pɪəriəd] Stunde; Unterrichtsstunde IV U2, 34
study hall period ['stʌdi hɔːl ˌpɪəriəd] Freistunde IV U2, 34
permanent ['pɜːmnənt] permanent; dauerhaft <IV U1, 24>
person ['pɜːsn] Person; Mensch II
personal ['pɜːsnl] persönlich III
perspective [pə'spektɪv] Perspektive; Blickwinkel <IV U3, 68>
pesticide ['pestɪsaɪd] Pestizid; Schädlingsbekämpfungsmittel <IV U4, 88>
pet [pet] Haustier I
phone [fəʊn] Telefon II
to answer the phone [ˌɑːnsə ðə 'fəʊn] ans Telefon gehen III
mobile (phone) ['məʊbaɪl (ˌfəʊn)] Handy; Mobiltelefon I
pay phone ['peɪ fəʊn] Münztelefon III
phone call ['fəʊn ˌkɔːl] Telefonanruf I
phone number ['fəʊn ˌnʌmbə] Telefonnummer III
to **phone** [fəʊn] anrufen; telefonieren II
photo ['fəʊtəʊ] Foto I
to take a photo [ˌteɪk‿ə 'fəʊtəʊ] ein Foto machen I
to take photos [ˌteɪk 'fəʊtəʊz] fotografieren; Fotos machen II
phrase [freɪz] Ausdruck; Redewendung; Satz <III>
PE (**Physical** Education) [ˌpiː'iː, ˌfɪzɪkl edʒʊ'keɪʃn] Sportunterricht I
to **pick** [pɪk] pflücken; herauslesen <IV U4, 88>; nehmen <IV U4, 93>
to pick up [ˌpɪk‿'ʌp] aufheben II; abholen IV U2, 43
to pick up the pieces [ˌpɪk‿ʌp ðə 'piːsiːz] wieder in den Griff bekommen <IV U2, 137>
mixed **pickles** [ˌmɪkst 'pɪklz] gemischtes Essiggemüse <IV U5, 112>
pick-up ['pɪkʌp] Abholung; Pick-up IV U5, 102
picnic ['pɪknɪk] Picknick I
picture ['pɪktʃə] Bild II; Film <IV U4, 140>
pie [paɪ] Kuchen; Pastete II
pie chart ['paɪ ˌtʃɑːt] Kuchendiagramm; Tortendiagramm <IV U1, 26>
piece [piːs] Stück II
a piece of [ə 'piːs‿əv] ein Stück <IV U1, 28>
piece of cake ['piːs‿əv keɪk] einfach <IV U3, 68>
pick up the pieces [ˌpɪk‿ʌp ðə 'piːsiːz] wieder in den Griff bekommen <IV U2, 137>
pierogi [pjɜ'rɔgi] Pirogge II
guinea **pig** ['gɪni ˌpɪg] Meerschweinchen I
pile [paɪl] Stapel; Haufen <IV U4, 93>
pilgrim ['pɪlgrɪm] Pilger- <IV U3, 139>
pinch [pɪntʃ] Prise II
pineapple ['paɪnæpl] Ananas III
pink [pɪŋk] pink; rosa I
pipe [paɪp] Rohr III
pirate ['paɪrət] Seeräuber; Seeräuberin; Pirat; Piratin I
pizza ['piːtsə] Pizza I
place [pleɪs] Platz; Stelle; Ort I
to take place [ˌteɪk 'pleɪs] stattfinden <IV U5, 108>
plain [pleɪn] Ebene <IV U2, 136>
plain [pleɪn] schlicht; einfach II
plan [plæn] Plan II
to **plan** [plæn] planen III
plane [pleɪn] Flugzeug II
planet ['plænɪt] Planet <IV U2, 48>
plank [plæŋk] Brett; Planke II
plant [plɑːnt] Pflanze I
plantain ['plæntеɪn] Kochbanane II
plantation [plæn'teɪʃn] Plantage IV U5, 97
plaster ['plɑːstə] Pflaster III
plastic ['plæstɪk] Plastik; Kunststoff III
plate [pleɪt] Teller II
play [pleɪ] Theaterstück II
role play ['rəʊl ˌpleɪ] Rollenspiel <II>
to **play** [pleɪ] spielen I
player ['pleɪə] Spieler; Spielerin II
playground ['pleɪgraʊnd] Schulhof; Pausenhof; Spielplatz I
playing card ['pleɪɪŋ ˌkɑːd] Spielkarte <IV U4, 92>
please [pliːz] bitte I
pledge [pledʒ] Versprechen IV U2, 45
pledge of allegiance [ˌpledʒ‿əv‿ə'liːdʒns] Treueeid IV U2, 45
pocket ['pɒkɪt] Tasche; Hosentasche II
pocketful ['pɒkɪtfʊl] Tasche voll <IV U1, 19>
podcast ['pɒdkɑːst] Podcast IV U4, 94
poem ['pəʊɪm] Gedicht III
lookout **point** ['lʊkaʊt ˌpɔɪnt] Aussichtspunkt II
starting **point** ['stɑːtɪŋ ˌpɔɪnt] Ausgangspunkt <III>
to **point** (at) [ˌpɔɪnt‿'ət] zeigen (auf) I
to point out [ˌpɔɪnt‿'aʊt] hinweisen auf <IV U1, 183>
police [pə'liːs] Polizei III
police officer [pə'liːs‿ɒfɪsə] Polizeibeamter; Polizeibeamtin I
Polish ['pəʊlɪʃ] polnisch; Polnisch; aus Polen IV U5, 99
polite [pə'laɪt] höflich II
polystyrene [ˌpɒlɪ'staɪriːn] Styropor <IV U3, 71>
swimming **pool** ['swɪmɪŋ ˌpuːl] Schwimmbad I
poor [pɔː] arm IV U1, 18
pop [pɒp] Pop <IV U5, 143>
popcorn ['pɒpkɔːn] Popcorn I
popular ['pɒpjələ] beliebt III
population [ˌpɒpjə'leɪʃn] Einwohner; Einwohnerzahl; Bevölkerung IV ZI, 8
pork [pɔːk] Schweinefleisch II
porridge ['pɒrɪdʒ] Haferbrei III
positive ['pɒzətɪv] positiv III

possessive pronoun [pə'sesɪv ˌprəʊnaʊn] Possessivpronomen <III>

post [pəʊst] Post *(online gestellte Nachricht)* IV U4, 80
post office ['pəʊst‿ɒfɪs] Postamt I

to **post** [pəʊst] aufgeben *(einen Brief)*; abschicken *(einen Brief)* III; online stellen; posten IV U4, 80

postcard ['pəʊstkɑ:d] Postkarte I

poster ['pəʊstə] Poster I

pot [pɒt] Topf III; Becher <IV U3, 71>

potato *(sg)* [pə'teɪtəʊ], **potatoes** *(pl)* [pə'teɪtəʊz] Kartoffel II
jacket potato [ˌdʒækɪt pə'teɪtəʊ] Ofenkartoffel II
mashed potatoes [ˌmæʃt pə'teɪtəʊz] Kartoffelbrei II

pound [paʊnd] Pfund *(brit. Währungseinheit)* I
... is £1.25. [ɪz 'wʌn paʊnd twentiˌfaɪv] ... kostet ein Pfund fünfundzwanzig. I

power ['paʊə] Energie; Kraft; Macht III

powerful ['paʊəfl] stark; mächtig; bedeutend; beeindruckend IV U1, 22

practical ['præktɪkl] praktisch IV U4, 89

practice ['præktɪs] Training; Übung I

to **practise** ['præktɪs] üben; trainieren III

prairie ['preəri] Prärie <IV U2, 136>

prayer [preə] Gebet IV U4, 85

to **prefer** [prɪ'fɜ:] vorziehen II

preparation [ˌprepr'eɪʃn] Zubereitung <IV U5, 112>

to **prepare** [prɪ'peə] zubereiten; vorbereiten III

prerequisite [ˌpri:'rekwɪzɪt] Voraussetzung <IV U2, 48>

present ['preznt] Geschenk I; Gegenwart; Präsens <IV U4, 140>
present perfect [ˌpreznt 'pɜ:fɪkt] das Perfekt <III>
present progressive [ˌpreznt prə'gresɪv] Verlaufsform der Gegenwart <III>
simple present [ˌsɪmpl 'preznt] Gegenwart; Präsens <III>

to **present** [prɪ'zent] vorstellen I; präsentieren <III>

presentation [ˌprezn'teɪʃn] Präsentation; Vortrag IV U2, 51

president ['prezɪdnt] Präsident; Präsidentin IV U3, 53

pretty ['prɪti] hübsch II

price [praɪs] Preis II

pride [praɪd] Stolz IV U5, 98

principal *(AE)* ['prɪnsɪpl] Schulleiter; Schulleiterin IV U2, 34

prison ['prɪzn] Gefängnis II

prize [praɪz] Preis II

probably ['prɒbəbli] wahrscheinlich III

problem ['prɒbləm] Problem I

process ['prəʊsəs] Prozess <IV U2, 48>

product ['prɒdʌkt] Produkt <III>

production [prə'dʌkʃn] Herstellung; Produktion <IV U4, 141>

profile ['prəʊfaɪl] Profil; Porträt; Steckbrief <III>

programme ['prəʊgræm] Programm; Sendung I

present **progressive** [ˌpreznt prə'gresɪv] Verlaufsform der Gegenwart <III>

project ['prɒdʒekt] Projekt III

to **promise** ['prɒmɪs] versprechen IV U3, 54

prompt card ['prɒmt ˌkɑ:d] Stichwortkarte <IV U2, 51>

possessive **pronoun** [pə'sesɪv ˌprəʊnaʊn] Possessivpronomen <III>

prop [prɒp] Requisit III

to **protect** [prə'tekt] schützen III

protective [prə'tektɪv] Schutz- <IV U2, 50>

protest ['prəʊtest] Protest; Demonstration IV U5, 96

to **protest** [prə'test] protestieren <IV U3, 138>

Protestant ['prɒtɪstnt] Protestant; Protestantin; protestantisch III

proud (of) [praʊd (əv)] stolz (auf) III

to **prove** [pru:v] beweisen IV U4, 84

pub [pʌb] Kneipe; Gasthaus III

public transport [ˌpʌblɪk 'trænspɔ:t] öffentliche Verkehrsmittel III

published ['pʌblɪʃt] veröffentlicht <IV U3, 72>

pudding ['pʊdɪŋ] Nachspeise; Pudding II

to **pull** [pʊl] ziehen I

pumpkin ['pʌmpkɪn] Kürbis; Kürbis- <IV U3, 72>

purple ['pɜ:pl] lila; violett I

on **purpose** [ɒn 'pɜ:pəs] absichtlich II

to **push** [pʊʃ] schieben; drücken I; schubsen; drängeln III

*to **put** [pʊt] setzen; legen; stellen I
to put a comment [ˌpʊt‿ə 'kɒment] einen Kommentar schreiben <I>
to put in [ˌpʊt‿'ɪn] einsetzen I
to put in the right order [ˌpʊt‿ɪn ðə 'raɪt ɔ:də] in die richtige Reihenfolge bringen I
to put on [ˌpʊt‿'ɒn] anlegen; anziehen III

put [pʊt] simple past von *to put* I

puzzle ['pʌzl] Rätsel; Puzzle <I>

Q

qualification [ˌkwɒlɪfɪ'keɪʃn] Qualifikation; Abschluss; Schulabschluss <IV U4, 88>

better **quality** food [ˌbetə 'kwɒləti ˌfu:d] qualitativ besseres Essen <IV U3, 72>

quarter ['kwɔ:tə] Viertel <IV U2, 50>
quarter past ['kwɔ:tə pɑ:st] Viertel nach I
quarter to ['kwɔ:tə tə] Viertel vor I

queen [kwi:n] Königin III

question ['kwestʃən] Frage I

queue [kju:] Warteschlange II

quick [kwɪk] schnell II

quiet ['kwaɪət] ruhig; leise; still III

quite [kwaɪt] ziemlich; ganz; völlig III

quiz [kwɪz] Quiz; Rätsel <I>

R

raccoon [rə'ku:n] Waschbär I
race [reɪs] Wettrennen; Rennen I
racism ['reɪsɪzm] Rassismus IV U5, 98
radiator ['reɪdieɪtə] Heizkörper IV U3, 59
radio ['reɪdiəʊ] Radio II
rafting ['rɑ:ftɪŋ] Rafting III
from **rags** to riches [frəm ˌræɡz tə‿'rɪtʃɪz] vom Tellerwäscher zum Millionär <IV U1, 28>
railway ['reɪlweɪ] Eisenbahn IV U4, 86
railway track ['reɪlweɪ ˌtræk] Gleis IV U3, 64
rain [reɪn] Regen IV U4, 85
to **rain** [reɪn] regnen I
rainbow ['reɪnbəʊ] Regenbogen III
raincoat ['reɪnkəʊt] Regenmantel III
rainy ['reɪni] regnerisch I
ran [ræn] simple past von *to run* III
rang [ræŋ] simple past von *to ring* III
to **rank** [ræŋk] einstufen <IV U3, 59>
ranking list ['ræŋkɪŋ lɪst] Rangliste; Rangfolge <IV U3, 59>
rap [ræp] Rap <I>
to **rap** [ræp] rappen II
rapper ['ræpə] Rapper; Rapperin III
raspberry ['rɑ:zbri] Himbeere III
to **rate** [reɪt] bewerten; einstufen III
I'd **rather** [aɪd 'rɑ:ðə] ich würde lieber III
rating ['reɪtɪŋ] Bewertung <III>
razor ['reɪzə] Rasierer; Rasierapparat IV U3, 59
RE (Religious Education) [ˌɑ:‿'ri:, rɪˌlɪdʒəs‿edʒʊ'keɪʃn] Religionsunterricht I
*to **read** [ri:d] lesen I
reading ['ri:dɪŋ] Lesen <I>
ready ['redi] fertig; bereit I
to get ready [ˌget 'redi] sich vorbereiten; sich fertig machen IV U3, 54
real [rɪəl] echt; richtig; wirklich II
reality [ri'æləti] Realität; Wirklichkeit <IV U1, 28>
really ['rɪəli] wirklich I; echt II
reason ['ri:zn] Grund III
to give reasons [ˌgɪv 'ri:znz] Gründe nennen; Gründe angeben III
*to **rebuild** [ˌri:'bɪld] wiederaufbauen <IV U2, 137>
receipt [ri'si:t] Quittung II
recipe ['resɪpi] Rezept II
to **record** [rɪ'kɔ:d] aufnehmen <III>
recording [rɪ'kɔ:dɪŋ] Aufnahme <III>
recording studio [rɪ'kɔ:dɪŋ ˌstju:diəʊ] Tonstudio I
recyclable [ˌri:'saɪkləbl] wiederverwertbar; recycelbar <IV U3, 71>
to **recycle** [ˌri:'saɪkl] recyceln; wiederverwerten <IV U3, 71>
red [red] rot I
redwood (tree) ['redwʊd (tri:)] Mammutbaum IV U4, 74
to **refuse** [rɪ'fju:z] ablehnen; sich weigern IV U5, 99
region ['ri:dʒn] Region; Gegend <IV U4, 79>
registration [ˌredʒɪ'streɪʃn] Überprüfung der Anwesenheit I; Anmeldung II
regular ['regjələ] regelmäßig; normal; üblich; gleichmäßig IV U4, 89
to **relax** [rɪ'læks] sich entspannen <IV U2, 47>
relaxed [rɪ'lækst] entspannt; locker; gelassen IV U4, 74
reliable [rɪ'laɪəbl] verlässlich; zuverlässig; vertrauenswürdig IV U5, 109
RE (**Religious** Education) [ˌɑ:‿'ri:, rɪˌlɪdʒəs‿edʒʊ'keɪʃn] Religionsunterricht I
religious freedom [ˌrɪlɪdʒəs 'fri:dəm] Religionsfreiheit <IV U3, 70>
to **remember** [rɪ'membə] sich merken; sich erinnern (an) II
to **remove** [rɪ'mu:v] entfernen IV U5, 98
rent [rent] Miete II
to **rent** [rent] mieten III
to **repair** [rɪ'peə] reparieren III
to **repeat** [rɪ'pi:t] wiederholen III
to **replace** [rɪ'pleɪs] ersetzen IV U1, 12
report [rɪ'pɔ:t] Bericht IV U4, 84
to **report** [rɪ'pɔ:t] berichten; wiedergeben; melden; sich melden; anzeigen <IV U5, 104>
reporter [rɪ'pɔ:tə] Reporter; Reporterin III
republic [rɪ'pʌblɪk] Republik III
required [rɪ'kwaɪəd] erforderlich; notwendig <IV U2, 48>
are required [rɪ'kwaɪəd] werden gebeten <IV U2, 48>
animal **rescue** shelter [ˌænɪml 'reskju: ˌʃeltə] Tierheim I
reservation [ˌrezə'veɪʃn] Reservierung IV U4, 76; Reservat IV U2, 32
to make a reservation [ˌmeɪk‿ə 'rezəveɪʃn] reservieren III
resident ['rezɪdnt] Bewohner; Bewohnerin; Anwohner; Anwohnerin; Einwohner; Einwohnerin <IV U1, 24>
to **respect** [rɪ'spekt] respektieren IV U4, 89
responsible [rɪs'pɒnsəbl] verantwortlich; verantwortungsvoll IV U2, 38
the **rest** [ðə 'rest] der Rest IV U1, 23
restaurant ['restrɒnt] Restaurant II
result [rɪ'zʌlt] Ergebnis II
*to **retell** [ˌri:'tel] nacherzählen; nochmals erzählen <IV U2, 42>
return ticket [rɪ'tɜ:n ˌtɪkɪt] Hin- und Rückfahrkarte III
to **return** [rɪ'tɜ:n] zurückkehren IV U4, 85
review [rɪ'vju:] Kritik III
rice [raɪs] Reis II
rich [rɪtʃ] reich III
ridden ['rɪdn] past participle von *to ride* II
ride [raɪd] Fahrt; Ritt IV U1, 14
*to **ride** [raɪd] fahren; reiten II
horse **riding** ['hɔ:s ˌraɪdɪŋ] Reiten I
right [raɪt] Recht IV U5, 96
civil rights *(pl)* [ˌsɪvl 'raɪts] Bürgerrechte IV U5, 96
right [raɪt] richtig; korrekt I; also II; rechts III; gerade; genau; in dem Moment als IV U2, 42
right ahead [ˌraɪt‿ə'hed] geradeaus IV U1, 15

right away [ˌraɪt‿əˈweɪ] sofort; gleich IV U4, 80
right now [ˌraɪt ˈnaʊ] gerade; jetzt gleich; sofort III
to be right [biː ˈraɪt] recht haben II
to do the right thing [ˌduː ðə ˈraɪt θɪŋ] das Richtige tun III
to turn right [ˌtɜːn ˈraɪt] (nach) rechts abbiegen I
all right [ˌɔːl ˈraɪt] in Ordnung; alles klar II
on the right [ɒn ðə ˈraɪt] auf der rechten Seite; rechts I
You're right. [jɔː‿ˈraɪt] Du hast recht. I
*to **ring** [rɪŋ] läuten; klingeln III
river [ˈrɪvə] Fluss I
road [rəʊd] Straße I
roadwork *(AE)* [ˈrəʊdwɜːk] Straßenbauarbeiten IV U1, 14
roast [rəʊst] gebraten <IV U3, 72>
roast beef [ˌrəʊst ˈbiːf] Roastbeef; Rinderbraten <IV U5, 112>
robotic [rəˈbɒtɪk] roboterhaft <IV U1, 134>
rock [rɒk] Fels; Stein III
rock climbing [ˈrɒk ˌklaɪmɪŋ] Klettern I
rock'n'roll [ˌrɒk‿ən ˈrəʊl] Rock 'n' Roll *(Musikrichtung)* IV U5, 97
rode [rəʊd] simple past von *to ride* II
role [rəʊl] Rolle IV U5, 107
role play [ˈrəʊl ˌpleɪ] Rollenspiel <II>
roller coaster [ˈrəʊlə ˌkəʊstə] Achterbahn II
the **Romans** [ðə ˈrəʊmənz] die Römer III
romance [ˈrəʊmæns] Liebesgeschichte III
Romanian [rʊˈmeɪniən] rumänisch; Rumänisch; aus Rumänien; Rumäne; Rumänin <IV U5, 206>
roof [ruːf] Dach II
room [ruːm] Zimmer; Raum I
rope [rəʊp] Seil I
rose [rəʊz] Rose IV ZI, 8
round **trip** [ˌraʊnd ˈtrɪp] Hin- und Rückflug; Hin- und Rückfahrt <IV U3, 66>
royal [ˈrɔɪəl] königlich II
rubber [ˈrʌbə] Gummi III
rubbish [ˈrʌbɪʃ] Müll; Abfall II
rude [ruːd] unhöflich; unverschämt IV U2, 39
rugby [ˈrʌgbi] Rugby III
to **ruin** [ˈruːɪn] ruinieren; zerstören II
rule [ruːl] Regel III
ruler [ˈruːlə] Lineal I
*to **run** [rʌn] rennen; laufen I; betreiben; leiten; führen III
to run about [ˈrʌn‿əˌbaʊt] herumrennen II
to run away [ˌrʌn‿əˈweɪ] weglaufen III
to run out of [ˌrʌn‿ˈaʊt‿əv] ausgehen *(Ware)* III
run [rʌn] past participle von *to run* III
rung [rʌŋ] past participle von *to ring* III
gold **rush** [ˈgəʊld ˌrʌʃ] Goldrausch IV U4, 84
to **rush** [rʌʃ] eilen; sich beeilen; stürzen III
to rush down [rʌʃ ˈdaʊn] hinuntereilen II
rush hour [ˈrʌʃ ˌaʊə] Hauptverkehrszeit IV U1, 14
Russian [ˈrʌʃn] russisch; Russisch; aus Russland; Russe; Russin IV U5, 99

S

sad [sæd] traurig III
safe [seɪf] sicher; ungefährlich III
safety [ˈseɪfti] Sicherheit IV U4, 75
safety measure [ˈseɪfti ˌmeʒə] Sicherheitsmaßnahme; Schutzmaßnahme <IV U2, 48>
safety net [ˈseɪfti ˌnet] Sicherheitsnetz IV U4, 75
said [sed] simple past von *to say* I
sail [seɪl] Segel <IV U3, 71>
to **sail** [seɪl] segeln <IV U3, 70>
sailing ship [ˈseɪlɪŋ ʃɪp] Segelboot <IV U3, 70>
saint [seɪnt] Heilige; Heiliger <IV U5, 108>
salad [ˈsæləd] Salat II
sale [seɪl] Schlussverkauf; Ausverkauf II
jumble sale [ˈdʒʌmbl ˌseɪl] Flohmarkt II
sales associate *(AE)* [ˌseɪlz əˈsəʊʃiət] Verkäufer; Verkäuferin IV U2, 38
salsa [ˈsælsə] Salsasoße <IV U5, 112>
salt [sɔːlt] Salz II
the **same** [ðə ˈseɪm] derselbe; gleich II
sample [ˈsɑːmpl] Probe <IV U1, 24>
sandal [ˈsændl] Sandale <IV U4, 77>
sandwich [ˈsænwɪdʒ] Sandwich; belegtes Brot I
sang [sæŋ] simple past von *to sing* II
sank [sæŋk] simple past von *to sink* III
sat [sæt] simple past, past participle von *to sit* IV U3, 63
satnav [ˈsætnæv] Navi I
Saturday [ˈsætədeɪ] Samstag I
sauce [sɔːs] Soße II
cocktail sauce [ˈkɒkteɪl ˌsɔːs] Cocktailsoße <IV U5, 112>
sausage [ˈsɒsɪdʒ] Wurst; Bratwurst II
sausage roll [ˌsɒsɪdʒ ˈrəʊl] Blätterteig mit Wurstfüllung II
to **save** [seɪv] speichern II; retten; bergen III; aufheben IV U3, 54
saw [sɔː] simple past von *to see* I
saxophone [ˈsæksəfəʊn] Saxofon I
*to **say** [seɪ] nachsprechen; nennen; sagen; sprechen I
to say hi to [ˌseɪ ˈhaɪ tə] grüßen; Grüße ausrichten I
to say sorry [ˌseɪ ˈsɒri] sich entschuldigen II
to **scan** [skæn] scannen; nach Details durchsuchen <III>
to **scare** [skeə] erschrecken II
scared [skeəd] verängstigt IV U3, 64
to be scared [biː ˈskeəd] Angst haben; erschrocken sein II

scarf *(sg)* [skɑ:f], **scarves** *(pl)* [skɑ:vz] Schal; Tuch I
scary ['skeəri] gruselig; beängstigend I
scene [si:n] Szene II
to set the scene [ˌset ðə 'si:n] beste Voraussetzungen schaffen <IV U3, 69>
schedule *(AE)* ['skedʒu:l] Stundenplan; Fahrplan IV U2, 33
school [sku:l] Schule I
at school [ət 'sku:l] in der Schule I
boarding school ['bɔ:dɪŋ ˌsku:l] Internat <IV U2, 137>
driving school ['draɪvɪŋ ˌsku:l] Fahrschule <IV U2, 44>
high school ['haɪ ˌsku:l] Highschool *(weiterführende Schule, Oberstufe)* IV U1, 18
school life ['sku:‿laɪf] Schulalltag <I>
school trip [ˌsku:l 'trɪp] Klassenfahrt I
schoolyard ['sku:ljɑ:d] Schulhof <IV U1, 28>
Science [saɪəns] Wissenschaft; Naturwissenschaft I
science fiction [ˌsaɪəns 'fɪkʃn] Science-Fiction I
scientist ['saɪəntɪst] Wissenschaftler; Wissenschaftlerin <IV U2, 48>
scissors *(pl)* ['sɪzəz] Schere III
nail scissors ['neɪl ˌsɪzəz] Nagelschere III
scone [skɒn] Scone *(eine Art süßes Brötchen)* II
score [skɔ:] Punktestand II; Punkten <IV U2, 50>
Scot [skɒt] Schotte; Schottin III
Scottish ['skɒtɪʃ] schottisch III
scrambled egg [ˌskræmbld‿'eg] Rührei II
to **scream** [skri:m] schreien; kreischen IV U3, 63
script [skrɪpt] Drehbuch; Skript <III>
sea [si:] Meer I
to **search** [sɜ:tʃ] durchsuchen <III>

at the **seaside** [ət ðə 'si:saɪd] am Meer I
season ['si:zn] Saison; Jahreszeit <IV U2, 50>
seat [si:t] Sitz; Sitzplatz IV U5, 106
Please have a seat. [ˌpli:z hæv‿ə‿ 'si:t] Bitte Platz nehmen. IV U3, 55
second ['sekənd] Sekunde II
second ['sekənd] zweite I
secret ['si:krət] Geheimnis II
secret ['si:krət] geheim II
section ['sekʃn] Abschnitt <III>
security [sɪ'kjʊərəti] Sicherheit <IV U1, 30>
*to **see** [si:] sehen I
to see friends [si: 'frendz] Freunde treffen I
I see. [aɪ 'si:] Ich verstehe. IV U5, 103
See you. ['si: ju:] Tschüss.; Bis bald. I
See you later. [ˌsi: jə 'leɪtə] Tschüss.; Bis bald. I
See you soon! ['si: ju ˌsu:n] Bis bald! I
seen [si:n] past participle von *to see* II
segregation [ˌsegrɪ'geɪʃn] Rassentrennung; Trennung IV U5, 106
self [self] selbst; sich III
selfie ['selfi] Selfie *(Schnappschuss von sich selbst)* IV U4, 83
selfish ['selfɪʃ] selbstsüchtig IV U2, 39
*to **sell** [sel] verkaufen III
semester [sɪ'mestə] Halbjahr; Schulhalbjahr; Semester <IV U2, 48>
*to **send** [send] schicken; senden I
senior citizen [ˌsi:njə 'sɪtɪzn] Rentner; Rentnerin <IV U5, 207>
sensation [sen'seɪʃn] Sensation <IV U5, 143>
sent [sent] simple past von *to send* I; past participle von *to send* II
sentence ['sentəns] Satz <I>
September [sep'tembə] September I
Serbian ['sɜ:biən] serbisch; Serbisch; aus Serbien; Serbe; Serbin <IV U5, 206>
serious ['sɪəriəs] ernst III

Are you serious? [ˌɑ: ju 'sɪəriəs] Im Ernst? III
to take sth seriously [ˌteɪk 'sɪəriəsli] etw. ernst nehmen IV U1, 18
to **serve** [sɜ:v] servieren IV U2, 33
service ['sɜ:vɪs] Dienst III
emergency service [ɪ'mɜ:dʒənsi ˌsɜ:vɪs] Notdienst; Rettungsdienst III
set [set] Satz <IV U4, 92>; Kulisse <IV U4, 141>
*to **set the scene** [ˌset ðə 'si:n] beste Voraussetzungen schaffen <IV U3, 69>
settler ['setlə] Siedler; Siedlerin IV U2, 32
seven ['sevn] sieben I
seventeen [ˌsevn'ti:n] siebzehn I
seventy ['sevnti] siebzig I
several ['sevrl] einige; mehrere; verschiedene IV U4, 80
shampoo [ʃæm'pu:] Shampoo III
shamrock ['ʃæmrɒk] Kleeblatt III
shape [ʃeɪp] Form <III>
to **share** [ʃeə] teilen III
shark [ʃɑ:k] Hai I
pencil **sharpener** ['pensl ˌʃɑ:pnə] Anspitzer I
she [ʃi:] sie I
sheep *(sg)* [ʃi:p], **sheep** *(pl)* [ʃi:p] Schaf I
sheet of paper ['ʃi:t‿əv ˌpeɪpə] Blatt Papier <IV U4, 92>
shelf *(sg)* [ʃelf], **shelves** *(pl)* [ʃelvz] Regal; Regalbrett I
walnut **shell** ['wɔ:lnʌt ˌʃel] Walnussschale <IV U3, 71>
animal rescue **shelter** [ˌænɪml 'reskju: ˌʃeltə] Tierheim I
*to **shine** [ʃaɪn] scheinen; glänzen IV ZI, 8
ship [ʃɪp] Schiff I
sailing ship ['seɪlɪŋ ʃɪp] Segelboot <IV U3, 70>
ship builder ['ʃɪp ˌbɪldə] Schiffsbauer; Schiffsbauerin III
shipyard ['ʃɪpjɑ:d] Werft III
shirt [ʃɜ:t] Hemd; Shirt I

shoe [ʃuː] Schuh I
shone [ʃɒn] simple past, past participle von *to shine* IV ZI, 8
***to shoot (a film)** [ˌʃuːt (ə 'fɪlm)] (einen Film) drehen <III>
to shoot (at) [ʃuːt (ət)] schießen (auf) IV U3, 63
shop [ʃɒp] Laden; Geschäft I
corner shop ['kɔːnə ˌʃɒp] Tante-Emma-Laden I
shop assistant ['ʃɒp‿əˌsɪstnt] Verkäufer; Verkäuferin II
sports shop ['spɔːts ˌʃɒp] Sportgeschäft I
shopping ['ʃɒpɪŋ] Einkaufen I
to do the shopping [ˌduː ðə 'ʃɒpɪŋ] Einkäufe machen; Besorgungen machen II
to go shopping [ˌgəʊ 'ʃɒpɪŋ] einkaufen gehen II
shopping centre ['ʃɒpɪŋ ˌsentə] Einkaufszentrum I
shopping list ['ʃɒpɪŋ ˌlɪst] Einkaufszettel I
short [ʃɔːt] kurz II
shortly ['ʃɔːtli] kurz III
shorts *(pl)* [ʃɔːts] Shorts; kurze Hose I
shot [ʃɒt] simple past, past participle von *to shoot* IV U3, 63
should [ʃʊd] sollte III
shout [ʃaʊt] Schrei I
to shout [ʃaʊt] schreien; rufen II
show [ʃəʊ] Show; Wettbewerb I; Schau; Aufführung IV U5, 102
talent show ['tælənt ˌʃəʊ] Talentwettbewerb I
talk show ['tɔːk ˌʃəʊ] Talkshow <IV U3, 68>
TV show [ˌtiː 'viː ˌʃəʊ] Fernsehsendung II
***to show** [ʃəʊ] zeigen II
to show up [ˌʃəʊ‿'ʌp] auftauchen; erscheinen IV U2, 42
shower ['ʃaʊə] Dusche III
shower gel ['ʃaʊə ˌdʒel] Duschgel III
shredded ['ʃredɪd] gehackt; klein gemacht <IV U5, 112>
shrimp [ʃrɪmp] Krabbe; Garnele <IV U5, 112>
***to shut up** [ˌʃʌt‿'ʌp] die Klappe halten IV U3, 63
shy [ʃaɪ] schüchtern IV U2, 42
***to be sick** [biː 'sɪk] sich übergeben I; krank sein *(AE)* III
side [saɪd] Seite I
sidewalk *(AE)* ['saɪdwɔːk] Gehweg; Bürgersteig IV U1, 15
sight [saɪt] Sehenswürdigkeit II
sightseeing ['saɪtsiːɪŋ] Besichtigungstour <IV U4, 201>
to go sightseeing [gəʊ 'saɪtsiːɪŋ] eine Besichtigungstour machen II
sign [saɪn] Schild; Zeichen III
sign language ['saɪn ˌlæŋgwɪdʒ] Gebärdensprache; Zeichensprache III
to sign [saɪn] unterschreiben; unterzeichnen IV U3, 53
to sign autographs [ˌsaɪn 'ɔːtəgrɑːfs] Autogramme geben IV U3, 53
signal ['sɪgnl] Empfang; Signal; Zeichen III
signature ['sɪgnətʃə] Unterschrift <IV U2, 44>
silence ['saɪləns] Stille; Schweigen; Ruhe III
silent ['saɪlənt] stumm; schweigsam III
silk [sɪlk] Seide III
silly ['sɪli] albern II; dumm; doof III
simple ['sɪmpl] einfach III
simple present [ˌsɪmpl 'preznt] Gegenwart; Präsens <III>
since [sɪns] seit; seitdem IV U4, 80
***to sing** [sɪŋ] singen I
singer ['sɪŋə] Sänger; Sängerin I
single ticket ['sɪŋgl ˌtɪkɪt] einfache Fahrkarte III
sink [sɪŋk] Becken; Spülbecken <IV U3, 71>
***to sink** [sɪŋk] untergehen; sinken III
siren ['saɪrən] Sirene; Martinshorn <IV U1, 19>
sister ['sɪstə] Schwester I
***to sit** [sɪt] sitzen I
site [saɪt] Seite *(im Internet)* IV U4, 80
construction site [kən'strʌkʃn ˌsaɪt] Baustelle IV U1, 15
situation [ˌsɪtju'eɪʃn] Situation II
six [sɪks] sechs I
sixteen [ˌsɪk'stiːn] sechzehn I
sixty ['sɪksti] sechzig I
size [saɪz] Größe II
skateboard ['skeɪtbɔːd] Skateboard III
to ski [skiː] Ski fahren II
skiing ['skiːɪŋ] Skifahren III
skill [skɪl] Fertigkeit <I>
to skim [skɪm] überfliegen <III>
skirt [skɜːt] Rock I
sky [skaɪ] Himmel <IV U2, 48>
skyline ['skaɪlaɪn] Skyline IV U1, 12
skyscraper ['skaɪskreɪpə] Wolkenkratzer IV U1, 14
slave [sleɪv] Sklave; Sklavin IV U4, 86
slavery ['sleɪvri] Sklaverei <IV U3, 138>
sled [sled] Schlitten <IV U1, 30>
sleep [sliːp] Schlaf III
***to sleep** [sliːp] schlafen I
sleepover ['sliːpˌəʊvə] Übernachtung I
slept [slept] simple past, past participle von *to sleep* II
slice [slaɪs] Scheibe; Stück <IV U5, 113>
sliced bread [ˌslaɪst 'bred] in Scheiben geschnittenes Brot III
slow [sləʊ] langsam III
small [smɔːl] klein I
small talk ['smɔːl ˌtɔːk] Smalltalk <IV U3, 55>
smart [smɑːt] schlau; klug; intelligent III
smartphone ['smɑːtˌfəʊn] Smartphone IV U4, 80
***to smell** [smel] riechen III
smelt [smelt] simple past, past participle von *to smell* III
to smile [smaɪl] lächeln <IV U1, 184>
smoke [sməʊk] Rauch III
smoked tofu ['sməʊkt ˌtəʊfuː] geräucherter Tofu <IV U5, 112>
smoothie ['smuːði] Smoothie <IV U3, 72>

smuggler ['smʌglə] Schmuggler; Schmugglerin II
smurf [smɜːf] Schlumpf I
snack [snæk] Snack; Imbiss I
snake [sneɪk] Schlange I
snow [snəʊ] Schnee IV U1, 14
so [səʊ] deshalb; also I; so II
so much [ˌsəʊ 'mʌtʃ] so sehr III
soap [səʊp] Seife III
social ['səʊʃl] sozial; gesellschaftlich <IV U1, 134>
social media [ˌsəʊʃl 'miːdiə] soziale Medien IV U4, 80
Social Studies ['səʊʃl ˌstʌdiz] Gesellschaftslehre; Sozialkunde I
society [sə'saɪəti] Gesellschaft <IV U2, 48>
sock [sɒk] Socke I
sofa ['səʊfə] Sofa II
software ['sɒftweə] Software II
solar ['səʊlə] Sonnen-; Solar-; solar III
solar system ['səʊlə] Sonnensystem <IV U2, 48>
sold [səʊld] simple past, past participle von *to sell* III
soldier ['səʊldʒə] Soldat; Soldatin III
solid ['sɒlɪd] fest III
solution [sə'luːʃn] Lösung IV U5, 98
to **solve** [sɒlv] lösen I
some [sʌm] einige; ein paar I; etwas II
somebody ['sʌmbədi] jemand IV U2, 38
somebody else [ˌsʌmbədi 'els] jemand anderes II
something ['sʌmθɪŋ] etwas I
sometimes ['sʌmtaɪmz] manchmal I
son [sʌn] Sohn III
song [sɒŋ] Lied I
soon [suːn] bald II
as soon as [əz 'suːn‿əz] sobald IV U4, 89
See you soon! ['siː ju ˌsuːn] Bis bald! I
sore [sɔː] schmerzhaft; wund II
sore throat [ˌsɔː 'θrəʊt] Halsschmerzen II
Sorry. ['sɒri] Tut mir leid.; Entschuldigung. I
to be sorry [biː 'sɒri] leidtun III
to feel sorry for [ˌfiːl 'sɒri] Mitleid haben mit; bedauern III
I'm sorry. [aɪm 'sɒrɪ] Es tut mir leid.; Entschuldigung. I
Sorry about … ['sɒri ˌəbaʊt] Es tut mir leid wegen … I
sort [sɔːt] Sorte; Art II
to **sort** [sɔːt] sortieren <III>
sound [saʊnd] Ton; Laut; Geräusch III
to **sound** [saʊnd] klingen II
soup [suːp] Suppe II
sweet and **sour** [ˌswiːt‿ən 'saʊə] süßsauer <IV U5, 206>
south [saʊθ] Süden III
south of ['saʊθ‿əv] südlich von IV ZI, 9
in the south of [ˌɪn ðə 'saʊθ‿əv] im Süden von III
southern ['sʌðən] südlich IV U5, 96
Southerner ['sʌðnə] Südstaatler; Südstaatlerin IV U5, 97
souvenir [ˌsuːvn'ɪə] Souvenir; Andenken III
souvenir shop ['suːvnɪə ˌʃɒp] Souvenirladen III
soy bean ['sɔɪ ˌbiːn] Sojabohne IV ZI, 9
spaghetti [spə'geti] Spaghetti II
Spanish ['spænɪʃ] spanisch; Spanisch; aus Spanien IV U5, 98
*to **speak** [spiːk] sprechen II
speaking ['spiːkɪŋ] Sprechen <I>
special ['speʃl] besonders; speziell I
special offer [ˌspeʃl‿'ɒfə] Sonderangebot III
with special needs [wɪð ˌspeʃl 'niːdz] mit Behinderung; mit besonderen Bedürfnissen III
spectacular [spek'tækjələ] spektakulär IV U4, 77
speech [spiːtʃ] Sprache; Rede III
direct speech [dɪˌrekt 'spiːtʃ] direkte Rede <IV U5, 110>
farewell speech [feə'wel spiːtʃ] Abschiedsrede II
speech bubble ['spiːtʃ ˌbʌbl] Sprechblase <III>
speech impaired ['spiːtʃ ɪmˌpeərd] sprachbehindert IV U5, 102
*to **spell** [spel] buchstabieren I
spelling ['spelɪŋ] Rechtschreibung I
*to **spend** [spend] ausgeben *(Geld)*; verbringen *(Zeit)* II
spent [spent] simple past, past participle von *to spend* II
spice [spaɪs] Gewürz II
spicy ['spaɪsi] würzig; pikant II
spider ['spaɪdə] Spinne III
splash [splæʃ] Platsch I
spoke [spəʊk] simple past von *to speak* II
spoken ['spəʊkn] past participle von *to speak* II
spoon [spuːn] Löffel II
sport [spɔːt] Sport I; Sportart III
sports shop ['spɔːts ˌʃɒp] Sportgeschäft I
sporting event ['spɔːtɪŋ ɪˌvent] Sportereignis; Sportveranstaltung <IV U2, 50>
*to **spread** [spred] streichen <IV U5, 112>
spring roll [ˌsprɪŋ 'rəʊl] Frühlingsrolle II
square [skweə] Platz II
square mile (= sq. mi.) [ˌskweə 'maɪl] Quadratmeile IV ZI, 8
stadium ['steɪdiəm] Stadion II
stage [steɪdʒ] Bühne II
at this stage [æt ðɪs 'steɪdʒ] zu diesem Zeitpunkt <IV U5, 108>
stairs *(pl)* [steəz] Treppe II
food **stall** ['fuːd ˌstɔːl] Essensstand II
market **stall** ['mɑːkɪt ˌstɔːl] Marktstand; Marktbude <IV U2, 191>
stallholder ['stɔːlˌhəʊldə] Standinhaber; Standinhaberin II
stamp [stæmp] Briefmarke III
*to **stand** [stænd] stehen II
to stand up [ˌstænd‿'ʌp] aufstehen; stehen IV U3, 63

standup paddleboarding ['stændʌp ˌpædlbɔ:dɪŋ] Stehpaddeln <IV U3, 72>
star [stɑ:] Star I; Stern III
start [stɑ:t] Start; Anfang III
to **start** [stɑ:t] anfangen; beginnen; starten II; gründen III
to start a band [ˌstɑ:t‿ə 'bænd] eine Band gründen II
starting point ['stɑ:tɪŋ ˌpɔɪnt] Ausgangspunkt <III>
to get **started** [ˌget 'stɑ:tɪd] anfangen <III>
starter ['stɑ:tə] Vorspeise II
state [steɪt] Staat; Bundesstaat; Land IV ZI, 8
state government ['steɪt ˌgʌvnmənt] Landesregierung IV U5, 98
State House *(AE)* ['steɪt ˌhaʊs] Regierungsgebäude IV U5, 98
statement ['steɪtmənt] Aussage; Behauptung <IV U3, 196>; Erklärung <IV U4, 87>
station ['steɪʃn] Haltestelle; Station; Bahnhof III
status ['steɪtəs] Status IV U4, 81
to **stay** [steɪ] übernachten; bleiben II
*to **steal** [sti:l] stehlen IV U2, 38
steam engine ['sti:m‿ˌendʒɪn] Dampfmaschine III
paddle **steamer** ['pædl ˌsti:mə] Raddampfer <IV U5, 142>
steel [sti:l] Stahl III
step [step] Schritt III; Stufe II
stereotype ['steriəʊtaɪp] Stereotyp; Klischee IV U2, 42
stick [stɪk] Stock II
sticker ['stɪkə] Aufkleber II
still [stɪl] noch; immer noch I; dennoch III
to **stir** [stɜ:] rühren; umrühren II
stocks [stɒks] Pranger III
stole [stəʊl] simple past von *to steal* IV U2, 38
stolen ['stəʊlən] past participle von *to steal* IV U2, 38
stomach ['stʌmək] Magen; Bauch II
stomach ache ['stʌmək ˌeɪk] Bauchweh; Bauchschmerzen II
stone [stəʊn] Stein III
stood [stʊd] simple past, past participle von *to stand* II
stop [stɒp] Haltestelle; Halt II
bus stop ['bʌs ˌstɒp] Bushaltestelle II
one stop [ˌwʌn 'stɒp] einmal Umsteigen <IV U3, 66>
to **stop** [stɒp] aufhören I
store *(AE)* [stɔ:] Laden; Geschäft IV U2, 33
department store [dɪ'pɑ:tmənt ˌstɔ:] Kaufhaus II
storm [stɔ:m] Sturm IV U2, 32
story ['stɔ:ri] Geschichte I
feature story ['fi:tʃə ˌstɔ:ri] Leitartikel; Sonderbericht <IV U5, 110>
straight [streɪt] gerade <IV U2, 47>
straight on [streɪt‿'ɒn] geradeaus I
hair **straightener** ['heə ˌstreɪtnə] Haarglätter I
strange [streɪndʒ] merkwürdig; seltsam II
straw [strɔ:] Trinkhalm II
drinking straw ['drɪŋkɪŋ ˌstrɔ:] Trinkhalm <IV U3, 71>
strawberry ['strɔ:bri] Erdbeere II
stream [stri:m] Bach <IV U2, 136>
to **stream** [stri:m] **streamen** *(im Internet)* IV U4, 80
street [stri:t] Straße III
street art ['stri:t ɑ:t] Straßenkunst IV U1, 13
street gang ['stri:t ˌgæŋ] Straßengang <IV U1, 134>
strict [strɪkt] streng; strikt IV U2, 34
striking ['straɪkɪŋ] bemerkenswert; auffallend III
comic **strip** ['kɒmɪk strɪp] Comicstrip <IV U2, 42>
strong [strɒŋ] stark III
structure ['strʌktʃə] Aufbau; Struktur III
to **structure** ['strʌktʃə] strukturieren; gliedern <IV U2, 46>
*to be **stuck** [bi: 'stʌk] feststecken; nicht weg können I
*to get **stuck** [ˌget 'stʌk] stecken bleiben IV U3, 54
student ['stju:dnt] Schüler; Schülerin; Student; Studentin I
studio ['stju:diəʊ] Studio IV U4, 75
recording studio [rɪ'kɔ:dɪŋ ˌstju:diəʊ] Tonstudio I
TV studio [ˌti:'vi: ˌstju:diəʊ] Fernsehstudio II
study hall period ['stʌdi hɔ:l ˌpɪəriəd] Freistunde IV U2, 34
study skills [ˌstʌdi 'skɪlz] Fertigkeit Lern- und Arbeitstechniken <I>
stunt [stʌnt] Stunt <IV U2, 50>
stuntman ['stʌntmæn] Stuntman IV U3, 53
style [staɪl] Stil III
subject ['sʌbdʒɪkt] Schulfach I
core subject [ˌkɔ: 'sʌbdʒɪkt] Pflichtfach IV U2, 35
submarine [ˌsʌbmr'i:n] U-Boot I
to **subscribe** [səb'skraɪb] abonnieren IV U4, 81
subtotal ['sʌbˌtəʊtl] Zwischensumme <IV U3, 66>
suburb ['sʌbɜ:b] Vorort IV U1, 15
subway *(AE)* ['sʌbweɪ] U-Bahn IV U1, 14
success [sək'ses] Erfolg IV U5, 107
successful [sək'sesfl] erfolgreich III
suddenly ['sʌdnli] plötzlich; auf einmal II
sugar ['ʃʊgə] Zucker I
to **suit** [su:t] stehen; passen II
suitable ['su:təbl] geeignet; passend <IV U2, 51>
suitcase ['su:tkeɪs] Koffer II
to **sum up** [ˌsʌm‿'ʌp] zusammenfassen IV U3, 73
to **summarize** ['sʌməraɪz] zusammenfassen <IV U3, 73>
summary ['sʌməri] Zusammenfassung <III>
summer ['sʌmə] Sommer II
sun [sʌn] Sonne III

to **sunbathe** ['sʌnbeɪð] sonnenbaden II
Sunday ['sʌndeɪ] Sonntag I
sunglasses *(pl)* ['sʌnˌglɑ:sɪz] Sonnenbrille II
sunk [sʌŋk] past participle von *to sink* III
sunny ['sʌni] sonnig I
super ['su:pə] super II
superhero ['su:pəˌhɪərəʊ] *(sg)*, **superheroes** ['su:pəˌhɪərəʊz] *(pl)* Superheld <IV U1, 135>
supermarket ['su:pəˌmɑ:kɪt] Supermarkt II
support [sə'pɔ:t] Unterstützung; Hilfe IV U1, 19
supporter [sə'pɔ:tə] Anhänger; Anhängerin; Fan <IV U2, 50>
sure [ʃʊə] sicher I
sure of oneself ['ʃʊər‿əv ˌwʌnself] selbstsicher III
to **surf** [sɜ:f] surfen; wellenreiten II
to surf the internet [ˌsɜ:f ði 'ɪntənet] im Internet surfen II
surfboard ['sɜ:fbɔ:d] Surfbrett IV U4, 76
surfer ['sɜ:fə] Wellenreiter; Wellenreiterin; Surfer; Surferin IV ZI, 9
surfing ['sɜ:fɪŋ] Wellenreiten; Surfen IV U4, 74
surprise [sə'praɪz] Überraschung I
surprised [sə'praɪzd] überrascht II
survey ['sɜ:veɪ] Umfrage II
to **survive** [sə'vaɪv] überleben III
sushi ['su:ʃi] Sushi <IV U5, 206>
swam [swæm] simple past von *to swim* II
swamp [swɒmp] Sumpf IV ZI, 9
to **swap** [swɒp] tauschen <IV U4, 92>
sweatshirt ['swetʃɜ:t] Sweatshirt I
*to **sweep** [swi:p] fegen II
sweet [swi:t] Süßigkeit; Bonbon I
sweet [swi:t] süß III
sweet and sour [ˌswi:t‿ən 'saʊə] süßsauer <IV U5, 206>
swept [swept] simple past, past participle von *to sweep* II
*to **swim** [swɪm] schwimmen II
*to go **swimming** [ˌgəʊ 'swɪmɪŋ] schwimmen gehen I
swimming pool ['swɪmɪŋ ˌpu:l] Schwimmbad I
Swiss [swɪs] schweizerisch; aus der Schweiz; Schweizer; Schweizerin IV U4, 84
sword [sɔ:d] Schwert III
swum [swʌm] past participle von *to swim* II
symbol ['sɪmbl] Symbol IV U1, 13
Syrian ['sɪriən] syrisch; aus Syrien; Syrer; Syrerin <IV U5, 206>

T

table ['teɪbl] Tisch I; Tabelle <III>
table tennis ['teɪbl ˌtenɪs] Tischtennis II
tablespoon ['teɪblspu:n] Esslöffel <IV U5, 113>
tablet ['tæblət] Tablette II
tactic ['tæktɪk] Taktik; Vorgehensweise III
take [teɪk] Aufnahme <III>
*to **take** [teɪk] nehmen; mitnehmen I; hinbringen II; dauern III; bringen IV U2, 43
to take a break [ˌteɪk‿ə 'breɪk] Pause machen II
to take a photo [ˌteɪk‿ə 'fəʊtəʊ] ein Foto machen I
to take a test [ˌteɪk‿ə 'test] eine Prüfung machen <IV U2, 44>
to take a trip [ˌteɪk‿ə 'trɪp] eine Fahrt machen III
to take notes [ˌteɪk 'nəʊts] sich Notizen machen I
to take off [ˌteɪk‿'ɒf] ausziehen III
to take out [ˌteɪk‿'aʊt] herausnehmen I
to take part (in) [ˌteɪk 'pɑ:t] teilnehmen (an) II
to take photos [ˌteɪk 'fəʊtəʊz] fotografieren; Fotos machen II
to take place [ˌteɪk 'pleɪs] stattfinden <IV U5, 108>
to take sth seriously [ˌteɪk 'sɪəriəsli] etw. ernst nehmen IV U1, 18
to take the dog for a walk [ˌteɪk ðə ˌdɒg fər‿ə 'wɔ:k] den Hund spazieren führen II
to take turns [ˌteɪk 'tɜ:nz] sich abwechseln <II>
Take care. ['teɪk ˌkeə] Macht's gut. I
takeaway ['teɪkəweɪ] Essen zum Mitnehmen II
takeaway ['teɪkəweɪ] zum Mitnehmen II
taken ['teɪkn] past participle von *to take* II
talent ['tælənt] Talent I
talent show ['tælənt ˌʃəʊ] Talentwettbewerb I
talk [tɔ:k] Gerede II; Vortrag; Rede <III>
to give a talk [ˌgɪv‿ə 'tɔ:k] einen Vortrag halten <III>
small talk ['smɔ:l ˌtɔ:k] Smalltalk <IV U3, 55>
talk show ['tɔ:k ˌʃəʊ] Talkshow <IV U3, 68>
to **talk** (to) ['tɔ:k tə] sprechen (mit); reden (mit) I
to talk about ['tɔ:k‿əˌbaʊt] sprechen über II
tall [tɔ:l] groß; hoch II
tape [teɪp] Klebeband <IV U3, 71>
task [tɑ:sk] Aufgabe; Auftrag <I>
taste [teɪst] Geschmack <IV U5, 112>
tasty ['teɪsti] lecker; schmackhaft III
tax [tæks] Steuer <IV U3, 66>
taxi ['tæksi] Taxi II
tea [ti:] Tee; (frühes) Abendessen I
tea bag ['ti: ˌbæg] Teebeutel <IV U5, 113>
tea light ['ti: ˌlaɪt] Teelicht <IV U3, 71>
teacher ['ti:tʃə] Lehrer; Lehrerin I
team [ti:m] Team; Mannschaft I
teamwork ['ti:mwɜ:k] Teamwork II
to **tease** [ti:z] hänseln; sticheln; reizen IV U2, 38
teaspoon *(tsp)* ['ti:spu:n] Teelöffel *(TL)* II

p pen • b bed • t ten • d dad • k cat • g grey • tʃ chair • dʒ joke • f fan • v very • θ three • ð the

technology [tek'nɒlədʒi] Technologie <IV U4, 90>
Design Technology (DT) [dɪˌzaɪn tek'nɒlədʒi, ˌdi:'ti:] Technik I
Welding Technology ['weldɪŋ ˌteknɒlədʒi] Schweißtechnik <IV U2, 48>
teen [ti:n] Jugend-; Teenager; Jugendliche; Jugendlicher II
teenager ['ti:nˌeɪdʒə] Teenager; Jugendliche; Jugendlicher III
telephone ['telɪfəʊn] Telefon III
telephone box ['telɪfəʊn ˌbɒks] Telefonzelle II
*to **tell** [tel] erzählen; sagen I
ten [ten] zehn I
tennis ['tenɪs] Tennis I
tent [tent] Zelt III
tepee ['ti:pi:] Tipi <IV U2, 136>
terrible ['terəbl] schrecklich; schlimm; furchtbar I
territory ['terɪtri] Gebiet; Revier; Territorium <IV U5, 142>
test [test] Test; Klassenarbeit I
to take a test [ˌteɪk‿ə 'test] eine Prüfung machen <IV U2, 44>
to **test** [test] testen; prüfen II
text [tekst] Text II
text message ['tekst ˌmesɪdʒ] SMS II
to **text** [tekst] eine SMS schreiben II
texter ['tekstə] SMS-Schreiber; SMS-Schreiberin II
than [ðæn] als II
thank God [ˌθæŋk‿'gɒd] Gott sei Dank <IV U3, 70>
Thank you. ['θæŋk ju] Danke. I
thanks [θæŋks] danke I
Thanks so much. [ˌθæŋk‿səʊ 'mʌtʃ] Vielen Dank.; Herzlichen Dank. IV U4, 94
Thanksgiving [ˌθæŋks'gɪvɪŋ] Erntedankfest IV U3, 53
that [ðæt] das I; dass III
after that ['a:ftə ðət] danach I
that night [ˌðæt 'naɪt] an jenem Abend; in jener Nacht II
That's £2.24. [ðæts 'tu: paʊndz ˌtwenti fɔ:] Das macht zwei Pfund und 24 Pence. I
the [ðə] der; die *(auch Pl.)*; das I
the same [ðə 'seɪm] derselbe; gleich II
theater *(AE)* ['θɪətə] Theater IV U1, 13
movie theater *(AE)* ['mu:vi ˌθi:ətə] Kino <IV U1, 134>
theatre ['θɪətə] Theater II
their [ðeə] ihr, ihre *(Pl.)* I
theirs [ðeəz] ihre III
them [ðem; ðəm] sie *(Pl.)*; ihnen I
theme park ['θi:m ˌpɑ:k] Freizeitpark I; Themenpark II
themselves [ðəm'selvz] selber; sie selbst; sich selbst; selbst III
then [ðen] dann; danach I; damals III
there [ðeə] da; dort I
down there [ˌdaʊn 'ðeə] dahin; da unten <IV U1, 183>
over there [ˌəʊvə 'ðeə] da drüben; dort drüben II
there are [ðeər‿'ɑ:] da sind; es gibt I
there is [ðeə 'ɪz] da ist; dort ist; es gibt I
these [ði:z] diese (hier) II
they [ðeɪ] sie *(Pl.)* I
thing [θɪŋ] Sache; Ding I
*to **think** [θɪŋk] denken; glauben I
to think of ['θɪŋk‿əv] sich ausdenken; sich etwas einfallen lassen <III>
third [θɜ:d] dritte I
thirsty ['θɜ:sti] durstig II
thirteen [θɜ:'ti:n] dreizehn I
thirty ['θɜ:ti] dreißig I
this [ðɪs] das; dies I
like this [laɪk 'ðɪs] so; auf diese Weise III
this way [ðɪs 'weɪ] in diese Richtung II
those [ðəʊz] jene II
thought [θɔ:t] simple past, past participle von *to think* II
a/one **thousand** [ə/wʌn 'θaʊznd] eintausend; tausend II
three [θri:] drei I
threw [θru:] simple past von *to throw* IV U2, 38
throat [θrəʊt] Hals II
sore throat [ˌsɔ: 'θrəʊt] Halsschmerzen II
through [θru:] durch II
*to **throw** [θrəʊ] werfen IV U2, 38
thrown [θrəʊn] past participle von *to throw* IV U2, 38
Thursday ['θɜ:zdeɪ] Donnerstag I
ticket ['tɪkɪt] Karte II; Fahrschein; Eintrittskarte III
return ticket [rɪ'tɜ:n ˌtɪkɪt] Hin- und Rückfahrkarte III
single ticket ['sɪŋgl ˌtɪkɪt] einfache Fahrkarte III
to **tidy (up)** [ˌtaɪdi 'ʌp] aufräumen; in Ordnung bringen II
tiger ['taɪgə] Tiger I
tight [taɪt] eng; fest II
time [taɪm] Zeit; Uhrzeit I; Mal III
brewing time ['bru:ɪŋ ˌtaɪm] Brühzeit <IV U5, 113>
free time [ˌfri: 'taɪm] Freizeit I
in time [ɪn 'taɪm] rechtzeitig I
on time [ɒn 'taɪm] pünktlich III
opening times ['əʊpnɪŋ ˌtaɪmz] Öffnungszeiten <IV U5, 207>
time travel ['taɪm ˌtrævl] Zeitreise III
time zone ['taɪm ˌzəʊn] Zeitzone IV ZI, 8
timeline ['taɪmlaɪn] Zeitstrahl <IV U4, 87>
timetable ['taɪmˌteɪbl] Stundenplan I; Fahrplan III
tin [tɪn] Dose; Büchse; Mülleimer IV U3, 63
tiny ['taɪni] klein; winzig III
tip [tɪp] Tipp; Ratschlag II
tired [taɪəd] müde I
to get tired of sth [ˌget 'taɪəd‿əv] etw. sattbekommen; etw. satthaben IV U1, 14
tissue ['tɪʃu:] Taschentuch III
title ['taɪtl] Titel; Überschrift <II>

job title ['dʒɒb ˌtaɪtl] Stellenbezeichnung; Berufsbezeichnung IV U2, 38

to [tu:; tʊ; tə] in; nach; zu; vor *(bei Uhrzeitangaben)* I; bis II

toast [təʊst] Toast II

today [tə'deɪ] heute I

together [tə'geðə] zusammen; gemeinsam I

toilet ['tɔɪlət] Toilette I

told [təʊld] simple past von *to tell* I

to **tolerate** ['tɒlreɪt] tolerieren; dulden IV U5, 98

tomato *(sg)* [tə'mɑ:təʊ], **tomatoes** *(pl)* [tə'mɑ:təʊz] Tomate II

tomorrow [tə'mɒrəʊ] morgen II

tongue twister ['tʌŋ ˌtwɪstə] Zungenbrecher <III>

tonight [tə'naɪt] heute Abend; heute Nacht II

tonne [tʌn] Tonne II

too [tu:] auch I; zu II

too much [ˌtu: 'mʌtʃ] zu sehr II

took [tʊk] simple past von *to take* II

tool [tu:l] Werkzeug; Gerät II

tooth *(sg)* [tu:θ], **teeth** *(pl)* [ti:θ] Zahn III

toothbrush ['tu:θbrʌʃ] Zahnbürste III

toothpaste ['tu:θpeɪst] Zahnpasta III

toothpick ['tu:θpɪk] Zahnstocher II

top [tɒp] Top; Oberteil II; Spitze IV U1, 13

topic ['tɒpɪk] Thema IV U2, 51

torch [tɔ:tʃ] Taschenlampe I

torn [tɔ:n] zerrissen; aufgerissen IV U4, 83

tornado [tɔ:'neɪdəʊ] Tornado; Wirbelsturm IV U2, 33

total ['təʊtl] Summe <IV U3, 66>

total ['təʊtl] Gesamt-; gesamt IV ZI, 8

*to keep in **touch** [ˌki:p ɪn 'tʌtʃ] in Verbindung bleiben II

touchdown ['tʌtʃdaʊn] Touchdown <IV U2, 50>

tough [tʌf] hart III

tour [tʊə] Tour; Fahrt; Reise IV U4, 76

guided tour ['gaɪdɪd ˌtɔ:] Führung <IV U1, 13>

tourist ['tʊərɪst] Tourist; Touristin I

Tourist Information Centre ['tʊərɪst ɪnfə'meɪʃn ˌsentə] Touristeninformation I

towel ['taʊəl] Handtuch III

tower ['taʊə] Turm II

clock tower ['klɒk ˌtaʊə] Uhrenturm II

town [taʊn] Stadt I

town centre [ˌtaʊn 'sentə] Stadtzentrum; Stadtmitte <IV U1, 15>

town hall [ˌtaʊn 'hɔ:l] Rathaus II

toy [tɔɪ] Spielzeug III

cuddly toy ['kʌdli ˌtɔɪ] Kuscheltier III

track [træk] Strecke IV U5, 102

railway track ['reɪlweɪ ˌtræk] Gleis IV U3, 64

tractor ['træktə] Traktor I

trader ['treɪdə] Händler; Händlerin <IV U2, 136>

tradition [trə'dɪʃn] Tradition III

traditional [trə'dɪʃnl] traditionell <IV U2, 136>

traffic ['træfɪk] Verkehr III

traffic jam ['træfɪk ˌdʒæm] Stau IV U1, 14

tragic ['trædʒɪk] tragisch <IV U2, 136>

trail [treɪl] Wanderweg; Spur IV U5, 102

train [treɪn] Zug I

trainer ['treɪnə] Turnschuh I; Trainer; Trainerin IV U5, 103

training ['treɪnɪŋ] Training III

tram [træm] Straßenbahn III

transcontinental [ˌtrænsˌkɒntɪ'nentl] transkontinental *(über den Kontinent hinweg)* IV U4, 86

transfer [træns'fɜ:] Transport; Transfer IV U5, 102

to **translate** [trænz'leɪt] übersetzen IV U5, 102

transparency [træn'spærnsi] Folie <IV U2, 51>

transport ['trænspɔ:t] Transport <IV U1, 30>

public transport [ˌpʌblɪk 'trænspɔ:t] öffentliche Verkehrsmittel III

travel ['trævl] (das) Reisen <IV U1, 30>

time travel ['taɪm ˌtrævl] Zeitreise III

to **travel** ['trævl] reisen II; fahren III

tray [treɪ] Tablett II

treasure ['treʒə] Schatz II

tree [tri:] Baum I

trend [trend] Trend; Entwicklung; Richtung IV U4, 80

tribe [traɪb] Stamm; Volksstamm <IV U1, 24>

trick [trɪk] Trick; Streich I; Kunststück III

Trick or treat! [ˌtrɪk‿ə 'tri:t] Süßes, sonst gibt's Saures! I

trip [trɪp] Ausflug I; Trip; Fahrt; Reise III

boat trip ['bəʊt ˌtrɪp] Bootsfahrt; Schiffsfahrt II

outgoing trip [ˌaʊtgəʊɪŋ 'trɪp] Hinfahrt <IV U3, 66>

return trip [ˌrɪtɜ:n 'trɪp] Rückfahrt <IV U3, 66>

round trip [ˌraʊnd 'trɪp] Hin- und Rückflug; Hin- und Rückfahrt <IV U3, 66>

school trip [ˌsku:l 'trɪp] Klassenfahrt I

to take a trip [ˌteɪk‿ə 'trɪp] eine Fahrt machen III

trouble ['trʌbl] Schwierigkeiten; Problem; Ärger III

trousers *(pl)* ['traʊzəz] Hose I

truck [trʌk] Wagen; Karre III

true [tru:] wahr II

to **trust** [trʌst] vertrauen IV U5, 109

to **try** [traɪ] probieren; versuchen II; ausprobieren III

to try on [ˌtraɪ‿'ɒn] anprobieren II

to try out [ˌtraɪ‿'aʊt] ausprobieren III

T-shirt ['ti:ʃɜ:t] T-Shirt I

tube [tju:b] Schlauch; Rohr III

Tuesday ['tju:zdeɪ] Dienstag I

on Tuesday [ˌɒn 'tju:zdeɪ] am Dienstag I

tuna ['tju:nə] Thunfisch II

tunnel ['tʌnl] Tunnel III
(wind) **turbine** [(wɪnd) 'tɜ:baɪn] Windrad III
turkey ['tɜ:ki] Truthahn; Pute IV U3, 53
Turkish ['tɜ:kɪʃ] türkisch; Türkisch; aus der Türkei IV U5, 99
*to take **turns** [ˌteɪk 'tɜ:nz] sich abwechseln <II>
to **turn** [tɜ:n] abbiegen III
to turn into [ˌtɜ:n‿'ɪntə] umwandeln in; verwandeln in <IV U1, 28>
to turn left [ˌtɜ:n 'left] (nach) links abbiegen I
to turn right [ˌtɜ:n 'raɪt] (nach) rechts abbiegen I
tutor ['tju:tə] Klassenlehrer; Klassenlehrerin I
tutor group ['tju:tə ˌgru:p] Klasse *(in einer englischen Schule)* I
tutorial [tju:'tɔ:riəl] Anleitung; Tutorial IV U4, 80
TV [ˌti:'vi:] Fernseher; Fernsehen I
TV show [ˌti: 'vi: ˌʃəʊ] Fernsehsendung II
TV studio [ˌti:'vi: ˌstju:diəʊ] Fernsehstudio II
to watch TV [ˌwɒtʃ ti:'vi:] fernsehen I
on TV [ɒn ˌti:'vi:] im Fernsehen IV U1, 13
tweet [twi:t] Pieps III
twelve [twelv] zwölf I
twenty ['twenti] zwanzig I
twenty-one [ˌtwenti'wʌn] einundzwanzig I
to **twist** [twɪst] verdrehen; verzerren II
two [tu:] zwei I
type [taɪp] Sorte; Typ; Art III
to **type** [taɪp] tippen <III>
typical ['tɪpɪkl] typisch <IV U2, 35>
tyre [taɪə] Reifen III

U

umbrella [ʌm'brelə] Regenschirm II
umpire ['ʌmpaɪə] Schiedsrichter; Schiedsrichterin <III>
unappealing [ˌʌnə'pi:lɪŋ] uninteressant IV U4, 77
uncle ['ʌŋkl] Onkel I
uncomfortable [ʌn'kʌmftəbl] unbequem; unangenehm II
under ['ʌndə] unter I
underground ['ʌndəgraʊnd] U-Bahn II
underlined [ˌʌndə'laɪnd] unterstrichen <III>
*to **understand** [ˌʌndə'stænd] verstehen II
understood [ˌʌndə'stʊd] simple past von *to understand* II
unemployed [ˌʌnɪm'plɔɪd] arbeitslos IV U1, 18
unfair [ʌn'feə] unfair III
unfashionable [ʌn'fæʃnəbl] unmodisch II
to **unfriend** [ʌn'frend] entfreunden *(jmdn. von seiner Freundesliste streichen)* IV U4, 81
unfriendly [ʌn'frendli] unfreundlich III
unhappy [ʌn'hæpi] unglücklich II
uniform ['ju:nɪfɔ:m] Uniform I
unit ['ju:nɪt] Lektion; Kapitel <I>
unmotivated [ˌʌn'məʊtɪveɪtɪd] unmotiviert IV U2, 39
until [ʌn'tɪl] bis I
unusual [ʌn'ju:ʒl] ungewöhnlich <II>; außergewöhnlich IV U4, 77
up [ʌp] hinauf; oben II
to pick up [ˌpɪk‿'ʌp] abholen IV U2, 43
to show up [ˌʃəʊ‿'ʌp] auftauchen; erscheinen IV U2, 42
to shut up [ˌʃʌt‿'ʌp] die Klappe halten IV U3, 63
to stand up [ˌstænd‿'ʌp] aufstehen; stehen IV U3, 63
to wash up [ˌwɒʃ‿'ʌp] abwaschen; abspülen <IV U2, 191>
to **update** ['ʌpdeɪt] updaten; auf den neuesten Stand bringen IV U4, 81
updated [ʌp'deɪtɪd] aktualisiert <IV U1, 30>
to **upload** ['ʌpləʊd] hochladen; ins Internet stellen II
upper ['ʌpə] obere III
upset [ʌp'set] aufgebracht; bestürzt I
upside-down [ˌʌpsaɪd 'daʊn] umgedreht; auf den Kopf gestellt <IV U4, 92>
us [ʌs] wir; uns I
US [ˌju:'es] US-amerikanisch IV U1, 18
to **use** [ju:z] benutzen; verwenden II
to get used to (sth) [ˌget 'ju:zd tə] sich an (etw.) gewöhnen IV U1, 18
used to (live) ['ju:st tə] (wohnte) früher III
useful ['ju:sfl] nützlich; hilfreich III
usually ['ju:ʒli] normalerweise; gewöhnlich II

V

vacation (AE) [və'keɪʃn] Ferien; Urlaub <IV U1, 15>
vacuum cleaner ['vækju:m ˌkli:nə] Staubsauger IV U3, 59
valid ['vælɪd] gültig III
van [væn] Lieferwagen; Transporter III
variety [və'raɪəti] Auswahl <IV U5, 112>
veganism *(no pl)* ['vi:gənɪzm] Veganismus IV U4, 83
vegetable (veg) ['vedʒtəbl] Gemüse II
vegetarian [ˌvedʒɪ'teəriən] Vegetarier; Vegetarierin I
veggie bean cake [ˌvedʒi 'bi:n keɪk] *vegetarisches Bohnengericht* II
version ['vɜ:ʃn] Version <IV U1, 135>
very ['veri] sehr I
vet [vet] Tierarzt; Tierärztin II
victim ['vɪktɪm] Opfer <IV U5, 108>
Victorian era [vɪkˌtɔ:riən 'ɪərə] viktorianisches Zeitalter III
video ['vɪdiəʊ] Video IV U4, 80
video chat ['vɪdiəʊ ˌtʃæt] Video-Chat III
Vietnamese [ˌvjetnə'mi:z] vietnamesisch; Vietnamesisch; aus Vietnam; Vietnamese; Vietnamesin IV U5, 98

view [vjuː] Aussicht; Sicht; Ausblick; Blick IV U1, 14
viewing [ˈvjuːɪŋ] Hör-/Sehverstehen <I>
the **Vikings** [ðə ˈvaɪkɪŋz] die Wikinger III
village [ˈvɪlɪdʒ] Dorf III
to **visit** [ˈvɪzɪt] besuchen II
visitor [ˈvɪzɪtə] Besucher; Besucherin II
vocabulary [vəˈkæbjəlri] Vokabular; Wortschatz II
voice [vɔɪs] Stimme III
volleyball [ˈvɒlibɔːl] Volleyball IV U4, 74
volunteer [ˌvɒlənˈtɪə] Freiwilliger; Freiwillige; ehrenamtlicher Helfer; ehrenamtliche Helferin III
to **vote** [vəʊt] abstimmen; wählen IV U2, 49
to vote for [ˈvəʊt fə] abstimmen über; wählen IV U2, 33
voyage [ˈvɔɪɪdʒ] Reise; Fahrt III

W

wage [weɪdʒ] Lohn IV U2, 38
to **wait** [weɪt] warten II
to wait for [ˈweɪt fɔː] warten auf II
waiter [ˈweɪtə] Kellner II
waitress [ˈweɪtrəs] Kellnerin; Bedienung IV U4, 89
*to **wake** up [ˌweɪk‿ˈʌp] aufwachen II
walk [wɔːk] Spaziergang III
night walk [ˌnaɪt ˈwɔːk] Nachtwanderung I
to take the dog for a walk [ˌteɪk ðə ˌdɒg fər‿ə ˈwɔːk] den Hund spazieren führen II
a five minute walk [ə ˈfaɪv mɪnɪt ˌwɔːk] fünf Minuten zu Fuß III
to **walk** [wɔːk] gehen I; laufen II
dog **walker** [ˈdɒg ˌwɔːkə] Hundeausführer; Hundeausführerin IV U2, 41
walking [ˈwɔːkɪŋ] Wandern III
wall [wɔːl] Mauer; Wand II
walnut shell [ˈwɔːlnʌt ˌʃel] Walnussschale <IV U3, 71>
to **want** (to) [wɒnt (tə)] wollen I
war [wɔː] Krieg <IV U1, 184>
Civil War [ˌsɪvl ˈwɔː] Bürgerkrieg <IV U3, 138>
wardrobe [ˈwɔːdrəʊb] Kleiderschrank I
warm [wɔːm] warm I
warning [ˈwɔːnɪŋ] Warnung IV U2, 33
was [wɒz] simple past von *to be* I
to **wash** [wɒʃ] (sich) waschen; spülen III
to wash up [ˌwɒʃ‿ˈʌp] abwaschen; abspülen <IV U2, 191>
*to do the **washing** up [ˌduː ðə ˈwɒʃɪŋ‿ʌp] abspülen II
to **watch** [wɒtʃ] anschauen; ansehen I; aufpassen auf; zuschauen; beobachten II
to watch TV [ˌwɒtʃ tiːˈviː] fernsehen I
bird **watching** [ˈbɜːd ˌwɒtʃɪŋ] Vogelbeobachtung III
water [ˈwɔːtə] Wasser I
bucket of water [ˈbʌkɪt‿əv ˌwɔːtə] Eimer Wasser I
mineral water [ˈmɪnrl ˌwɔːtə] Mineralwasser III
water level [ˈwɔːtə ˌlevl] Wasserpegel; Wasserstand <IV U5, 142>
waterproof [ˈwɔːtəpruːf] wasserfest <IV U3, 71>
wave [weɪv] Welle IV ZI, 9
to **wave** [weɪv] winken II
way [weɪ] Art und Weise III; Weg IV U2, 34
way in [ˌweɪ ˈɪn] Einstieg <I>
way to go [ˈweɪ tə ˌgəʊ] super II
asking the way [ˈɑːskɪŋ ðə ˌweɪ] nach dem Weg fragen I
No way! [ˌnəʊ ˈweɪ] Auf keinen Fall!; Was?!; Echt?! III
on the way [ˌɒn ðə ˈweɪ] auf dem Weg; unterwegs I
this way [ðɪs ˈweɪ] in diese Richtung II
we [wiː; wi] wir I
weak [wiːk] schwach III
wealth [welθ] Reichtum III
*to **wear** [weə] tragen *(Kleidung)* I
weather [ˈweðə] Wetter I
web [web] Spinnennetz; Netz III
website [ˈwebsaɪt] Website II
wedding [ˈwedɪŋ] Hochzeit II
Wednesday [ˈwenzdeɪ] Mittwoch I
on Wednesdays [ɒn ˈwenzdeɪz] mittwochs I
week [wiːk] Woche I
on **weekdays** [ɒn ˈwiːkdeɪz] unter der Woche; an Werktagen III
weekend [ˈwiːkend] Wochenende I
at the weekend [ˌət ðə ˈwiːkend] am Wochenende I
weekly [ˈwiːkli] wöchentlich III
to **weigh** [weɪ] wiegen II
to **welcome** [ˈwelkəm] willkommen heißen IV U4, 80
You're **welcome**. [jɔː ˈwelkəm] Gern geschehen. I
welcome (to) [ˈwelkəm (tʊ)] willkommen (bei/in) I
Welding Technology [ˈweldɪŋ ˌteknɒlədʒi] Schweißtechnik <IV U2, 48>
well [wel] na ja I; gut II
Well done! [ˌwel ˈdʌn] Gut gemacht! I
welly [ˈweli] Gummistiefel I
Welsh [welʃ] walisisch; Walisisch; Waliser; Waliserin III
went [went] simple past von *to go* I
were [wɜː] simple past von *to be* I
west [west] Westen III
west of [ˈwest‿əv] westlich von IV ZI, 9
country and **western** music [ˌkʌntri ənd ˈwestən ˌmjuːzɪk] Countrymusik <IV U5, 143>
wet [wet] nass I
what [wɒt] was I; welche II; wie III
What a … [ˈwɒt‿ə] Was für ein/eine … I
What about …? [ˈwɒt‿əˌbaʊt] Was ist mit …? I
What about you? [ˌwɒt‿əbaʊt ˈjuː] Und du? II

what else [ˌwɒtˌˈels] was sonst; was noch <I>
What else can you …? [ˌwɒtˌˈels kæn juː] Was kannst du noch …? <I>
What time is it? [ˌwɒt ˈtaɪmˌɪzˌɪt] Wie spät ist es?; Wie viel Uhr ist es? I
What to … [ˈwɒt tə] Was man … II
What's up? [ˌwɒtsˌˈʌp] Wie geht's? IV U3, 54
What's wrong? [ˌwɒts ˈrɒŋ] Was ist los?; Was stimmt nicht? II
What's your name? [ˌwɒts jə ˈneɪm] Wie heißt du? I
wheel [wiːl] Rad II
big wheel [ˌbɪg ˈwiːl] Riesenrad II
wheelchair [ˈwiːltʃeə] Rollstuhl III
when [wen] wann I; wenn; als II
where [weə] wo; wohin; woher I
Where are you from? [ˌweərˌə ju ˈfrɒm] Woher kommst du? I
wherever [weəˈrevə] wo(hin) auch immer; egal wo(hin); überall wo(hin) III
which [wɪtʃ] welche II; die; der; dem; den; das III
while [waɪl] während II
to whisper [ˈwɪspə] flüstern <IV U5, 104>
white [waɪt] weiß I
who [huː] wer I; die; welche II; der; dem; den III
whole [həʊl] ganz IV U3, 63
whom [huːm] wem; wen IV U3, 58
whose [huːz] dessen; deren III
why [waɪ] warum I
wife Ehefrau IV U4, 85
the wild [ðə ˈwaɪld] Wildnis; freie Wildbahn IV U5, 102
wild [waɪld] wild IV U3, 63
wilderness [ˈwɪldənəs] Wildnis IV U4, 85
wildlife [ˈwaɪldlaɪf] Tierwelt *(in freier Wildbahn)* IV U5, 102
will [wɪl] werden II
***to win** [wɪn] gewinnen; siegen I
wind [wɪnd] Wind I
wind farm [ˈwɪnd fɑːm] Windpark III
window [ˈwɪndəʊ] Fenster I
windy [ˈwɪndi] windig I
wine [waɪn] Wein IV U3, 62
winner [ˈwɪnə] Sieger; Siegerin; Gewinner; Gewinnerin I
winter [ˈwɪntə] Winter I
wish [wɪʃ] Wunsch <III>
Best wishes, [ˌbest ˈwɪʃɪz] Viele Grüße, I
to wish [wɪʃ] wünschen III
witch [wɪtʃ] Hexe I
with [wɪð] mit I
with special needs [wɪð ˌspeʃl ˈniːdz] mit Behinderung; mit besonderen Bedürfnissen III
within [wɪˈðɪn] innerhalb <IV U2, 136>
without [wɪˈðaʊt] ohne III
witness [ˈwɪtnəs] Zeuge; Zeugin IV U5, 107
woke up [ˌwəʊkˌˈʌp] simple past von *to wake up* II
woman *(sg)* [ˈwʊmən], **women** *(pl)* [ˈwɪmɪn] Frau I
won [wʌn] simple past von *to win* I; past participle von *to win* II
won't (= will not) [wəʊnt] nicht werden II
wonderful [ˈwʌndəfl] wunderbar III
wood [wʊd] Holz I; Wald III
wood [wʊd] Holz III
wool [wʊl] Wolle I
word [wɜːd] Wort <I>
key word [ˈkiː ˌwɜːd] Stichwort; Schlüsselbegriff <IV U3, 68>
linking word [ˌlɪŋkɪŋ ˈwɜːd] Verbindungswort <IV U3, 73>
work [wɜːk] Arbeit I
to work [wɜːk] arbeiten I; funktionieren II
workbook [ˈwɜːkbʊk] Arbeitsheft I
worker [ˈwɜːkə] Arbeiter; Arbeiterin II
working hours *(pl)* [ˈwɜːkɪŋ ˌaʊəz] Arbeitszeit IV U2, 39
workshop [ˈwɜːkʃɒp] Workshop II
acting workshop [ˈæktɪŋ ˌwɜːkʃɒp] Schauspielworkshop II
world [wɜːld] Welt II
in the world [ɪn ðə ˈwɜːld] auf der Welt II
world-class [ˈwɜːldˌklɑːs] weltklasse <IV U1, 134>
worn [wɔːn] past participle von *to wear* II
worried [ˈwʌrid] beunruhigt; besorgt II
to worry [ˈwʌri] sich Sorgen machen I
worst [wɜːst] schlimmste; schlechteste III
would [wʊd] würde(n) II
would like [wʊd ˈlaɪk] würde(n) gern; hätte(n) gern II
I wouldn't like (to) … [aɪ ˈwʊdnt laɪk (tə)] Ich möchte nicht …; Ich würde nicht gerne … I
Would you like (to) …? [ˌwʊd jə ˈlaɪk (tə)] Möchtest du? I
wrap [ræp] Wrap II
bubble wrap [ˈbʌbl ˌræp] Luftpolsterfolie <IV U3, 71>
wrist [rɪst] Handgelenk IV U3, 63
***to write** [raɪt] schreiben I
writer [ˈraɪtə] Schriftsteller; Schriftstellerin II; Verfasser; Verfasserin; Autor; Autorin III
writing [ˈraɪtɪŋ] Schreiben <I>
written [ˈrɪtn] past participle von *to write* <IV U3, 72>; schriftlich <IV U2, 44>
wrong [rɒŋ] falsch I
wrote [rəʊt] simple past von *to write* I

Y

year [jɪə] Jahr; Jahrgangsstufe; Klasse I
yearbook [ˈjɪəbʊk] Jahrbuch <IV U2, 49>
yellow [ˈjeləʊ] gelb I
yes [jes] ja I
yesterday [ˈjestədeɪ] gestern I
yet [jet] schon II
not … yet [nɒt … ˈjet] noch nicht II
yogurt [ˈjɒgət] Joghurt II

you [ju:] du; Sie; ihr; euch; dich; dir; Ihnen I
You're right. [jɔ:‿'raɪt] Du hast recht. I
You're welcome. [jɔ: 'welkəm] Gern geschehen. I
young [jʌŋ] jung II
your [jɔ:] dein, deine; euer, eure; Ihr, Ihre I
yours [jɔ:z] deine; eure; Ihre I
Yours, [jɔ:z] Eure *(als Briefabschluss)* I
yourself [jɔ:'self] dich selbst II
by yourself [baɪ 'jɔ:self] allein II
yourselves [jɔ:'selvz] selber; ihr/euch/Sie/sich (selbst) III
youth *(no pl)* [ju:θ] Jugend-; Jugend III

Z

zebra ['zebrə] Zebra I
zero ['zɪərəʊ] null I
zip line ['zɪp ˌlaɪn] Seilrutsche III
ZIP Code ['zɪp kəʊd] Postleitzahl <IV U2, 44>
time **zone** ['taɪm ˌzəʊn] Zeitzone IV ZI, 8
zoo [zu:] Zoo; Tierpark I
zookeeper [ˌzu:'ki:pə] Tierpfleger; Tierpflegerin I
to **zoom** in ['zu:m‿ɪn] heranzoomen <I>

Boys' names

Alaqua ['ælækwə] <IV U2, 137>
Chris [krɪs] IV U3, 62
CJ ['siːˌdʒeɪ] IV U2, 45
Daniel ['dænjəl] IV U4, 76
David ['deɪvɪd] IV U1, 14
Derek ['derɪk] IV U4, 80
Edward ['edwəd] IV U4, 85
Ethan ['iːθn] IV U5, 102
Finn [fɪn] <IV U3, 72>
Gordie ['gɔːdi] IV U3, 62
Jacob ['dʒeɪkəb] IV U3, 54
José [həʊ'zeɪ] IV U1, 18
Matt [mæt] IV U5, 102
Matteo [mə'tɪəʊ] <IV U4, 88>
Michael ['maɪkl] IV U2, 38
Pablo ['pæbləʊ] IV U1, 20
Ramon [rə'mɒn] <IV U4, 88>
Robert ['rɒbət] IV U3, 54
Ronan ['rəʊnən] IV U1, 25
Roy [rɔɪ] IV U2, 45
Teddy ['tedi] IV U3, 63
Vern [vɜːn] IV U3, 63
Warren ['wɒrn] IV U2, 33
Wesley ['wezli] IV U1, 25

Girls' names

Amy ['eɪmi] <IV U2, 44>
Angela ['ændʒlə] IV U1, 19
Anna ['ænə] IV U5, 98
Becky ['beki] IV U4, 79
Brenda ['brendə] IV U3, 54
Caitlin ['keɪtlɪn] <IV U2, 44>
Claudette [klɔː'det] IV U5, 106
Emma ['emə] <IV U3, 72>
Jennifer ['dʒenɪfə] IV U3, 58
Jessica ['dʒesɪkə] IV U1, 25
Julia ['dʒuːliə] IV U3, 54
Lily ['lɪli] IV U3, 54
Linda ['lɪndə] IV U2, 40
Marie [mə'riː] IV U2, 39
Pam [pæm] <IV U3, 72>
Pat [pæt] <IV U2, 137>
Ruby ['ruːbi] IV U2, 45
Ruth [ruːθ] IV U3, 58
Sandy ['sændi] IV U4, 79
Stacey ['steɪsi] IV U2, 39

Surnames

Beeman ['biːmən] IV U3, 64
Blanco ['blænkəʊ] IV U1, 18
Colvin ['kɒlvɪn] IV U5, 106
Lachance ['læʃɑːns] IV U3, 63
Lee [liː] IV U4, 80
Miller ['mɪlə] IV U3, 54
Singh [sɪŋ] IV U1, 14
Sutter ['sʌtə] IV U4, 84
Warner ['wɔːnə] <IV U3, 72>
Williams ['wɪljəmz] IV U5, 98

Place names

Africa ['æfrɪkə] Afrika II
Alabama (AL) [ælə'bæma] *Bundesstaat in den USA* IV ZI, 9
Alaska (AK) [ə'læskə] Alaska IV ZI, 8
America [ə'merɪkə] Amerika II
Arkansas (AR) ['ɑːkənsɔː] *Fluss und Bundesstaat in den USA* <IV U2, 136>
Asia ['eɪʒə] Asien IV U4, 74
Australia [ɒs'treɪliə] Australien I
Bishop ['bɪʃəp] *Ortsname* IV U4, 76
Bodie ['bəʊdi] *Ortsname* IV U4, 86
Boston ['bɒstən] *Stadt in den USA* III
The **British Isles** [ðə ˌbrɪtɪʃ 'aɪlz] die Britischen Inseln III
the **Bronx** [ðə 'brɒŋks] *Stadtteil von NYC* IV U1, 12
Brooklyn ['brʊklɪn] *Stadtteil von NYC* IV U1, 12
California (CA) [ˌkælɪ'fɔːniə] Kalifornien IV ZI, 9
Canada ['kænədə] Kanada III
Cape Cod [ˌkeɪp 'kɒd] *Ortsname* <IV U3, 70>
Cardiff ['kɑːdɪf] *Hauptstadt von Wales* III
Charleston ['tʃɑːlstən] *Stadt in den USA* IV U5, 98
Chicago [ʃɪ'kɑːgəʊ] *Stadt in den USA* <IV U2, 44>
China ['tʃaɪnə] China IV U1, 23
Clearwater ['klɪəwɔːtə] *Stadt in den USA* IV U5, 104
Coloma [kə'ləʊmə] *Ortsname* IV U4, 84
Colorado (CO) [ˌkɒlər'ɑːdəʊ] *Bundesstaat in den USA* IV ZI, 10
Cuba ['kjuːbə] Kuba IV U1, 18
The **Czech Republic** [ðə ˌtʃek rɪ'pʌblɪk] Tschechien II
Daytona [deɪ'təʊnə] *Stadt in den USA* IV U5, 102
Del Mar [ˌdel 'mɑː] *Ortsname* <IV U4, 77>
Denmark ['denmɑːk] Dänemark III
Doheny [də'hiːni] *Strand in Kalifornien* <IV U4, 77>
Dominican Republic [ðə dəˌmɪnɪkn rɪ'pʌblɪk] Dominikanische Republik IV U1, 23
Eastern Europe ['iːstn ˌjʊərəp] Osteuropa IV U1, 23
England ['ɪŋglənd] England I
Europe ['jʊərəp] Europa II
Florida (FL) ['flɒrɪdə] *Bundesstaat in den USA* IV U5, 96
Florida Keys ['flɒrɪdə ˌkiːz] *Inselkette in den USA* IV U5, 143
France [frɑːns] Frankreich II
Germany ['dʒɜːməni] Deutschland I
Great Britain [ˌgreɪt 'brɪtn] Großbritannien III
Greece [griːs] Griechenland IV U1, 23
Harlow ['hɑːləʊ] *Stadt in den USA* IV U3, 64
Hawaii [hə'waɪiː] *Inselkette im Pazifischen Ozean* IV ZI, 9
Huntsville ['hʌntsvɪl] *Ort in den USA* IV ZI, 10
Illinois (IL) [ˌɪlɪ'nɔɪ] *Bundesstaat in den USA* <IV U2, 44>
India ['ɪndiə] Indien I
Indiana (IN) [ˌɪndi'ænə] *Bundesstaat in den USA* IV ZI, 10
Ireland ['aɪələnd] Irland IV U1, 23
Italy ['ɪtəli] Italien II
Jamaica [dʒə'meɪkə] Jamaika II
Japan [dʒə'pæn] Japan <IV U4, 90>
Kentucky (KY) [ken'tʌki] *Bundesstaat in den USA* IV ZI, 10
Las Vegas [ˌlæs 'veɪgəs] *Großstadt in den USA* IV ZI, 10

Latin America [ˌlætɪn əˈmerɪkə] Lateinamerika IV U1, 18

Little Italy [ˌlɪtl ˈɪtli] *Stadtteil von NYC* IV U1, 25

London [ˈlʌndən] London I

Los Angeles [lɒs‿ˈændʒɪliːz] *Stadt in den USA* IV U3, 52

Louisiana (LA) [luˌiːziˈænə] *Bundesstaat in den USA* IV ZI, 9

Maine (ME) [meɪn] *Bundesstaat in den USA* IV U3, 53

Manhattan [mænˈhætn] *Stadtteil von NYC* IV U1, 12

Massachusetts [ˌmæsəˈtʃuːsɪts] *Bundesstaat in den USA* <IV U3, 66>

Mexico [ˈmeksɪkəʊ] Mexiko IV U1, 23

Miami [maɪˈæmi] *Stadt in den USA* IV U3, 57

The **Midwest** [ˌðə ˈmɪdwest] der Mittlere Westen IV ZI, 8

Mississippi (MS) [ˌmɪsɪˈsɪpi] *Bundesstaat in den USA* IV ZI, 9

Montgomery [mɑːntˈɡʌmri] *Stadt in den USA* IV U5, 106

Narrabeen [ˈnærəbiːn] *Strand in Australien* <IV U4, 77>

Nashville [ˈnæʃvɪl] *Ort in den USA* IV U5, 97

The **Netherlands** [ðə ˈneðələndz] die Niederlande II

Nevada (NV) [nəˈvɑːdə] *Bundesstaat in den USA* IV ZI, 10

New England [ˌnjuː‿ˈɪŋɡlənd] Neuengland IV ZI, 8

New Mexico (NM) [njuː ˈmeksɪkəʊ] *Bundesstaat in den USA* IV ZI, 10

New Orleans [ˌnjuː‿ɔːˈliənz] *Stadt in den USA* IV U5, 97

New York City (NYC) [ˌnjuː jɔːk ˈsɪti] *Großstadt in den USA* IV U1, 12

North America [ˌnɔːθ‿əˈmerɪkə] Nordamerika IV ZI, 8

North Dakota (ND) [ˌnɔːθ dəˈkəʊtə] *Bundesstaat in den USA* IV ZI, 10

Northern Ireland [ˌnɔːðn‿ˈaɪələnd] Nordirland III

Norway [ˈnɔːweɪ] Norwegen III

Oklahoma (OK) [ˌəʊkləˈhəʊmə] *Bundesstaat in den USA* <IV U2, 137>

Panama [ˌpænəˈmɑː] *Ortsname* IV U4, 85

Park Ridge [ˈpɑːk ˌrɪdʒ] *Ortsname* <IV U2, 44>

Pennsylvania (PA) [ˌpensɪlˈveɪniə] *Bundesstaat in den USA* IV ZI, 10

Philadelphia [ˌfɪləˈdelfiə] *Stadt in den USA* <IV U3, 66>

The **Philippines** [ˌðə ˈfɪlɪpiːnz] die Philippinen IV U1, 19

Plymouth [ˈplɪməθ] *Ortsname* <IV U3, 70>

Poland [ˈpəʊlənd] Polen II

Queens [kwiːnz] *Stadtteil von NYC* IV U1, 12

The **Republic of Ireland** [ðə rɪˌpʌblɪk‿əv‿ˈaɪələnd] Irland III

Russia [ˈrʌʃə] Russland IV U1, 23

Sacramento [ˌsækrəˈmentəʊ] *Ortsname* IV U4, 84

San Francisco [ˌsæn frənˈsɪskəʊ] *Stadt in den USA* IV U4, 74

Santa Cruz [ˌsæntə ˈkruːz] *Stadt in den USA* <IV U4, 77>

Scandinavia [ˌskændɪˈneɪviə] Skandinavien IV U1, 23

Scotland [ˈskɒtlənd] Schottland III

Seattle [siˈætl] *Großstadt in den USA* IV ZI, 10

Siberia [saɪˈbɪəriə] Sibirien <IV U2, 136>

South Carolina (SC) [ˌsaʊθ kærˈlaɪnə] *Bundesstaat in den USA* IV U5, 98

South Dakota (SD) [ˌsaʊθ dəˈkəʊtə] *Bundesstaat in den USA* IV U2, 34

Spain [speɪn] Spanien II

Staten Island [ˌstætn‿ˈaɪlənd] *Stadtteil von NYC* IV U1, 12

Trestles [ˈtreslz] *Strand in Kalifornien* <IV U4, 77>

Turkey [ˈtɜːki] Türkei II

The **United Kingdom (UK)** [ðə juːˌnaɪtɪd ˈkɪŋdəm] Vereinigtes Königreich von Großbritannien und Nordirland III

USA (United States of America) [ˌjuːesˈeɪ (juːˌnaɪtɪd ˌsteɪts‿əv əˈmerɪkə)] USA (Vereinigte Staaten von Amerika) III

Venice Beach [ˌvenɪs ˈbiːtʃ] *Stadtteil von Los Angeles* <IV U1, 26>

Vietnam [ˌvjetˈnæm] Vietnam IV U1, 23

Wales [weɪlz] Wales III

Washington (WA) [ˈwɒʃɪŋtən] *Bundesstaat in den USA* IV ZI, 10

Washington, D.C. [ˌwɒʃɪŋtən ˌdiːˈsiː] *Hauptstadt der USA* IV ZI, 8

West Coast [ˌwest ˈkəʊst] Westküste <IV U1, 24>

Other names

Academy Award [əˌkædəmi‿əˈwɔːd] *Filmpreis* <IV U4, 140>

The **Appalachian Mountains** [ðə ˌæpəleɪʃən ˈmaʊntɪnz] Die Appalachen IV ZI, 8

Batman [ˈbætmæn] *Filmtitel* <IV U1, 135>

Baxendale Road [ˈbæksndeɪl ˌrəʊd] *Straßenname* <IV U2, 44>

bento [ˈbentəʊ] *Kästchen für Speisen* <IV U4, 90>

Bird Highway [ˌbɜːd ˈhaɪweɪ] *Straßenname* <IV U2, 44>

Bollywood [ˈbɒliwʊd] *indische Filmindustrie: Bombay + Hollywood* II

Broadway [ˈbrɔːdweɪ] *Straße in NYC* IV U1, 14

Brooklyn Bridge [ˌbrʊklɪn ˈbrɪdʒ] *Brücke in NYC* IV U1, 14

California Star [ˌkælɪfɔːniə‿ˈstɑː] *Name einer Zeitung* IV U4, 84

Census Bureau [ˈsensəs ˌbjʊərəʊ] Statistisches Bundesamt <IV U1, 26>

Central Park [ˌsentrl ˈpɑːk] *Park in NYC* IV U1, 14

Chief Ten Bears [ˌtʃiːf ˈten beəz] Häuptling Zehn Bären <IV U2, 136>

Chinatown [ˈtʃaɪnətaʊn] *chinesisches Stadtviertel* IV U4, 74

Colorado River [ˌkɒlərɑːdəʊ ˈrɪvə] *Fluss in den USA* IV ZI, 8

Christopher **Columbus** [ˌkrɪstəfə kəˈlʌmbəs] *Personenname* <IV U2, 136>

Columbus Day [kəˌlʌmbəs ˈdeɪ] *Feiertag in den USA* <IV U3, 139>

The **Confederate Flag** [ðə kənˈfedrət ˌflæg] Konföderiertenflagge IV U5, 98

Declaration of Independence [ˌdekləreɪʃn‿əv‿ɪndɪˈpendəns] Unabhängigkeitserklärung IV ZI, 10

Denali [dəˈnɑːli] *höchster Berg in Nordamerika (neuer Name)* IV ZI, 8

Department of Homeland Security [dɪˌpɑːtmənt‿əv ˌhəʊmlænd sɪˈkjʊərəti] Heimatschutzbehörde IV U1, 23

Ellis Island [ˌelɪs‿ˈaɪlənd] *Insel vor NYC* IV U1, 20

Empire State Building [ˌempaɪə steɪt ˈbɪldɪŋ] *Gebäude in NYC* IV U1, 14

Empire State of Mind (Part II) Broken Down [ˌempaɪə ˌsteɪt‿əv ˈmaɪnd (pɑːt ˈtuː) ˌbrəʊkn ˈdaʊn] *Liedname* <IV U1, 19>

European Union [ˌjʊərəpiːən ˈjuːnjən] Europäische Union III

The **Everglades** [ði ˈevəgleɪdz] *Nationalpark in den USA* IV U5, 102

Fort Knox [ˌfɔːt ˈnɒks] *Lager für die Goldreserven des Schatzamtes der USA* IV ZI, 10

Fruit4U [ˌfruːtfəˈjuː] *Firmenname* IV U2, 39

Mahatma **Gandhi** [məˌhɑːtmə ˈgændi] *Personenname* IV U5, 108

Gold Rush [ˈgəʊld ˌrʌʃ] **Goldrausch in Kalifornien** IV U4, 75

The **Golden Gate Bridge** [ðə ˌgəʊldn ˌgeɪt ˈbrɪdʒ] *berühmte Brücke in San Francisco* IV U4, 74

Gotham City [ˌgɒθəm ˈsɪti] *fiktiver Ort im Film Batman* <IV U1, 135>

Grand Canyon [ˌgrænd ˈkænjən] *Sehenswürdigkeit in den USA* IV U4, 76

Grand Central Station [ˌgrænd sentrl ˈsteɪʃn] *Hauptbahnhof in NYC* IV U1, 14

Grand Central Terminal [ˈgrænd ˌsentrl ˌtɜːmɪnl] *alter Name des Hauptbahnhofs in NYC* IV U1, 16

Gulf Coast [ˈgʌlf ˌkəʊst] Golfküste IV U5, 96

Hollywood [ˈhɒliwʊd] *Zentrum der amerikanischen Filmindustrie (in Los Angeles)* II

Huarache [ˌhuːəˈrɑːtʃə] *Name einer Schuhfirma* <IV U4, 77>

Hurricane Katrina [ˌhʌrɪkən kəˈtriːnə] *Name eines Wirbelsturms* <IV U5, 108>

Independence Day [ˌɪndɪˈpendəns ˌdeɪ] amerikanischer Unabhängigkeitstag <IV U3, 138>

Indy 500 [ˌɪndi faɪvˈhʌndred] *Name eines Autorennens* IV ZI, 10

Iron Man [ˈaɪən ˌmæn] *Filmtitel* <IV U1, 135>

Martin Luther King [ˌmɑːtɪn ˌluːθə ˈkɪŋ] *Personenname* <IV U3, 138>

Stephen **King** [ˌstiːvn ˈkɪŋ] *US-amerik. Schriftsteller* IV U3, 62

King Kong [ˈkɪŋ ˌkɒŋ] King Kong <IV U4, 141>

Ku Klux Klan [ˌkuː klʌks ˈklæn] *ein rassistischer Geheimbund in den Südstaaten der USA* IV U5, 107

Lexington Avenue [ˈleksɪŋtn ˌævənjuː] *Straße in NYC* IV U1, 14

Abraham **Lincoln** [ˌeɪbrəhæm ˈlɪŋkən] *16. Präsident der USA (1861–1865)* <IV U3, 138>

Long Island [ˌlɒŋ‿ˈaɪlənd] *Teilort von NYC* <IV U1, 135>

Malcolm X [ˌmælkəm ˈeks] *Personenname* <IV U5, 108>

Mardi Gras [ˌmɑːdi ˈgrɑː] Faschingsdienstag IV U5, 98

Martin Luther King Day [ˌmɑːtɪn ˌluːθə ˌkɪŋ ˈdeɪ] *Feiertag in den USA zu Ehren Martin Luther Kings* <IV U3, 138>

Mayflower [ˈmeɪflaʊə] *Schiffsname* <IV U3, 70>

Mesa Verde [ˌmeɪsə ˈvɜːdi] *US-Nationalpark* IV ZI, 10

Mississippi River [ˌmɪsɪsɪpi ˈrɪvə] *Fluss in den USA* IV ZI, 8

Missouri River [mɪˌzʊəri ˈrɪvə] *Fluss in den USA* IV ZI, 8

Mt. McKinley [ˌmaʊnt məˈkɪnli] *höchster Berg in Nordamerika (alter Name)* IV ZI, 8

NASCAR (National Association for Stock Car Racing) [ˈnæzkɑː] *amerikanischer Motorsportverband* IV U5, 102

New World [ˌnjuː ˈwɜːld] *alter Name für Amerika* <IV U3, 70>
Niagara Falls [naɪˌægrə ˈfɔːlz] Niagarafälle IV U3, 52
One World Trade Center [ˌwʌn ˈwɜːld ˌtreɪd ˌsentə] *Gebäude in NYC* IV U1, 12
Oscar [ˈɒskə] *Filmpreis* <IV U4, 140>
Pacific Ocean [pəˌsɪfɪk‿ˈəʊʃn] Pazifischer Ozean IV ZI, 9
Rosa **Parks** [ˌrəʊzə ˈpɑːks] *amerikanische Bürgerrechtlerin* IV U5, 107
Presidents' Day [ˌprezɪdnts ˈdeɪ] *Feiertag in den USA* <IV U3, 138>
Rio Grande [ˌriːəʊˈgrænd] *Fluss in den USA* <IV U2, 136>
River Thames [ˌrɪvə ˈtemz] *Fluss in London* II
the **Rockies** (= the Rocky Mountains) [ðə ˈrɒkiz] *Gebirge in Nordamerika* <IV U4, 89>
Rocky Mountains [ˌrɒki ˈmaʊntɪnz] *Gebirge in Nordamerika* IV ZI, 9
Silicon Valley [ˌsɪlɪkən ˈvæli] *Ort, wo viele Computerfirmen ihren Sitz haben* IV U4, 75
Sitting Bull [ˌsɪtɪŋ ˈbʊl] *Name des Häuptlings eines Indianerstammes* IV ZI, 10
Space Needle [ˈspeɪs ˌniːdl] *Sehenswürdigkeit in Seattle* IV ZI, 10
Statue of Liberty [ˌstætʃuː‿əv ˈlɪbəti] *Freiheitsstatue in NYC* IV U1, 13
Joseph **Strauss** [ˌdʒəʊzɪf ˈstraʊs] *Architekt* IV U4, 75
Super Bowl [ˈsuːpə bəʊl] *Meisterschaftsendspiel des NFL* <IV U2, 50>
Surfin' USA [ˈsɜːfɪn ˌjuːesˈeɪ] *Liedtitel* <IV U4, 77>
Taylor **Swift** [ˌteɪlə ˈswɪft] *Personenname* IV U5, 97
Universal Studios [ˌjuːnɪˈvɜːsl ˌstjuːdiəʊz] *bekanntes Filmstudio in den USA* <IV U4, 141>
US Space & Rocket Center [ˌjuːes ˌspeɪs‿ən ˈrɒkɪt ˌsentə] *Raumfahrtmuseum in den USA* IV ZI, 10
Ventura County Line [venˌtʊərə ˌkaʊnti ˈlaɪn] *Name einer Bahnlinie* <IV U4, 77>
Very Large Array [ˌveri lɑːdʒ‿əˈreɪ] *Radioteleskop in den USA* IV ZI, 10
Walk of Fame [ˌwɔːk‿əv ˈfeɪm] *Straße in Hollywood mit Sternen für bekannte Leute* IV U4, 75
Wall Street [ˈwɔːl ˌstriːt] *Straße in NYC* IV U1, 14
George **Washington** [ˌdʒɔːdʒ ˈwɒʃɪŋtən] *1. Präsident der USA (1789–1797)* <IV U3, 138>
The **White House** [ðə ˈwaɪt ˌhaʊs] das Weiße Hause IV U3, 53
World Trade Center [ˌwɜːld ˈtreɪd ˌsentə] *Gebäude in NYC bis 2001* IV U1, 12
World Wide Web [ˌwɜːld waɪd ˈweb] *ein über das Internet abrufbares System* IV U4, 80
Malala **Yousafzai** [ˌməlælæ ˈjuːsæfzaɪ] *Personenname* IV U5, 108

A

abbiegen to turn III
abdecken to cover IV U3, 58
Abend evening I
an jenem Abend that night II
heute Abend tonight II
Abendessen dinner II
(frühes) **Abendessen** tea I
abends in the evenings III
Abenteuer adventure I
aber but I
abfahren leave II
Abfall rubbish II
abholen to pick up IV U2, 43
Abholung pick-up IV U5, 102
ablehnen to refuse IV U5, 99
abonnieren to subscribe IV U4, 81
abräumen to clear IV U2, 33
den Tisch abräumen to clear the table II
abschicken *(einen Brief)* to post III
Abschieds- leaving II
Abschiedsrede farewell speech II
abschließen to lock I
sich **abseilen** to abseil II
absichtlich on purpose II
absolut absolutely IV U3, 59
abspülen to do the washing up II
abstimmen über to vote for IV U2, 33
Abteilung department II
acht eight I
Achterbahn roller coaster II
achtzehn eighteen I
achtzig eighty I
Ackerboden farmland IV U2, 32
Ackerland farmland IV U2, 32
Adapter adaptor III
Adjektiv adjective III
Adresse address II
Affe monkey I
Afroamerikaner African American IV U5, 96
afroamerikanisch African-American IV U5, 106
Ahnung idea I
Aktenkoffer briefcase III
Aktentasche briefcase III
Aktivität activity I
akzeptieren to accept IV U5, 99
albern silly II
Alkohol alcohol *(no pl)* IV U3, 58
alle all I; everyone II; every III; everybody IV U2, 43
Allee avenue IV U1, 14
allein alone I; by yourself II
ganz allein all alone I
Allergie allergy II
allergisch gegen allergic to II
alles everything II
alles klar all right II
Alligator alligator IV ZI, 9
Alphabet alphabet I
als than; as II; when II
also so I; right II
alt old I
Alter age I
Altglascontainer bottle bank II
am Dienstag on Tuesday I
am Schluss by the end II
am Wochenende at the weekend I
Amerikaner American IV ZI, 9
Amerikanerin American IV ZI, 9
Amerikanisch American IV ZI, 9
amerikanisch American IV ZI, 9
amisch Amish IV U3, 58
die **Amischen** the Amish IV U3, 53
Ampel lights IV U1, 14
amüsiert amused IV U3, 63
an on; at I; by IV U3, 63
an Bord on board III
an der Spitze (von) at the front of II
Ananas pineapple III
anbauen to grow IV U3, 58
anbieten to offer IV U2, 38
Anblick look IV U1, 14
andauern to last IV U4, 86
Andenken souvenir III
andere other I; others II
ein anderer another II
die anderen the others I
anderer Meinung sein to disagree II
(sich) **ändern** to change III
seine Meinung ändern to change one's mind III
anders different I
Anfang start; beginning III
anfangen to start II
Anführer leader III
Anführerin leader III
angenehm comfortable II
angezogen (wie) dressed III
angreifen to attack IV U2, 42
Angriff attack IV U1, 12
Angst haben to be scared; to be afraid II
ängstlich afraid II
anhalten to last IV U4, 86
anhören to listen (to) I
ankommen to arrive II
Ankündigung announcement II
anlegen to put on III
Anleitung tutorial IV U4, 80
anmalen to paint II
Anmeldeformular entry form II
Anmeldung registration II
annehmen to accept IV U5, 99
Annonce ad(vert) (= advertisement) IV U4, 76
Anordnung layout IV U4, 77
anprobieren to try on II
Anruf call III
anrufen to call I; to phone II
Anrufer caller II
Anruferin caller II
anschauen to watch; to look at I; to have a look II
sich **anschließen** to join III
ansehen to watch I
Anspitzer pencil sharpener I
morgendliche **Ansprache** morning message IV U2, 34
ansprechend appealing IV U4, 77
anstelle von instead IV U4, 80
anstoßen to hit III
(sich) **stoßen** to hit III
Antenne antenna III
Antwort answer II
antworten to answer I
Anzahl number IV U4, 75
Anzeige advertisement II

anziehen to put on III
sich anziehen to get dressed II
April April I
Arbeit work I; job II
arbeiten to work I
Arbeiter worker II
Arbeiterin worker II
Arbeitsheft workbook I
Arbeitskollege co-worker IV U2, 38
Arbeitskollegin co-worker IV U2, 38
arbeitslos unemployed IV U1, 18
arbeitsreich busy I
Arbeitszeit working hours *(pl)* IV U2, 39
Architekt architect IV U4, 75
Architektin architect IV U4, 75
Archiv archive II
Areal area IV ZI, 9
Ärger trouble III
Arm arm I
arm poor IV U1, 18
Armee army III
armselig miserable III
Art sort II; type III
Art und Weise way III
Arzt doctor II
Ärztin doctor II
Astronomie astronomy IV U2, 34
atmen to breathe III
Attacke attack IV U1, 12
auch too; also I
auch nicht not either III
auf on; at I
auf dem Land in the country I
auf dem Weg on the way I
auf der linken Seite on the left I
auf der rechten Seite on the right I
auf der Welt in the world II
auf diese Weise like this III
auf einmal suddenly II
Auf keinen Fall! No way! III
Auf Wiedersehen! Goodbye. I
Aufbau structure III
auffallend striking III
Aufführung show IV U5, 102
Aufgabe job II
aufgeben to give up IV U1, 18
aufgeben *(einen Brief)* to post III
aufgebracht upset I
aufgeregt excited; nervous II
aufgerissen torn IV U4, 83
aufheben to pick up II; to save IV U3, 54
jmdn. **aufheitern** to cheer sb up III
aufhören to stop I; to finish II
Aufkleber sticker II
aufmachen to open I
jmdn. **aufmuntern** to cheer sb up III
aufpassen to look after II
aufpassen auf to watch II
aufräumen to tidy (up) II
aufregend exciting I
aufschauen to look up II
aufstehen to get up I; to stand up IV U3, 63
auftauchen to show up IV U2, 42
aufwachen to wake up II
aufwachsen to grow up III
Aufzug elevator *(AE)* IV U1, 13
Auge eye II
Augenblick moment II
August August I
im August in August I
aus from I
aus ... heraus out of II
Ausbildung education IV U2, 38
Ausblick view IV U1, 14
auschecken to check out III
Auseinandersetzung argument II; conflict IV U5, 99
ausfallen to fail IV U1, 19
Ausflug trip I
ausgeben *(Geld)* to spend II
ein **ausgefüllter** Tag a busy day I
ausgehen *(Ware)* to run out of III
(aus)gehen mit to go out with IV U3, 58
ausländisch foreign IV U1, 18
ausleihen to borrow II
ausprobieren to try; to try out III
ausräumen to clear IV U2, 33
Ausrüstung equipment III
aussehen to look II
außer except III
außergewöhnlich unusual IV U4, 77
außerhalb outside IV U2, 38
außerhalb des Lehrplans extracurricular IV U2, 34
Außerirdische alien I
Außerirdischer alien I
außerunterrichtlich *(Zusatzunterricht)* extracurricular IV U2, 34
Aussicht view IV U1, 14
Aussichtspunkt lookout point II
aussteigen to get off II
Austausch exchange IV U2, 34
Ausverkauf sale II
auswählen to choose II
auswandern to emigrate IV U1, 19
Ausweis ID III
Auswirkung impact IV U4, 80
Auto car I
Autofahrt drive III
Autogramm autograph IV U3, 53
Autogramme geben to sign autographs IV U3, 53
Automat machine II
Autor writer III
Autorin writer III

B

Baby baby II
Babysitter babysitter IV U2, 41
Babysitterin babysitter IV U2, 41
einen Kuchen **backen** to make a cake I
Bäcker baker III
Bäckerei baker's III
Bäckerin baker III
Backofen oven II
Bad bathroom I
Badezimmer bathroom I
Bahnhof station I
bald soon II
Ball ball II
Banane banana I
Band band II
Bank bench III
Bär bear I
Bargeld cash II
Baseball baseball IV U1, 13
Basketball basketball II
Bauarbeiter builder II

Bauarbeiterin builder II
Bauch stomach II
Bauchschmerzen stomach ache II
Bauchweh stomach ache II
bauen to build II
Bauer farmer I
Bäuerin farmer I
Bauernhof farm I
Baum tree I
Baumwolle cotton III
Baustelle construction site IV U1, 15
beängstigend scary I
beantworten to answer I
bedauern to feel sorry for III
bedecken to cover IV U3, 58
bedeuten to mean III
bedeutend major IV ZI, 8; powerful IV U1, 22
sich **bedienen** to help oneself III
Bedienung waitress IV U4, 89
Bedingung condition IV U1, 22
mit besonderen **Bedürfnissen** with special needs III
sich **beeilen** to hurry II; to rush III
beeindrucken to impress III
beeindruckend powerful IV U1, 22
beenden to finish II
befolgen to follow III
befördern to carry II
befragen to interview I
Befrager interviewer IV U1, 18
Befragerin interviewer IV U1, 18
Befragung interview II
befreunden *(jmdn. zu seiner Freundesliste hinzufügen)* to friend IV U4, 81
begeistert excited II
Beginn beginning III
beginnen to start II; to begin IV U1, 18
begnadigen to pardon IV U3, 53
Begnadigung pardon IV U3, 67
mit **Behinderung** with special needs III
bei at I
bei Bewusstsein awake III
Bein leg II
beinahe almost III
Beispiel example IV U5, 98
zum Beispiel for example IV U2, 34
sich **beklagen** to complain IV U1, 18
Bekleidungsvorschriften dress code IV U2, 36
bekommen to get I
bekräftigen to confirm IV U4, 84
beliebt popular III
bemerkenswert striking III
benennen to name IV ZI, 9
benutzen to use II
beobachten to watch II
bequem comfortable II
bereit ready I
bereits already II
Berg mountain III; hill IV U4, 74
Bergarbeiter miner III
Bergarbeiterin miner III
bergen to save III
Bergwerk mine III
Bericht report IV U4, 84
Beruf job II; career IV U1, 18
Berufsbezeichnung job title IV U2, 38
berühmt famous I
Besatzung crew III
beschäftigt busy I
sich **beschweren** to complain IV U1, 18
eine **Besichtigungstour** machen to go sightseeing II
besitzen to own; to have got II
mit **besonderen** Bedürfnissen with special needs III
besonders special I; especially II
besorgt worried II
Besorgungen machen to do the shopping II
besser better I
bestätigen to confirm IV U4, 84
bestbezahlt best-paid IV U5, 97
beste best II
die besten the best II
besteigen to climb III
bestellen to order II
bestürzt upset I
besuchen to visit II
Besucher visitor II
Besucherin visitor II
Beton concrete III
betreiben to run III
betreten to enter IV U3, 54
betrunken drunk IV U3, 62
Bett bed I
ins Bett gehen to go to bed I
Bettdecke blanket IV U3, 62
beunruhigt worried II
Bevölkerung population IV ZI, 8
bevor before II
(sich) **bewegen** to move IV U1, 22
Bewegung move III; movement IV U5, 96
beweisen to prove IV U4, 84
sich **bewerben** (für/um) to apply (for) IV U2, 38
bewerten to rate III
Bewohner inhabitant III
Bewohnerin inhabitant III
bei **Bewusstsein** awake III
Bezahlautomat payment machine II
bezahlen to pay II
Bezirk borough IV U1, 12
Bibliothek library III
Bild picture II
bilden to make I
Bildung education IV U2, 38
billig cheap II
Biologie Biology I
bis to II; until I
bis zu before II
Bis bald! See you soon! I
Bis bald. See you later.; See you. I
bis (spätestens) by III
ein **bisschen** a little; a bit II
bitte please I
Bitte schön. Here you are. I
bitten um to ask for II
blau blue I
bleiben to stay II
etw. bleiben lassen to give sth a miss III
in Verbindung bleiben to keep in touch II
stecken bleiben to get stuck IV U3, 54
Bleistift pencil I
Blick look; view IV U1, 14
Blog blog II
Blume flower III

Bluse blouse I
bluten to bleed III
Boden ground III
Bonbon sweet I
Boot boat II
Bootsfahrt boat trip II
an **Bord** on board III
böse angry II; naughty III
Boss boss II
Botschaft message II
Boulevard avenue IV U1, 14
Bowlen bowling IV U3, 58
Box box I
braten to fry IV U5, 98
Bratwurst sausage II
brauchen to need I
nicht brauchen needn't I
braun brown I
brechen to break II
brennen to be on fire II; to burn III
Brett plank II
Brief letter III
Briefmarke stamp III
bringen to bring II; to take IV U2, 43
britisch British II
Broschüre brochure III; booklet IV U5, 102
Brot bread II
belegtes Brot sandwich I
Brotlaib loaf III
Brücke bridge II
Bruder brother I
Buch book I
buchen to book IV U4, 76
Bücherei library III
Büchse tin IV U3, 63
Buchstabe letter III
buchstabieren to spell I
Bucht bay IV U4, 75
Büfett buffet III
Bühne stage II
Bundesstaat state IV ZI, 8
bunt colourful II
Buntstift pencil I
Burg castle II
Bürgerrechte civil rights *(pl)* IV U5, 96
Bürgersteig sidewalk *(AE)* IV U1, 15
Büro office II
Bus bus I
im Bus on the bus II
Bushaltestelle bus stop II
Butter butter I

C

Café café I
Cafeteria cafeteria I
Camp camp II
campen gehen to go camping II
Camping camping III
Campingplatz campsite III
Cartoon cartoon IV U4, 81
Center centre III; center *(AE)* IV U1, 13
Chance chance II
chatten to chat II
Cheerleader *(Mädchen, das in einer Gruppe eine Sportmannschaft anfeuert)* cheerleader IV U2, 34
Chef boss II
Chefin boss II
Chefkoch head chef II
Chili chilli II
chillen to chill out IV U4, 76
Chinese Chinese IV U5, 99
Chinesin Chinese IV U5, 99
Chinesisch Chinese IV U5, 99
chinesisch Chinese IV U5, 99
christlich Christian IV U3, 53
circa about II
Cola coke I
College college IV U1, 19
Comic(heft) comic II
Computer computer I
Courage courage IV U5, 107
Cousin cousin II
Cousine cousin II
Crew crew III
Curry curry II
Cyber-Mobbing cyberbullying IV U4, 80

D

da there I
da drüben over there II
da ist there is I
da sind there are I
da because I
Dach roof II
Dachboden attic I
damals then III
Dame lady II
Dampfmaschine steam engine III
danach then; after that I; after III
Herzlichen **Dank**. Thanks so much. IV U4, 94
Vielen **Dank**. Thanks so much. IV U4, 94
danke thanks I
Danke. Thank you. I
dann then I
das the; this; that I; which III
dass that III
Date date IV U2, 42
Datei file II
Datum date I
dauern to take III; to last IV U4, 86
davor in front of II
Decke blanket IV U3, 62
decken to lay II
dein your I
deine yours I; your I
dem who; which III
Demonstration protest IV U5, 96
den who; which III
denken to think I
Denkmal monument II
dennoch still III
deprimiert down III
der the I; who; which III
deren whose III
derselbe the same II
Desaster disaster III
deshalb so I
dessen whose III
Detail detail IV U5, 102
deutlich clear IV U4, 77
Deutsch German I
deutsch German III
Dezember December I
dich you I
dich selbst yourself II
die *(auch Pl.)* the I; who II; which III
Diele hall II

Dienst service III
Dienstag Tuesday I
am Dienstag on Tuesday I
dies this I
diese (hier) these II
Ding thing I
dir you I
Distanz distance IV ZI, 9
Dollar *(amer. Währungseinheit)* dollar IV ZI, 8
Donnerstag Thursday I
doof silly III
Dorf village III
dort there I
dort drüben over there II
dort ist there is I
Dose can I; tin IV U3, 63
Dr. *(Anrede)* Dr III
Drama drama III
drängeln to push III
Draufgänger daredevil IV U3, 53
Draufgängerin daredevil IV U3, 53
draußen outside II
draußen halten to keep out III
dreckig dirty I
Drehort location III
drei three I
dreißig thirty I
dreizehn thirteen I
drinnen in II; inside IV U1, 25
dritte third I
drücken to push I
Dschungel jungle IV U4, 85
du you I
Dudelsack bagpipes *(pl)* III
dulden to tolerate IV U5, 98
dumm silly III
dunkel dark I
Dunkelheit the dark III
durch through II
quer durch across IV U3, 54
Durcheinander mess I
Durchsage announcement II
durchschnittlich average IV U3, 58
dürfen may II; to be allowed to IV U2, 34
nicht dürfen mustn't III
nicht/nie dürfen must not/never III
Darf es sonst noch etwas sein? Anything else? I
durstig thirsty II
Dusche shower III
Duschgel shower gel III

E

echt real II; really II
Echt?! No way! III
Ecke corner III
Es ist **egal.** It doesn't matter. II
egal wo(hin) wherever III
Ehefrau wife IV U4, 85
Ehemaligentreffen Homecoming *(AE)* IV U2, 33
Ehemann husband IV U3, 54
Ehre honor *(AE)* IV U1, 25
ehrenamtliche Helferin volunteer III
ehrenamtlicher Helfer volunteer III
ehrlich honestly IV U3, 63
Ei egg I
eifersüchtig jealous II
eigene own II
Eigenschaftswort adjective III
eigentlich actually III; anyway IV U1, 14
Eigentümer landlord II
eilen to rush III
Eimer Wasser bucket of water I
ein a; an I
ein bisschen a bit II
ein paar a few III
ein wenig a bit II
einander each other III
Einbrecher burglar I
Einbrecherin burglar I
einchecken to check in III
eindeutig clear IV U4, 77
eindringen (in) to invade III
einfach easy I; plain II; simple III
einfache Fahrkarte single ticket III
Einfluss impact IV U4, 80; influence IV U5, 98
einflussreich important II
einfügen to paste II
eingängig catchy IV U4, 77
Eingangstor gateway IV U1, 12
einhundert a/one hundred I
einige some I; a few III; several IV U4, 80
Einkäufe machen to do the shopping II
Einkaufen shopping I
einkaufen gehen to go shopping II
Einkaufszentrum shopping centre I
Einkaufszettel shopping list I
einladen to invite I
Einladung invitation I
einmal once IV U1, 25
noch einmal once more II
einmarschieren (in) to invade III
einpacken to pack; to pack up II
einprägsam catchy IV U4, 77
eins one I
einsam lonely III
einschlafen to fall asleep III
einsetzen to put in I
einst once IV U1, 25
einsteigen (in den Bus) to get on (the bus) IV U5, 106
Einstellung attitude IV U4, 89
einstufen to rate III
Eintrag entry IV U4, 86
eintreten to enter IV U3, 54
Eintrittskarte ticket III
nicht **einverstanden** sein to disagree II
Einwanderer immigrant IV U1, 13
Einwanderin immigrant IV U1, 13
einwandern to immigrate IV U1, 18
Einwohner inhabitant III; population IV ZI, 8
Einwohnerin inhabitant III
Einwohnerzahl population IV ZI, 8
Einzelheit detail IV U5, 102
einzige only II
Eis ice cream I
Eisberg iceberg III
Eiscreme ice cream I
Eisenbahn railway IV U4, 86
Elefant elephant I
elegant chic I
elektrisch electric IV U3, 59

Elektrizität electricity III
elend miserable III
elf eleven I
Eltern parents *(pl)* II
E-Mail e-mail I
emigrieren to emigrate IV U1, 19
Empfang signal III
Ende end II; ending III
enden to finish II; to end IV U5, 107
endlich at last II
Energie power III
eng tight II
die **Engländer** the English III
Englisch English I
englisch English I
Entdeckung discovery IV U4, 84
entfernen to remove IV U5, 98
entfernt away II
Entfernung distance IV ZI, 9
entfreunden *(jmdn. von seiner Freundesliste streichen)* to unfriend IV U4, 81
entlang along I; down III
(sich) **entscheiden** to decide III
Entscheidung decision IV U1, 18
entschuldigen to pardon IV U3, 53
  sich entschuldigen to say sorry II
Entschuldigung pardon IV U3, 67
Entschuldigung! Excuse me! I
Entschuldigung. Sorry.; I'm sorry. I
sich **entspannen** to chill out IV U4, 76
entspannt relaxed IV U4, 74
Entwicklung trend IV U4, 80
Enzyklopädie encyclopedia IV U4, 86
er he I
  er selbst himself III
Erdbeere strawberry II
Erdboden ground III
Erdkunde Geography I
Erdnussbutter peanut butter III
Ereignis event IV U4, 86
etwas **erfahren** über to learn about sth III
erfinden to invent III
Erfinder inventor III
Erfinderin inventor III
Erfindung invention III
Erfolg success IV U5, 107
erfolgreich successful III
erforschen to explore II
Ergebnis result II
ergreifen to grab III
sich **erinnern** (an) to remember II
erklären to explain III
erkunden to explore II
sich **erkundigen** nach to ask about II
erlauben to allow IV U4, 84
ernst serious III
  etw. ernst nehmen to take sth seriously IV U1, 18
  Im Ernst? Are you serious? III
Erntedankfest Thanksgiving IV U3, 53
erraten to guess II
erscheinen to show up IV U2, 42
erschöpft exhausted III
erschrecken to scare II; to jump III
erschrocken sein to be scared II
ersetzen to replace IV U1, 12
erstaunlich amazing II
erste first I
  erste Stunde *(in der Schule)* homeroom IV U2, 45
erstellen to make I
als **Erstes** first I
Erwachsene adult III
Erwachsener adult III
erwarten to expect III
erzählen to tell I
Erzähler narrator I
Erzählerin narrator I
Erziehung education IV U2, 38
es it I
  es gibt there are; there is I
  Es tut mir leid wegen … Sorry about … I
  Es tut mir leid. I'm sorry. I
Essen food I; meal II; dinner IV U3, 53
  Essen zum Mitnehmen takeaway II
essen to eat I; to have II
Essensstand food stall II
Esszimmer dining room I
etwa about II
etwas something I; some II
euch you I
euer your I
eure yours I; your I
Eure *(als Briefabschluss)* Yours, I
Euro *(Währung)* euro III
Europäer European IV U2, 32
Europäerin European IV U2, 32
europäisch European IV U2, 32
Europäisch European IV U2, 32
ewig forever II
exakt exact III
existieren to be around IV U4, 80
explodieren to explode III
Explosion explosion III

F

Fabel fable III
Fabrik factory III
Fahne flag II
fahren to go I; to ride II; to travel III; to drive IV U3, 52
  gegen etw. fahren to hit III
  Ski fahren to ski II
Fahrer driver III
Fahrerin driver III
einfache **Fahrkarte** single ticket III
Fahrplan timetable III; schedule *(AE)* IV U2, 33
Fahrpreis fare III
Fahrrad bike I
Fahrschein ticket III
Fahrt ride IV U1, 14; drive; trip; voyage; journey III; tour IV U4, 76
  eine Fahrt machen to take a trip III
Fakt fact II
Fall case IV U5, 107
fallen to fall I; to fall (over) III
falls if II
falsch wrong I
Faltblatt flyer II
Familie family I
Fan fan I
fangen to catch II
Fantasie fantasy II
fantastisch fantastic II
Fantasy fantasy II
Farbe colour I; color *(AE)* IV ZI, 8
Fasching carnival IV U5, 98

Fass barrel IV U3, 53
fast almost III
Fastfood fast food I
faszinierend fascinating IV U4, 77
Februar February I
Federmäppchen pencil case I
Feedback feedback IV U2, 39
fegen to sweep II
fehlschlagen to fail IV U1, 19
Feier party I; celebration IV U3, 52
feiern to celebrate I
Feind enemy III
Feindin enemy III
Feld field IV ZI, 9
Fels rock III
Fenster window I
Ferien holiday I
in der **Ferne** in the distance IV U1, 15
Fernsehen TV I
  im Fernsehen on TV IV U1, 13
fernsehen to watch TV I
Fernseher TV I
Fernsehsendung TV show II
Fernsehstudio TV studio II
fertig ready I
  sich fertig machen to get ready IV U3, 54
fertigstellen to finish II
fest tight II; solid III
festhalten to hold III
festnehmen to arrest IV U5, 107
feststecken to be stuck I
Feuer fire I
Feuerwehrauto fire engine II
Fieber fever IV U4, 86
Film film; movie I
Filzstift felt-tip I
Finanz- financial IV U1, 14
finanziell financial IV U1, 14
finden to find I
Finger finger III
Fingerabdruck fingerprint II
Firma company II
Fisch fish I
fit fit III
Fitnessraum gymnasium III
Fläche area IV ZI, 9
Flagge flag II
Flamingo flamingo I
Flasche bottle I
Fledermaus bat I
Fleisch meat I
fleißig hard-working IV U2, 39
fliegen to fly II
fließend fluent III
Flohmarkt jumble sale II
Flug flight II
Flughafen airport II
Flugzeug plane II
Flur hall; corridor II
Fluss river I
flüssig fluent III
Flyer flyer II
folgen to follow III
Fön hairdryer III
in **Form** fit III
Foto photo I
  ein Foto machen to take a photo I
  Fotos machen to take photos II
fotografieren to take photos II
Frage question I
fragen to ask I
  fragen nach to ask about II
  nach dem Weg fragen asking the way I
die **Franzosen** the French *(pl)* IV U5, 98
Französisch French I
Frau woman I; lady II
Frau *(Anrede)* Mrs; Ms I
frech cheeky; naughty III
freie Wildbahn the wild IV U5, 102
Land der **Freien** land of the free IV U3, 53
Freiheit freedom *(no pl)* IV U1, 23
Freiland- free range II
Freiluft- outdoor III
Freistunde study hall period IV U2, 34
Freitag Friday I
Freiwillige volunteer III
Freiwilliger volunteer III
Freizeit free time I
Freizeitpark theme park I
fremd foreign IV U1, 18
Freude fun I
Freund friend I
  Freunde treffen to see friends I
Freund *(in einer Paarbeziehung)* boyfriend IV U2, 42
Freundin friend I
Freundin *(in einer Paarbeziehung)* girlfriend IV U2, 38
freundlich kind II; friendly III
Freundschaften schließen to make friends I
Frieden peace III
friedlich peaceful IV U5, 96
frieren to freeze; to get cold III
Frisbee frisbee I
Frisbeescheibe frisbee I
frisch fresh II
Friseur hairdresser II
Friseurin hairdresser II
frittieren to fry IV U5, 98
froh glad IV U3, 54
Frucht fruit I
früh early I
  früher earlier I
  (wohnte) früher used to (live) III
Frühlingsrolle spring roll II
Frühstück breakfast I
frühstücken to have breakfast I
Frühstückspension bed and breakfast (B & B) III
(sich) **fühlen** to feel II
führen to run III
Führer guide II; leader III
Führerin guide II; leader III
Führerschein driver's license *(AE)* IV U2, 38
Füller pen I
fünf five I
fünfzehn fifteen I
fünfzig fifty I
funktionieren to work II
für for I
  für immer forever II
furchtbar awful; terrible I; horrible; dreadful III
sich **fürchten** to be afraid II
Fuß foot I
  zu Fuß on foot I
Fußball football I
Fußboden floor I

Fußgelenk ankle II
Fußknöchel ankle II
füttern to feed I

G

Gabel fork II
Gang corridor II
ganz all II; quite III; whole IV U3, 63
ganz allein all alone I
den ganzen Tag all day III
gar nicht not at all II
Garten garden I
Gas gas III
Gast guest III
Gastfamilie host family IV U2, 34
Gasthaus pub III
Gebärdensprache sign language III
Gebäude building II
geben to give I; to be around IV U4, 80
Autogramme geben to sign autographs IV U3, 53
jmdm. das Gefühl geben, etw. zu sein to make sb feel like sth III
es gibt there are; there is I
Gebet prayer IV U4, 85
Gebiet area IV ZI, 9
geboren werden to be born III
(in der Pfanne) **gebraten** fried II
Geburtstag birthday I
Alles Gute zum Geburtstag! Happy birthday! I
Gedicht poem III
geduldig patient III
gefährlich dangerous III
Gefängnis prison II
gefrieren to freeze III
jmdm. das **Gefühl** geben, etw. zu sein to make sb feel like sth III
gegen against II; around III
gegen etw. fahren to hit III
Gegend area IV ZI, 9
sich **gegenseitig** each other III
gegenüber opposite I
geheim secret II
Geheimnis mystery I; secret II
gehen to go; to walk I
gehen um to be about III
ins Bett gehen to go to bed I
gehörlos deaf III
Gehweg sidewalk *(AE)* IV U1, 15
Geist ghost II
Gel gel III
gelassen relaxed IV U4, 74
gelb yellow I
Geld money I
Geldschein note II
Gelegenheit chance II
gemein mean IV U3, 63
Gemeinde community IV U1, 18
gemeinsam together I
Gemeinschaft community IV U1, 18
Gemüse vegetable (veg) II
Obst- und **Gemüseladen** greengrocer's III
gemustert patterned II
gemütlich cosy III
genannt werden to be called II
genau exact III; right IV U2, 42
Genau. Exactly. IV U3, 59
genießen to enjoy II
genug enough III
genügend enough III
Geocaching geocaching I
Geografie Geography I
gerade right now III; right IV U2, 42
gerade (eben) just II
geradeaus straight on I; right ahead IV U1, 15
Gerät tool II; device IV U3, 58
Geräusch noise I; sound III
Gerede talk II; gossip IV U3, 58
Gericht dish II; court IV U5, 107
Gerichtsverhandlung court case IV U5, 107
Gern geschehen. You're welcome. I
gern mögen to love I
hätte(n) gern would like II
Ich würde nicht gerne … I wouldn't like (to) … I
würde(n) gern would like II
gesamt total IV ZI, 8
Gesamt- total IV ZI, 8
Geschäft shop I; store *(AE)* IV U2, 33
Geschäftsführer manager IV U2, 38
Geschäftsführerin manager IV U2, 38
Geschäftsmann businessman IV U4, 84
geschehen to happen II
Geschenk present I
Geschichte History; story I; history III
Geschoss bullet IV U3, 63
Gesellschaft company II
Gesellschaftslehre Social Studies I
gestatten to allow IV U4, 84
gestern yesterday I
Getränk drink II
Getreide corn IV ZI, 9
gewinnen to win I
Gewinner winner I
Gewinnerin winner I
sich an (etw.) **gewöhnen** to get used to (sth) IV U1, 18
gewöhnlich usually II
Gewürz spice II
Gips cast III
Giraffe giraffe I
Gitarre guitar III
glänzen to shine IV ZI, 8
Glas glass II; jar III
glauben to think I; to believe II
gleich the same II; right away IV U4, 80
jetzt gleich right now III
gleichmäßig regular IV U4, 89
Gleis railway track IV U3, 64
Glocke bell II
Glück haben to be lucky III
viel **Glück** good luck II
glücklich happy I
glücklicherweise luckily II
Glückstag lucky day II
Glückszahl lucky number I
Glückwunsch! Congratulations! II
Glühbirne light bulb III
Gold gold III
Gold- gold III; golden IV U5, 98
golden gold III; golden IV U5, 98
Goldrausch gold rush IV U4, 84
Grab grave III
Gras grass I
grau grey I
greifen to grab III

Grenze border IV U3, 52
Griechisch Greek IV U5, 99
griechisch Greek IV U5, 99
Grill barbecue I
Grillparty barbecue I
groß big; high I; tall; large II
großartig great I; fantastic II
Größe size II
Großeltern grandparents *(pl)* II
Großmutter grandmother III
Großstadt city II
Großvater grandfather II
großzügig generous IV U2, 39
grün green I
Grund reason III
Gründe angeben to give reasons III
Gründe nennen to give reasons III
Grundbesitzer landowner IV U4, 84
Grundbesitzerin landowner IV U4, 84
gründen to start III; to found IV U5, 98
Gruppe group I
gruselig scary I; creepy IV U3, 53
Grüß dich. Hello there. I
Grüße ausrichten to say hi to I
Viele Grüße, Best wishes, I
grüßen to say hi to I
gültig valid III
Gummi rubber III
Gummistiefel welly I
gut good I; fine II; well II; nice III
gut sein in/bei to be good at I
Guten Morgen. Good morning. II
Gut gemacht! Well done! I

H

Haar hair III
Haare hair III
sich die Haare schneiden lassen to have a haircut II
Haargel hair gel III
Haarglätter hair straightener I
Haarschnitt haircut II
haben to have I; to have got II
Glück haben to be lucky III
hätte(n) gern would like II
Mitleid haben mit to feel sorry for III
Du hast recht. You're right. I
Hafen harbour II; harbor *(AE)* IV U1, 22
Hafer oat III
Haferbrei porridge III
Hai shark I
halb half III
halb (drei) half past (two) I
eine halbe Million half a million III
(die) Hälfte half IV U4, 80
Hallen- indoor III
Hallo. Hello.; Hi.; Hello there. I
Hals throat II
Halsband collar I
Halsschmerzen sore throat II
Halt stop II
halten to keep II; to hold III
die Klappe halten to shut up IV U3, 63
draußen halten to keep out III
Haltestelle stop II
Haltung attitude IV U4, 89
Hamburger burger II
Hand hand I
handeln von to be about III
Handgelenk wrist IV U3, 63
Handtuch towel III
Handy mobile (phone) I
hängen to hang II
hänseln to tease IV U2, 38
hart hard II; tough III
hassen to hate I
häufig often I
Haupt- major IV ZI, 8
Hauptgericht main course II
Hauptstadt capital (city) III
Hauptverkehrszeit rush hour IV U1, 14
Haus house I
im Haus around the house I
nach Hause home I
zu Hause at home I
Hausaufgabe(n) homework I
Hausaufgabe(n) machen to do homework I
Häuschen cottage III
Hausmeister caretaker I
Hausmeisterin caretaker I
Haustier pet I
Heer army III
Heft book I; booklet IV U5, 102
Heim home I
Heimweh haben to be homesick III
heiraten to get married II
heiß hot I
heißen to be called II
willkommen heißen to welcome IV U4, 80
Heizkörper radiator IV U3, 59
Held hero III
helfen to help I
Helfer helper IV U4, 89
Helferin helper IV U4, 89
Helikopter helicopter I
hell bright IV ZI, 8
Helm helmet III
Hemd shirt I
heraus out II
aus … heraus out of II
herausfallen aus to fall out of IV U2, 42
herausfinden to find; to find out I
herauskommen to get out III
herausnehmen to take out I
Herberge hostel III
Herbst fall *(AE)* IV ZI, 8
hereinkommen to get in I; to enter IV U3, 54
hergestellt sein aus to be made of III
Herr *(Anrede)* Mr I
herrlich lovely II
herüber across IV U3, 54
herum around I
herumkommen to get around III
herumrennen to run about II
herunter down III
herunterladen to download II
Herzlichen Dank. Thanks so much. IV U4, 94
heute today I
heute Abend tonight II
heute Nacht tonight II
heutzutage now II
Hexe witch I

Hi. Hi. I
hier here I
hiesig local III
Highschool *(weiterführende Schule, Oberstufe)* high school IV U1, 18
Hightech- high-tech IV U4, 75
Hilfe help II; support IV U1, 19
hilfreich useful III; helpful IV U2, 38
hilfsbereit helpful IV U2, 38
Himbeere raspberry III
Hin- und Rückfahrkarte return ticket III
hinauf up II
hinbringen to take II
in … **hinein** inside II
hineingehen to go on II; to enter IV U3, 54
hineingelangen to get into IV U1, 14
hineinkommen to get into IV U1, 14
hinfallen to fall (over) III
hinnehmen to accept IV U5, 99
hinter behind II
Hinter- back IV U3, 62
Hintergrund background III
im Hintergrund in the background III
Hinterteil back IV U5, 106
hinüber across IV U3, 54
hinunter down III
hinuntereilen to rush down II
Hinweis clue I
hinzufügen to add II
zu … hinzufügen to bookmark II
Hip-Hop *(Musik)* hip hop III
Hitparade charts *(pl only)* IV U5, 97
Hitze heat IV U5, 102
Hobby hobby III
hoch high I; tall II
hochladen to upload II
Hochzeit wedding II
hoffen to hope I
Hoffnung hope IV U1, 13
hoffnungsvoll hopeful III
höflich polite II
Höhe height II
Höhle cave II
holen to get II
Holz wood III
hören to listen (to); to hear I
Hose trousers *(pl)* I
kurze Hose shorts *(pl)* I
Hosentasche pocket II
Hospital hospital I
Hot Dog *(Würstchen im Brötchen)* hot dog IV U1, 14
Hotel hotel II
Hotelfachschule catering college II
hübsch beautiful I; pretty; lovely II
Hubschrauber helicopter I
Hügel hill IV U4, 74
Huhn chicken I
Hühnchen chicken II
Hund dog I
Hundeausführer dog walker IV U2, 41
Hundeausführerin dog walker IV U2, 41
Hundekeks dog biscuit II
hundert a/one hundred I
hungrig hungry I
husten to cough III
Hut hat II
hüten to look after II

I

ich I; me I
Ich heiße … My name is … I
Ich komme aus … I'm from … I
Ich weiß (es) nicht! I don't know! I
ich würde lieber I'd rather III
Idee idea I
ihm him I
ihn him I
Ihnen you I
ihnen them I
ihr you I; her I; its III
Ihr your I
ihr *(Pl.)* their I
Ihre yours I; your I
ihre their I; her I; hers II; theirs III
im August in August I
im Bus on the bus II
Im Ernst? Are you serious? III
im Freien outside II
im Haus around the house I
im Stadtzentrum downtown *(AE)* IV U1, 14
im Süden von in the south of III
im vorderen Bereich at the front of II
Imbiss snack I
immer always I
für immer forever II
immer noch still I
Immigrant immigrant IV U1, 13
Immigrantin immigrant IV U1, 13
Immigration immigration IV U1, 22
immigrieren to immigrate IV U1, 18
in in; to; at I; inside III
in der Ferne in the distance IV U1, 15
in der Mitte in the centre of III
in der Pause at break I
in der Schule at school I
in Form fit III
in Ordnung fine; all right II
in … hinein inside II
Indianer Native American IV U2, 32
Indianerin Native American IV U2, 32
indianisch Native American IV U2, 32
indisch Indian II
indisch Indian I
Industrie industry III
industrielle Revolution Industrial Revolution III
Informatik IT (Information Technology) I
Information information *(no pl)* I; information desk II
Informationen information *(no pl)* I
informativ informative IV U4, 77
Ingenieur engineer II
Ingenieurin engineer II
Inhalt content III
innen in inside III
innen inside IV U1, 25
Innen- indoor III
im **Innern** inside III
Insekt insect III
Insel island II
Institut college IV U1, 19
intelligent clever I; smart; intelligent III
interessant interesting I

sich **interessieren** für to be interested in III
interessiert sein an to be interested in III
Internet internet II
im Internet surfen to surf the internet II
ins Internet stellen to upload II
Internettagebuch blog II
Interview interview II
interviewen to interview I
Interviewer interviewer IV U1, 18
Interviewerin interviewer IV U1, 18
irgendein any II
irgendetwas anything II
irgendwelche any II
Irisch Irish III
irisch Irish III
Italiener Italian II
Italienerin Italian II
Italienisch Italian II
italienisch Italian II

J

ja yes I
na ja well I
Jacke coat I; jacket II
Jäger chaser IV U2, 33; hunter IV U4, 85
Jägerin chaser IV U2, 33; hunter IV U4, 85
Jahr year I
Jahrgangsstufe year I
Jahrhundert century III
jamaikanisch Jamaican II
jämmerlich miserable III
Januar January I
Japaner Japanese IV U5, 99
Japanerin Japanese IV U5, 99
Japanisch Japanese IV U5, 99
japanisch Japanese IV U5, 99
Jeans jeans *(pl)* I
jeder every; everyone I; everybody IV U2, 43
jedoch however III
jemals ever II
jemand somebody IV U2, 38
jemand anderes somebody else II
jene those II
jetzt now I
jetzt gleich right now III
Job job I
Joghurt yogurt II
Journalismus journalism IV U2, 34
Journalistik journalism IV U2, 34
Jugend youth *(no pl)* III
Jugend- teen II; youth *(no pl)* III
Jugendliche teen II; teenager III
Jugendlicher teen II; teenager III
Jugendzentrum activity centre III
Juli July I
jung young II
Junge boy I
Juni June I
Juror judge II
Jurorin judge II

K

Käfig cage I
kalt cold I
Kamel camel I
Kamm comb III
Kampf fight; battle III
kämpfen to fight III
Kanarienvogel canary III
Kanone cannon II
Kanonenkugel cannon ball II
Kanufahren canoeing I
Kapitän captain I
Kapitänin captain I
Kappe cap I
Karate karate III
Karneval carnival IV U5, 98
Karotte carrot II
Karre truck III
Karriere career IV U1, 18
Karte card I; ticket II
Kartoffel potato II
Kartoffelbrei mashed potatoes II
Kartoffelchip crisp I
Karton cardboard III
Käse cheese I
Käsekuchen cheesecake II
Katastrophe disaster III
Katholik Catholic III
Katholikin Catholic III
katholisch Catholic III
Katze cat I
kaufen to buy I
Kaufhaus department store II
Kaugummi chewing gum I
kein no I; not … any II
Keks biscuit II
Kellner waiter II
Kellnerin waitress IV U4, 89
kennen to know I
kennen lernen to meet I; to get to know II
Kerl guy IV U2, 42
Kerze candle I
Ketchup ketchup II
Kidneybohne kidney bean II
Kilogramm (kg) kilogram (kg) I
sieben Kilogramm täglich 7 kilograms a day I
Kilometer (km) kilometre (km) I
40 Kilometer pro Stunde 40 kilometres an hour I
Kilt kilt III
Kind child; kid II
Kinder children *(pl)* II
Kinderzimmer bedroom I
Kino cinema I
Kirche church II
Kiste box I
die **Klappe** halten to shut up IV U3, 63
klar clear IV U4, 77
alles klar all right II
Klasse year I; class III; grade *(AE)* IV U2, 33
Klasse *(in einer englischen Schule)* tutor group I
Klassenarbeit test I
Klassenfahrt school trip I
Klassenlehrer tutor I
Klassenlehrerin tutor I
Klassenzimmer classroom I
Klatsch gossip IV U3, 58
Klebstoff glue I
Kleeblatt shamrock III
Kleid dress I
Kleider *(Pl.)* clothes *(pl)* I
Kleiderordnung dress code IV U2, 36

Kleiderschrank wardrobe I
Kleidung clothes *(pl)* I; outfit III
klein small I; little II; tiny III
Klettern rock climbing I
klettern to climb III
klicken to click I
klingeln to ring III
klingen to sound II
Klischee stereotype IV U2, 42
Kloß dumpling II
Klub club II
Klubhaus clubhouse IV U3, 62
klug clever I; smart; intelligent III
Kneipe pub III
Knie knee III
Knoblauch garlic II
knuddelig cuddly III
Koch chef II
Kochbanane plantain II
Kochen cooking II
kochen to cook II
Köchin chef II
Koffer suitcase II
Kohl cabbage II
Kohle coal III
Kokosnuss coconut II
Kombination combination II
kommen to come I
Kommentar comment IV U4, 80
Komödie comedy III
Kompromiss compromise IV U5, 99
Konfitüre jam III
Konflikt conflict IV U5, 99
König king III
königlich royal II
Konkurrenz competition IV U2, 34
können can I; may II
nicht können can't I; cannot III
nicht weg können to be stuck I
konnte could III
Ich konnte nicht anders als … I couldn't help but … III
könnte could III
Konto account IV U4, 80
Kontrolle check IV U1, 22
kontrollieren to check III
(sich) **konzentrieren** to concentrate IV U3, 58
Konzert concert II
Kopf head II
Kopfhörer headphones *(pl)* IV U3, 59
Kopfsalat lettuce II
Kopfschmerzen headache II
kopfüber head first III
Kopfweh headache II
Kopie copy II
kopieren to copy II
Korbball netball I
Korn corn IV ZI, 9
Körper body III
Körperlotion body lotion III
korrekt right I
Korridor hall II
kosten to cost III
… kosten 99 Pence. … are 99p. I
… kostet ein Pfund fünfundzwanzig. … is £1.25. I
kostenlos free III
köstlich delicious II
Kostüm costume; fancy dress I
Kraft power III
krank sein (AE) to be sick III
krank ill II
Krankenhaus hospital I
Krankenpfleger nurse II
Krankenschwester nurse II
Krankenwagen ambulance III
Krankheit disease IV U1, 22
Kraut cabbage II
Kreis circle III
kreischen to scream IV U3, 63
Kricket cricket II
Kritik review III
Krokodil crocodile I
Kubaner Cuban IV U1, 18
Kubanerin Cuban IV U1, 18
kubanisch Cuban IV U1, 18
Küche kitchen I
Kuchen cake I; pie II
einen Kuchen backen to make a cake I
Kugel bullet IV U3, 63
Kuh cow III
kühl cool I
kühlen to cool III
Kühlschrank fridge III
Kultur culture IV U1, 13
sich **kümmern** (um) to care (for) III
Kumpel buddy *(infml)* IV U2, 45
Kunde customer III
Kundin customer III
Kunst Art I
Kunststoff plastic III
Kunststück trick III
Kuppel dome II
Kurs course III; class IV U2, 34
kurz short II; shortly III
kurze Hose shorts *(pl)* I
Kuscheltier cuddly toy III
Kuss kiss II
Küste coast III
an der Küste on the coast III

L

lachen to laugh II
Ladegerät charger III
Laden shop I; store *(AE)* IV U2, 33
Tante-Emma-Laden corner shop I
Lage location III
Lager camp II
Lamm lamb II
Lampe lamp I
Land country I; land II; countryside III; state IV ZI, 8
auf dem Land in the country I
Land der Freien land of the free IV U3, 53
landen to land IV U3, 54
Landesregierung state government IV U5, 98
Landkarte map III
ländliche Gegend country I
Landschaft countryside III; landscape IV ZI, 9
Landwirt farmer I
Landwirtin farmer I
Landwirtschaftsflächen farmland IV U2, 32
lang long I
langsam slow III
langweilig boring I
Laptop laptop I
Lasagne lasagne II

lassen leave II
etw. bleiben lassen to give sth a miss III
lass uns let's I
Laufbahn career IV U1, 18
laufen to run I; to walk II
Wie läuft's? How's it going? IV U3, 54
Laut sound III
laut noisy; loud III
läuten to ring III
Layout layout IV U4, 77
Leben life I; lifetime IV U4, 76
leben to live I
Lebensart lifestyle IV U4, 74
Lebensmittel food I; groceries *(pl)* IV U4, 89
Lebenszeit lifetime IV U4, 76
lecker nice; tasty III
Leder leather III
leer empty IV U4, 86
legen to put I; to lay II
Lehrer teacher I; instructor III
Lehrerin teacher I; instructor III
Leiche body IV U3, 62
leicht easy I
Es tut mir **leid.** I'm sorry. I
Es tut mir **leid** wegen … Sorry about … I
Tut mir **leid.** Sorry. I
leidtun to be sorry III
leihen to lend II
Leine lead I
leise quiet III
leiten to run III
Leiter ladder I
lernen to learn II
kennen lernen to get to know II
lesen to read I
zu guter **Letzt** at last II
letzte last I
leuchtend bright IV ZI, 8
Leute people *(pl)* I; guys II
Lexikon encyclopedia IV U4, 86
Licht light IV U1, 13
Liebe/Lieber …, *(Anrede in Briefen)* Dear …, I
Liebe love IV U4, 85
lieben to love I
ich würde **lieber** I'd rather III
Liebesgeschichte romance III
Lieblings- favourite I; favorite *(AE)* IV U3, 53
Lied song I
Lieferwagen van III
Lifestyle lifestyle IV U4, 74
Lift elevator *(AE)* IV U1, 13
lila purple I
Limonade lemonade II
Lineal ruler I
Linie line II
Link link IV U4, 80
links on the left I; left III
Liste list II
LKW-Fahrer lorry driver II
LKW-Fahrerin lorry driver II
Loch hole I
locker relaxed IV U4, 74; loose II
Löffel spoon II
Lohn wage IV U2, 38
lokal local III
lose loose II
lösen to solve I
Lösung solution IV U5, 98
Löwe lion I
Luft air IV U1, 22
Luftballon balloon I
Lunchpaket packed lunch II
lustig funny I

M

machen to do; to make I
ein Foto machen to take a photo I
Hausaufgabe(n) machen to do homework I
sich Notizen machen to take notes I
Gut gemacht! Well done! I
Mach dir nichts draus. Never mind. II
Macht nichts. Never mind. II
Macht's gut. Take care. I
Macht power III
mächtig powerful IV U1, 22
Mädchen girl I
Magen stomach II
Magie magic II
magisch magic II
Mahlzeit meal II
Mai May I
Mais corn IV ZI, 9
Make-up make-up IV U3, 58
Mal time III
malen to paint II
Mama mum I; mama II
Mammutbaum redwood (tree) IV U4, 74
Manager manager IV U2, 38
Managerin manager IV U2, 38
manchmal sometimes I
Mann man I
Mannschaft team I; crew III
Märchen fable III
Marke brand III
Markt market II
Marmelade jam III
März March I
Maschine machine II
Mathe Maths I; Math *(AE)* IV U2, 34
Mathematik Maths I; Math *(AE)* IV U2, 34
Matsch mud III
Mauer wall II
Maus mouse I
Mayonnaise mayonnaise II
meckern to nag III
soziale **Medien** social media IV U4, 80
Medikamente medicine III
Medizin medicine III
Meer sea I; ocean IV ZI, 9
am Meer at the seaside I
Meerschweinchen guinea pig I
Mehl flour II
in Mehl wenden to cover in flour IV U5, 98
mehr more I
nicht mehr not … any more III
mehrere several IV U4, 80
Mehrheit majority IV U1, 23
die Mehrheit most I
Meile mile II
mein my I
meine my I; mine II

meinen to mean III
Meinung opinion III
einer Meinung sein (mit) to agree (with) III
seine Meinung ändern to change one's mind III
anderer Meinung sein to disagree II
am **meisten** most II
die **meisten** most I
eine **Menge** a lot of I
jede **Menge** lots of I; lots III
Mensa cafeteria I
Mensch person II
Menschen people *(pl)* I
Menschenmenge crowd II
sich **merken** to remember II
merkwürdig strange; funny II
Messer knife II
Metall metal III
Meter metre I
Methode method II
Metzgerei butcher's III
mich me I
Miete rent II
Mikrowelle microwave IV U3, 59
Milch milk I
Milchmischgetränk milkshake III
Milchshake milkshake III
mild mild I
Milliarde billion IV U1, 13
Million million III
eine halbe Million half a million III
Minderheit minority IV U1, 22
Mindest- minimum IV U2, 38
Mineralwasser mineral water III
minimal minimum IV U2, 38
Minimum minimum IV U2, 38
Minute minute II
mir me I
von mir of mine II
mischen to mix IV U5, 98
mit with I
mit *(dem Zug)* by *(train)* I
mit Behinderung with special needs III
mit besonderen Bedürfnissen with special needs III
mitbringen to bring II
Mitleid haben mit to feel sorry for III
zum **Mitnehmen** takeaway II
mitnehmen to take I
Mittagessen lunch I
Mittagspause lunchtime I
Mittagszeit lunchtime I
Mitte centre; middle III; center *(AE)* IV U1, 13
in der Mitte in the centre of; in the middle III
Mitternacht midnight III
Mittwoch Wednesday I
mittwochs on Wednesdays I
mixen to mix IV U5, 98
Mobiltelefon mobile (phone) I
Mode fashion *(no pl)* IV U3, 58
modern modern I
modisch fashionable II
mögen to like I; to enjoy III
am liebsten mögen to like … best I
am meisten mögen to like … best I
gern mögen to love I
nicht mögen to hate I; to dislike IV U4, 81
Ich möchte … I'd like (to) … (= I would like to) I
Ich möchte nicht … I wouldn't like (to) … I
Möchtest du? Would you like (to) …? I
Möglichkeit chance IV U1, 18
Moment moment II
in dem Moment als right IV U2, 42
Monat month I
monatlich monthly III
Monster monster III
Montag Monday I
Mörder murderer III
Mörderin murderer III
Morgen morning I
Guten Morgen. Good morning. II
morgen tomorrow II
morgendliche Ansprache morning message IV U2, 34
Moschee mosque II
Motorrad motorbike I
Moussaka moussaka II
müde tired I
Müll rubbish II
Mülleimer tin IV U3, 63
multikulturell multicultural IV U5, 98
Mund mouth II
Münze coin III
Münzgeld change II
Münztelefon pay phone III
Museum museum II
Musik music I
Musik- musical III
musikalisch musical III
Musikgruppe band II
Müsli cereal III
Muslim Muslim I
Muslimin Muslim I
müssen must I; to have to II
nicht müssen needn't I
Mut courage IV U5, 107
mutig brave III
Mutter mother I
Mütze cap I

N

nach to; after I
nach Hause home I
nach dem Weg fragen asking the way I
nach *(bei Uhrzeitangaben)* past II
Nachbar neighbour III; neighbor *(AE)* IV U3, 54
Nachbarin neighbour III; neighbor *(AE)* IV U3, 54
Nachmittag afternoon I
nachmittags in the afternoon I
nachmittags *(Uhrzeit)* p.m. II
Nachricht message II
Nachricht(en) news II
nachschauen to look I; to look up II
Nachsitzen detention IV U2, 45
Nachspeise dessert; pudding II
nachsprechen to say I

nächste next I
als **Nächstes** next II
Nacht night I
heute Nacht tonight II
in jener Nacht that night II
Nachtwanderung night walk I
Nagel nail III
Nagelschere nail scissors III
nah near III
in der **Nähe** close IV U3, 53
in der **Nähe** von near I
nahe close IV U3, 53
Nahrung food I
Name name I
Nase nose I
die Nase voll haben (von) to be fed up (with) III
nass wet I
national national III
National- national III
Natur nature III
natürlich of course I
Naturwissenschaft Science I
Navi satnav I
neben next to I
neblig foggy I
nehmen to take I
etw. ernst nehmen to take sth seriously IV U1, 18
Bitte Platz nehmen. Please have a seat. IV U3, 55
neidisch jealous II
nein no I
nennen to say I
nervös nervous II
nett nice I; kind II; friendly III
Netz web III; net IV U4, 75
neu new I
auf den neuesten Stand bringen to update IV U4, 81
Neuigkeit(en) news II
neun nine I
neunzehn nineteen I
neunzig ninety I
nicht not I
auch nicht not either III
nicht brauchen needn't I
nicht dürfen mustn't III
nicht einverstanden sein to disagree II
nicht können can't I; cannot III
nicht mehr not … any more III
nicht mögen to hate I; to dislike IV U4, 81
nicht müssen needn't I
nicht wahr? isn't it? II
nicht werden won't (= will not) II
Nichte niece III
nichts nothing IV U3, 63
nie never I
niederbrennen to burn down II
niedlich cute I
niedrig low II
niemals never I
niemand no one I; nobody III
nirgendwo nowhere IV U2, 34
nirgendwohin nowhere IV U2, 34
noch still I; even II
noch ein another II
noch einmal again; once more II
noch nicht not … yet II
Norden north III
nördlich von north of IV ZI, 9
Nordwesten northwest III
nordwestlich northwest of III
nörgeln to nag III
normal regular IV U4, 89
normalerweise usually II
die **Normannen** the Normans III
Normanne Norman III
Normannin Norman III
Notdienst emergency service III
Note grade *(AE)* IV U2, 33
Notfall emergency III
sich **Notizen** machen to take notes I
Notruf emergency call III
November November I
Nudelauflauf pasta bake II
Nudeln pasta II
null zero I
null *(bei Uhrzeiten und Telefonnummern)* oh I
Nummer number I
nun now I
nur only I; just II
Nuss nut I
nützlich useful III; helpful IV U2, 38

O

oben up II
obere upper III
Oberteil top II
Obst fruit I
Obst- und Gemüseladen greengrocer's III
oder or I
Ofenkartoffel jacket potato II
öffentliche Verkehrsmittel public transport III
offiziell official IV U4, 84
öffnen to open I
oft often I
ohne without III
Ohr ear II
okay OK I
Oktober October I
Öl oil IV U5, 98
Oma grandma II
Onkel uncle I
online online II
online stellen to post IV U4, 80
Opa grandad III
Operation operation III
optimistisch optimistic III
Orange orange I
orange orange I
Orchester orchestra III
in **Ordnung** fine; all right II
in Ordnung bringen to tidy (up) II
organisieren to organize II
Ort place I
örtlich local III
Osten east III
östlich von east of IV ZI, 9
Outdoor- outdoor III
Outfit outfit III
Ozean ocean IV ZI, 9

P

ein **Paar** a pair of II
ein **paar** some I; a few III

packen to pack; to pack up II
Packung packet I
Paket package IV U5, 102
panisch werden to panic II
Papa dad I
Papagei parrot I
Papier paper III
Papiere papers *(pl)* IV U1, 19
Pappe cardboard III
Parade parade III
Paradies paradise IV ZI, 9
Parfüm perfume III
Park park I
Parkplatz parking lot *(AE)* IV U1, 15
Partner partner III
Partnerin partner III
Party party I
Passagier passenger II
Passagierin passenger II
passen to suit; to fit II
passieren to happen II
Pasta pasta II
Pastete pasty; pie II
Patient patient II
Patientin patient II
Pause break I
  in der Pause at break I
  Pause machen to take a break II
Pausenhof playground I
peinlich embarrassing IV U2, 42
Pekannuss pecan IV U3, 67
Pence *(brit. Währungseinheit)* pence I
  Das macht zwei Pfund und 24 Pence. That's £2.24. I
  ... kosten 99 Pence. ... are 99p. I
perfekt perfect IV ZI, 9
Person person II
Personalausweis ID III
persönlich personal III
Pfannkuchen pancake II
Pfeffer pepper II
Pferd horse I
Pfirsich peach I
Pflanze plant I
Pflaster plaster III
Pflichtfach core subject IV U2, 35
Pfund *(brit. Währungseinheit)* pound I
  Das macht 2 Pfund und 24 Pence. That's £2.24. I
  ... kostet ein Pfund fünfundzwanzig. ... is £1.25. I
Picknick picnic I
Pick-up pick-up IV U5, 102
Pieps tweet III
pikant spicy II
Pinguin penguin I
pink pink I
Pirat pirate I
Piratin pirate I
Pirogge pierogi II
Pizza pizza I
Plan plan II
planen to plan III
Planke plank II
Plantage plantation IV U5, 97
Plastik plastic III
Platsch splash I
Platz place I; square II
  Bitte Platz nehmen. Please have a seat. IV U3, 55
plaudern to chat II
plötzlich suddenly II
Podcast podcast IV U4, 94
Polizei police III
Polizeibeamter police officer I
Polizeibeamtin police officer I
polnisch Polish IV U5, 99
Polnisch Polish IV U5, 99
Pommes frites chips *(pl)* I
Popcorn popcorn I
positiv positive III
Post *(online gestellte Nachricht)* post IV U4, 80
Postamt post office I
posten to post IV U4, 80
Poster poster I
Postkarte postcard I
praktisch practical IV U4, 89
Praline chocolate IV U3, 54
Pranger stocks III
Präsentation presentation IV U2, 51
Präsident president IV U3, 53
Präsidentin president IV U3, 53
Preis prize; price II
Prise pinch II
pro per IV U2, 41
  pro Stück each II
probieren to try II
Problem problem I; trouble III
Programm programme I
Projekt project III
Propellerboot airboat IV U5, 102
Prospekt brochure III
Protest protest IV U5, 96
Protestant Protestant III
Protestantin Protestant III
protestantisch Protestant III
Prozent percent (%) IV U1, 23
prüfen to test II
Pudding pudding II
Punktestand score II
pünktlich on time III
Pute turkey IV U3, 53
putzen to clean I

Q

Quadratmeile square mile (= sq. mi.) IV ZI, 8
quer durch across IV U3, 54
Quittung receipt II

R

Rad wheel II
Radfahren cycling III
Radiergummi eraser I
Radio radio II
Rafting rafting III
rappen to rap II
Rapper rapper III
Rapperin rapper III
Rasierapparat razor IV U3, 59
Rasierer razor IV U3, 59
Rassentrennung segregation IV U5, 106
Rassismus racism IV U5, 98
Rat advice III
raten to guess II
Rathaus town hall II
Ratschlag advice III; tip II
Rätsel mystery I
Rauch smoke III

Raum room I
Rechner calculator I
Rechnung bill III
Recht right IV U5, 96
  recht haben to be right II
  Du hast recht. You're right. I
rechts on the right I; right III
Rechtschreibung spelling I
Rechtsfall court case IV U5, 107
rechtzeitig in time I
Rede speech III
reden (mit) to talk (to) I
Regal shelf I
Regalbrett shelf I
Regel rule III
regelmäßig regular IV U4, 89
Regen rain IV U4, 85
Regenbogen rainbow III
Regenmantel raincoat III
Regenschirm umbrella II
Regierungsgebäude State House *(AE)* IV U5, 98
Regisseur director II
Regisseurin director II
regnen to rain I
regnerisch rainy I
reich rich III
reichen to pass II
Reichtum wealth III
Reifen tyre III
in die richtige **Reihenfolge** bringen to put in the right order I
Reis rice II
Reise trip; voyage; journey III; tour IV U4, 76
reisen to travel II
Reiten horse riding I
reiten to ride II
reizen to tease IV U2, 38
Religionsunterricht RE (Religious Education) I
rennen to run I
reparieren to repair III
Reporter reporter III
Reporterin reporter III
Republik republic III
Requisit prop III
Reservat reservation IV U2, 32
reservieren to make a reservation III; to book IV U4, 76
Reservierung reservation IV U4, 76
respektieren to respect IV U4, 89
der **Rest** the rest IV U1, 23
Restaurant restaurant II
retten to save III
Rettungsboot lifeboat III
Rettungsdienst emergency service III
Rezept recipe II
richtig right I; real II
das **Richtige** tun to do the right thing III
Richtung trend IV U4, 80
  in diese Richtung this way II
riechen to smell III
Riese giant III
Riesen- giant IV U4, 74
riesengroß huge IV ZI, 9
Riesenrad big wheel II
riesig huge IV ZI, 9; giant IV U4, 74
Rindfleisch beef II
Ring circle III
Ritt ride IV U1, 14
Ritter knight III
Rock skirt I
Rohr tube; pipe III
Rolle part II; role IV U5, 107
Rollstuhl wheelchair III
Rolltreppe escalator II
die **Römer** the Romans III
rosa pink I
Rose rose IV ZI, 8
rot red I
Hin- und **Rückfahrkarte** return ticket III
Rückmeldung feedback IV U2, 39
Rucksack backpack IV U3, 62
Ruf call III
rufen to call I; to shout II
Rugby rugby III
Ruhe silence III
ruhig quiet III
Rührei scrambled egg II
rühren to stir II
ruinieren to ruin II
Russe Russian IV U5, 99
Russin Russian IV U5, 99
Russisch Russian IV U5, 99
russisch Russian IV U5, 99
Rüstung armour III

S

Sache thing I
Sack bag I
Saft juice II
sagen to say; to tell I
Salat salad II
Salz salt II
sammeln to collect I
  (sich) sammeln to gather IV U3, 64
Samstag Saturday I
Sandwich sandwich I
Sänger singer I
Sängerin singer I
etw. **sattbekommen** to get tired of sth IV U1, 14
etw. **satthaben** to get tired of sth IV U1, 14
sauber clean I
  sauber machen to clean I
sauer sein to be fed up (with) III
Saxofon saxophone I
Schachtel box I
Schaf sheep I
Schal scarf I
Schälchen bowl II
Schale bowl II
Schatz treasure II
schätzen to guess IV U3, 59
Schau show IV U5, 102
schauen to look I
Schauspielen acting III
Schauspieler actor II
Schauspielerei acting III
Schauspielerin actor II
Schauspielworkshop acting work shop II
scheinen to shine IV ZI, 8
Schere scissors *(pl)* III
schick chic I
schicken to send I
schieben to push I
schießen (auf) to shoot (at) IV U3, 63

Schiff ship I
Schiffsbauer ship builder III
Schiffsbauerin ship builder III
Schiffsfahrt boat trip II
Schild sign III
Schimmelkäse blue cheese II
Schinken ham II
Schlacht battle III
Schlaf sleep III
schlafen to sleep I; to be asleep III
Schlafzimmer bedroom I
schlagen to hit II; to beat III
Schlagzeile headline IV U4, 77
Schlamm mud III
schlammig muddy I
Schlange snake I
schlau clever I; smart III
Schlauch tube III
schlecht bad I; ill II
schlechteste worst III
schleifen to drag IV U5, 107
schleppen to drag IV U5, 107
schlicht plain II
schließen to close I
Schließfach locker IV U2, 34
schließlich in the end; finally II
schlimm terrible I
schlimmste worst III
Schloss castle II
Schlumpf smurf I
Schluss end II; ending III
am Schluss by the end II
zum Schluss in the end; finally II
Schlussfolgerung conclusion III
Schlussverkauf sale II
schmackhaft tasty III
schmerzhaft sore II
Schminke make-up IV U3, 58
Schmuck jewellery II
Schmuggler smuggler II
Schmugglerin smuggler II
schmutzig dirty I
Schnäppchen bargain II
schnappen to grab III
Schnee snow IV U1, 14
(sich) **schneiden** to cut II
sich die Haare schneiden lassen to have a haircut II
schnell fast; quick II
der/die/das schnellste the fastest I
Schokolade chocolate I
Tafel Schokolade bar of chocolate I
schon already; yet II
Schon gut. Never mind. II
schön nice; beautiful I; fine; lovely II
Schotte Scot III
Schottenrock kilt III
Schottin Scot III
schottisch Scottish III
Schrank cupboard III
schrecklich awful; terrible I; horrible III
Schrei shout I
schreiben to write I
eine SMS schreiben to text II
Schreibtisch desk IV U3, 62
schreien to shout II; to scream IV U3, 63
Schriftsteller writer II
Schriftstellerin writer II
Schritt step III
schubsen to push III
schüchtern shy IV U2, 42
Schuh shoe I
Schule school I
in der Schule at school I
Schüler student I
Schülerin student I
Schulfach subject I
Schulhof playground I
Schulleiter principal *(AE)* IV U2, 34
Schulleiterin principal *(AE)* IV U2, 34
Schulstunde lesson I
Schüssel bowl II
Schusswaffe gun IV U3, 62
schützen to protect III
schwach weak III
schwarz black I
Schweigen silence III
schweigsam silent III
Schweinefleisch pork II
Schweizer Swiss IV U4, 84
Schweizerin Swiss IV U4, 84
schweizerisch Swiss IV U4, 84
schwer heavy; hard II
schwerhörig deaf III
Schwert sword III
Schwester sister I
schwierig difficult III; hard II
Schwierigkeiten trouble III
Schwimmbad swimming pool I
schwimmen to swim II
schwimmen gehen to go swimming I
Science-Fiction science fiction I
Scone *(eine Art süßes Brötchen)* scone II
sechs six I
sechzehn sixteen I
sechzig sixty I
See lake III
Seeräuber pirate I
Seeräuberin pirate I
sehen to see I; to look II
Sehenswürdigkeit sight II
sehr very I; a lot II
so sehr so much III
zu sehr too much II
Seide silk III
Seife soap III
Seil rope I
Seilbahn cable car IV U4, 74
Seilrutsche zip line III
sein to be I
sauer sein to be fed up (with) III
sein his I; its III
seit for IV U4, 80; since IV U4, 80
seitdem since IV U4, 80
Seite page; side I
Seite *(im Internet)* site IV U4, 80
Sekunde second II
selber myself; ourselves; themselves; yourselves III
selbst myself; self III
dich selbst yourself II
ihr/euch/Sie/sich (selbst) yourselves III
sie selbst themselves; herself III
selbstbewusst confident III
selbstsicher confident; sure of oneself III
selbstsüchtig selfish IV U2, 39

selbstverständlich of course I
Selfie *(Schnappschuss von sich selbst)* selfie IV U4, 83
seltsam strange; funny II
senden to send I
Sendung programme I
Senf mustard II
September September I
servieren to serve IV U2, 33
Serviette napkin II
setzen to put I
Shampoo shampoo III
Shirt shirt I
Shorts shorts *(pl)* I
Show show I
sich each other; self III
sich beeilen to rush III
sich beklagen to complain IV U1, 18
sich beschweren to complain IV U1, 18
sich gegenseitig each other III
sicher sure I; safe III
Sicherheit safety IV U4, 75
Sicherheitsnetz safety net IV U4, 75
Sicht look; view IV U1, 14
Sie you I
sie her; she I
sie *(Pl.)* they; them I
sie selbst herself III
sieben seven I
siebzehn seventeen I
siebzig seventy I
Siedler settler IV U2, 32
Siedlerin settler IV U2, 32
siegen to win I
Sieger winner I
Siegerin winner I
Signal signal III
singen to sing I
sinken to sink III
Situation situation II
Sitz seat IV U5, 106
Sitzbank bench III
sitzen to sit I
Sitzplatz seat IV U5, 106
Skateboard skateboard III
Ski fahren to ski II
Skifahren skiing III
Sklave slave IV U4, 86
Sklavin slave IV U4, 86
Skyline skyline IV U1, 12
Smartphone smartphone IV U4, 80
SMS message; text message II
eine SMS schreiben to text II
SMS-Schreiber texter II
SMS-Schreiberin texter II
Snack snack I
so like this I; so II
so ... wie as ... as II
so sehr so much III
sobald as soon as IV U4, 89
Socke sock I
soeben just II
Sofa sofa II
sofort right now III; right away IV U4, 80
Software software II
sogar even II
Sohn son III
Sojabohne soy bean IV ZI, 9
solar solar III
Solar- solar III
Soldat soldier III
Soldatin soldier III
sollte should III
Sommer summer II
Sonderangebot special offer III
Sonne sun III
Sonnen- solar III
sonnenbaden to sunbathe II
Sonnenbrille sunglasses *(pl)* II
sonnig sunny I
Sonntag Sunday I
sich **Sorgen** machen to worry I
sorgfältig careful II
Sorte sort II; type III
Soße sauce II
Souvenir souvenir III
Souvenirladen souvenir shop III
soweit as far as IV U3, 59
soziale Medien social media IV U4, 80
Sozialkunde Social Studies I
Spaghetti spaghetti II
spanisch Spanish IV U5, 98
Spanisch Spanish IV U5, 98
spannend exciting I
Spaß fun I
zum Spaß for fun III
(zu) **spät** late I
später later I; after III
den Hund **spazieren** führen to take the dog for a walk II
Spaziergang walk III
speichern to save II
Speise dish II
Speisekarte menu II
spektakulär spectacular IV U4, 77
speziell special I
Spiegel mirror III
Spiel match; game I
spielen to play I; to act II
Spieler player II; gamer II
Spielerin player II; gamer II
Spielfeld court III
Spielkarte card I
Spielplatz playground I
Spielzeug toy III
Spind locker IV U2, 34
Spinne spider III
Spinnennetz web III
Spitze top IV U1, 13
an der Spitze (von) at the front of II
spitze awesome IV U2, 34
Sport sport I
Sportart sport III
Sportgeschäft sports shop I
Sportunterricht PE (Physical Education) I
sprachbehindert speech impaired IV U5, 102
Sprache language II; speech III
sprechen to say I; to speak II
sprechen (mit) to talk (to) I
sprechen über to talk about II
springen to jump IV U3, 63
Spritze injection III
spülen to wash III
Spülmaschine dishwasher IV U3, 59
Spur clue I; trail IV U5, 102
Staat state IV ZI, 8
Staatsangehörige citizen IV U1, 18
Staatsangehöriger citizen IV U1, 18
Staatsbürger citizen IV U1, 18

T

Taschenrechner calculator I
Taschentuch tissue III
Tasse cup II
Tätigkeit job II
tatkräftig energetic IV U4, 89
Tatsache fact II
tatsächlich actually III
taub deaf III
tausend a/one thousand II
Taxi taxi II
Team team I
Teamwork teamwork II
Technik Design Technology (DT) I
Techniker engineer II
Technikerin engineer II
Tee tea I
Teelöffel *(TL)* teaspoon *(tsp)* II
Teenager teen II; teenager III
Teil part II
teilen to share III
teilnehmen (an) to take part (in) II
Telefon phone II; telephone III
  ans Telefon gehen to answer the phone III
Telefonanruf phone call I
telefonieren to phone II
Telefonnummer phone number III
Telefonzelle telephone box II
Teller plate II
Tennis tennis I
Teppich carpet I
Test test I
testen to test II
teuer expensive II
Text lines *(pl)*; text II
Theater theatre; drama II; theater *(AE)* IV U1, 13
Theaterstück play II
Thema topic IV U2, 51
Themenpark theme park II
Thunfisch tuna II
Tier animal I
Tierarzt vet II
Tierärztin vet II
Tierheim animal rescue shelter I
Tierpark zoo I
Tierpfleger zookeeper I
Tierpflegerin zookeeper I
Tierwelt *(in freier Wildbahn)* wildlife IV U5, 102
Tiger tiger I
Tipp tip II
Tisch table I
  den Tisch decken to lay the table II
Tischler carpenter II
Tischlerin carpenter II
Tischtennis table tennis II
Toast toast II
Tochter daughter I
tod- deadly III
tödlich deadly III
Toilette toilet I
tolerieren to tolerate IV U5, 98
toll great; brilliant I; amazing II
Tomate tomato II
Ton sound III
Tonne tonne II; barrel IV U3, 53
Tonstudio recording studio I
Top top II
Topf pot III
Tor gateway IV U1, 12
Tornado tornado IV U2, 33
tot dead III
töten to kill III
Tour tour IV U4, 76
Tourist tourist I
Touristin tourist I
Touristeninformation Tourist Information Centre I
Tradition tradition III
tragen to carry II
tragen *(Kleidung)* to wear I
Trainer trainer IV U5, 103
Trainerin trainer IV U5, 103
trainieren to practise III
Training practice I; training III
Traktor tractor I
Transfer transfer IV U5, 102
transkontinental *(über den Kontinent hinweg)* transcontinental IV U4, 86
Transport transfer IV U5, 102
Transporter van III
Tratsch gossip IV U3, 58
Traum dream I
träumen to dream III
traurig sad III
treffen to meet I; to hit II
  Freunde treffen to see friends I
treiben to drive IV U3, 52
Trend trend IV U4, 80
Trennung segregation IV U5, 106
Treppe stairs *(pl)* II
Treue allegiance IV U2, 45
Treueeid pledge of allegiance IV U2, 45
Trick trick I
trinken to drink II
Trinkhalm straw II
Trip trip III
trocken dry III
trocknen to dry IV U5, 98
Trommel- drumming III
Truthahn turkey IV U3, 53
Tschüss. See you later.; Bye.; See you. I
T-Shirt T-shirt I
Tuch scarf I
tun to do; to make I
  Tut mir leid. Sorry. I
Tunnel tunnel III
Tür door I
Türkisch Turkish IV U5, 99
türkisch Turkish IV U5, 99
Türklingel doorbell IV U3, 54
Turm tower II
Turnhalle gym(nasium) IV U2, 42
turnieren to joust III
Turnierzweikampf jousting III
Turnschuh trainer I
Tüte bag; packet I
Tutorial tutorial IV U4, 80
Typ type III; guy IV U2, 42

U

U-Bahn underground II; subway *(AE)* IV U1, 14
U-Boot submarine I
üben to practise III
über about I; over IV U1, 12; across IV U3, 54
überall all over IV U4, 85
  überall wo(hin) wherever III

überfüllt crowded IV U1, 22
sich **übergeben** (BE) to be sick III
sich übergeben to be sick I
überhaupt nicht not at all II
überleben to survive III
überlegen to guess II
übernachten to stay II
Übernachtung sleepover I
überprüfen to check III
Überprüfung der Anwesenheit registration I
überqueren to cross III
überrascht surprised II
Überraschung surprise I
Überschrift headline IV U4, 77
übersetzen to translate IV U5, 102
überzeugt convinced IV U3, 59
üblich regular IV U4, 89
Übung exercise; practice I
Übungsheft exercise book I
Uhr clock II
Uhr *(Zeitangabe bei vollen Stunden)* o'clock I
Uhrenturm clock tower II
Uhrzeit time I
um at I
um ... herum around IV U1, 14
ungefähr um around III
umfallen to fall (over) III
Umfrage survey II
umher around I
umrühren to stir II
umsteigen to change III
umziehen to move (house) II
Umzug parade III
Unabhängigkeit independence IV U1, 13; freedom *(no pl)* IV U1, 23
unangenehm uncomfortable II
unbequem uncomfortable II
und and I
unfair unfair III
Unfall accident III
unfreundlich unfriendly III
ungefähr about II
ungefähr um around III
ungefährlich safe III
Ungeheuer monster III
ungewöhnlich unusual IV U4, 77
unglaublich amazing II
Unglück disaster III
unglücklich unhappy II
unhöflich rude IV U2, 39
Uniform uniform I
uninteressant unappealing IV U4, 77
unmodisch unfashionable II
unmöglich impossible III
unmotiviert unmotivated IV U2, 39
Unordnung mess I
uns us I
unschuldig innocent IV U3, 63
unser our I
unsere ours III; our I
unter under I
unter der Woche on weekdays III
unterbrechen to interrupt IV U4, 94
untere lower III
untergehen to sink III
Unterlagen papers *(pl)* IV U1, 19
Unterricht class; lesson I
Unterrichtsstunde class; period IV U2, 34
unterschiedlich different I
unterschreiben to sign IV U3, 53
Unterstützung support IV U1, 19
unterwegs on the way; out and about I
unterzeichnen to sign IV U3, 53
unverschämt rude IV U2, 39
updaten to update IV U4, 81
Ureinwohner Amerikas Native American IV U2, 32
Ureinwohnerin Amerikas Native American IV U2, 32
Urgroßeltern great-grandparents IV U1, 25
Urlaub holiday I
Ururopa great-great-grandad I
US-amerikanisch US IV U1, 18

V

Vanillesauce custard II
Vater father I
Veganismus veganism *(no pl)* IV U4, 83
Vegetarier vegetarian I
Vegetarierin vegetarian I
Ventilator fan IV U3, 59
sich mit jmdm. **verabreden** to ask sb out IV U2, 42
Verabredung date IV U2, 42
veraltet outdated IV U4, 81
verändern to change III
verängstigt scared IV U3, 64
Veranstaltung event IV U4, 86
verantwortlich responsible IV U2, 38
verantwortungsvoll responsible IV U2, 38
verärgert angry II; annoyed III
Verband bandage III
verbessern to correct I
verbinden to attach; to connect III
Verbindung link IV U4, 80
in Verbindung bleiben to keep in touch II
verboten forbidden IV U3, 58
verbrennen to burn down II; to burn III
verbringen *(Zeit)* to spend II
verdienen to earn IV U2, 38
verdrehen to twist II
Verein club II
Vereinsheim clubhouse IV U3, 62
Verfasser writer III
Verfasserin writer III
Verfolger chaser IV U2, 33
Verfolgerin chaser IV U2, 33
Vergangenheit past III
vergessen to forget I
vergleichen to compare I
vergnügt amused IV U3, 63
verhaften to arrest IV U5, 107
sich **verirren** to get lost I
verkaufen to sell III
Verkäufer shop assistant II; assistant III; sales associate *(AE)* IV U2, 38
Verkäuferin shop assistant II; assistant III; sales associate *(AE)* IV U2, 38
Verkehr traffic III
öffentliche **Verkehrsmittel** public transport III
verkleidet (als) dressed III
Verkleidung fancy dress I

V

verlassen leave II
verlässlich reliable IV U5, 109
verlegen embarrassed II
verletzen to hurt II
verletzt hurt II
sich **verlieben** (in) to fall in love (with) III
verlieren to lose II
vermischen to mix IV U5, 98
vermissen to miss II
Vermittlung operator III
vermuten to guess IV U3, 59
vernünftig intelligent III
verpassen to miss II
verrückt crazy I
jmdn. **verrückt** machen to drive sb crazy III
versagen (in/bei) to **fail** (at) IV U1, 19
verschiedene several IV U4, 80
verschwinden to disappear IV U3, 62
Versprechen pledge IV U2, 45
versprechen to promise IV U3, 54
(sich) **verstecken** to hide III
verstehen to understand II; to get III; to know IV U5, 103
etw. verstehen to get sth IV U5, 102
Versuch experiment II
versuchen to try II
vertrauen to trust IV U5, 109
vertrauenswürdig reliable IV U5, 109
vervollständigen to complete I; to finish II
verwenden to use II
verwirrt confused III
verzeihen to pardon IV U3, 53
Verzeihung pardon IV U3, 67
verzerren to twist II
auf etw. **verzichten** to give sth a miss III
Vesper packed lunch II
Video video IV U4, 80
Video-Chat video chat III
viel a lot; much; lots of I; a lot of I; lots III
viel Glück good luck II
viele many II
wie viele how many II
Viele Grüße, Best wishes, I
Vielen Dank. Thanks so much. IV U4, 94
vielleicht maybe I; may II
vier four I
vierte fourth I
Viertel nach quarter past I
Viertel vor quarter to I
vierzehn fourteen I
vierzig forty I
Vietnamese Vietnamese IV U5, 98
Vietnamesin Vietnamese IV U5, 98
Vietnamesisch Vietnamese IV U5, 98
vietnamesisch Vietnamese IV U5, 98
viktorianisches Zeitalter Victorian era III
violett purple I
Vogel bird I
Vogelbeobachtung bird watching III
Vokabular vocabulary II
voll full IV U5, 106
Volleyball volleyball IV U4, 74
völlig quite III; absolutely IV U3, 59
vollkommen perfect IV ZI, 9
von from; of I; by II
von hinten from behind I
von ... weg off IV U5, 107
vor ago; in front of II; before IV U3, 61
vor *(bei Uhrzeitangaben)* to I
vor allem especially II
vorbei past III
vorbereiten to prepare III
sich vorbereiten to get ready IV U3, 54
Vordergrund foreground III
im Vordergrund in the foreground III
Vorgehensweise tactic III
vorhaben to be up to III
vorher before II
vorhersagen to foretell III
Vormittag morning I
vormittags *(Uhrzeit)* a.m. II
Vorort suburb IV U1, 15
Vorrichtung device IV U3, 58
vorsichtig careful II
Sei vorsichtig! Be careful! I
Vorsingen audition II
Vorspeise starter II
Vorspielen audition II
Vorsprechen audition II
vorstellen to present I
Vorstellungsgespräch interview IV U2, 38
Vortanzen audition II
Vortrag presentation IV U2, 51
vorziehen to prefer II

W

wach awake III
wachsen to grow IV U3, 58
Wagen truck III
wählen to choose II; to vote for IV U2, 33
Wahlfach elective IV U2, 34
wahr true II
während while II; during III
wahrscheinlich probably III
Währung currency IV ZI, 8
Wald wood III; forest IV U3, 53
Waliser Welsh III
Waliserin Welsh III
walisisch Welsh III
Walisisch Welsh III
Wand wall II
Wandern hiking; walking III
wandern to hike II
Wanderweg trail IV U5, 102
Wandgemälde mural III
wann when I
warm warm I
Warnung warning IV U2, 33
warten to wait II
warten auf to wait for II
Warteschlange queue II
warum why I
was what I
Was?! No way! III
Was für ein/eine ... What a ... I
Was ist los? What's wrong? II
Was ist mit ...? What about ...? I
Was man ... What to ... II
Was stimmt nicht? What's wrong? II
Waschbär raccoon I
(sich) **waschen** to wash III

Wasser water I
Eimer Wasser bucket of water I
Website website II
Wechselgeld change II
wechseln to change II
Wecker alarm clock I
Weg way IV U2, 34
auf dem Weg on the way I
weg away II
nicht weg können to be stuck I
wegen because of III
weglaufen to run away III
weh tun to hurt II
Weide field IV ZI, 9
sich **weigern** to refuse IV U5, 99
Weihnachten Christmas I
Weihnachtstheaterstück pantomime II
weil because I
Wein wine IV U3, 62
Art und **Weise** way III
auf diese **Weise** like this I; like this III
weiß white I
Weißkopfseeadler bald eagle IV ZI, 8
weit far III
weitere other I
weitergehen to keep going IV U4, 85
weitermachen to keep going IV U4, 85
welche which; what; who II
Welle wave IV ZI, 9
Wellenreiten surfing IV U4, 74
wellenreiten to surf II
Wellenreiter surfer IV ZI, 9
Wellenreiterin surfer IV ZI, 9
Welt world II
auf der Welt in the world II
wem whom IV U3, 58
wen whom IV U3, 58
in Mehl **wenden** to cover in flour IV U5, 98
ein **wenig** a bit II
wenige a few III
weniger less III
wenn when; if II
wer who I
Werbespot advertisement II; ad(vert) IV U4, 76
werden to get I; will; to become II
genannt werden to be called II
nicht werden won't (= will not) II
werfen to throw IV U2, 38
Werft shipyard III
Werk factory III
an **Werktagen** on weekdays III
Werkzeug tool II
Westen west III
westlich von west of IV ZI, 9
Wettbewerb show I; competition II
Wetter weather I
wichtig important II; major IV ZI, 8
wie like I; how I; as II; what III
Wie alt bist du? How old are you? I
Wie bitte? Pardon? I
Wie geht es dir? How are you? I; How are you doing? IV U3, 54
wie geht's how are things going IV U3, 55
Wie geht's? What's up?; How's it going? IV U3, 54
Wie heißt du? What's your name? I
wie läuft's how are things going IV U3, 55
Wie läuft's? How's it going? IV U3, 54
Wie man … How to … II
Wie spät ist es? What time is it? I
Wie viel (kostet/kosten) …? How much (is/are) …? I
Wie viel Uhr ist es? What time is it? I
wie viele how many II
Wie wäre es mit …? How about …? II
so … wie as … as II
wieder again II
wiederholen to repeat III
Auf **Wiedersehen**. Goodbye. I
wiegen to weigh II
Wiese field IV ZI, 9
die **Wikinger** the Vikings III
wild wild IV U3, 63
freie **Wildbahn** the wild IV U5, 102
Wildnis wilderness IV U4, 85; the wild IV U5, 102
willkommen (bei/in) welcome (to) I
willkommen heißen to welcome IV U4, 80
Wind wind I
windig windy I
Windpark wind farm III
Windrad (wind) turbine III
winken to wave II
Winter winter I
winzig tiny III
wir we; us I
Wirbelsturm tornado IV U2, 33
wirklich really I; real II; actually III
wirr confused III
wissen to know I
Ich weiß (es) nicht! I don't know! I
Wissenschaft Science I
Witz joke I
witzig funny I
wo where I
wo(hin) auch immer wherever III
Woche week I
unter der Woche on weekdays III
Wochenende weekend I
am Wochenende at the weekend I
wöchentlich weekly III
woher where I
Woher kommst du? Where are you from? I
wohin where I
wohnen to live I
Wohnung flat I
Wohnwagen caravan III
Wohnzimmer living room I
Wolke cloud IV U2, 33
Wolkenkratzer skyscraper IV U1, 14
wolkig cloudy I
Wolldecke blanket IV U3, 62
Wolle wool I
wollen to want (to) I
Workshop workshop II
Wortschatz vocabulary II
Wrap wrap II
wund sore II
wünschen to wish III
würde(n) would II

würde(n) gern would like II
Ich würde gerne ... I'd like (to) ... (= I would like to) I
Ich würde nicht gerne ... I wouldn't like (to) ... I
Wurst sausage II
würzig spicy II
wütend angry II; furious III

Z

Zahl number I
Zahn tooth III
Zahnbürste toothbrush III
Zahnpasta toothpaste III
Zahnstocher toothpick II
Zauber- magic II
Zauberei magic II
Zebra zebra I
zehn ten I
Zeichen sign; signal III
Zeichensprache sign language III
Zeichentrickfilm cartoon IV U4, 81
zeichnen to draw II
zeigen to show II
Zeile line II
Zeit time I
viktorianisches **Zeitalter** Victorian era III
Zeitreise time travel III
Zeitschrift magazine I
Zeitschriftenladen newsagent's III
Zeitung newspaper II
Zeitungsausträger paperboy IV U2, 41
Zeitungsausträgerin papergirl IV U2, 41
Zeitzone time zone IV ZI, 8
Zelt tent II
Zelten camping III
zelten to go camping II
Zeltplatz campsite III
Zentimeter (cm) centimetre (cm) I
Zentrum centre III; center *(AE)* IV U1, 13
zerbrechen to break II
zerrissen torn IV U4, 83
zerstören to ruin II
Zeuge witness IV U5, 107
Zeugin witness IV U5, 107
Ziege goat III
Ziegelstein brick II
ziehen to pull I; to grow IV U3, 58; to drag IV U5, 107
Ziel ambition II
ziemlich quite III
Zimmer room I
Zimmerdecke ceiling I
Zimmerin carpenter II
Zimmermann carpenter II
Zitrone lemon II
Zoo zoo I
zornig angry II
zu to I; too II
zu Fuß on foot I
zu Hause at home I; back home II
zu sehr too much II
zubereiten to prepare III
züchten to grow IV U3, 58
Zucker sugar I
zuerst first I
Zug train I
Zuhause home I
zuhören to listen (to) I
Zuhörer listener II
Zuhörerin listener II
Zukunft future IV U1, 18
zum Schluss finally II
zum Spaß for fun III
zumachen to close I
zuordnen to match I
zurück back I
zurückkehren to return IV U4, 85
zurückzahlen to pay back II
zusammen together I; everyone II
zusammenfassen to sum up IV U3, 73
zusammenzucken to jump III
Zusatz- extra II
zusätzlich extra II
zuschauen to watch II
Zustand condition IV U1, 22
zustimmen to agree II; to agree (with) III
Zutat ingredient II
zuverlässig reliable IV U5, 109
zuvor before II
Zuwanderung immigration IV U1, 22
zwanzig twenty I
zwei two I
zweite second I
Zwiebel onion II
zwischen between II
zwölf twelve I

Lösungen

Lösungen Mediation

1. It said that the United States is free (from Great Britain).
2. President …
3. November
4. political, religious, economic reasons
5. Africans; people from Africa
6. New Hampshire, Massachusetts, Rhode Island, Connecticut, New York, New Jersey, Pennsylvania, Delaware, Maryland, Virginia, North Carolina, South Carolina, Georgia
7. Cherokee, Navajo, Sioux, Chippewa, Choctaw, Pueblo, Apache, Iroquois, Creek, Blackfeet, Seminole, Cheyenne, Arawak, Shawnee, Mohegan, Huron, Oneida, Lakota, Crow, Teton, Hopi, Inuit
8. Pacific (Ocean)
9. because there are 50 states
10. New Year's Day, Martin Luther King, Jr. Day, Presidents' Day, Memorial Day, Independence Day, Labor Day, Columbus Day, Veterans Day, Thanksgiving, Christmas

Lösungen Grammatik – TEST YOURSELF

G1
1. had
2. liked
3. did not / didn't take
4. did … do
5. Were
6. was not / wasn't

G2
1. had left
2. had not / hadn't done
3. had … started
4. had watched
5. had lived
6. had not / hadn't seen

G3
1. could not / couldn't / was not allowed to / wasn't allowed to
2. had to
3. could / was allowed to
4. did not / didn't have to
5. could / were allowed to
6. could not / couldn't

G4
1. will / 'll help
2. will / 'll be
3. does not / doesn't come
4. will not / won't find
5. meet
6. read

G5
1. Do
2. does
3. will
4. Did
5. –
6. did

G6
1. would be
2. would not / wouldn't meet
3. was / were
4. did not / didn't come
5. would not / wouldn't worry
6. would be

G7
1. goes
2. is not / isn't surfing
3. Are … listening
4. do not / don't like
5. do … do
6. meet

G8
1. has … met
2. have not / haven't seen
3. hasn't … called
4. Have … forgotten
5. have not / haven't been
6. Have … watched

G9
1. is cooked
2. is made
3. are not / aren't cooked
4. are organized
5. is not / isn't accepted
6. are not / aren't grown

G10
1. Anna says (that) they prefer the Everglades.
2. She says (that) she wants to go on a boat tour.
3. She says (that) she doesn't like all those crowds.
4. She says (that) she doesn't want to feed the alligators.
5. She says (that) she knows Florida.
6. She says (that) they can't visit the zoo at night.

Bildquellennachweis

Cover.1 Getty Images (The Image Bank), München; **Cover.2** Getty Images (Photographer's Choice), München; **2.1** Getty Images (Photolibrary/Maremagnum), München; **3.1** Alamy Stock Photo (World History Archive), Abingdon, Oxon; **3.2** plainpicture GmbH & Co. KG (Michael Runkel), Hamburg; **4.1** Getty Images (Lonely Planet/jean pierre lescourret), München; **5.1** Getty Images (Stockbyte), München; **5.2** Getty Images (Daniel Zuchnik), München; **8.6** Getty Images (Corbis), München; **8.7** Getty Images RF (The Image Bank), München; **8.3** Getty Images (Perspectives), München; **8.4** Getty Images (First Light), München; **8.8** plainpicture GmbH & Co. KG (Ableimages/David Harrigan), Hamburg; **8.5** Getty Images (National Geographic Magazines), München; **8.9** plainpicture GmbH & Co. KG (Aurora Photos/Josh Miller), Hamburg; **8.1** Getty Images (Iconica), München; **8.2** Getty Images (E+/Ron Thomas), München; **10.10** By Orlando Scott Goff, Bismarck, Dakota Territory - Heritage Auctions, Public Domain, https://commons.wikimedia.org/w/index.php?curid=27530348; **10.5** By John Dunlap, text by Thomas Jefferson et al. - http://lcweb2.loc.gov/cgi-bin/ampage?collId=rbc3&fileName=rbc0001_2004pe76546page.db, Public Domain, https://commons.wikimedia.org/w/index.php?curid=33408334; **10.6** Getty Images (The Image Bank), München; **10.12** Getty Images (Lonely Planet), München; **10.3** Getty Images (Bettmann), München; **10.11** Getty Images (Lonely Planet), München; **10.13** Getty Images (Universal Images Group), München; **10.1** Getty Images (DigitalGlobe), München; **10.2** Getty Images (The Image Bank), München; **10.9** Getty Images (Tim Fitzharris), München; **10.7** plainpicture GmbH & Co. KG (Image Source/Gu), Hamburg; **10.14** Getty Images (Science Source), München; **10.15** Getty Images (Photodisc), München; **10.16** Getty Images (Alan Copson), München; **10.17** Getty Images (David Sucsy), München; **10.4** plainpicture GmbH & Co. KG (Fancy Images/Whisson/Jordan), Hamburg; **10.8** Getty Images (Corbis Documentary), München; **10.18** Getty Images (Cameron Davidson), München; **12.1** Getty Images (Photolibrary/Maremagnum), München; **12.2** plainpicture GmbH & Co. KG (Gine Seitz), Hamburg; **13.1** Avenue Images GmbH (ponton), Hamburg; **13.2** Getty Images (Lonely Planet/Michael Marquand), München; **13.3** Getty Images (Moment/© 2014 Noppon Umnajwannaphan), München; **14.2** Alamy Stock Photo (Etcheverry Images), Abingdon, Oxon; **14.1** Thinkstock (LUNAMARINA), München; **18.1** Corbis (Duane Osborn/Somos Images), Berlin; **19** Song: Empire State of Mind, Text: CARTER, SHAWN/HUNTE, ANGELA/KEYES, BERT/Keys, Alicia/Robinson, Sylvia/SEWELL, JANET ANDREA/SHUCKBURGH, ALEXANDER WILLIAM, Verlag: Carter Boys Music / EMI April Music / Foray Music / Gambi Music Inc / Global Talent Publishing / J Sewell Publishing / Lellow Productions Inc / Masani El Shabazz EMI Music Publishing Germany GmbH, Berlin / Rolf Budde Musikverlag GmbH, Berlin / Neue Welt Musikverlag GmbH, Hamburg; **19.1** Corbis (PT Images/Tetra Images), Berlin; **19.2** plainpicture GmbH & Co. KG (Kniel Synnatzschke), Hamburg; **21.1** Corbis (Duane Osborn/Somos Images), Berlin; **22.1** Alamy Stock Photo (The Print Collector), Abingdon, Oxon; **25.2** Alamy Stock Photo (Michael Dwyer), Abingdon, Oxon; **25.1** shutterstock (Vacclav), New York, NY; **25.3** Thinkstock (stu99), München; **25.4** Thinkstock (iStockphoto), München; **26.1** Getty Images (Lonely Planet/jean pierre lescourret), München; **27.1** Ulrike Beutel, Mitarbeiterin, Stuttgart; **28.1** Getty Images (Hulton Archive), München; **29.2** Fotolia.com (Robert Wilson), New York; **29.4** Fotolia.com (tharun15), New York; **29.3** Fotolia.com (gguy), New York; **29.1** Alamy Stock Photo (Randy Duchaine), Abingdon, Oxon; **30.2** Getty Images (Gallo Images), München; **30.1** Getty Images (First Light), München; **30.3** Thinkstock (mlharing), München; **32.2** Alamy Stock Photo (World History Archive), Abingdon, Oxon; **32.1** Thinkstock (welcomia), München; **33.1** Thinkstock (IPGGutenbergUKLtd), München; **33.2** Alamy Stock Photo (Martin Shields), Abingdon, Oxon; **33.3** Getty Images (J. Meric), München; **34.1** plainpicture GmbH & Co. KG (Fancy Images/Hero), Hamburg; **35.3** Getty Images (E+/Pamela Moore), München; **35.5** Alamy Stock Photo (Marjorie Kamys Cotera/Bob Daemmrich Photography /), Abingdon, Oxon; **35.2** Getty Images (Universal Images Group), München; **35.1** Thinkstock (alexfedo), München; **35** Song: Cool Kids, Text: Dzwonek, Jesiah/Sierota, Graham/Sierota, Jamie/Sierota, Jefery/Sierota, Noah/Sierota Sydney, Verlag: Echosmith Songs/WB Music Corp./Jeffery David Songs/Upcast Music D/A/CH Neue Welt Musikverlag GmbH, Hamburg/Roba Music Verlag GmbH, Hamburg, Reach Music Publishing, Burbank CA; **35.6** shutterstock (Jim Lopes), New York, NY; **36.6** Thinkstock (Ramsey), München; **36.5** Thinkstock (StandbyPictures), München; **36.4** Thinkstock (Jupiterimages), München; **36.2** Thinkstock (xantuanx), München; **36.1** Thinkstock (Wylius), München; **36.3** Thinkstock (Antonius_), München; **45.1** JDM Productions Inc, New York; **47.1** Getty Images (E+/Steve Debenport), München; **48.2** Thinkstock (michal-rojek), München; **48.1** Thinkstock (Digital Vision.), München; **49.1** Getty Images (Roger Lecuyer), München; **50.1** Thinkstock (Mike Watson Images), München; **50.2** Thinkstock (Enterline Design Services LLC), München; **50.3** plainpicture GmbH & Co. KG (Image Source), Hamburg; **52.1** plainpicture GmbH & Co. KG (Michael Runkel), Hamburg; **52.2** Getty Images (Corbis), München; **53.1** plainpicture GmbH & Co. KG (NaturePL/Edwin Giesbers), Hamburg; **53.2** Getty Images (Aurora), München; **53.3** f1 online digitale Bildagentur, Frankfurt; **56.1** Getty Images (Thomas M. Barwick INC), München; **58.2** Thinkstock (Flying Colours Ltd), München; **58.1** Alamy Stock Photo (brt PHOTO), Abingdon, Oxon; **59.1** iStockphoto (RF/Sascha Burkard), Calgary, Alberta; **59.3** Thinkstock (Oleksiy Mark), München; **59.5** MEV Verlag GmbH, Augsburg; **59.2** Avenue Images GmbH (stock disc), Hamburg; **59.4** shutterstock (Maxx-Studio), New York, NY; **61.1** Getty Images (Taxi/Troy Aossey), München; **62** From: The body, Stephen King, retold by Robin Waterfield; **62.1** Ullstein Bild GmbH (United Archives / KPA), Berlin; **63.1** Ullstein Bild GmbH (United Archives), Berlin; **67.3** JDM Productions Inc, New York; **67.1** JDM Productions Inc, New York; **67.2** JDM Productions Inc, New York; **67.4** JDM Productions Inc, New York; **68.1** Alamy Stock Photo (Hero Images Inc.), Abingdon, Oxon; **70.1** Alamy Stock Photo (North Wind Picture Archives), Abingdon, Oxon; **74.1** shutterstock (mariakraynova), New York, NY; **74.2** plainpicture GmbH & Co. KG (Cl2/Joel Bear Studios), Hamburg; **75.3** Getty Images (Lonely Planet/jean pierre lescourret), München; **75.1** Getty Images (E+/Johnny Greig), München; **75.2** Getty Images (Kiyoshi Ota/Bloomberg), München; **76.4** Getty

Images (Blend Images), München; **76.1** shutterstock (bikeriderlondon), New York, NY; **76.2** Thinkstock (1001Love), München; **76.3** Thinkstock (somchaij), München; **77** Song: Surfin' U.S.A., Text: Brian Wilson, Verlag: ARC Music Corp. Good Tunes Music AG; **77.1** Ullstein Bild GmbH (Rolf Schulten), Berlin; **79.3** Beutel, Ulrike, Stuttgart; **79.4** Beutel, Ulrike, Stuttgart; **79.2** Beutel, Ulrike, Stuttgart; **79.1** Reis, Axel, Oberderdingen; **80.1** Getty Images (Hero Images), München; **81.1** Getty Images (South_agency), München; **83.1** Thinkstock (McIninch), München; **85.1** Alamy Stock Photo (Granger Historical Picture Archive), Abingdon, Oxon; **86.1** Alamy Stock Photo (Russ Bishop), Abingdon, Oxon; **87.1** Getty Images (E+/Steve Debenport), München; **88.1** Alamy Stock Photo (nik wheeler), Abingdon, Oxon; **89.1** JDM Productions Inc, New York; **91.1** Thinkstock (littlewormy), München; **93.1** Reis, Axel, Oberderdingen; **94.2** Reis, Axel, Oberderdingen; **94.1** Reis, Axel, Oberderdingen; **96.2** Alamy Stock Photo (World History Archive), Abingdon, Oxon; **96.1** Getty Images (Stockbyte), München; **97.3** Getty Images (2013 Kevin Mazur), München; **97.1** Getty Images (Hulton Archive/The Print Collector), München; **97.2** Getty Images (Blend Images), München; **98.2** Thinkstock (emarto), München; **98.1** shutterstock (Michael Rosebrock), New York, NY; **99.4** Geoatlas, Hendaye; **99.2** Klett-Archiv-RF-HF, Stuttgart; **99.3** Klett-Archiv-RF-HF, Stuttgart; **99.5** Geoatlas, Hendaye; **99.1** Klett-Archiv-RF-HF, Stuttgart; **102.1** Getty Images (Jon Feingersh Photography 2011), München; **102.2** Getty Images (Stocktrek Images), München; **104.1** Getty Images (The Image Bank), München; **105.1** Getty Images (kristian sekulic), München; **106.1** laif (Richard Harbus/Polaris), Köln; **106.2** Picture-Alliance (Everett Collection), Frankfurt; **108.1** Getty Images (Sean Gardner), München; **109.3** February Films, London; **109.4** JDM Productions Inc, New York; **109.2** JDM Productions Inc, New York; **109.1** JDM Productions Inc, New York; **112.1** Fotolia.com (lubashi), New York; **113.^6; "shutterstock (Suslik1983), New York, NY; 113.5** shutterstock (jultud), New York, NY; **113.1** iStockphoto (RF/Dmitry Bezkorovayny), Calgary, Alberta; **113.3** Corbis (Matthias Kulka), Berlin; **113.4** shutterstock (George W. Bailey), New York, NY; **113.2** iStockphoto (sspopov), Calgary, Alberta; **113.7** Thinkstock (pilipphoto), München; **116.1** plainpicture GmbH & Co. KG (Kniel Synnatzschke), Hamburg; **118.1** plainpicture GmbH & Co. KG (Fancy Images/Hero), Hamburg; **119.1** Getty Images (Fuse), München; **119.3** Alamy Stock Photo (Marjorie Kamys Cotera/Bob Daemmrich Photography), Abingdon, Oxon; **119.5** Getty Images (E+/Pamela Moore), München; **119.2** Alamy Stock Photo (Image Source Plus), Abingdon, Oxon; **119.4** Getty Images (View Pictures/UIG), München; **125.1** iStockphoto (RF/Sascha Burkard), Calgary, Alberta; **125.2** Avenue Images GmbH (stock disc), Hamburg; **125.5** MEV Verlag GmbH, Augsburg; **125.4** shutterstock (Maxx-Studio), New York, NY; **125.3** Thinkstock (Oleksiy Mark), München; **127.4** Getty Images (Blend Images), München; **127.1** shutterstock (bikeriderlondon), New York, NY; **127.3** Thinkstock (somchaij), München; **127.2** Thinkstock (1001Love), München; **129.1** Getty Images (Hero Images), München; **131.5** Geoatlas, Hendaye; **131.4** Geoatlas, Hendaye; **131.2** Klett-Archiv-RF-HF, Stuttgart; **131.3** Klett-Archiv-RF-HF, Stuttgart; **131.1** Klett-Archiv-RF-HF, Stuttgart; **133.1** Getty Images (Moment Mobile), München; **134.1** Getty Images RF (The Image Bank), München; **134.6** Getty Images (WireImage), München; **134.5** Alamy Stock Photo (PYMCA), Abingdon, Oxon; **134.4** Getty Images (Hulton Archive), München; **134.3** Getty Images (Michael Ochs Archives), München; **134.2** Corbis (Owaki - Kulla), Berlin; **135.1** Corbis (Bo Zaunders), Berlin; **135.2** Getty Images (Daniel Zuchnik), München; **136.1** Getty Images RF (The Image Bank), München; **136.3** Getty Images (Dorling Kindersley RF), München; **136.2** Kansas Historical Society, Topeka; **137.1** Getty Images (The Image Bank), München; **138.1** Getty Images RF (The Image Bank), München; **138.2** Getty Images (Popperfoto), München; **138.3** Getty Images (National Geographic Magazines), München; **138.4** Getty Images (M_a_y_a), München; **139.2** iStockphoto (circlePS), Calgary, Alberta; **139.1** Getty Images (De Agostini Picture Library), München; **140.1** Getty Images RF (The Image Bank), München; **140.2** Getty Images (Corbis Documentary), München; **140.3** Getty Images (Jemal Countess), München; **140.4** Getty Images (Albert L. Ortega), München; **141.2** Getty Images (DreamPictures), München; **141.1** Alamy Stock Photo (FORRAY Didier/SAGAPHOTO.COM), Abingdon, Oxon; **142.1** Getty Images RF (The Image Bank), München; **142.2** Getty Images (Lonely Planet), München; **142.3** Getty Images (Corbis Documentary), München; **143.1** Getty Images (Photographer's Choice), München; **143.2** Getty Images (Corbis Documentary), München; **144.1** Getty Images (Spencer Sutton), München; **144.3** Getty Images (Lonely Planet), München; **144.2** Getty Images (Photolibrary), München; **144.4** Getty Images (Jiji Press / AFP), München; **145.1** Getty Images (Gary S. Chapman), München; **147.1** Getty Images (Blend Images), München; **148.1** The Absolutely True Diary of a Part-Time Indian, Author: Sherman Alexie, Illustrator: Ellen Forney, Andersen Press.; **148** The Absolutely True Diary of a Part-Time Indian, Sherman Alexie, Andersen Press; **149.1** The Absolutely True Diary of a Part-Time Indian, Author: Sherman Alexie, Illustrator: Ellen Forney, Andersen Press.; **150.1** The Absolutely True Diary of a Part-Time Indian, Author: Sherman Alexie, Illustrator: Ellen Forney, Andersen Press.; **150.2** The Absolutely True Diary of a Part-Time Indian, Author: Sherman Alexie, Illustrator: Ellen Forney, Andersen Press.; **182.9** Fotolia.com (naughtynut), New York; **182.8** Fotolia.com (blondsteve), New York; **182.7** iStockphoto (Dominic Burke RF), Calgary, Alberta; **182.6** Fotolia.com (thorabeti), New York; **182.5** Fotolia.com (Pavel Losevsky), New York; **182.4** iStockphoto (Marcel Pfost), Calgary, Alberta; **182.3** Fotolia.com (axeldrosta), New York; **182.2** iStockphoto (Michael Utech), Calgary, Alberta; **182.1** iStockphoto (stockcam), Calgary, Alberta; **183.3** Bananastock, Watlington / Oxon; **183.2** Das Fotoarchiv RF (RF), Essen; **183.1** Thinkstock (Owat Tasai), München; **188.11** iStockphoto (Alejandro Rivera), Calgary, Alberta; **188.10** Klett-Archiv (Weccard), Stuttgart; **188.9** Avenue Images GmbH (StockDisc), Hamburg; **188.8** shutterstock (igor.stevanovic), New York, NY; **188.7** Thinkstock (Stockbyte), München; **188.6** Avenue Images GmbH (Digital Vision), Hamburg; **188.5** Fotolia.com (Michael Shake), New York; **188.4** iStockphoto (Steve Debenport), Calgary, Alberta; **188.1** Fotosearch Stock Photography (Digital Vision), Waukesha, WI; **188.3** iStockphoto (herreid), Calgary, Alberta; **188.2** shutterstock (bikeriderlondon), New York, NY;

199.14 iStockphoto (Linda Steward), Calgary, Alberta; **199.13** Fotolia.com (Markus Mainka), New York; **199.12** iStockphoto (kodachrome25), Calgary, Alberta; **199.11** shutterstock (AXL), New York, NY; **199.10** iStockphoto (RF/Lukasz Janicki), Calgary, Alberta; **199.9** Thinkstock (iStock/Wojciech Gajda), München; **199.8** shutterstock (hadot 760), New York, NY; **199.7** Fotolia.com (Angela Jones), New York; **199.6** iStockphoto (David Mathies), Calgary, Alberta; **199.5** Fotolia.com (pondchao), New York; **199.4** shutterstock (Alex Melnick), New York, NY; **199.3** iStockphoto (Marcel Pfost), Calgary, Alberta; **199.2** Fotolia.com (Sharpshot), New York; **199.1** Fotolia.com (Achim Thomae), New York; **204.27** shutterstock (Campre83), New York, NY; **204.26** shutterstock (Various-Everythings), New York, NY; **204.25** shutterstock (Niyazz), New York, NY; **204.24** shutterstock (Steve Allen), New York, NY; **204.23** shutterstock (argus), New York, NY; **204.22** shutterstock (Anchiy), New York, NY; **204.21** shutterstock (NAN SKYBLACK), New York, NY; **204.20** shutterstock (Various-Everythings), New York, NY; **204.19** shutterstock (Various-Everythings), New York, NY; **204.18** shutterstock (Various-Everythings), New York, NY; **204.17** shutterstock (Daboost), New York, NY; **204.16** shutterstock (Niyazz), New York, NY; **204.15** shutterstock (Various-Everythings), New York, NY; **204.14** shutterstock (PhotoStockImage), New York, NY; **204.13** shutterstock (Irina Rumyantseva), New York, NY; **204.12** shutterstock (ArpornSeemaroj), New York, NY; **204.11** shutterstock (Various-Everythings), New York, NY; **204.10** shutterstock (Aleksandar Mijatovic), New York, NY; **204.9** shutterstock (Visionsi), New York, NY; **204.8** shutterstock (stockcreations), New York, NY; **204.7** shutterstock (hlphoto), New York, NY; **204.6** shutterstock (rj lerich), New York, NY; **204.5** shutterstock (Aleksandra Duda), New York, NY; **204.4** shutterstock (Troscha), New York, NY; **204.3** shutterstock (stocksolutions), New York, NY; **204.2** shutterstock (Anna Mandrikyan), New York, NY; **204.1** shutterstock (Iryna Denysova), New York, NY; **205.16** Fotolia.com (Stefano Gasparotto), New York; **205.15** Fotolia.com (Kzenon), New York; **205.14** iStockphoto (Lya_Cattel), Calgary, Alberta; **205.13** shutterstock (Kzenon), New York, NY; **205.12** Fotolia.com (Iuliia Sokolovska), New York; **205.11** shutterstock (Scott Sanders), New York, NY; **205.10** Thinkstock (Jupiterimages), München; **205.9** iStockphoto (Linda Steward), Calgary, Alberta; **205.8** shutterstock (gorillaimages), New York, NY; **205.7** Fotolia.com (Thaut Images), New York; **205.6** Fotolia.com (Robert Pernell), New York; **205.5** Fotolia.com (Sharpshot), New York; **205.4** shutterstock (AXL), New York, NY; **205.3** shutterstock (Alex Melnick), New York, NY; **205.2** Fotolia.com (pondchao), New York; **205.1** iStockphoto (Marcel Pfost), Calgary, Alberta

Textquellennachweis

S. 19: Song: Empire State of Mind, Text: CARTER, SHAWN/HUNTE, ANGELA/KEYES, BERT/Keys, Alicia/Robinson, Sylvia/SEWELL, JANET ANDREA/SHUCKBURGH, ALEXANDER WILLIAM, Verlag: Carter Boys Music / EMI April Music / Foray Music / Gambi Music Inc / Global Talent Publishing / J Sewell Publishing / Lellow Productions Inc / Masani El Shabazz EMI Music Publishing Germany GmbH, Berlin / Rolf Budde Musikverlag GmbH, Berlin / Neue Welt Musikverlag GmbH, Hamburg
S. 35: Song: Cool Kids, Text: Dzwonek, Jesiah/Sierota, Graham/Sierota, Jamie/Sierota, Jefery/Sierota, Noah/Sierota Sydney, Verlag: Echosmith Songs/WB Music Corp./Jeffery David Songs/Upcast Music D/A/CH Neue Welt Musikverlag GmbH, Hamburg/ Roba Music Verlag GmbH, Hamburg, Reach Music Publishing, Burbank CA
S. 62: From: The body, Stephen King, retold by Robin Waterfield
S. 77: Song: Surfin' U.S.A., Text: Brian Wilson, Verlag: ARC Music Corp. Good Tunes Music AG
S. 148–151: The Absolutely True Diary of a Part-Time Indian, Sherman Alexie, Andersen Press

Sollte es in einem Einzelfall nicht gelungen sein, den korrekten Rechteinhaber ausfindig zu machen, so werden berechtigte Ansprüche selbstverständlich im Rahmen der üblichen Regelungen abgegolten.

CANADA
ALASKA
Denali
CANADA
Seattle
Portland
WASHINGTON
OREGON
IDAHO
MONTANA
WYOMING
NORTH DAKOTA
SOUTH DAKOTA
NEBRASKA
Rocky Mountains
NEVADA
UTAH
COLORADO
Denver
KANS
San Francisco
CALIFORNIA
Las Vegas
HOLLYWOOD
Los Angeles
San Diego
Phoenix
ARIZONA
NEW MEXICO
OKLAHOM
TEXAS
Pacific Ocean
HAWAII
MEXICO